HOMEMADE MEN IN POSTWAR AUSTRIAN CINEMA

Film Europa: German Cinema in an International Context
Series Editors: **Hans-Michael Bock** (CineGraph Hamburg);
Tim Bergfelder (University of Southampton); **Sabine Hake**
(University of Texas, Austin)

German cinema is normally seen as a distinct form, but this series
emphasizes connections, influences, and exchanges of German cinema
across national borders, as well as its links with other media and art
forms. Individual titles present traditional historical research (archival
work, industry studies) as well as new critical approaches in film and
media studies (theories of the transnational), with a special emphasis on
the continuities associated with popular traditions and local perspectives.

**The Concise Cinegraph: An
Encyclopedia of German Cinema**
General Editor: Hans-Michael Bock
Associate Editor: Tim Bergfelder

**International Adventures:
German Popular Cinema and
European Co-Productions
in the 1960s**
Tim Bergfelder

**Between Two Worlds: The Jewish
Presence in German and Austrian
Film, 1910–1933**
S.S. Prawer

**Framing the Fifties: Cinema in a
Divided Germany**
Edited by John Davidson and
Sabine Hake

**A Foreign Affair: Billy Wilder's
American Films**
Gerd Gemünden

**Destination London:
German-speaking Emigrés and
British Cinema, 1925–1950**
Edited by Tim Bergfelder and
Christian Cargnelli

**Michael Haneke's Cinema:
The Ethic of the Image**
Catherine Wheatley

Willing Seduction:
The Blue Angel, **Marlene
Dietrich, and Mass Culture**
Barbara Kosta

**Dismantling the Dream Factory:
Gender, German Cinema, and the
Postwar Quest for a New Film
Language**
Hester Baer

Belá Balázs: Early Film Theory.
Visible Man and *The Spirit of Film*
Belá Balázs, edited by Erica Carter,
translated by Rodney Livingstone

**Screening the East: Heimat,
Memory and Nostalgia in German
Film since 1989**
Nick Hodgin

**Peter Lorre: Face Maker.
Stardom and Performance
between Hollywood and Europe**
Sarah Thomas

**Turkish German Cinema in
the New Millennium: Sites,
Sounds, and Screens**
Edited by Sabine Hake
and Barbara Mennel

**Postwall German Cinema: History,
Film History and Cinephilia**
Mattias Frey

**Homemade Men in Postwar
Austrian Cinema: Nationhood,
Genre and Masculinity**
Maria Fritsche

HOMEMADE MEN IN POSTWAR AUSTRIAN CINEMA

Nationhood, Genre and Masculinity

Maria Fritsche

berghahn
NEW YORK · OXFORD
www.berghahnbooks.com

First edition published in 2013 by

Berghahn Books

www.berghahnbooks.com

© 2013 Maria Fritsche

Library of Congress Cataloging-in-Publication Data

Fritsche, Maria, 1969-
    Homemade men in postwar Austrian cinema : nationhood, genre and masculinity / Maria Fritsche. -- First edition.
        pages cm. -- (Film Europa: German cinema in an international context)
    Includes filmography.
    Includes bibliographical references and index.
    ISBN 978-0-85745-945-9 (hardback : alk. paper)
-- ISBN 978-0-85745-946-6 (institutional ebook)
    1. Masculinity in motion pictures. 2. Nationalism in motion pictures. 3. Motion pictures--Austria--History--20th century. I. Title.
    PN1995.9.M34F85 2013
    791.4309436′1309045--dc23
                                 2013006282

British Library Cataloguing in Publication Data

A catalogue record for this book is available from the British Library

Printed in the United States on acid-free paper
ISBN: 978-0-85745-945-9 (hardback)
ISBN: 978-0-85745-946-6 (institutional ebook)

CONTENTS

LIST OF ILLUSTRATIONS

Figures

Tables

Acknowledgements

Thanks to the many reruns of Austrian films on national television, the images of pre- and postwar Austrian cinema have accompanied me from an early age. My interest on the postwar era had grown while I was investigating the life of Austrian soldiers during the Second World War. I came to wonder how a society that was so deeply unsettled by the war and by its involvement in terrible crimes could (ostensibly) recover so quickly from its wounds and the wounds it had inflicted on others. Studying the developments of Austrian society after the Second World War, and familiarising myself with the dominant discourses of the time, I realised that Austrian cinema must have played an important role in shaping postwar society by evaluating and modifying societal norms and values.

Yet it was only after I had left Austria and started studying postwar cinema in more depth while living in England that I came to understand why Austrian cinema held such an appeal to contemporary audiences and learnt which multiple functions it fulfilled in postwar society. Looking at a subject from a distance usually enables one to form a clearer, more complete picture. So my new perspective from across the English Channel granted me many revelatory insights into postwar Austrian cinema and its complex relationship with society which I otherwise would not have had. This monograph thus combines a 'close-up' with a 'long shot' perspective, bringing together an intimate knowledge of the films with a detached, analytical view of the film industry and postwar society. The result of this scholarly endeavour is presented here to the interested reader.

As anyone who has ever produced a work of a similar kind knows, a book involves many more hands, brains and eyes than just those of the author. There are a number of people who actively supported this project over the years with their knowledge, advice, encouragement and practical help. Without them, this book could not have been brought to completion and it is thus to them all I want to express my gratitude.

This book would not exist without the marvellous support of Sue Harper. She has inspired me intellectually and encouraged me to think differently, and it is to her that I am most indebted. I would like to thank her especially for freely and generously sharing with me her vast knowledge of British cinema, for accompanying me through the writing process by asking the right questions, guiding me out of dead ends and pointing out worthwhile inquiries. My heartfelt thanks also go to Deborah Shaw and Petra-Uta Rau, whose critical interest and encouragement gave me the necessary stamina to see the work through. Their expertise and different intellectual background have greatly added to this book. Another person whose help was crucial for this study is Christian Cargnelli. Nobody knows this book better than Christian, who took it upon himself to read the different chapters several times and discuss them with me at length. His precise and straightforward, but always kindly-meant criticism has greatly helped to sharpen my argument and iron out inconsistencies. I am also grateful to Justin Smith for reading my work with a critical eye and asking me many useful questions; I am particularly thankful for his great help in finding the title for this book while he was visiting me in Berlin. I also want to thank Tim Bergfelder, both for his constructive criticism and for his support in getting this study published. I owe much to Jeremy Lowe, who did a wonderful job as a proof reader and gently smoothed stylistic edges. I would also like to express my thanks to Berghahn Books for their interest in the subject, and especially to their senior editor Mark Stanton, who has been supportive and helpful throughout the bookmaking process. Last but not least, I would like to express my gratitude to the two anonymous referees who reviewed my manuscript so thoroughly and who offered fair and extremely helpful criticism in a friendly manner!

Any historian who endeavours to dig deep in order to produce new and revealing findings cannot work without original sources. Like all my colleagues I very much depend on the help of knowledgeable and interested archivists and librarians. They deserve special thanks for providing me with the materials needed, for sharing their knowledge and for pointing out sources of potential interest. I would thus like to thank, first and foremost, the staff of the Filmarchiv Austria in Vienna, and in particular Thomas Ballhausen, for generously providing me with copies of many films without which I could not have written this book. I would also like to thank Christian Dewald and Karin Moser for valuable advice on various questions, and Miriam Frühstück and Peter Spiegel for their friendly help in finding suitable stills for this book. A big thank-you also goes to the Österreichische Mediathek in Vienna, and particularly to Johannes Kapeller and Hubert Rainer who were most helpful and cut the red tape to give me access to a number of important films. Finally, I would like to thank my kind friends and colleagues Martina Aicher, Barbara Eichinger and Judith Scheiring for getting hold of some of the films I needed for this book.

There are many more people who have offered not only intellectual stimulus but also invaluable emotional support during the years I have worked on this book. First and foremost I want to thank my dear colleagues at the Centre of European and International Studies and the University of Portsmouth, many of whom have become close friends, for their encouragement, interest and sometimes much needed diversion, in particular (in alphabetical order) Ivano Bruno, Yung-Fang Chen, Assaf Givati, Brigitte Leucht, Vijay Pereira, Fazlinah Said, Eva Sanchez-Turro, Katja Seidel, Kristian Steinnes and Cevdet Zengin. Their interest, kindness and openness made my five years in Portsmouth truly memorable. I also want to thank Mario Daniels for giving much needed intellectual advice and practical support while I reworked the manuscript under a looming deadline. I am very grateful to my sister Lisa Manneh for believing in this book and for providing continuous and generous support in all matters, be it by providing accommodation during my research visits to Vienna or by offering her wonderful skills in graphic design. And finally, I would like to thank Jakob Schindegger, not only for his excellent work on the cover design and the images for this book, but also for accompanying me through the last production stages of this book with so much kindness and understanding.

INTRODUCTION

In the Austrian costume comedy *Die Deutschmeister* (The Deutschmeister, 1955), a case of mistaken identity leaves the slightly quirky Baron Zorndorf, played by comedian Gunter Philipp, accidentally engaged to Countess Nanette. The night before, Zorndorf has fallen for the naïve charm of country girl Constanze Hübner (Romy Schneider) at a masquerade. Mistaking her for the offspring of wealthy Countess Burgstetten, he comes the next morning to ask for her hand in marriage. To his dismay he finds out that Burgstetten's daughter, Nanette (Susi Nicoletti), is not the same girl that he met the night before. Yet Countess Burgstetten, delighted at having finally found a suitor for her daughter, immediately busies herself arranging the engagement, leaving Zorndorf little choice but to stand by his proposal in order to save face. Nanette cannot remember any encounter with Zorndorf, and convinces herself that she must have been sleep-walking; she then questions him over a glass of champagne about the night they spent together, in order to find out why he is so eager to marry her. When Zorndorf, feeling slightly uncomfortable with Nanette's advances as she moves closer and closer, truthfully denies that he kissed her during their first encounter, she replies, rather indignantly: 'What kind of man are you? To *what* did I get engaged?'[1]

This scene, from one of the most popular Austrian costume films of the 1950s, is a useful illustration of contemporary views on masculinity and allows us to analyse how masculinity was treated in popular cinema. The dialogue shows that Nanette expects her partner to take the initiative in sexual matters – a form of behaviour that is typically regarded as masculine in Western culture. The fact that he does not meet these expectations suggests he might be somehow deficient in masculine attributes. To Nanette, Zorndorf's apparent lack of sexual interest is more than just an indicator that he is not a very masculine man: it signals that he is no man at all, which is why she refers to him as a thing – 'to *what* did I get engaged?' The fact that his appearance (he looks like a man) does not match his behaviour (he does not try to kiss her) causes tension. To resolve this confusion, Nanette sets out to test his manliness by then pulling him over and kissing him. His immediate, somatic and involuntary reaction – a strand of hair pops up, a metaphor for sexual arousal – reassures her, as well as the audience, that Baron Zorndorf is a 'real' – that is, heterosexual – man.

Significantly, *Die Deutschmeister* is a costume film, a genre that, with lavish costumes and high emotional content, has traditionally attracted female audiences.[2] Like in *Die Deutschmeister*, Austrian historical costume film often presents men as passive, which is a result both of generic and cinematic traditions and of Austria's particular political situation at the time. Masculinity could be mocked in *Die Deutschmeister* because men's position of power was secure by 1955. This had not always been the case. Masculinity, as this book will show, was an issue of major concern in postwar Austria, as the Second World War had caused dramatic social shifts and destabilised traditional gender relations in Austria. Men have traditionally been looked upon as pillars of society and nation, and so the loss of men's political, economic and symbolic power following the military defeat and occupation of the country was perceived as a threat to social order.[3]

This book will show how popular cinema tackled the pressing issues of masculinity and national identity, in order to establish how cinema intervened in and shaped popular discourses and thus helped to stabilise and modernise Austrian society. It investigates whose views cinema endorsed, promoted or contested, and asks whether the film industry largely followed its own (economic or artistic) agenda or allied itself with other social institutions, and for what purpose. My analysis demonstrates that due to the precarious economic conditions of the domestic film industry, as well as the specific political context of Allied occupation and the people's desire for national independence, popular cinema acquired a key role in formulating ideas about Austrian nationhood and masculinity.

The fact that Austria has a long cinematic tradition, and that its films once enjoyed great popularity inside Austria, in Germany and in some other neighbouring countries, has almost been forgotten. As has the fact that Austrian artists also left their imprint on other European cinemas and on Hollywood through co-operation, exchange of personnel and the (voluntary as well as forced) emigration of filmmakers, scriptwriters, musicians, actors and designers.[4] After the Second World War, Austrian film productions continued to draw large audiences in Austria, at least up to the late 1950s; it also remained successful in West Germany, traditionally Austria's main export market. The unbroken popularity of Austrian films in postwar Germany dumbfounded external observers, such as the US High Commissioner for Austria, who tried to explain the films' appeal by suggesting that 'the Austrian films, though artistically inferior, were in a lighter vein, whereas most of the German films, though artistically better, were serious and gloomy'.[5]

The Austrians' well documented preference for domestic over foreign productions after the war suggests that Austrian cinema offered something unique to its audience. So what was the appeal of Austrian cinema? Did it lie in the strong stylistic and personal continuities with pre-1945 cinema, which rewarded the audiences' longing for the familiar? Were audiences attracted by the genres of historical costume film, *Heimatfilm*, musical comedies and melodrama, which were typical of Austrian cinema? Was it in the way Austrian cinema engaged with pressing social issues, such as conflicted gender relations, the rapid modernisation of society or the trauma of war, by making light of gender troubles or by presenting the challenges of modernity in an optimistic light? Or was it that Austrian cinema evaded complicated subjects by glossing over the traumatic Nazi past, substituting it with images of a glorious imperial history or showcasing a rural idyll untainted by war or modernity, thereby providing reassurance or escape?

By analysing the aesthetics, narratives and themes of the films produced in the first decade after the war, then, I want to establish what made Austrian cinema so attractive to contemporary audiences; after all, it was the immense appeal of Austrian cinema which gave wide publicity to the notions of masculinity and national identity it advertised. To be sure, its attraction did not lie in artistic invention. Unlike other European cinemas Austrian cinema more or less continued where it had broken off in 1945.[6] It did not follow the German lead in trying its hand at what came to be known as the (short-lived) genre of the 'rubble film'.[7] Nor was the old guard of Austrian filmmakers inspired by Italian neorealism to find new forms of artistic expression; the two young filmmakers, Harald Röbbeling and Kurt Steinwendner, who attempted a neorealist approach, became targets of heated controversies and their films failed at the box office.[8] The influence of French and Hollywood *noir*-cinema, too, was very limited; it provided inspiration for two crime films but left no lasting imprint on Austrian cinema. Experimental or avant-garde cinema did not exist in Austria until the 1950s: Wolfgang Kudranovsky and the above-mentioned Steinwendner took the first hesitant steps in avant-garde cinema in 1951 with their filmic interpretation of Edgar Allan Poe's poem *Der Rabe* (The Raven), and Peter Kubelka, who presented his first film, *Mosaik im Vertrauen* (Mosaic in Confidence), in 1955, became Austria's pioneer in experimental cinema.[9] Yet the fact that most Austrian filmmakers did not seek novel forms of expression after the war did not impede the films' commercial success in the 1950s.

The period between 1945 and 1955 marked not only the last heyday of commercial Austrian cinema, but was also a most momentous historical period, as 1945 marked the end of German dictatorship and 1955 the regaining of national independence. Austria, from 1938 a part of Nazi Germany, came out of the Second World War as a defeated country whose economy and social structures lay in ruins, and whose future as an independent state was uncertain. With the ruling Nazi elites overthrown, a sizeable part of the population gone due to casualties and imprisonment and the Allied Forces now holding supreme power, society was in turmoil.[10] Apart from the urgent need to rebuild the economy and infrastructure, issues of both gender and national identity emerged as fields of particular concern. As in postwar Germany, men had lost their status as 'protectors, providers and procreators'.[11] Women had taken over men's roles during the war, which resulted in conflict when the men, often traumatised by the experiences of war and perhaps imprisonment, finally returned.[12] Men's loss of power was the subject of intense debate in the media, as well as in political, medical and Church circles, albeit often addressed indirectly in discussions about divorce rates, the issue of fraternisation, the problems of war veterans or the so-called youth problem.[13] The way in which the issue of masculinity was addressed, namely as a normative ideal that had become destabilised, and which needed to be strengthened in order to guarantee the functioning of society, suggests that there was much more at stake than domestic peace: the issue of masculinity was entangled with the question of political autonomy and the desire to instil a sense of Austrian identity in the people.

John Tosh's argument that in periods of emerging national identity the 'dominant masculinity is likely to become a metaphor for the political community as a whole' seems a fitting description of the national discourse in postwar Austria.[14] The question of nationhood occupied a prominent place in political and media discourses after the war. As a union with Germany was no longer desired (or opportune) after the downfall of the Third Reich, Austria's elites made considerable efforts to highlight the differences between Germany and Austria and promote a unique Austrian identity. This construction of an Austrian nation was first of all directed at the Austrian people, many of whom still considered themselves (at least culturally) German; although an Austrian sentiment existed in parts of the population, a clear concept of Austrian nationhood had yet to be actively produced. Furthermore, Austria's political and cultural elites also sought to convince the international community that Austria was different from Nazi Germany, an 'innocent victim' rather than a perpetrator, and thus deserving of being granted a better treatment.[15]

Due to the historical intertwining of nation, citizenship and masculinity, the latter played an influential role in the national rebuilding process.[16] Within the specific context of social destabilisation and confusion over national identity, the issue of masculinity acquired double significance: on the one hand, the dominant masculine ideal as embodiment of the nation needed to be strengthened in order to stabilise social order; on the other hand, this traditional ideal had to be adapted to changing political and economic circumstances and infused with new 'national' values in order to foster identification with the emerging Austrian nation. Popular cinema, as this book will show, played a key role in this nation-building process in that it formulated and promoted national ideals of masculinity, and thereby decisively shaped the discourse on nationhood.

Gender as a Category of Analysis

However, in order to establish how popular cinema engaged in this complex process of social reorganisation and nation building, and to understand why it represented masculinity in particular ways and repressed or omitted other possibilities, we need to assess the significant role of gender as a defining element of relationships of power. Gender, as a cultural construction, 'designates social relations between the sexes'; it also, as the feminist theorist Joan W. Scott argues in her seminal article 'Gender: A Useful Category of Historical Analysis', signifies relationships of power.[17] Hence, 'changes in the organisation of social relationships always correspond to changes in representations of power', which explains why in postwar Austria the established elites were so concerned about the destabilisation of traditional gender relations.[18]

Feminist historians were the first ones to explain the unequal distribution of power between men and women, by pointing to the constructedness of gender. Nira Yuval-Davis insists that gender 'should not be understood as a "real" difference between men and women, but as a mode of discourse' which defines the social roles of subjects on the basis of constructed differences.[19] Research into women's history showed how men and women were assigned specific gender roles and characteristics on the basis of biological differences, which granted or withheld access to political and economic power. By providing historical evidence that gender is socially created, feminist historians rebutted the claim upon which the legitimacy of patriarchy rests, namely that masculinity and femininity are natural and thus unchangeable. Anthropological and historical research have provided ample evidence that masculinity and femininity are not fixed entities, but mean different things to different people at different times.[20]

Gender is a relational category that interacts with concepts such as class or race, but also with other categories, such as age, religion or national or regional affiliations, the result of which is a wide variety of gender concepts and identities.[21] Because gender identities and gender ideals are varied and pluralistic, it is necessary to speak of masculinities and femininities in the plural. Gender is also relational in the sense that it seems impossible to speak about masculinity without speaking about femininity – it is, at least superficially, a matter of binary opposition. This idea, however, has been challenged and complicated by feminist theorists like Scott or Judith Butler, who questioned the 'fixed and permanent quality' of a binary opposition and called for a 'genuine historicization and deconstruction of the terms of sexual difference'.[22] By arguing that gender and even the biological sex itself are products of a cultural discourse which turns the material body into an embodiment of norms, Butler triggered a controversial but inspiring discussion about the validity of the binary system.[23] This debate serves to show that masculinities and femininities are neither one-dimensional nor fixed categories, but nuanced, unstable constructs that are open to change.

How do the abstract concepts of masculinity and femininity, which are produced and shaped through discourses (including the cinematic discourse), become 'real' and meaningful to individuals and societies? Construction, as Butler reminds us, is not a single act but a 'temporal process which operates through the reiteration of norms'.[24] Candace West and Sarah Fenstermaker have developed the theory of 'doing gender' to illustrate how individuals appropriate gender norms through socialisation and constant interaction with others. The concept of doing gender, which is based on the assumption that gender identities need to be affirmed on a daily basis, emphasises that the production of gender is neither a unidirectional process, from top to bottom, nor reducible to individual agency.[25] While masculinities and femininities are constructed within an institutional context and inscribed onto the individual, for example, through education, military service or the media, the practice of acknowledging and identifying with these norms also reproduces, reinforces or subverts the conditions in which gender is produced.[26] West and Fenstermaker highlight the element of human agency in the construction of gendered identities, and thus move a step away from earlier theories that ascribed considerably more power to discourses and institutions.

The power of cinema to produce gendered subjects and affirm the patriarchal system is highlighted by feminist film theorist Laura Mulvey in her seminal (and controversial) article 'Visual Pleasure and Narrative Cinema', published in 1975. Based on Jean-Louis Baudry's theory of the ideological effects of the cinematic apparatus, Mulvey introduced the concept of the 'male gaze', according to which cinema imposes the look of the male protagonist on the audience.[27] According to Mulvey, mainstream cinema operates in such a way that the spectator (whether male or female) has no choice but to identify with the gaze of the active male protagonist, which forces the female character into passivity and turns women into a 'sexual spectacle'.[28]

The concept of the male gaze was helpful in reconsidering how cinematic codes and conventions reinforce gender norms. However, it also caused fierce controversy because it denied that women possess an active gaze or can experience pleasure by looking at other females or at males.[29] The concept was also criticised for setting the gaze of the heterosexual white man on white women as the absolute norm, thereby ignoring other structures of oppression in mainstream cinema and the victimisation of other groups.[30]

Presenting mainstream cinema as an ideological apparatus that objectifies women to secure patriarchy obscured the system of dominance and suppression that exists among men. This is where the emerging field of theories of masculinities, and in particular R.W. Connell's influential concept of hegemonic masculinity, has covered new ground.[31] Based on Antonio Gramsci's theory of cultural hegemony, Connell argues that different categories of masculinity are situated within a hierarchical system in which all compete for dominance and power; the form of masculinity that achieves the hegemonic position subordinates other masculinities in order to assert its position.[32] Connell thus makes clear that hegemonic masculinity is 'always constructed in relation to various subordinated masculinities', and that some masculinities are sidelined or even suppressed. What manages to sustain this system is the demarcation from women and their subordination, which unites all forms of masculinities, even those at the margins.[33]

Hegemonic masculinity, it needs to be pointed out, is less a social practice than a cultural ideal – an ideal that, nevertheless, has real power to shape society because it embodies the 'masculine norms and practices which are most valued by the politically dominant class'.[34] In order to win the consent of the majority, hegemonic masculinity needs to convince it of the desirability of its norms. Influence is exerted on a number of levels, and although the pressure is usually subtle, it is so powerful that even marginalised men aspire to the ideal of normative masculinity in order to overcome their exclusion, as Jürgen Martschukat and Olaf Stieglitz point out.[35] Tosh hence describes hegemonic masculinity aptly as those 'masculine attributes which are most widely subscribed to – and least questioned – in a given social formation'.[36]

Gramsci's assumption that hegemony is established by cultural means rather than by the application of brute force points to the influential role of cultural media in sustaining the hegemonic ideal. By endorsing the views held by the ruling elites and presenting them as desirable, popular cinema often allies itself with those in power and helps to promote consensus in order to gain recognition. The broad consensus, in turn, does not allow cinema to stray away too far from the hegemonic views which the majority has adopted as its own.[37] Gramsci does not deny the subversive potential of institutions such as cinema, broadcasting or the press: under certain circumstances, cinema may contest dominant ideologies and social practices. After all, the position of hegemony is never secure and can be challenged at any time.[38] We thus have to be careful not to view cinema as a simple propaganda tool of dominant ideology. As Sue Harper points out in her illuminating study *Picturing the Past*, films have a range of functions apart from providing pleasure and textual comfort for their audience. Films may secure the power of the ruling elite by winning over marginalised groups, for instance, through incorporating them into the narrative. They may also strengthen a 'politically centrist position by excluding dissident groups or discourses'.[39] We thus need to ask whom cinema addresses, and how. Is it inclusive in the sense of making concessions to differences of class, age, religion or regional affiliation – an inclusivity that is reflected in a diversity of representations? Or does it marginalise or repress alternative possibilities and thus enforce a homogeneous view of society, which bolsters the position of those in power but might leave parts of the audience dissatisfied? Scott points out that gender is created first of all on the symbolic level, which is why it is crucial to investigate which culturally available symbols film uses, which symbolic representations it invokes to define gender norms and how it limits and contains the 'metaphoric possibilities' of symbols through interpretation.[40]

Film and Society

The relationship between popular cinema and society is clearly a complex one. Films, as Anton Kaes notes, comment on society, but they are also agents in that 'they intervene in on-going debates and often give shape to dominant discourses'.[41] Robert Allen and Douglas Gomery's suggestion that films 'derive their images and sounds, themes and stories ultimately from their social environment' implies that cinema is not simply an instrument of ideological domination, but both the product and instigator of discourse.[42] It responds to the 'fears, hopes and hidden anxieties' of a society by offering reassurance and orientation; not necessarily by promising a better world, but by limiting choices or by promoting role models.[43] The success of the *Heimatfilm* genre after the war arguably was down to the fact that it gave the audiences a glimpse of an unspoilt world that was governed by simple rules and that knew no confusion over women's or men's roles.

The desires, fears and concerns of a society can be traced by deciphering the fictional world of film. This means investigating the various layers of meaning in the filmic text, in particular the aesthetics, narrative modes and choice of themes. It involves studying the factors that shape cinematic representations – that is, the filmic traditions and modes of production which impact on the content and style of films, as well as producers' economic interests and market strategies or the aesthetic conceptions of those involved in the making of a film.[44] The audience's positive or negative response at the box office also affects future film productions. Last but not least, cinematic representations are influenced by the degree of control the film industry is subjected to, for example, through censorship, the amount of financial support it receives from governmental authorities or private investors and the cultural prestige a society ascribes to popular cinema.

In order to understand which social and political functions popular cinema fulfils, apart from providing entertainment, it is necessary to establish its status in society and its relation to the ruling elites. A state that ascribes a high economic value and level of influence to its cinema, as was the case in postwar Austria, will attempt to mobilise the support of the film industry through financial support, favourable legislation or specific forms of recognition – whether a film industry is willing to play to the wishes of those in power is again largely (but not solely) dependent on strategic considerations, such as the need for funding or the desire to increase one's social status. Although Austria's governing elites were unable (and largely also unwilling) to provide any financial backing, they nevertheless considered Austrian cinema to be a matter of national importance, as the regular presence of high-ranking officials at film premieres illustrates.[45] The elites saw Austrian cinema as a lucrative source of income, as well as a useful tool to foster the people's identification with the new nation. The film industry, on the other hand, fighting for economic survival, first of all looked towards governmental institutions for support, especially with regard to the taxation of cinemas and the lifting of export restrictions. As can be glimpsed from the lively and ongoing discussions in the trade papers, the industry was in agreement with the governing elites that its films should promote a positive image of Austria, assuming that this would also increase box-office takings, both in the domestic and export markets.

However, the controversies over films such as Fritz Kortner's gloomy depiction of the late Austro-Hungarian Empire in *Sarajevo* (1955), G.W. Pabst's discussion of anti-Semitism in *Der Prozess* (The Trial, 1948) or Harald Röbbeling's social-problem film *Asphalt* (1951) show that the consensus was not total. These films were exceptions to the norm, but they indicate that conflict existed over how to interpret history and/or social reality: on the margins of the dominant cinematic discourse, they are thus as important as the discourse itself, as they illustrate the variety of views that actually existed in Austrian cinema; the controversies they provoked also show why their interpretations could not win through.

Austrian Cinema – a National Cinema?

Like any other national cinema, Austrian cinema negotiated notions of nationhood – that 'distinct, familiar sense of belonging which is shared by people from different social and regional backgrounds'.[46] However, in postwar Austria the question of nationhood acquired perhaps an even greater significance than in other national cinemas because of the urgency with which the issue was debated. National cinema plays a key role in the construction and affirmation of national identity, and, as Andrew Higson suggests, it does so by homogenising internal differences and contradictions and by 'standardising' and 'naturalising' conceptions of the national.[47] Jill Forbes and Sarah Street argue that the 'double address' of national cinema, which makes films appeal to both domestic and foreign audiences, helps to reinforce a sense of national identity by promoting clichés which reflect back on domestic audiences.[48] According to Georg Tillner, the popular clichés of waltz, charm and *Gemütlichkeit*, which Wien-Film sold successfully as embodiments of the Austrian or Viennese spirit to the Germans during the era of the Third Reich, also strongly shaped the national discourse in postwar Austria.[49] Austrian audiences, encouraged by a political leadership that was keen to win recognition for the nation from the Allied Forces, often internalised these stereotypes, which were promoted through the media, education and political discourse.

Thomas Elsaesser categorises Austrian cinema as a national cinema due to Austria's long cinematic tradition and the 'special kind of continuity in its themes and genres over a lengthy period'; Austrian cinema boasts 'distinctive cinematic and aural signifiers', such as the Viennese dialect and Viennese stereotypes, as well as the typical genres of operetta films, musical biopics and musical comedies.[50] The 'Viennese' film, so called because of its celebration of a mythologised Vienna, and best represented by Willi Forst's costume melodramas, became the trademark of Austrian cinema in the 1930s and throughout the era of the Third Reich.[51] Austrian cinema did not break free from these cinematic traditions after the Second World War, but showed strong stylistic continuities. While they were in fact more diverse than often acknowledged, the films produced after 1945 displayed characteristics which contemporaries regarded as typical of Austrian cinema: a light-hearted narrative style, an emphasis on music and on the beautiful landscape, recurring motifs of Vienna (such as the waltz and a distinctive local charm), particular gestural codes and a standardised Viennese accent. Pondering which formulae might sell best abroad, a representative of the film industry concluded in 1950 that Austrian cinema offered something which 'others are not capable of', namely: 'musicality, charm, a light touch'.[52] A contemporary writer, offering a satirical analysis of the representation of romance in different national cinemas in the West German paper *Frankfurter Allgemeine* in 1953, mused that 'the lovely love film only exists in Austria', traditionally featuring a girl with a diminutive name, a father played by Hans Moser or Paul Hörbiger and a musical genius such as Schubert, Beethoven or Strauss as a fiancé, with all complications resolved in a beautiful, open setting and accompanied by a cheerful, touching melody.[53]

The film producers and Austria's political and cultural elites were united in the belief that Austrian cinema should convey a positive image of Austria. By constructing as well as reinforcing existing cultural myths, popular cinema fulfilled two tasks at the same time: it provided a source of shared identification for Austrians, many of whom were still confused about their national affiliation, and it ensured that Austrian cinema was a recognisable brand.[54] Nationhood was inscribed not only in the filmic texts, but also on the level of consumption: Austrian audiences, as one critic insisted in 1955, 'naturally ... like Austrian films best, as the number of cinema visits show'.[55] This strong identification with filmic traditions across all levels of society, the distinct aesthetics and themes of Austrian film and its specialisation in certain genres are evidence that Austrian cinema was a cinema in its own right – close to but still distinct from German cinema, at least until the mid-1950s.

The notion of national cinema, however, is not unproblematic. This goes in particular for Austrian cinema, whose claims in this regard have been disputed by international – and especially by German – scholarship, which tends to classify Austrian films, especially those produced in the first decades after the Second World War, as German, and considers Austrian cinema to be a mere sub-category of German cinema.[56] Undoubtedly, many links exist between German and Austrian cinema, as the following chapter illustrates: a shared language, a long tradition of economic cooperation and exchange of personnel, as well as the persistent, strong historical and cultural links between the two countries. The common language and the frequent screenings of Austrian films in German cinemas and, subsequently, on West German TV, mean that Austrian film has certainly become a part of the German cultural heritage. Nevertheless, to consider Austrian cinema simply as a variation of German cinema disregards its clear differences, and overlooks its influential role in Austrian society in the first half of the twentieth century.

There is further controversy: employing the concept of national cinema inevitably leads to the debate on transnational versus national cinema. Advocates of transnationality question the validity of the term 'national cinema', which presupposes a unity in the films produced in a particular nation-state and assumes that these films display cultural characteristics typical of that nation.[57] The argument put against the idea of a national cinema is that film is a commercial product of mass entertainment that seeks to penetrate national borders in order to maximise its profits. International film distribution and co-operation between different national industries, as well as the more-or-less universally understood visual language, make film a very mobile medium. Bergfelder, for example, argues that the steep rise in multinational co-productions and a preference for foreign settings in West German cinema in the 1960s 'challenge the very validity of national cinema as a means of classification'; he thus considers West German film from the 1960s onwards as transnational and part of a European cinema.[58]

So what about the close ties between the Austrian and the West German film industries? From the 1920s onwards, the Austrian film industry relied on the German market, and there were periods when German financiers invested strongly in Austrian film production. However, in the period covered here – the time between the end of the Second World War and the regaining of national independence in 1955 – Austrian cinema was, at least in the immediate postwar years, strongly inwardly oriented and largely cut off from the German market due to strict trade restrictions imposed by the Allied Forces. The situation only changed after a trade agreement was reached with the newly independent West Germany in 1950, which facilitated exports and opened the doors to German investors. This resulted in a gradual increase in Austrian-German co-productions, which reached an average of about one fifth of the overall film production in Austria in the mid-1950s; still, in about half of these productions Austria assumed the dominant role and provided the main artistic and creative input, through the use of Austrian directors, actors and technical personnel. Thus, up to the mid-1950s, about 90 per cent of domestic output was still initiated and dominated by Austrians.

Around the mid-1950s, however, this changed considerably, as West German distributors who financed films by granting distribution guarantees gained more influence and the exchange of personnel between the two industries intensified. The German and Austrian film industries became more intertwined, financially as well as artistically, producing remakes and sequels of each other's films.[59] It was only around this time that Austrian cinema acquired a transnational, or, more precisely, a binational quality. Both film production and film aesthetics increasingly lost their national imprint, making a distinction between Austrian and West German film more difficult. Cinema's rapid decline in Austria in the early 1960s was not a direct result of this close and almost exclusive cooperation with West Germany, but this interconnection was certainly influential in its demise in that the Austrian industry ignored aesthetic trends outside the German-speaking market, such as the emergence of the French New Wave, and underestimated the impact of technical developments such as the quickly growing popularity of television.

A transnational perspective on cinema has the undisputable advantage of bringing into focus the cultural exchange of ideas and styles and the economic 'interpenetration' of otherwise seemingly distinct national film industries; it also highlights the historical variability and cultural hybridity of national cinemas.[60] However, recognising the benefits of a transnational approach does not necessarily mean discarding the concept of national cinema as a whole, as long as it remains clear that national cinema is not a stable or closed entity, but a negotiated space often without firm boundaries. National cinema is always subject to other cultural influences and responds to wider international developments, both artistic and technological, by appropriating these trends or by countering them. Most film industries seek to maximise profits by accessing new markets, but an industry also needs to keep up with the international (usually Hollywood) standard of filmmaking to secure the domestic market against competition.[61] Thus, drawing a strict line between transnational and national cinema may not be possible at all because of the 'fluid, contingent and hybrid quality of any cultural formation'.[62]

We can, however, establish how open and flexible a national cinematic culture is, and how it engages with the nation and its cultural heritage. Whether a cinema should be considered as national also depends on who is in control of the production, distribution and exhibition of films. Other important questions are whether the film industry, or the state as a subsidising or legislative body, actively promotes domestic productions, and whether audiences prefer national productions over foreign ones. The national can also be located in the filmic texts themselves, which evoke national characteristics through their visuals, narratives, themes or symbols.[63] So, rather than just identifying the national through aesthetics or determining it on the level of production and consumption, all these elements need to be taken into account when applying the term 'national cinema'. The fact that this book considers postwar Austrian cinema as a national cinema in its own right does not mean that it fetishises the national or celebrates Austrian cinema as superior. Nor does it, as the next chapter will show, ignore the 'cultural cross-breeding' across borders, or the consequences of Austrian economic dependency on the West German market.[64]

The body of films made between 1946 and 1955 constitutes the primary source of this book. During that period, 212 feature-length films were produced; I was able to analyse 140 films, almost two-thirds of this total output – a solid basis from which to draw valid and representative conclusions. Because my main research questions involve uncovering patterns and themes, I opt for a broader, generic approach rather than focusing on a few selected films. Analysing representations of masculinity in different genres allows me to uncover differences and similarities; such an approach gives due consideration to generic and cinematic traditions that shape representations of masculinity, and factors audience expectations into the analysis. Masculinity, as mentioned earlier, is a relational category and constructed in differentiation from femininity. Cinematic representations of masculinity can thus never be investigated in isolation, but need to be analysed in how they are differentiated from, and overlap with, concepts of femininity, as well as how they relate to the definitions of gender roles and gender relations cinema proposed. The reason why some chapters pay more attention to femininity than others is largely due to the dominant themes and conventions of the chosen genres. Masculinity, however, lies at the centre of this study, largely because scholarly interest in women has produced some insightful studies on the representation of women in Austrian cinema, whereas the analysis of masculinities is largely uncharted territory.[65]

This book explores the role of popular cinema in a society in transition. Analysing the cinematic discourses on masculinity and the way they are interwoven with other popular discourses, this study brings into view the changing notions of gender and acceptable gendered behaviour, and thus helps to understand how popular cinema is involved in the construction of gender norms. This is crucial to establish whether cinematic representations of masculinity were the products of social consensus, or whether they conflicted with the masculine ideals endorsed by Austria's political or cultural elites.[66] Yet Tosh has rightly cautioned that studying discourses and representations may become 'a curiously detached kind of cultural analysis'.[67] Discourses are always historically specific, and therefore the meaning and influence of cinematic representations of masculinity can only be assessed within their wider historical context and with regard to other contemporary discourses, such as those on Austria's involvement in Nazi crimes or on the role of women. In order to be able to make valid assumptions about how the films were understood and which meanings they carried for contemporary audiences, the analysis has to be firmly grounded in the social, political and economic context from which the films emerged.

This book seeks to bridge the gap between the textual and contextual levels by giving equal consideration to the filmic texts and to the context in which they were produced and consumed. To establish the significance of cinematic representations it is essential to investigate which films were particularly popular with audiences and which films were rejected. Studies focusing on cinema audiences, such as Harper's analysis of exhibition patterns of local British cinemas in the 1940s, or Robert James's investigation of the cinema-going habits of the British working-class in the 1930s, have demonstrated how much audience taste varies in terms of class, sex or location.[68] For Germany, Joseph Garncarz's evaluation of box-office rankings and statistical data has provided hard evidence of the audience's preference for domestic films in the 1950s and 1960s, and thus revised the theory of a total dominance of Hollywood cinema in Europe.[69] Hester Baer's analysis of the West German film magazine *Film und Frau* (Film and Woman) shows how the magazine not only aimed to meet the tastes of 1950s female audiences, but also tried to train the artistic eye of the female spectator.[70] It is, of course, very difficult to ascertain what audiences really thought or liked about a film; even oral-history studies, such as Annette Kuhn's interview-based analysis of cinema-going habits in 1930s Britain, cannot reconstruct the actual feelings of contemporary audiences.[71] However, analysing contemporary film reviews and trade journals and assessing the coverage in fan magazines and daily newspapers – as, for example, Janet Thumin and Janet Staiger have done in their studies on British and Hollywood cinema respectively – can uncover which cinematic representations were acceptable and which provoked controversy.[72] Thus, as Thumin aptly puts it, 'if we cannot meet the audience, we can reconstruct the discursive contexts of their cinema going and their readings of films'.[73]

A look at the trade journal *Österreichische Film und Kinozeitung* reveals that in postwar Austria the main debates revolved around three related topics: the financial and critical success of Austrian films in the domestic and international markets; the financial difficulties of the Austrian film industry; and the problems it faced with regard to export regulations and restrictions imposed by the Allied Forces. In contrast, the general press coverage, although also expressing a strong interest in the financial problems of the film industry, debated at length the possibly damaging effect of films on young people and the question of censorship. The Austrian film and fan magazines *Film, Mein Film, Funk und Film* and *Illustrierter Filmkurier*, on the other hand, ignored these issues, and instead catered to those fans who looked for information on the private lives of their favourite film stars, thereby giving equal consideration to national and international films and stars. Analysing these materials reveals the often contradictory emotions that cinema triggered in Austrian society, and demonstrates how the debates surrounding the medium of film interconnected with contemporary discourses on youth, the role of women and the influence of US American culture.

I am well aware that an approach that aims to identify patterns, and which traces the interconnectedness of discourses, carries the risk of achieving comprehensiveness at the expense of analytical depth; each genre-led chapter is therefore complemented with detailed case studies to illustrate my argument. The book's structure reflects my historicist approach to film. The first chapter analyses postwar Austrian audiences and their preferences, the historical developments in the film industry and the economic and political conditions of film production after the war, and assesses the role of cinema within wider society. The chapter opens with an analysis of audience taste and discusses why Austrian cinema specialised in certain genres and neglected others, such as crime, war and social-problem films. The second part briefly describes the developments in the Austrian film industry up to 1945, investigates the modes of film production and distribution and considers the economic and artistic challenges the film industry faced after the war. It also shows how the occupying Allied Forces intervened by controlling the distribution of films and restricting exports to West Germany, and discusses the impact of the industry's continuing dependence on the West German market. The last part looks at the role of popular cinema within its wider social context by analysing how cinematic discourse responded to issues of major concern in postwar Austrian society.

Chapter Two is devoted to historical costume film, which was one of the most popular genres in postwar Austria. This film genre arguably fulfilled three major functions: promoting a new Austrian identity, glossing over the dark Nazi past with images of a glorified, multi-cultural Empire, and popularising the image of a 'cultured', 'softer' Austrian masculinity to demarcate it from 'hard' German masculinity. By analysing depictions of the military man I seek to demonstrate how the genre – expressed through the popular figure of Austrian musicality – helped to depoliticise the military and substantiate the claim that Austria was a victim of Nazi aggression, and not a perpetrator.

Chapter Three considers *Heimatfilm*, a genre that is regarded as archetypal of 1950s Austrian and West German cinema. Even though *Heimatfilm* has attracted considerable scholarly interest, a focus on representations of masculinity can still produce new insights into the social functions of the genre. Centring on the discourses of purity and dirt, and guilt and repentance, my analysis shows how the films took up pressing social issues and helped the audience to work through these problems. Through the portrayal of archetypal male figures, Austrian *Heimatfilm* helped to ease the specific guilt of the Austrian nation and a more general guilt about men's actions in the Second World War.

Chapter Four looks at tourist film – a type of film that is not an industrial category, but a term I apply retrospectively to describe those films that deal with the holiday experiences of urban tourists. Because of its focus on the landscape, tourist film has often been categorised as a sub-genre of *Heimatfilm*, and has thus been awarded very little critical attention. I argue that it is important to look at the tourist film as a critical category in its own right, not only because it displays crucial differences in narrative patterns and visual style from *Heimatfilm*, but also because it fulfilled a very different function. Focusing on the genre's dominant narrative themes of mobility and modernity, I will show that tourist film, unlike any other genre in postwar Austria, promoted modern masculinities and equal gender relations, if only for a limited time.

Chapter Five covers comedy, a genre that has often been neglected as an object of study, even though it accounted for the largest share of films produced in postwar Austria. In response to Jean-Pierre Jeancolas's suggestion that humour is 'inexportable', I discuss the double address of Austrian comedies which made them appeal to both German and Austrian audiences.[74] Focusing on the dominant narrative themes of mistaken identity and troubled gender relations, I explore how comedy addressed pressing social issues and thus engaged in popular discourses on fatherhood, consumerism or gender relations. The chapter also reveals the ambiguous and often contradictory role of Austrian comedy: while it promoted new, liberal father figures, it also endorsed traditional patriarchal structures and female submission; it thus played a crucial part in the stabilisation of society that was accompanied by a return to more conservative gender roles from the late 1940s onwards.

Finally, Chapter Six ties the different strands of analysis together, and asks how postwar cinema shaped popular notions of gender and national identity. By tracing the developments in Austrian cinema after the country gained national independence in 1955, this concluding chapter discusses the reasons for the demise of Austrian cinema in the 1960s and its inability to respond to international trends in filmmaking. It also analyses why it failed to leave an impact on future generations of filmmakers, and why the new Austrian cinema that started to emerge in the 1970s and gathered in strength in the 1990s cut itself off from older cinematic traditions and pursued new forms of artistic expression. Answers to these questions can be found in the development and economic and artistic orientation of the Austrian film industry, which is the topic of the next chapter.

Notes

1. My emphasis.
2. See S. Harper. 1997. 'Bonnie Prince Charlie Revisited: British Costume Film in the 1950s', in R. Murphy (ed.), *The British Cinema Book*, London: BFI, 133.

3. Erna Appelt has convincingly demonstrated the links between gender, citizenship and nation. See E. Appelt. 1999. *Geschlecht - Staatsbürgerschaft - Nation. Politische Konstruktionen des Geschlechterverhältnisses in Europa*, Frankfurt am Main: Campus, 143–146.

4. See G. Heiss and I. Klimeš. 2003. *Obrazy Času / Bilder der Zeit. Tschechischer und Österreichischer Film der 30er Jahre*, Prague: Národní Filmový Archiv, VPS; T. Bergfelder and C. Cargnelli. 2008. *Destination London: German-speaking Emigrés and British Cinema, 1925–1950*, New York: Berghahn; J.C. Horak and E. Tape. 1986. *Fluchtpunkt Hollywood. Eine Dokumentation zur Filmemigration nach 1933* (2nd ed.), Münster: MAKS.

5. Cited by U. Halbritter. 1993. *Der Einfluss der Alliierten Besatzungsmächte auf die österreichische Filmwirtschaft und Spielfilmproduktion in den Jahren 1945 bis 1955*, unpublished master's thesis (Diplomarbeit), University of Vienna, 59, 62.

6. See W. Fritz. 1991. *Kino in Österreich 1929–1945. Der Tonfilm*, Vienna: ÖBV, 210.

7. See E. Carter. 2000. 'Sweeping up the Past: Gender and History in the Postwar German "Rubble" Film', in U. Sieglohr (ed.), *Heroines without Heroes: Reconstructing Female and National Identities in European Cinema, 1945–51*, London: Continuum International Publishing Group; R.R. Shandley. 2001. *Rubble Films: German Cinema in the Shadow of the Third Reich*, Philadelphia: Temple University Press.

8. See U. Döge. 2004. 'ASPHALT 1951–1953 in Österreich, Frankreich und der Schweiz', in C. Dewald (ed.), *Der Wirklichkeit auf der Spur. Essays zum österreichischen Nachkriegsfilm ASPHALT*, Vienna: Filmarchiv Austria, 63–74.

9. B. Wegenstein. 2008. 'The Embodied Film: Austrian Contributions to Experimental Cinema', in R. Halle and R. Steingröver (eds), *After the Avant-Garde: Contemporary German and Austrian Experimental Film*, Rochester, N.Y.: Camden House, 51; R. Dassanowsky. 2005. *Austrian Cinema: A History*, Jefferson, N.C.: McFarland & Co, 195.

10. See E. Bruckmüller. 1985. *Sozialgeschichte Österreichs*, Vienna: Herold, 520.

11. H. Fehrenbach. 1998. 'Rehabilitating Fatherland. Race and German Remasculinisation', *Signs*, 24(1), 109.

12. See, e.g., I. Bandhauer-Schöffmann and E. Hornung. 1996. 'War and Gender Identity: The Experience of Austrian Women, 1945–1950', in D.F. Good, M. Grandner and M.J. Maynes (eds), *Austrian Women in the Nineteenth and Twentieth Centuries*, Providence, R.I.: Berghahn; E. Langthaler. 1996. 'Ländliche Lebenswelten von 1945 bis 1950', in R. Sieder, H. Steinert and E. Tálos (eds), *Österreich 1945–1995: Gesellschaft, Politik, Kultur*, Vienna: Verlag für Gesellschaftskritik.

13. See I. Bauer and R. Huber. 2007. 'Sexual Encounters across (Former) Enemy Borderlines', in G. Bischof, A. Pelinka and D. Herzog (eds), *Sexuality in Austria*, New Brunswick, N.J.: Transaction Publishers; Österreichisches Statistisches Zentralamt. 1959a. *Die Ehescheidung. Eine statistisch-soziologische Untersuchung*, Vienna, 41–43; For Germany see, e.g., F. Biess. 2006. *Homecomings: Returning POWs and the Legacies of Defeat in Postwar Germany*, Princeton, N.J.: Princeton University Press; Fehrenbach, 1998; M. Höhn. 2002. *GIs and Fräuleins: The German-American Encounter in 1950s West Germany*, Chapel Hill, N.C.: University of North Carolina Press; R.G. Moeller. 1998. '"The Last Soldiers of the Great War" and Tales of Family Reunions in the Federal Republic of Germany', *Signs*, 24(1); R.G. Moeller. 1997. 'Reconstructing the Family in Reconstruction Germany: Women and Social Policy in the Federal Republic 1949/1955', in R.G. Moeller (ed.), *West Germany under Construction: Politics, Society, and Culture in the Adenauer Era*, Ann Arbor: University of Michigan Press; R.G. Moeller. 2001. 'Heimkehr ins Vaterland: Die Remaskulierung Westdeutschlands in den fünfziger Jahren', *Militärgeschichtliche Zeitschrift*, 2(1).

14. J. Tosh. 2004. 'Hegemonic Masculinity and the History of Gender', in S. Dudink, K. Hagemann and J. Tosh (eds), *Masculinities in Politics and War: Gendering Modern History*, Manchester: Manchester University Press, 49.

15. See E. Brix. 1988. 'Zur Frage der österreichischen Identität am Beginn der Zweiten Republik', in G. Bischof and J. Leidenfrost (eds), *Die bevormundete Nation. Österreich und die*

Alliierten 1945–1949, Innsbruck: Haymon; E. Bruckmüller. 1997. *Symbole österreichischer Identität zwischen 'Kakanien' und 'Europa'*, Vienna: Picus Verlag, 42–45.

16. See U. Frevert. 1996. 'Soldaten, Staatsbürger. Überlegungen zur historischen Konstruktion von Männlichkeit', in T. Kühne (ed.), *Männergeschichte - Geschlechtergeschichte. Männlichkeit im Wandel der Moderne*, Frankfurt am Main: Campus, 69–87, 80–82; Tosh, 2004, 49; S.O. Rose. 2007. 'Fit to Fight but Not to Vote? Masculinity and Citizenship in Britain, 1832–1918', in S. Dudink, K. Hagemann and A. Clark (eds), *Representing Masculinity: Male Citizenship in Modern Western Culture*, New York: Palgrave Macmillan, 141; A. Forrest. 2007. 'Citizenship and Masculinity: The Revolutionary Citizen-Soldier and his Legacy', in S. Dudink, K. Hagemann and A. Clark (eds), *Representing Masculinity: Male Citizenship in Modern Western Culture*, New York: Palgrave Macmillan, 124.

17. J.W. Scott. 1986. 'Gender: A Useful Category of Historical Analysis', *The American Historical Review*, 91(5), 10–56.

18. See Scott, 1986, 1067.

19. N. Yuval-Davis. 1997. *Gender & Nation*, London: Sage, 9.

20. See R.W. Connell. 1996. *Masculinities*, Cambridge: Polity Press, 47.

21. J. Martschukat and O. Stieglitz. 2008. *Geschichte der Männlichkeiten*, Frankfurt am Main: Campus, 55–56.

22. Scott, 1986, 1065.

23. J. Butler. 1993. *Bodies that Matter: On the Discursive Limits of 'Sex'*, London: Routledge, 10–11.

24. Butler, 1993, 10.

25. See C. West and S. Fenstermaker. 1995. 'Doing Difference', *Gender & Society*, 9(1), 21.

26. See R.W. Connell. 1993. 'The Big Picture: Masculinities in Recent World History', *Theory and Society*, 22(5), 602.

27. L. Mulvey. 2004 [1975]. 'Visual Pleasure and Narrative Cinema', in L. Braudy and M. Cohen (eds), *Film Theory and Criticism: Introductory Readings*, Oxford: Oxford University Press, 842. First published in *Screen*, 16(3).

28. M. Jancovich. 1995. 'Screen Theory', in J. Hollows and M. Jancovich (eds), *Approaches to Popular Film*, Manchester: Manchester University Press, 143.

29. Jancovich, 1995, 144.

30. J. Gaines. 1988. 'White Privilege and Looking Relations', *Screen*, 29(4), 16; E.A. Kaplan. 1997. *Looking for the Other: Feminism, Film, and the Imperial Gaze*, New York: Routledge, 7.

31. See Connell, 1996.

32. See Connell, 1996, 76–81; Connell, 1993, 603; E. Hanisch. 2005. *Männlichkeiten*, Vienna: Böhlau, 26–28, 267–274, 301–332; G.L. Mosse. 1998. *The Image of Man. The Creation of Modern Masculinity*, Oxford: Oxford University Press, 56–76; H. Schissler. 1992. 'Männerstudien in den USA', *Geschichte und Gesellschaft*, 18(2), 204–205.

33. R.W. Connell. 1987. *Gender and Power: Society, the Person, and Sexual Politics*, Cambridge: Polity Press, 183. For the demarcation from homosexual masculinity see also M. Dinges. 2005. '"Hegemoniale Männlichkeit" – Ein Konzept auf dem Prüfstand', in M. Dinges (ed.), *Männer-Macht-Körper. Hegemoniale Männlichkeiten vom Mittelalter bis heute*, Frankfurt am Main: Campus, 9, 12, 16f.; W. Schmale. 2003. *Geschichte der Männlichkeit in Europa (1450–2000)*, Vienna: Böhlau, 227–230.

34. Tosh, 2004, 48.

35. See Martschukat and Stieglitz, 2008, 65.

36. Tosh, 2004, 47.

37. See A. Gramsci. 1971 [1935]. 'Notes on Italian History', in A. Gramsci, Q. Hoare and G. Nowell-Smith (eds), *Selections from the Prison Notebooks of Antonio Gramsci*, London: Lawrence and Wishart, 80.

38. Connell, 1996, 77; see also Tosh, 2004, 45; Dinges, 2005, 11.

39. S. Harper. 1994. *Picturing the Past: The Rise and Fall of the British Costume Film*, London: BFI, 3.
40. Scott, 1986, 1067.
41. A. Kaes. 1995. 'German Cultural History and the Study of Film: Ten Theses and a Postscript', *New German Critique*, 65, 51.
42. R.C. Allen and D. Gomery. 1985. *Film History: Theory and Practice*, New York: McGraw-Hill, 158.
43. Kaes, 1995, 51; also Allen and Gomery, 1985, 165.
44. See M. Lagny. 1997. 'Kino für Historiker', *Österreichische Zeitschrift für Geschichte*, 8(4), 466.
45. Austria's president, chancellor and a number of ministers attended the premiere of *Der Engel mit der Posaune* (The Angel with the Trumpet, 1948); the premiere of *Vagabunden* (Vagabonds, 1949) was honoured with the presence of the president and members of the government; that of *Wiener Mädeln* (Viennese Girls, 1949) was attended by the chancellor, members of the government and the vice-mayor; members of the government also came to the premiere of the comedy *Es schlägt dreizehn* (That's the Limit! 1950). See 'Der Engel mit der Posaune', *Wiener Tageszeitung*, 17 October 1948; 'Uraufführung des Films "Vagabunden"', *Das Kleine Volksblatt*, 22 October 1949; 'Die langerwarteten "Wiener Mädeln"', *Wiener Zeitung*, 24 December 1949; 'Als es dreizehn schlug', *Arbeiterzeitung*, 23 September 1950.
46. See S. Street. 1997. *British National Cinema*, London: Routledge, 1.
47. See A. Higson. 2002 [1989]. 'The Concept of National Cinema', in C. Fowler (ed.), *The European Cinema Reader*, London: Routledge, 139.
48. J. Forbes and S. Street. 2000. *European Cinema: An Introduction*, Basingstoke: Palgrave, 41.
49. See G. Tillner. 1996. 'Österreich, ein weiter Weg. Filmkultur zwischen Austrofaschismus und Wiederaufbau', in R. Beckermann and C. Blümlinger (eds), *Ohne Untertitel: Fragmente einer Geschichte des österreichischen Kinos*, Vienna: Sonderzahl, 184.
50. T. Elsaesser. 1999. 'Austria', in T. Elsaesser (ed.), *The BFI Companion to German Cinema*, London: BFI, 26, 28.
51. See W. Fritz. 1996. *Im Kino erlebe ich die Welt. 100 Jahre Kino und Film in Österreich*, Vienna: Verlag Christian Brandstätter, 149–172.
52. See A. Schuchmann. 1950. 'Filmwirtschaft: Der österreichische Film im Ausland', *Film-Kunst. Zeitschrift für Filmkultur und Filmwissenschaft*, 5, 246.
53. F. Hrastinik. 'Im Film dreht sich alles um die Liebe', *Frankfurter Allgemeine*, 6 March 1953, 6.
54. E. Hanisch. 1994. *Der lange Schatten des Staates. Österreichische Gesellschaftsgeschichte im 20. Jahrhundert*, Vienna: Ueberreuter, 161–163.
55. My emphasis. 'Rückschau auf das Filmjahr 1954 in Österreich?', *Wiener Zeitung*, 9 January 1955.
56. See, for example, C. Seidl. 1987. *Der deutsche Film der fünfziger Jahre*, Munich: Heyne; T. Bergfelder. 2006. *International Adventures: German Popular Cinema and European Co-productions in the 1960s*, New York: Berghahn, 31, 40. Mary Wauchope regards Austrian cinema as an important contributor to West German cinema in the 1950s, rather than as a separate national cinema. She also introduces the concept of 'regional cinema' to provide a more accurate description of the close relationship between Austrian and German cinema, especially with regard to the production of *Heimatfilm* in the 1950s. This is a regionality, however, that is only evident in film texts and locations, and not in the companies that produced the films. See M. Wauchope. 2007. 'The Other "German" Cinema', in J.E. Davidson and S. Hake (eds), *Framing the Fifties: Cinema in a Divided Germany*, New York: Berghahn, 214–217.
57. See Higson, 2002, 137–139; see also A. Higson. 2000. 'The Limiting Imagination of National Cinema', in M. Hjort and S. MacKenzie (eds), *Cinema and Nation*, London:

Routledge; T. Bergfelder. 2005. 'National, Transnational or Supranational Cinema? Re-thinking European Film Studies', *Media, Culture & Society*, 27(3).

58. See Bergfelder, 2006, 4, 10.
59. See Wauchope, 2007, 214.
60. See S. Crofts. 1998. 'Concepts of National Cinema', in J. Hill and Church Gibson (eds), *Oxford Guide to Film Studies*, Oxford: Oxford University Press, 386.
61. Higson, 2002, 136.
62. A. Higson and R. Maltby. 1999. '"Film Europe" and "Film America": An Introduction', in A. Higson and R. Maltby (eds), *'Film Europe' and 'Film America': Cinema, Commerce and Cultural Exchange 1920–1939*, Exeter: University of Exeter Press, 18.
63. See ibid., 132f; also S. Hake. 2002. *German National Cinema*, London: Routledge, 3f.
64. Higson, 2000, 67.
65. See, e.g., E. Büttner and C. Dewald. 1997a. *Anschluß an Morgen. Eine Geschichte des öster-reichischen Films von 1945 bis zur Gegenwart*, Salzburg: Residenz; S. Schachinger. 1993. *Der österreichische Heimatfilm als Konstruktionsprinzip nationaler Identität in Österreich nach 1945*, unpublished master's thesis (Diplomarbeit), University of Vienna.
66. See Scott, 1986, 1068.
67. Tosh, 2004, 52.
68. See S. Harper. 2006. 'Fragmentation and Crisis: 1940s Admission Figures at the Regent Cinema, Portsmouth, UK', *Historical Journal of Film, Radio and Television*, 26(3); R. James. 2006. *Working-class Taste in 1930s Britain: A Comparative Study of Film and Literature*, un-published PhD thesis, University of Portsmouth.
69. J. Garncarz. 1994. 'Hollywood in Germany: The Role of American Films in Germany, 1925–1990', in D.W. Ellwood and R. Kroes (eds), *Hollywood in Europe: Experiences of a Cul-tural Hegemony*, Amsterdam: VU University Press.
70. See H. Baer. 2007. '*Film und Frau* and the Female Spectator in 1950s West German Cin-ema', in J.E. Davidson and S. Hake (eds), *Framing the Fifties: Cinema in a Divided Germany*, New York: Berghahn.
71. Kuhn may not have been able to reconstruct the actual cinema-going experience, but she provides a colourful and detailed picture of cinema memory. See A. Kuhn. 2002. *An Everyday Magic: Cinema and Cultural Memory*, London: I.B. Tauris.
72. See J. Thumin. 2002. 'The "Popular", Cash and Culture in the Postwar British Cinema Industry', in C. Fowler (ed.), *The European Cinema Reader*, London: Routledge; J. Staiger. 1992. *Interpreting Films: Studies in the Historical Reception of American Cinema*, Princeton, N.J: Princeton University Press.
73. Thumin, 2002, 198.
74. J.P. Jeancolas. 1992. 'The Inexportable: The Case of French Cinema and Radio in the 1950s', in R. Dyer and G. Vincendeau (eds), *Popular European Cinema*, London: Routledge, 143f.

Chapter 1

POPULAR CINEMA AND SOCIETY

Austrian Cinema and the Audience

In January 1946, eight months after Nazi Germany's downfall, the shooting of the first Austrian postwar film began. The film's serious title, *Glaube an mich* (Believe in Me), a plea to put trust in the future of Austria, contrasted with its content. *Glaube an mich* was directed by the Austrian-Hungarian revue specialist Géza von Cziffra, and was a light-hearted winter sports comedy (see Chapter Four for more details) that had little to say about the immediate Nazi past, the war or the deprivations from which people were still suffering. Traditional in choice of theme as well as aesthetic style, it was meant to provide distraction for an audience that looked with pessimism into the future.

Glaube an mich is also illustrative of the circumstances under which films were produced in the immediate postwar years. It was shot on location in the Alps in the French Occupation Zone and then completed in the Sievering studio in Vienna, in the US Zone, with the Soviet Army providing most of the film stock; the owner of a racing stable, who had made his fortune on the black market, financed the production.[1]

The difficulties in getting the film produced were indicative of the state of the film industry at the time. However, even though it struggled with shortages of material and equipment and (at least initially) depended on the goodwill of the Allied Forces (who occupied Austria until 1955), Austria's film industry recovered fairly quickly. Whereas West German filmmakers, faced with the widespread destruction (both social and physical) of their country, felt compelled 'to seek out a film language strong enough to confront recent German history', their Austrian counterparts looked to a more distant imperial past for orientation.[2] Where Austrian filmmakers did attempt to find new ways of expression, the changes were usually subtle and remained within the confines of Austria's cinematic tradition. As a result, postwar Austrian cinema displays no immediately visible break with the cinema of the Third Reich, neither aesthetically nor in terms of

narrative. Only on closer scrutiny do the films reveal ruptures and inconsistencies which can be read as the traces of a severe trauma.[3]

A Matter of Taste: The Popularity of
Cinema in Postwar Austria

From the early twentieth century up to the 1960s, cinema was the most
popular form of entertainment in Austria. The number of cinemas rose
from only twelve in 1906 to 839 in 1936, with the eastern province of Lower
Austria holding the largest number (314), and the most western province
of Vorarlberg the smallest number (14). Vienna, Austria's capital, was the
centre of film production, and also accounted for about half of all box office
takings in Austria.[4] More and more cinemas were built, and the Austrian
film industry as a whole thrived under Nazi occupation: in 1944, despite
(or perhaps because of) the looming defeat of Nazi Germany, the 222 Viennese cinemas allegedly counted around sixty million visitors.[5] While
Vienna's traditional theatres closed in September 1944, cinemas continued
to play almost to the final defeat, and resumed business a few weeks after
the Soviet troops had freed Vienna on 13 April 1945. The glamorous Apollo
cinema was among the first to re-open, premiering with a German film,
Der Engel mit dem Saitenspiel (The Angel with the Harp), produced in 1944, a
fact which illustrates the fairly smooth transition between the Third Reich
and postwar Austria with regard to film production and exhibition.

The impressive number of cinemas and tickets sold during the postwar
years in Austria, which then counted a population only of approximately
6.9 million people, is evidence of cinema's unbroken popularity.[6] Even
though cinema operators complained about the tax burden and shrinking
incomes, largely due to the growing number of cinemas, film boomed after
the war. The number of cinemas in postwar Vienna, with a population of
about 1.8 million people in the early 1950s, quickly rose from 207 in 1949
to an all-time high of 228 in 1953.[7] After that, numbers started to decline in
the capital, but continued to grow in the rest of the country: in 1953, there
were 1,143 cinemas in Austria, with a total of about 108 million visitors;
five years later, the number had increased to 1,244 cinemas, with almost
120 million visitors.[8] Cinema, as the Austrian producer Erich von Neusser
noted in 1954, was not just a leisure pursuit, but a 'necessity', at least for city
dwellers.[9] Going to the cinema was considered a basic need, second only
to eating and sleeping, according to the newspaper *Wiener Tageszeitung*.[10]
A comparison with other forms of mass entertainment underlines the
popularity of cinema. In 1954, Viennese cinemas counted 48.3 million tickets sold (that is more than thirty visits per citizen a year), whereas sports
events sold only 2.5 million and Viennese theatres 2.67 million tickets.[11]
Nineteen-year-olds were the keenest cinema-goers in the mid-1950s;[12] a
survey conducted among teenage apprentices in Vienna in 1955 showed

that male teenagers went to the cinema on average 4.7 times per month, and females 3.6 times a month.[13]

Going to the cinema was, then, one of the most popular leisure pursuits in the postwar era, and, despite the influx of foreign films after the war, domestic productions were much in demand with Austrian audiences. Austrian films even outdid glamorous Hollywood productions at the box office, even though they were usually slower and more dialogue-based.[14] Austrian audiences were not alone in their preference for domestic productions, as Garncarz's study demonstrates for West Germany.[15] A survey conducted by the German and Austrian Section of the Research Department of the US Foreign Office in May 1946 found that 'old German films [which includes Austrian films] seem considerably more popular than the average of Allied imports and an imported film must be outstandingly good to attract anything like the audiences of the more popular German films'.[16] Higson and Maltby explain the popularity of domestic cinema across Europe by suggesting that national films addressed their audiences with 'greater intimacy'. An audience study undertaken by the Information Division of the Military Government for Germany in May 1949 confirmed that audiences preferred domestic films for their subject matter, for being 'more true to life' and easier to understand 'from a cultural as well as a language point of view'.[17] Whether European audiences also preferred domestic productions because they provided 'narratives of resistance to American commercial culture' seems doubtful, but national productions certainly fulfilled desires that were very different from those satisfied by Hollywood cinema, which appealed to audiences through its glamour and technical superiority.[18]

The first box-office hit after the war, the tourist film *Der Hofrat Geiger*, directed by Hans Wolff and featuring the comedy duo Paul Hörbiger and Hans Moser in the leading roles, struck a chord with Austrian audiences. This light-hearted comedy was set in the idyllic countryside by the Danube and certainly touched on contemporary problems, but provided reassurance that everything was going to be alright. It premiered in December 1947 and drew 2.3 million Austrian visitors over the following twenty-nine months, an extraordinary number considering that a film was regarded as lucrative in postwar Austria when it attracted 800,000 visitors or more.[19] But *Der Hofrat Geiger* was also popular in West Germany and even in cinemas across the Netherlands, where it sold out for weeks, which suggests that images of beautiful countryside combined with a narrative that conveyed an optimistic outlook had broad appeal.[20]

Another huge success for Austrian cinema was the historical costume film *Wiener Mädeln* (Viennese Maidens), by the famous director Willi Forst, which began shooting in 1944 but could only be completed in 1949 because the Allied Forces had confiscated the reels. Interestingly, two versions premiered in Vienna in 1950: one in the Western zones, completed by the director himself, and one in the Soviet zone, finished by the Soviets (reportedly with much better colours, as Western critics conceded grudg-ingly).[21] *Wiener Mädeln* seemed to embody the superiority of Austrian culture while at the same time promoting harmony: a harmony that, as Karsten Witte acidly remarked, was more a *'diktat* of unanimity'.[22] The press celebrated the film as a symbolic reawakening of the Austrian na-tion, 'a tribute to a true, rejuvenated Austria', as one reviewer wrote jubi-lantly, exclaiming: '"Wiener Mädeln", a colour film? No! An Austrian Film? Yes, yes, yes!' The thunderous applause at the premiere was interpreted as a 'patriotic demonstration' and the Apollo Cinema sold more than 300,000 tickets during the first eleven weeks of its run.[23] The critics' excitement shows that Austrian films were infused with national meaning: popular cinema was assigned the role of an advertising vehicle for Austrian culture and looked upon with pride. However, if it did not deliver, either because the entertainment was considered too shallow or because it touched on uncomfortable issues (as 'social problem' films did), it was criticised for being the harbinger of Austria's cultural demise.

The fact that domestic productions were so successful does not mean that Austrian audiences rejected foreign films. In fact, the large number of tickets sold demonstrates a general 'hunger' for entertainment; audiences went to see domestic as well as foreign productions, especially those from Hollywood, which soon acquired a dominant position in the Austrian film market. Particularly lucrative were British and US children's films, such as *The Thief of Baghdad* (GB, 1940), *Bambi* (US, 1942) and *The Jungle Book* (US, 1942), probably because they brought whole families into the cinemas.[24] *Snow White and the Seven Dwarfs* (US, 1937), which opened in 1948, was the most successful international film, attracting almost 300,000 visitors to the Apollo during its first twelve weeks, despite being screened in the summer.[25] An unexpected run on tickets for the Esther Williams musical *Bathing Beauty* (US, 1944) led to them being sold for a premium on the black market in January 1949.[26]

The different national cinemas appealed to different desires: while American stars offered the glamour of Hollywood, local stars embodied domestic ideals of masculinity and femininity.[27] Hollywood productions, which often only reached Austrian cinemas with considerable delay, were particularly popular with young, working-class men, who favoured the genres of adventure, crime or western, which were almost non-existent in domestic film production.[28] Hollywood films also appealed to the younger, urban middle-class because they advertised what Lawrence Napper called a 'culture of aspiration'.[29]

Audience tastes varied according to gender, age, class and regional background. Historical costume films, if we can generalise from findings in British film studies, were a favourite with female audiences;[30] the Austri-an variety, however, had a broader appeal and also attracted men because of its celebration of Austrian culture.[31] Female spectators particularly liked *Heimatfilm* and musical revues, whereas men preferred crime and adventure, and also more 'serious' drama.[32] Gender preferences were, of course, not really as clear cut; the cinema was a prime dating site, and men would often accompany women to films they might not otherwise have chosen, and vice versa. Moreover, audiences were attracted by genre films for different reasons: while melodrama was traditionally considered a typical women's genre because of its emotional content and female perspective, the melodramas featuring the famous Austrian actress Paula Wessely as the heroine were a must-see for the cultured Austrian middle-class, regardless of gender, as the press reports indicate.[33]

For the industry, the orientation towards genre helped to reduce economic risk. Producers could increase the chances of financial success by adhering to generic formulas which attracted specific audiences.[34] Comedies were a safe choice because they appealed to both genders and all ages. When a survey asked Viennese teenagers in 1953 which films they liked best, they predominantly named Austrian and West German comedies, such as the Austrian *Der Feldherrnhügel* (Grandstand for General Staff, 1953), *Hannerl* (1952) and *Knall und Fall als Hochstapler* (Knall and Fall as Impostors, 1952), or the West German *Das verliebte Kleeblatt* (I Can't Marry Them All, 1952) and *Fanfaren der Liebe* (Fanfares of Love, 1951). Even these were trumped by the most popular comedy by far: *Don Camillo und Peppone* (The Little World of Don Camillo, 1952), an Italian film about a feisty Italian priest fighting with a Communist mayor. Its popularity was not surprising given that Austria was still a devout Catholic country at that time.[35]

Genres that were traditionally popular with female audiences, such as melodramas, remained popular, especially in the immediate postwar years, when women represented a clear majority in the population and presumably also in the audience: by the end of 1945, women accounted for 64.2 per cent of eligible voters, and in 1951, they still constituted 53.6 per cent of the population.[36] The unusually high number of melodramas produced in 1948 and 1949 suggests that the industry paid heed to the strong presence of women, who were attracted by films that presented a female point of view. Yet did their strength in numbers also affect the way the genders were represented in films? The fact that positive depictions of independent, self-reliant women and equal relationships between men and women were much more frequent in the early post war years shows that the film industry – although dominated by men – took note of the erosion of traditional gender roles and tried to cater to the tastes of modern women. Admittedly, the showcasing of feisty, independent heroines in early postwar films did not mark an actual break with the cinema of the Third Reich, where Goebbels had endorsed similar depictions, especially during the war, to support the large-scale recruitment of women into the arms industry.[37] However, the energetic, self-confident female protagonists of Ufa cinema had to direct their energies for the benefit of the community or the family, and were not allowed to pursue 'selfish' interests.[38] Linda Schulte-Sasse thus describes the examples of female independence in Nazi cinema (which existed alongside more conservative interpretations of women's roles) as the 'fascist delusion of female autonomy'.[39]

In contrast, early postwar Austrian cinema often allowed women to enjoy their independence, which they retained even if they entered a relationship. Although there were some films that presented female autonomy as a state that had to be remedied (as the discussion of *Der Hofrat Geiger* in Chapter Four illustrates), the majority of films favoured strong women. The real break occurred around the early 1950s when Austrian cinema responded to societal changes that saw more and more women relegated to the domestic sphere by increasingly restricting female independence in its films.

The audiences' views were also influenced by representations of gender in other national cinemas, whose films were entering the Austrian market in growing number. Film imports more than doubled between 1947 and 1949: whereas only 122 foreign films were imported in 1947 (thirty-nine French films and thirty-one each from the United States and the Soviet Union), the number rose to 280 film imports in 1949 – 150 alone from the US. By 1949, West Germany had regained its position as the second largest supplier of films to the Austrian market, and it retained this position for many years to come.

The evident popularity of West German productions in Austria, however, was often downplayed by contemporary critics for reasons of national pride.[40] From 1953 onwards, we can access more detailed records on the films that were screened at 107 Viennese cinemas (Table 1.1). The records of the Central Bureau of Statistics show that among the films screened in 1953 (including reruns) were 488 US films, 178 West German and 57 domestic productions. British films came fourth (40), followed by French (37) and Italian films (32).[41]

Country of origin	Number of film titles	Days of exhibition per title
USA	488	29.0
West Germany	178	65.4
Austria	57	81.3
UK	40	25.4
France	37	44.4
Italy	32	46.7
Sweden	13	42.4
Soviet Union	9	17.7
Switzerland	5	60.6

Table 1.1: Film exhibition in Vienna in 1953 (based on evaluation of 107 cinemas)
Source: Österreichisches Statistisches Zentralamt. 1959b. Beiträge zur österreichischen Statistik, Vienna, vol. 39, 143.

Yet, these numbers offer only limited information on audience preferences; they need to be complemented with an analysis of the exhibition patterns indicating the value distributors attributed to specific films (and therefore exhibited more widely); only then will we be able to establish the popularity of different national cinemas. So, while Hollywood dominated in terms of quantity, Austrian films ranked highest in the category of the most frequently screened films. With around eighty-one days of exhibition on average, Austrian films were shown for the longest period, followed by West German films (sixty-five days on average) and Swiss films (almost sixty-one days on average). US films, in comparison, changed much more frequently and were only on offer for twenty-nine days on average.[42] Table 1.2, which shows the most frequently screened (and presumably also seen) films in Viennese cinemas in 1953, lists six Austrian but only one US film: *Gone With the Wind* (1939). With a total of 358 days of screening at 107 cinemas, it came second only to one Austrian film, *1. April 2000* (1953), with 387 days.[43] The following years saw a similar predominance of domestic films.

Ranking	Country of origin	Film title	Days of exhibition
1.	Austria	*1. April 2000*	387
2.	USA	*Gone with the Wind*	358
2.	Austria	*Grandstand for General Staff*	358
3.	Italy	*The Little World of Don Camillo*	350
4.	Austria	*Punktchen and Anton*	320
5.	West Germany	*The White Horse Inn*	278
6.	Austria	*Me and My Wife*	270
7.	Austria	*Hannerl*	269
8.	West Germany	*Mask in Blue*	259
9.	Austria	*The Emperor's Waltz*	249

Table 1.2: Most frequently screened films in Vienna in 1953 (based on evaluation of 107 cinemas)
Source: Österreichisches Statistisches Zentralamt. 1959b. *Beiträge zur österreichischen Statistik*, Vienna, vol. 39, 146.

The popularity of traditional Austrian cinema with mass audiences in Austria and West Germany explains the industry's reliance on 'tried and tested' models of filmmaking. After the war, Austrian filmmakers revived the aesthetic traditions and modes of narration that had become synonymous with the so-called Viennese-Film in the 1930s and 1940s.

Postwar Austrian cinema was certainly much poorer for the irreplaceable loss of Jewish talent and technical expertise that the expulsion and murder of Jews during Nazi dictatorship had caused. Only a few Jewish artists, more of whom would have injected much-needed new blood into the industry, returned after the war to a country that was in general not very welcoming to the survivors.[44] Thus, at the outset of 1946, the film industry was in the hands of seasoned filmmakers, producers and actors who had been in the business for many years and who had weathered political changes or, indeed, had successfully furthered their careers during Nazi rule. They undoubtedly represented a pool of considerable talent, and a new generation of actors and actresses provided new faces.[45] However, new filmmakers with different ideas found it hard to gain a foothold. The *Wiener Kurier*, published by the US Forces, gave voice to the young filmmaker Georg Tressler, who in 1949 criticised the industry for 'sticking too much to the old ways'; Tressler made documentaries for government organisations and several US information services in Austria before emigrating to West Germany, where his career took off with the youth film *Die Halbstarken* (Teenage Wolfpack, 1956).[46] Other critics referred to Austrian scriptwriters as a 'closed clique that excels in keeping away every newcomer'; the Social Democratic *Welt am Montag* acidly described Austrian cinematographers and cutters as people who 'have been filming and cutting for ages. They weren't good then and haven't improved since […]; they remain immoveable like their cameras'.[47]

Innovation was also hampered by the precarious financial situation and the organisation of film production. Whereas in the United States and Great Britain the large production companies owned their studios and managed the distribution of their films, the Austrian film industry was decentralised and therefore in a more disadvantageous position. With very few exceptions, Austrian production companies did not own studios or have fixed distribution contracts; instead, they had to rent studios and staff and negotiate the distribution for each film separately.[48] As a consequence, neither production companies nor studios were able to undertake any long-term planning or to rationalise their production methods. It is not surprising, then, that many producers opted for 'safe films of average quality' rather than for taking artistic and financial risks.[49] The industry itself often blamed the dominance of Hollywood and the pressures of the West German market for producers' reluctance to enter new artistic territory and cross national boundaries.[50]

In the end, the lack of artistic daring and the disconnection from wider cinematic developments proved fateful for Austrian film production; the spread of television sets in the 1960s (television was introduced in 1955) compounded these problems and sent Austrian cinema into rapid decline.[51] Commenting on the certain demise of Austrian cinema in 1961, the conservative newspaper *Die Presse*, referring to the highly lucrative *Sissi*-trilogy, stated dryly: 'The *Sissi*-streams of gold have dried up'.[52]

What we find, then, is that Austrian cinema did not innovate, but remained entrenched in traditional forms. As we have seen, postwar Austrian cinema was largely oriented towards genres, and specialised in film modes for which the traditional Viennese film, with its specific social milieu, Viennese dialect and emotional content, provided the template. After the war, the genres were cleansed of National Socialist traces, and plot, characters and mise-en-scène were modernised to fit the new political and economic context. The visual and narrative techniques remained largely unchanged.[53] One of the most important genres of postwar Austrian cinema was the historical costume film, for example. A favourite with the industry and audiences alike, it played a particular influential role after the war in helping to promote the idea of Austrian nationhood through its showcasing of Austria's rich musical tradition and imperial past. Comedy was another traditional format and made up the largest share of postwar Austrian film production. It often took the form of the musical-style romantic comedy, a modernised version of the operetta and revue film. The stereotypical representations of Austrian characters, the ample use of cliché, the use of the Viennese dialect and a beautiful setting in either the Austrian countryside or in Vienna made them recognisably Austrian; these comedies often served as star vehicles for comedians such as Hans Moser and Paul Hörbiger, who guaranteed success at the box office. From the mid-1950s Austrian comedies increasingly merged with tourist film to become vehicles for pop stars and their hit songs (*Schlager*), branded under the name of *Schlagerfilme*. The genre of *Heimatfilm*, whose success was due to circumstance rather than planning, only became a defining genre of Austrian cinema after the Second World War. But once the industry found that these rural dramas, which debated conflicts between tradition and modernity, carried great appeal for postwar audiences, it quickly exploited the financial success of *Der Förster vom Silberwald* (1954) by more or less replicating the same formula until the genre was exhausted by the late 1950s. Melodramas were yet another staple of Austrian cinema and chiefly linked (as noted above) with the actress Paula Wessely. She had her breakthrough in film in 1934 with Willi Forst's *Maskerade* opposite Anton Walbrook (then Adolf Wohlbrück); she became the best-paid actress in Nazi Germany and after the war continued to attract large audiences, who flocked to the cinema to see the newest 'Wessely film', as these melodramas were commonly called.

While innovation was not a distinguishing mark of Austrian film production in the 1950s, then, there were, of course, exceptions. As mentioned in the introduction, films were produced that deviated from the mainstream, questioned the dominant ideology or experimented with new techniques, examples of which are Fritz Kortner's cynical historical drama *Sarajevo* (1955), discussed in Chapter Two, or Karl Paryla's class-conscious historical biopic *Der Komödiant von Wien* (Girardi, 1954). However, their number was relatively small, and their impact was never strong enough to establish a new school of filmmaking or to spark decisive aesthetic changes in Austrian cinema.

As significant as the films that ran counter to the cinematic mainstream was the absence of particular genres in Austrian cinema. The fact that some genres clearly dominated while others were sidelined or missing altogether shows how popular cinema gives weight to specific views not merely through representation, but also by omitting or evading issues. The remarkable absence of war films in Austrian cinema, for instance, has to be seen in connection with the official efforts to represent the Austrian people as peaceful and cultured. Apart from the internationally acclaimed anti-war drama *Die letzte Brücke* (The Last Bridge, 1953), an Austrian-Yugoslav co-production directed by the German Helmut Käutner, no war films were produced in Austria between 1945 and 1955. This lack was largely a re-sult of national film traditions, as the war film had never been a genre that appealed to Austrian filmmakers; yet the traumatic experience of the Second World War, and especially the military defeat which had brought the Austrians into a precarious situation, only increased their reluctance to make them, even though the genre boomed in postwar Britain and the US.[54] West Germany's rearmament and joining of NATO in 1955 were ac-companied by a revival of the war film, starting off in 1954 with the success of the West German military comedy *08/15*, directed by Paul May, and its two sequels in 1955, but the Austrian film industry continued to give the war genre a wide berth.[55] This careful avoidance of the genre correspond-ed with official government policies to present Austria as a pacifistic and harmonious nation, and thus illustrates how popular cinema was entan-gled in the ideological project of cleansing Austria of its Nazi past. Postwar cinema never depicted Austrian men as combatants in the war, but only as victims, mostly as returning POWs who struggle to adapt to civilian life, as in the dramas *Der weite Weg* (The Long Way Home, 1946) and *Arlberg-Express* (1948). Such narratives gave credibility to the government's efforts to present Austria as the first victim of Nazi aggression in order to improve its status under Allied occupation, and lent this idea wider publicity. The exculpatory message of *Der Weite Weg* prompted the exile newspaper *Der Aufbau* to quip: 'This "long way" is a "long way off" the truth'.[56]

Another genre severely underrepresented was the crime film, despite its popularity with Austrian audiences.[57] A similar absence of domestic crime productions can be found in German cinema, where the number of domestic crime or *noir* productions remained small after the war, perhaps a legacy of the suppression of the genre by the Nazis, as Bergfelder has suggested.[58] 'Where is the Austrian murder film?' inquired the newspaper *Welt am Montag* in 1948 – an ironic question, as the lack of domestic crime films ('We watch farmers' films, revue films [and] funny films, but nobody is murdered in an Austrian film') was presented as a virtue rather than as a shortcoming, because their lack was proof of the non-violent char-acter of the Austrian.[59] The sidelining of the genre partly had to do with national film traditions, and with the fact that Austrian filmmakers, as one critic commented in 1951, had not mastered the crime genre.[60] Even though crime film was popular with audiences, only five crime films were produced between 1946 and 1955, the majority in the late 1940s; they were small-scale productions with low production values: *Zyankali* (1948), *Schuss durchs Fenster* (Shot Through the Window, 1949) and *Lambert fühlt sich bedroht* (Lambert Feels Threatened, 1949), as well as the two *noirish Prämien auf den Tod* (Bonus on Death, 1949) and *Abenteuer in Wien* (Stolen Identity, 1952, an Austrian-US co-production). Even though the latter two are well crafted, their success at the box office was limited, as they were no match for the stylistically impressive and suspenseful US or British *film noirs* or the dark Swiss *Matto regiert* (Madness Rules, 1947), directed by the Austrian exile Leopold Lindtberg.

However, the main reason why there were no attempts to produce more, or indeed better, crime films lies in the heated debates about the dangerous effects of such films on young people. In 1951, the federal government of the Austrian province of Styria even declared a state of 'moral emergency' and appealed to cinema owners to abstain from exhibiting crime and gangster films for half a year 'to curb crime'.[61] The avoidance of crime films was thus meant to imply that violence and dark passions were simply not in the Austrian character.

The refusal to acknowledge the existence of a dark underworld, or social tensions giving rise to violence, was also the reason why the *Problemfilm* ('social problem' film), a genre that dealt with contemporary problems in a realistic manner, never succeeded in Austria the way it did in Germany – regardless of the fact that it was, as the critic Claudius Seidl sarcastically noted, the darling of all film critics.[62] In countless reviews, Austrian critics pleaded with directors to make more films that touched upon contemporary issues. Like other national cinemas, the Austrian social problem film focused on the so-called youth problem, a theme that preoccupied many postwar societies. British films such as *Cosh Boy* (1952) or *Beat Girl* (1960), US films such as *The Wild One* (1953) or *Rebel Without a Cause* (1955) and the West German film *Die Halbstarken* (Teenage Wolfpack, 1956) depicted well off, bored youngsters who lack values and orientation and thus turn to crime.

The young Austrian filmmakers Harald Röbbeling and Kurt Steinwendner took Italian Neorealism as the model for their films *Asphalt* (1951) and *Wienerinnen* (Viennese Girls, 1952), which addressed the problems of contemporary adolescents, but the films triggered uproar among the political and religious elites who condemned their 'voyeurism' and negative portrayal of Austria's youth.[63] Film reviews appreciated the films' aesthetics, interpreting them as a sign that Austria could gain ground on leading European cinemas, but criticised the verisimilitude of the subject matter, an intrinsic part of neorealism, as un-Austrian, and as giving a false image of Austrian society.[64] Showing abused, disillusioned and rebellious youth obviously stood in sharp contrast to the positive image of Austria which officials wanted to convey; the films were therefore classified as dangerous, and suspected of corrupting Austria's youth. The negative response to these social problem films illustrates that the Austrian public had clearly no appetite for confronting hard realities or, indeed, for self-critical engagement with the anxieties that manifested themselves in the discourse on the youth problem. Even at the box office, the films failed, which discouraged other filmmakers from entering the same territory.[65]

The mainstream audience, as these examples show, enjoyed the familiar and well known, and the film industry complied willingly. At first glance, audience tastes appear to have remained stable throughout the 1950s, which fostered an inertia within the industry that would prove fatal. Having underestimated the importance of television, and having overlooked the growing dissatisfaction of the audience with a cinema that seemed stuck in a cycle of repetitions, Austria's film industry went into rapid decline in the late 1950s and reached its (temporary) end in the late 1960s.

The Austrian Film Industry

From an economic perspective, this trajectory from boom to bust was not new. In fact, the history of Austrian cinema can be described as a continuous cycle of financial crises. Early Austrian cinema is intrinsically linked to the illustrious Count Alexander (Sascha) Kolowrat-Krakowsky, a wealthy aristocrat and filmmaker, whose company Sascha-Film, founded in 1910, became one of the most important production companies in Austria.[66] During the early 1920s, the film industry was a thriving business, producing an impressive output of 138 feature films in 1921/1922.[67] In the 1920s Vienna was home to a large film industry that attracted talents from different corners of the erstwhile empire, and from part of what Elsaesser described as the 'creative axis Vienna–Berlin–Hollywood'.[68]

But economic depression hit the industry hard. In order to support the domestic film industry, the Austrian government implemented measures to restrict imports; production slowly picked up again, only to be shaken anew by the worldwide economic crisis and the introduction of sound in 1928, which demanded a refitting of the studios. The financial crisis and rise in production costs put huge pressure on the industry: only eleven films were produced in 1930, and only two of them with sound. The number of distributors also dropped, from seventy in the mid-1920s to about thirty companies by the mid-1930s.[69] Indicative of the industry's dire financial situation was that the most powerful production company, Sascha-Film, went bankrupt in 1931; it was eventually acquired by the Austrian Pilzer brothers, who secured the German Tobis-Film as investor.[70]

Since the demise of the Austro-Hungarian Empire, Austria's film industry had relied on exports, gaining only around 10 per cent of its profits from the small domestic market. Germany was a key partner to Austria's film industry and its largest export market. A lively exchange of personnel, finances and films had existed between the two countries since the 1920s, which was further intensified when the introduction of sound reduced the export opportunities for both countries. This growing economic dependency on its German neighbour gave rise for concern in the Austrian industry, which was already suffering from the worldwide economic crisis. The National Socialists' rise to power in Germany in 1933 triggered hope that the Austrian film industry might attract foreign investors who boycotted Nazi Germany; indeed, a reorientation towards new markets became even more pressing given that Austrian companies could no longer access their box-office takings in Germany: Germany's propaganda minister, Joseph Goebbels, had declared these assets frozen to pressure Austrian production companies to implement anti-Semitic regulations and oust their Jewish shareholders.[71] While some producers succumbed early to these pressures, others who employed Jewish personnel looked for cooperation elsewhere and found partners in Hungary, Czechoslovakia and the Netherlands. The results of these cooperations were twenty-four film productions, most of them produced between 1934 and 1936 – evidence of a creative boost triggered by the sudden influx of middle-European Jewish artists who had been driven out of Nazi Germany.[72]

The stance of the Austrian fascist government that held power between 1933 and 1938 towards the film industry was ambiguous. On the one hand, the Austrian Minister of Trade tried to support independent film production by restricting German influence, forging links to investors from other countries, promoting Austrian films and advertising Austria as a production site in the USA; on the other hand, he continued to negotiate with the German Reich Film Chamber.[73] Under the continuing economic strain, the Austrian film industry increasingly ceded to German pressure and finally ceased to employ Jews in 1936 in order to secure the release of Austrian films in Nazi Germany – a de facto annexation of Austria's film industry two years before the official *Anschluss* in 1938.[74] It would be wrong to say that no efforts were made in Austria to minimise dependency on Germany, but it seems that a total separation from the German market was perceived as neither possible nor necessary by those in power, particularly in view of the economic boom in Nazi Germany and the intensifying anti-Semitism in Austria. Even so, between 1934 and 1937 about 20 per cent of all Austrian feature films – namely those predominantly made by Jewish film personnel – were produced in the knowledge that they had no chance of being shown in Germany.[75]

Immediately after Austria had been annexed by Nazi Germany on 12 March 1938, Austrian production companies were liquidated or taken over by German firms. Almost all of the thirty Austrian distributors, as well as about half of the 189 Viennese cinema operators, were stripped of their assets because they were categorised as Jewish.[76] After the war, the municipality of Vienna would take full advantage of this 'Aryanisation', refusing to give back the cinema licenses to the heirs of murdered owners; as cinemas were worthless without a license, the city of Vienna could buy the cinemas cheaply from the surviving relatives and hand them over to its own distribution company, Kiba, thus profiting immensely from Nazi extermination policies.[77] The *Anschluss* also brought about the immediate dismissal of Jewish artists from the stage and from film sets and their expulsion from Austria. Sometimes it was Austrian colleagues who took matters into their own hands to further their careers. The Viennese actors Erik Frey and Robert Horky turned up at the Josefstadt theatre in their SA uniforms and intimidated the Jewish director Ernst Lothar; weeks later, Frey and his colleague Robert Valberg forced the actor and theatre director Rudolf Beer to leave a performance, and handed him over to the SA troops.[78] Beer committed suicide in May 1938, after having been tortured by the Nazis, whereas Frey was able to continue as a much esteemed actor in postwar Austria, never apologising for his deed.[79]

Austria's biggest production company, Tobis-Sascha, was seized and changed into Wien-Film in 1938. Goebbels put it under direct control of the state-owned Ufa-Film GmbH, also known as UFI-trust, and appointed the successful Austrian director Karl Hartl as its executive producer.[80] Through the brutal elimination of business rivals, as well as through Goebbels' huge financial investments, Austria's film industry, now largely centralised under Wien-Film, experienced a period of boom.[81] Wien-Film continued in the Austrian tradition and specialised in seemingly apolitical comedies, operetta films and melodramas that emanated the mythological Viennese charm. While it also produced a few anti-Semitic propaganda films, such as *Leinen aus Irland* (Linen for Ireland, 1939), *Wien 1910* (Vienna 1910, 1943) and the infamous *Heimkehr* (Homecoming, 1941), which detailed the apparent plight of ethnic Germans in Poland and thus justified Germany's invasion of Poland, the name of Wien-Film became synonymous with light-hearted musicals and comedies, often set in the past and oscillating between slight melancholy and carefree optimism. Goebbels needed this kind of escapist entertainment films, whose political content was obscured by their cheerful tenor, to distract the German people from oppressive politics and the hardships of the war.[82] Wien-Film thus became the feel-good factory of the German Reich that helped to keep the war machine running.[83]

Yet, after 1945, many film artists, foremost among them the famous Austrian director Willi Forst, exculpated the personnel of Wien-Film from any involvement in Nazi politics by constructing the myth of Wien-Film as a place of 'charming Austrian resistance' against the Nazis.[84] Forst even accused those forced to emigrate of opportunism, and suggested that those who had stayed and furthered their careers in Nazi Germany were actually heroes of resistance.[85] Clearly, by presenting themselves as 'apolitical', many Austrian artists wanted to bury the fact that they had been far from opposed to the National Socialist regime: the Austrian comedian Oskar Sima (since 1933 a member of the then illegal Nazi party and the SA) had publicly expressed his delight about the *Anschluss*; the heart-throb Wolf Albach-Retty, the actress Hilde Krahl, the producer Erich von Neusser and the comedian Hans Olden were members of the Nazi party, the latter three long before the *Anschluss*; the Hungarian-born musical star Marika Rökk was a fervent admirer of Hitler, as her letters to him reveal; and the actress Magda Schneider was a regular at Hitler's Alpine retreat at the Obersalzberg.[86] The Austrian artists' involvement with Nazi politics ranged from willing support of the Nazis to enforced cooperation, as in the case of the comedian Hans Moser, whose Jewish wife made him vulnerable to Goebbels' demands.

Passing judgement on their conduct with the benefit of hindsight might not be appropriate, but their refusal to reflect critically on their involvement with the Nazi regime (Hans Olden was among the very few who freely admitted his previous admiration for the Nazis) and their self-stylisation as upright, patriotic Austrians deserve criticism.[87] Distinguished directors who had worked for Wien-Film – Willi Forst, Gustav Ucicky, E.W. Emo, Hans Thimig, Hubert Marischka, Géza von Bolvary and Géza von Cziffra – continued to play an influential role in postwar Austrian cinema. The same goes for the big Austrian film stars of the Third Reich, such as Paula Wessely, Attila and Paul Hörbiger, Hans Moser, Maria Andergast, Marika Rökk and Wolf-Albach Retty, producers such as Karl Hartl or Erich von Neusser, the composers Willy Schmidt-Gentner and Anton Profes, the cinematographers Hans Schneeberger, Sepp Ketterer and Günther Anders and the art directors Friedrich Jüptner-Jonstorff and Julius von Borsody. They were able to resume their careers almost as soon as the tumult of the war had subsided, carrying into the new era the style and traditions of the old.

Postwar Austrian Cinema and the Allied Forces

At the end of 1944, with the collapse of the *Reich* drawing closer, film production in Vienna came to a temporary halt. Much of the studio equipment and many of the films were evacuated to the western provinces of Salzburg and Upper Austria, later to be seized by US Forces on their advance. The Soviet Army liberated Vienna on 13 April 1945 and captured the film studios and their remaining equipment. As early as May 1945, the provisionally installed Austrian government made its first attempts to revive film production, which illustrates the industry's importance to the state. However, the government's move to centralise film production by claiming the assets of Wien-Film as Austrian property and found the distribution company Austria Film-Verleih und Vertriebsgesellschaft met with fierce opposition from the US. American opposition to a centralised production and distribution system was not just ideological, bearing in mind that the Soviets supported Austria's centralising efforts, but very much economically motivated, as the US had a vested interest in securing the Austrian market for its own film exports. Upon the arrival of the Western Allies in

Vienna at the end of August 1945 and the division of Vienna into four Allied occupation zones, the US Information Services Branch (ISB) took immediate control of the production and distribution companies, which were mostly located in US-controlled territory. The US military government banned the Austrian Film-Verleih und Vertriebsgesellschaft, confiscated Wien-Film's property and, in December 1945, annulled governmental regulations that taxed and restricted film imports intended to strengthen the film industry.[88] At the same time, the ISB secured the distribution rights not only for American and confiscated German films, but also for British, French and Soviet productions. Thus, by the end of 1945, the ISB had gained full control over production and distribution in Austria, including the Rosenhügel studio in the Soviet zone.[89]

The fact that the ISB did not consult the Soviets on the liquidation of Wien-Film and the takeover of the Austrian film companies created considerable tension between the US and the Soviet Union.[90] A battle over the Austrian film industry ensued, which was played out against the growing political tensions of the Cold War and led to the British and French administrations siding with the US.[91] The Soviets responded to the Americans' aggressive actions by presenting themselves as saviours of the Austrian film industry; they demonstrated their support by presenting much-needed film stock to the Austrian government in November 1945. Four months later, the Soviets also withdrew from joint film distribution with the US and founded their own distribution enterprise, Sovexport.[92] The US military government returned the studios Sievering and Schönbrunn to the Austrian government in 1946 in order to make it clear that the US, too, was in favour of reviving Austria's film industry, and finally, at the end of 1946, handed over the confiscated capital of Wien-Film; this, however, was only done after the Austrian government had signed a contract that gave US films unrestricted access to the Austrian market.[93] In the meantime the Soviets had put the Rosenhügel studio under Soviet management to demonstrate their power, which led to the emergence of two parallel film industries in Austria – a split that would last for nine years (Figure 1.1).

The Austrian film industry had thus become a pawn in the battle between the US and the Soviet Union, which was as much about ideological influence as about market share. Ultimately, it profited from this conflict, at least on the level of film production, and regained most of its film stock, studios and films by the end of 1946. It remains unclear whether the Austrian officials strategically intervened to benefit from the quarrels between the Western Allies and the Soviets, or whether they were more or less innocent bystanders who picked up what the two enemies dropped during their fight. But despite the precarious relations between the Soviets and the Western Allies, Austrian film production remained largely free from any form of political intervention. Only the Soviets exerted some control on film production in their territory, and demanded that the production company Wien-Film am Rosenhügel submit all film scripts for inspection.

Some of the films produced at Wien-Film displayed a few overt ideological references to workers' solidarity and class conflict, such as the melodrama *Das Herz einer Frau* (Heart of a Woman, 1951) or the musical *Abenteuer im Schloss* (Adventures in the Castle, 1953), but overall the emphasis was clearly on apolitical entertainment.

The US Office of Information, on the other hand, left it to the Austrians to ensure that the films did not contain Nazi or anti-Western propaganda, or feature actors or actresses who had starred in Nazi propaganda films, even though the latter restriction was soon ignored.[94] However, while the Western Allies did not interfere in film production, they still exercised control on the distribution level. Shortly after they had taken over supreme power, the Allied Forces reintroduced censorship to 'denazify' and re-educate the Austrians, and banned a large number of films produced during the Nazi era.[95] Until 1948, each film, regardless whether it was an Austrian or international production, had to be approved for screening by the Film Sections of the Allied Forces. The British Forces lifted these restrictions on 1 May 1948, with the US Forces following suit on 10 June 1948, on condition that the Austrian government took measures to regulate film screening, in particular by imposing audience age limits.[96]

The Soviets continued to control distribution in their zone until January 1955, but their control was patchy.[97] Hollywood films were screened in cinemas in the Soviet zone to full houses, as the head of the US Motion Picture

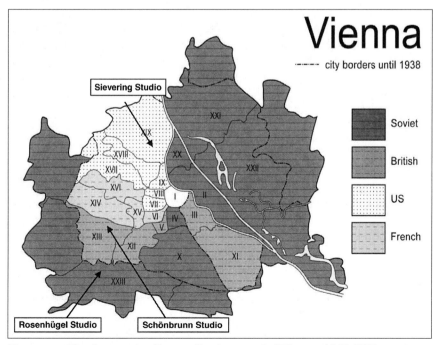

Figure 1.1: The three major film studios in occupied Vienna, 1945–1955.

Export Association (MPEA), which had taken over distribution from the ISB, gleefully reported in July 1948.[98] It seems clear that the Americans and the British were more prohibitive when it came to the exhibition of Soviet films than vice versa. The US military government, backed by the powerful US distributors, generally refused to give screening permissions for Soviet films in the Western zones. It did not, however, merely exclude Soviet films from cinemas. As Reinhold Wagnleitner has shown, it extended its censorship to US productions and aimed to ban Hollywood films that did not 'depict US life in its most favourable light', in order to protect America's image abroad. However, the US Army's attempts to restrict the exhibition of American westerns, gangster and horror films, and films that presented the USA in a negative light, came into conflict with Hollywood's commercial interests and, in the end, Hollywood prevailed.[99]

All things considered, there was very little interference in Austrian film production by the Allied Forces. The Soviets exerted only limited influence on the production company Wien-Film am Rosenhügel and control was almost non-existent in the zones occupied by the Western Allies. On the level of distribution, no Austrian film produced between 1946 and 1955 was banned from exhibition by the Allies, which was probably also due to the fact that Austrian filmmakers, having grown accustomed to strict censorship under Nazi dictatorship, applied a certain amount of self-censorship in their productions in order not to offend the Allied Forces.

Despite the economic privations that marked the early postwar years, the industry recovered swiftly: seventeen new Austrian films premiered in 1947; twenty-eight in 1948. A large number of production companies were founded soon after the war (the commercial register listed 110 production firms in 1947), but little more than one-tenth of them actually produced films.[100] Karl Hartl, the former director of Wien-Film, was appointed head of the new Sascha-Film, a production and distribution company relaunched by the bank Creditanstalt in 1947. Hartl also functioned as curator of his former employer Wien-Film, which continued to exist only nominally, as most of its assets were now located in the Soviet zone.[101]

While the US and British Forces handed over the studios Sievering and Schönbrunn to the Austrians, the former Wien-Film studio Rosenhügel remained under Soviet control. Renamed Wien-Film am Rosenhügel, the production company rented out its studio, but also produced its own films from 1950; the first production, which was also the first colour film produced in Austria after the war, was the musical *Kind der Donau* (Child of the Danube, 1950), starring Marika Rökk, the dancing star of the Third Reich.[102] Wien-Film am Rosenhügel chiefly produced entertainment fare in colour, such as revue and costume films, and avoided ideology in most, though not all, of its films.[103] However, its productions were labelled political by the Western Allied Forces as well as by Austria's conservative elites. Denounced as Soviet propaganda and boycotted by distribution companies in the Western zones, the financial success of the Wien-Film productions was limited in Austria and West Germany, whereas they sold well in the newly founded German Democratic Republic.[104] Nevertheless, Wien-Film am Rosenhügel was the only financially stable film company in postwar Austria, because its productions were financed by the Soviets until 1955. In comparison, most Austrian companies in the Western zones were short-lived enterprises, usually ceasing business after a few films, a situation resembling that in West Germany.[105] The main founders were private businessmen and banks, but also directors, such as Johannes Hübler-Kahla, Geza von Cziffra, Willi Forst and Ernst Marischka, or actors, such as Paula Wessely, who established production companies chiefly to produce their own films.[106] G.W. Pabst formed a partnership with the municipal distribution company Kiba to establish Pabst-Kiba-Filmproduktion, which produced four films. Among the bigger Austrian enterprises were Ring-Film and Nova-Film (operating until 1955), each of which produced eight films, and Vindobona-Film and Neusser-Film, with seven films each.[107] Only a few companies were in business for longer than four or five years: one of the most persistent was Schönbrunn-Film, which was set up in 1950 and did business until 1980, producing nine films before 1955. Styria-Film Wien, founded in 1934, was the only Austrian production company that continued to produce films throughout the Third Reich and up to 1953.

Film production remained a risky business in Austria, and the absence of any notable financial support from the Austrian government meant that a film's projected commercial success was crucial to win investors. In the first years after the war, productions were primarily financed through bank loans. A film cost between 1 and 3.5 million Austrian schillings in the late 1940s, but as the national market was small, the Austrian box office revenues of one season usually only covered 15 to 25 per cent of a film's costs; however, as Austrian films were very popular with its audiences, they were often screened for a longer period and thus earned more money over time.[108] Still, as in the inter-war years, the industry relied on foreign, and especially the West German, markets for survival. The West German industry, however, was grappling with its own economic problems, suffered from a 'deficit-driven overproduction' and complained about an oversupply of foreign films.[109] German producers thus welcomed the regulations set out by the Allied Forces, made in an attempt to prevent the revival of pan-Germanic relations, severely restricting access of Austrian films to the West German market. The Austrian industry, heavily in debt by the end of 1948, lobbied the government intensely to lift the ban on exporting their films to West Germany.[110]

The trade restrictions with West Germany imposed by the Allied Forces could have acted as an incentive to open up other foreign markets, and the press repeatedly called on the Austrian film industry to be stylistically more innovative in order to make their films more attractive in other countries.[111] Yet the critics' voices were largely ignored. While the industry reacted with pride when some Austrian films were exported to non-

German speaking countries, their circulation abroad was limited, and the producers made very few attempts to build up new markets or to make the films more accessible to foreign audiences. Of the twenty-one films exported to the USA from the end of the war to the beginning of 1953, only two had English subtitles, which suggests that the films were aimed at expatriates.[112] 'Austrian Film – Where To?' asked the *Neuer Kurier*, rather disheartedly, in December 1954. Ever since the Austrian film industry had resumed business after the war, Austrian producers invested their energies in trying to facilitate an exchange with West Germany rather than in establishing new cooperations with other partners.[113] The reasons for their persistence lay in the fairly long history of producing for the German market, but also in personal continuities and close networks – the strong ties that had been established between the two industries during the Third Reich and before – and their common language, which allowed producers to save on expensive dubbing or subtitling costs. Moreover, the Austrian government lacked both the financial means and the will to provide strong incentives that would encourage producers to strike new paths in film-making.[114] Instead, the government and representatives of the Austrian film industry were in continuous negotiations with the British and US Allied Forces to facilitate film exports to West Germany.

On 1 October 1947, a first agreement was reached that granted the Austrian government permission to export a small quota of films to the British and the US zones in Germany, under the condition that Austria imported four West German films for every film they exported.[115] The first eight Austrian films chosen by the German distributors in 1948 were mainly comedies, tourism films and costume melodramas, among them *Wiener Melodien* (Viennese Melodies, 1947), *Kleine Melodie aus Wien* (Little Melody from Vienna, 1948), *Rendezvous im Salzkammergut* (Rendezvous in the Salzkammergut, 1948), *Der Hofrat Geiger* (Privy Councillor Geiger, 1947) and *Der himmlische Walzer* (The Heavenly Waltz, 1948). The titles indicate what the West German audiences liked about Austrian cinema: waltz and wine, a beautiful landscape, carefree laughter mixed with a touch of melancholy and stars such as Paul Hörbiger or Hans Moser.[116] The exchange agreement was widely criticised in Austria, not only because the (initial) conversion rate of one German Mark to one Austrian schilling disadvantaged the Austrians.[117] Even more detrimental was the fact that Austrian producers could not access their considerable box-office takings from West Germany, as these were offset against the West German profits in Austria and put into frozen accounts.[118] As the Austrian film industry was unable to reinvest its profits into new productions, the financial crisis deepened. Banks, which had been the prime investors, largely refused to finance new productions. The press coverage of the time reveals considerable unease about the industry's future, expressing the fear that a weak or non-existent Austrian film industry might have a detrimental effect on Austrians as a whole. The underlying concern was that if the industry should cease to produce, it would no longer provide orientation or be able to project a positive image of Austria abroad. These arguments illustrate how strongly national cinema was invested with cultural meaning, regardless of the fact that government authorities considered Austrian cinema primarily to be a lucrative economic asset rather than a cultural institution.[119]

By May 1949, even the US High Commissioner noted with concern that in Austria 'production had practically ceased, and little or no future production was planned'.[120] The films produced in summer 1949 – the screwball comedies *Ein bezaubernder Schwindler* (A Charming Fraud, 1949) and *Mein Freund Leopold* (My Friend Can't Say No, 1949), and the tourist film *Kleiner Schwindel am Wolfgangsee* (Little Swindle at Lake Wolfgang, 1949) – were economical productions mostly filmed on location.[121] *Kleiner Schwindel* was one of the cheapest films at the time, produced with a budget of only 800,000 Austrian schillings – a loaf of bread cost about two schillings and one kilo of butter twenty-two schillings at the time.[122]

The film crisis reached its height in 1950, when three Viennese studios in the Western zones faced closure.[123] In an alarmist tone, the press warned that a number of actresses and actors, directors and technical personnel had already sought employment elsewhere, most often in West Germany or, even worse, at the Rosenhügel studio in the Soviet zone, which had more capital to hand.[124] The conservative *Die Presse* lamented that 'one has lost trust in the stability and looks for affiliation elsewhere. It comes as no surprise that directors of distinction enter commitments abroad, Hartl in London, E.W. Emo in Germany, Bolvary in Rome. One also looks on in dismay as great actors cross the borders'.[125] The government and the industry tried (unsuccessfully) to release their frozen profits from West German accounts. They met resistance from US authorities, who feared that Austrian film imports would hamper the sales of US films in West Germany, as well as from German producers, who lobbied to modify the exchange quota – again to Austria's disadvantage.[126] Austrian films, the German producer Günther Stapenhorst complained to the Americans, would hamper the success of German films abroad; he made the exaggerated claim that 'Austria has swamped the market with mass products which have done more harm than good to the long-expected German film'.[127]

Austria's industry started to recover when an agreement with the now independent Federal Republic of Germany was reached in August 1950, which allowed Austrian producers to access the revenues gained in West Germany: 'Austrian film secured', sighed *Die Presse* with relief.[128] And, roused by the crisis, the Austrian government made an effort to boost domestic film production by offering liability for export credits of up to 30 per cent of the production costs if the producer could win a foreign distributor to cover the remainder. This change in financing resulted in a change in production patterns, as Austrian producers increasingly entered into distribution agreements with West German distributors, who paid an advance on the production costs, with Austrian banks or investors contributing the rest. In economic terms, both sides profited from the deal: Austrian filmmakers were able to realise their projects and were guaranteed distribution in the lucrative West German market, while the German distributors profited from the popularity of Austrian films in West Germany. However, as was the case in the West German industry, the distributors consequently gained more influence on the production process, and could, for example, demand changes to the script or make casting suggestions.[129] Nonetheless, the Austrian film industry experienced a veritable boom around the mid-1950s as a result of the facilitated access to the German market and the influx of West German capital: not only did the number of Austrian films increase, but also the size of the budgets, as lavish historical costume films such as *Sissi* or *Der Kongress tanzt* illustrate. This growth, however, came at the cost of reduced autonomy.

Because postwar Austrian cinema was originally barred from the German market by Allied law, it remained a national cinema in its address, choice of themes and visual and narrative style. The political changes in West Germany, which led to the lifting of trade bans and influx of West German capital into the Austrian industry, brought the two film industries closer together. Yet the visual and narrative style of Austrian film was affected more strongly by this growing exchange than was that of West German cinema, which had a much larger domestic market. A noticeable 'Germanisation' of the language spoken in Austrian films and an increasingly monotonous replication of themes and storylines deemed popular with German audiences can be detected from around 1953 in comedies such as *Auf der grünen Wiese* (On the Green Meadow, 1953) or *Fräulein Casanova* (Miss Casanova, 1953), but the trend became more manifest from the mid-1950s.

However, the exchange of personnel and the rising German investment in Austrian film production ultimately impacted on both industries, and would eventually lead to a stronger harmonisation of film production. While Austrian cinema did not step outside the confines of typical Austrian genres, such as the historical costume film and romantic (musical) comedies, both industries interacted with and borrowed from each other by producing remakes or sequels of films that had been produced in the other country. *Heimatfilm* was the genre that most manifestly bridged the barriers between Austria and Germany by evading any reference to nationality, but West German cinema also adapted the successful, typical Viennese costume film for its own purpose.[130]

Austria's cultural elites voiced concern about the growing cultural interconnectedness of Austrian and German cinema. Like the newspaper *Neues Österreich*, which lamented that 'cultural ambition is sacrificed for the West German market', contemporary critics addressed the cultural exchange primarily in terms of loss.[131] The Soviet-backed *Österreichische Zeitung* complained in 1955 that due to growing West German investment 'Austrian film has not only lost its sophistication, but most of its national imprint', making it 'almost impossible for the audience to distinguish whether a film is West German or Austrian'.[132] The charge of a cultural decline, however, was nothing new. Ever since the industry had resumed production in 1946, journalists such as H. Krikovsky, from the left-wing *Arbeiterzeitung*, repeatedly lamented its impoverishment; Krikovsky complained that 'nine-tenths of Austrian film production are deeply provincial' and that the films gave a falsified image of Austria and its people.[133] Critics bemoaned filmmakers' reluctance to depart from the 'standardised pseudo-Viennese style' ('*reichseinheitlicher Pseudowienerstil*') that they had adopted during the Third Reich.[134] As part of the cultural elite, the critics accused filmmakers of succumbing to the lure of money and churning out the same old 'so-called Viennese film with the waltz, *Heurigen* [wine taverns] and musical military parades'.[135] Yet, the incessant calls from the press for more artistic innovation, the opening up of new markets, more state sponsorship for independent productions and altogether different films seemingly fell on deaf ears. Neither the producers nor the Austrian government felt under immediate pressure to make such efforts after the 1950 agreement with West Germany had consolidated the industry's economic situation.

Class, Gender, National Identity and Other Issues of Major Concern

Even though the role of popular cinema is ambiguous and often contradictory, it is at certain times more affirmative of social order than at others. The fact that postwar Austrian cinema was largely in accord with the governing elites on major issues such as nationhood, class or gender can be explained by its particular vulnerability: Austria's film industry, due to its precarious financial situation and initial dependence on the goodwill of the Allied Forces, looked, as it had done before, to the state for protection and support. The government authorities, who relied on cinema to support their nation-building policies, could only offer limited financial support, but rewarded the industry symbolically. Members of the government or the Church gave support to Austrian cinema by regularly attending premieres of Austrian films and by complimenting the filmmakers on positive representations of Austria and Austrian culture, thus winning their consent. Looking at the films made in the 1950s (the late 1940s were a different matter), it almost seems as if the ruling elites and the film industry had a tacit agreement to work hand in hand to present Austria and the Austrian people in a way that would strengthen Austrian identity and help to fend off any allegations of Nazi collaboration.

Film both expresses and represses themes and ideas, and what it represses is often as significant as what it shows. This goes for the specialisation in genres, mentioned above, but also for the content of the films.

Hence, the fact that postwar Austrian cinema generally avoided the issue of class conflict and presented Austria as a homogeneous, middle-class society while largely omitting the working-class, is quite significant. The filmmakers clearly depicted an aspirational image of Austrian society rather than giving an accurate description of contemporary social reality. By presenting decent, middle-class prosperity as standard, popular cinema indirectly fed the government's attempts to bridge class conflict and to secure social peace. The absence of class in this cinematic discourse is particularly remarkable given that it had been the predominant issue in the inter-war years, with class conflict bringing Austrian society to the brink of destruction. Yet, after 1945, this was almost completely buried by a policy of consent, largely because the former antagonists, the Social Democratic Party and the conservative Christian Socialist Party (now called the Austrian People's Party), were now bound together in a coalition and by the shared experience of Nazi persecution. What is more, the ruling elites felt it necessary to show unity against the Allied Forces in order to demonstrate that Austria could govern itself. 'Compromise' and 'harmony' were therefore the watchwords of the day. The ideological divide between the classes was bridged by means of proportional democracy and 'social partnership', which integrated trade unions and representatives of the industry into the political decision-making process. The majority of Austrians, weary of conflict and politics in general, welcomed this enforced consensus, as it guaranteed the political and social stability much yearned for after years of turmoil, albeit at the expense of democratic participation and openness.[136] Against this background it becomes clearer why harmony was also such a dominant theme in postwar Austrian films. Popular cinema responded to the desire of the Austrian audience for stability and material comfort by focusing on a prosperous, middle-class, consumer society. It did not portray a classless society, but one in which class was insignificant.

Whereas political measures smoothed over the class divide in postwar Austria, the gap between the genders, after a brief phase of female empowerment in the early postwar years, grew visibly during the 1950s.[137] As mentioned in the introduction, the war had challenged the purportedly natural gender-based division of labour between (unpaid) female housework and (paid) male work, and had thus strengthened women's independence whilst Austrian men (temporarily) suffered a loss of power. Many men, in Austria as well as in Germany, experienced the defeat and occupation of their country by the former enemy – unconsciously or consciously – as a blow to their masculine identity, and even akin to emasculation.[138] However, men's ability to adapt to civilian life after years of military service varied greatly.[139] The frequently used notion of a masculine crisis, a shorthand term to describe the disorientation of men after the war, has hence to be employed with caution. What certainly was in crisis after the war was the once powerful soldierly ideal of hard, virile masculinity, which for many still represented the quintessence of manhood.[140] This temporary destabilisation of the hegemonic ideal, along with conflicting expectations of gender roles and the divergence of male and female experiences, put considerable strain on the relations between men and women in the early postwar years.[141] Heated controversies erupted over women's intimate relations with members of the Allied Forces, as Ingrid Bauer's illuminating study on 'Ami brides' illustrates. The arrival of the Western Allied soldiers brought Austrian women into contact with attractive, healthy and, above all, carefree, smiling men who looked very different from the emaciated Nazi prisoners and haggard and gloomy Austrian soldiers who had started to return. The Allied soldiers' status as victors, along with their material power, certainly added to their appeal, as did their gentlemanly conduct towards women: British and American soldiers were considered to be less macho than Austrian men.[142] Women who took up with the former enemy were generally frowned upon, but it was the veterans who displayed particular aggression towards 'fraternising' women, accusing them of besmirching their country. The men's reactions arose not only from wounded male pride but, as Bauer argues, were also a projection of their own guilt over their actions in the war onto the women.[143]

There was a widespread feeling that the political and economic system, after a temporary stabilisation under Nazi rule, had again 'gone out of joint' with the end of the war.[144] Instead of trying to build a new, more equal society on the ruins of the collapsed one, the predominantly male ruling elites hastened to bring society back to normal as soon as possible. This involved the rebuilding of Austria's economy and infrastructure, as well as the reconstruction of society along pre-war gender lines.[145] Women's groups and the Socialists called for a reform of family and matrimonial law, but the conservative elites successfully thwarted these efforts.[146] The widespread circulation of images of vigorous, virile men on murals and election posters, as detailed in Wolfgang Kos's inspiring analysis of public iconography, is illustrative of the efforts the establishment made to strengthen weakened male positions by promoting an ideal of muscular masculinity.[147] Indeed, as Siegfried Mattl argues, the fetishisation of work and production in postwar Austria can be seen as an attempt to compensate for lost virility.[148] Despite its tarnished reputation, the ideal of hard masculinity still exerted considerable influence. Yet it needed to be adapted to the demands of a new era. In public discourse, the outdated masculine ideal of the warrior was swiftly replaced with the 'hero of work'. Popular cultural imports from the US also supplied positive images of hard masculinity, substituting the military hero with heroes of westerns, adventurers and sailors that provided orientation for Austria's youth.[149] It is highly interesting, then, that images of hard, virile men, so dominant in the public sphere, were largely absent from postwar Austrian films. This helps to show that the function of Austrian cinema was different to that of, for instance, public imagery: popular cinema sought to appease and harmonise, and thus promoted a distinct, cultured, softer masculinity to imbue Austrian identity with new meaning.

However, representations of gender and gender relations in Austrian cinema were not static, but continually changed, indicative of the fact that the eventual reaffirmation of traditional gender order in the 1950s was a lengthy, gradual and by no means straightforward process. In the early postwar years, when Austrian women constituted the majority of the population and were often the primary providers for their families, popular cinema showcased strong, independent women in melodramas, comedies and tourist films.[150] It did not entirely dispense with traditional role models, as the example of the early tourist film *Der Hofrat Geiger* illustrates, which relegates the feisty single mother to the position of an obedient housewife at the end of the film; yet contemporary female audiences might have perceived the heroine's progress from the independent but precarious state of being single to the safety of a marriage, at the cost of independence, as a welcome return to normality, with the man assuming responsibility for his family; still, the film remains ambiguous in that regard. With the economic upswing and the modernisation of the Austrian economy, political and public discourse put increasing pressure on women to retreat to the private sphere and give up paid work in order to make room for job-seeking men. Accompanying this gradual transformation into a modern consumer society, cinematic discourse promoted the nuclear middle-class family with the 'breadwinner-husband and mother-housewife' couple as a role model for all classes, and thus played an influential role in this transformation of society.[151] Rising living standards combined with an increasing mechanisation of the household, the introduction of family benefits for the male breadwinner and higher incomes for men, and the widespread advertising extolling the joys of being a housewife and consumer helped to consolidate the unequal relations between men and women in the 1950s. The increase in marriages and birthrates from the mid-1950s on indicates that the marketing of the modern nuclear family model and the concept of companionate marriage across all levels of society were successful, and appealed to most men and women.[152] By showcasing specific family and gender models, then, Austrian cinema both commented on social developments and offered orientation to audiences struggling with the rapid transformations in Austrian society.

Austrian cinema was still more influential in the construction of a new Austrian identity. The concept of an Austrian nation, despite Austria's long history, is relatively young.[153] While an Austrian sentiment did exist in parts of the population, the majority had no clear concept of Austrian identity up to the Second World War. Interestingly, it was the much desired unification with Germany in 1938 which would eventually awaken a national Austrian spirit; the actual experience of living in a German state, which had been favoured by a considerable percentage of the population, resulted in disillusionment and, consequently, a gradual dissociation from the Germans.[154] After the defeat of Nazi Germany, Austria's political elites hastened to argue for an independent Austrian nation to evade responsibility. Based on a highly selective interpretation of the wording of the Moscow Declaration of 1943, the Austrian government highlighted Austria's status as a victim, and inferred from it that Austria deserved a different and more lenient treatment than Germany.[155] This so-called victim myth formed the core of the newly formulated Austrian identity; it was drafted to convince the international community of Austria's innocence and, as a result, to help Austria regain national independence and avoid reparation payments and the return of property confiscated by the Nazis to its rightful owners.[156] While the 'ideological project of (re)-conceptualising Austria as a nation in its own right' was launched by the political elites, it was also strongly supported by the cultural elites, the popular media and the Church, and could thus be seen as a collective effort to define Austrianness and assert the existence of a distinct 'Austrian mentality'.[157]

The fact that representations of masculinity played a key part in the formulation of Austrian nationhood is in line with Appelt's findings of the close linkage between masculinity and the historical development of the idea of the nation, which was meant to reflect male autonomy.[158] Unlike femininity, which was perceived as natural and stable, the dominant masculine norm had come under threat through the war, as we have seen. Both to give form to the imagined Austrian nation and to strengthen the weakened masculine norm, masculinity was infused with national values, and men's role as national citizens was reaffirmed. Of course, femininity also had a place in the formulation of Austrian nationhood, but it was more symbolic than political: in order to distance Austria from the German nation, political discourse highlighted the feminine aspects of the Austrian character, describing the typical Austrian as harmonious, peace-loving, passive and homely. To attest to the feminine character of Austria, the discourse called upon historical personae, such as Austria's only female empress, Maria Theresia, and revived well-worn clichés of Austrian sensitivity. Yet it was men, because of their ties to the public and political spheres, who were regarded as representatives of the nation, which partly explains why after the war masculine norms were reconceptualised to support the claim of Austrian nationhood.

Postwar Austrian cinema largely abstained from a critical discussion of pressing social issues; still, as the following analysis will show, it responded strongly to societal changes, and promoted views of nationality and social order that fed back into popular discourse. By smoothing over social conflicts and endorsing harmony in its films, popular cinema accompanied the political efforts to create a peaceful society that would not suffer from the ideological strife of the inter-war years. This harmony, however, which the state enforced through careful politics of checks and balances and 'social partnership', came at a price. Individualism or dissenting views were regarded as threats to social peace in postwar Austria.

The much debated threat of the *Halbstarke* – rebellious youth with leather jackets and a love for rock 'n' roll – or the massive campaign against 'dirt and trash' in the cinema and the media, which resulted in the passing of the 'Dirt and Trash Act' in 1950 (*Schmutz- und Schundgesetz*), are illustrative of this moral panic.[159] Considerable unease arose from the popularity of cinema with teenagers, who were seen as particularly impressionable and thus easily affected by films that showed acts of violence or sex. The allegedly damaging effects of films were widely debated in the press, revealing a fear that was directly linked to other popular cultural imports, especially from the USA. Hollywood gangster and crime films were, according to the press, directly responsible for the increase in youth crime, as a headline from *Neues Österreich* – 'Two Gangster Films – 215 Young Bandits' – illustrates.[160] Austria's cultural elites felt that the Western Allied Forces could not be relied on to protect Austria's youth because they lacked 'the proper understanding of what our youth, contaminated by Nazi ideology, should be allowed to see'.[161] According to *Neues Österreich*, the Austrian teenager needed, because of his experience of war and Nazism, more guidance than 'a sated sixteen-year-old in New York who can watch a gangster movie without the danger of turning into a burglar'.[162] As the Austrian constitution prohibited any censorship, control could only be exercised through the imposition of age restrictions. The installation of two classifying bodies – the advisory councils in provincial governments (*Filmbeiräte*) and the Ministry of Education's film board (*Filmbegutachtungsstelle*) – was intended to keep young people away from films deemed unsuitable.[163] However, a survey conducted among fifteen-year-old youths in Vienna in 1955 showed that 30 per cent of the films teenagers watched were actually banned for their age group.[164] Cinema operators, thinking in business terms, often took a pragmatic approach when it came to complying with age regulations.[165]

The debates about the dangerous effects of film and the campaign against dirt and trash reveal a strong anti-American sentiment, but are also indicative of a collective uneasiness about the Nazi past and the lost war. Society needed to be cleansed, but the purification efforts targeted public expressions of sexuality and loose moral behaviour.[166] The film industry responded to the moral panic by offering reassuring images: happy teenagers instead of rowdy hooligans and neat bikini girls instead of wicked women populated 1950s comedies, tourist films and the emerging genre of *Schlagerfilme*, which were directed at young people. Austrian cinema tried to divest masculinity and femininity of physicality, as the body was perceived as dangerous, harbouring dark passions or erupting in violent acts that would unsettle a harmonious society. There were, of course, films that subverted this unspoken rule of representation; some, like the aforementioned social problem films, which showed half-naked women or brutal and abusive fathers, were publicly denounced for undermining morality; others, such as the aesthetically poor farmers' comedies (*Bauernschwänke*), replete with crude sexual allusions, caused outrage among Catholic circles and were dismissed by the critics as the lowest form of entertainment.[167] Exceptional in many ways was Arthur Maria Rabenalt's formidable costume film *Die Fiakermilli* (1953), which featured the feisty and sexually liberal music hall singer Fiakermilli (Gretl Schörg) as the heroine. One might have suspected that the point-of-view shots onto the audience through Fiakermilli's silk-stockinged legs, or the suggestive gestures which accompany a song about sexual awakening performed by her rival competitor, Antonie Mannsfeld (Erni Mangold), would cause outrage, but critics and audiences were thrilled. Using the format of the historical costume film, Rabenalt could be more daring because the audience watched the erotic spectacle placed in a bygone era from a safe distance.[168]

While sexuality and violence disquieted Austrian society, another issue was even more unsettling: the Nazi past. It is impossible to evaluate the state of Austrian postwar society without taking into account Austria's involvement in Nazi crimes and the attempts to come to terms with it. The renowned Austrian historian Friedrich Heer noted from his own experience that during the Allied occupation the Austrians united in an effort not to speak publicly about what he called 'inner conflicts', referring to the shared guilty conscience about the acquiescence to or outright complicity with the Nazi regime, in an attempt to present Austria in the most positive light.[169] However, even a brief glance at the press and radio coverage of the time shows that the war and the Third Reich were by no means taboo subjects in postwar Austria. Popular cinema, too, discussed the Nazi past and the question of guilt in the early postwar years in dramas such as *Das andere Leben* (The Other Life, 1948), *Die Frau am Weg* (The Woman by the Road, 1948) or *Duell mit dem Tod* (Duell with Death, 1949). Interestingly, the films often centred on the hardships of an upright heroine whose moral purity exculpated the Austrian nation. So the Nazi past was discussed constantly in public, but in a highly selective way. Politicians debated it mainly under two rubrics – 'moving on' or 'we must not forget' – without being explicit about what it was that should or should not be forgotten.[170] Among the general public, the discourse was dominated by veterans and their experiences as prisoners of war, while the experiences of victims of Nazi persecution and those of women and children at the home front were gradually excluded. The public discourse highlighted the suffering of the Austrian people, while downplaying the fact that many had collaborated with or approved of the Nazi regime, a complicity which had in part enabled the Nazi atrocities. The desire to suppress this bad conscience was so powerful that many Austrians not merely presented themselves as, but actually convinced themselves that they were victims who had suffered from a double injustice, at the hands of the Nazis as well as from the occupying Allied Forces.[171]

Austrian postwar society thus suffered from a fundamental insecurity, as the widespread anxieties about the Nazi past and 'foreign' cultural influences, the yearning for harmony and stability and the aversion to open conflict indicate. We need to be aware of this particular state of mind in order to comprehend the meanings and significance of popular Austrian film for its audience. Films cannot be reduced to the role of an ally of the ruling elites; nor are they pure products of artistic genius and therefore free from ideological or economic influence. Many, sometimes conflicting, interests are at work, which is reflected in the fact that Austrian cinema did not give equal importance to all social concerns. Some issues, such as class, were almost elided, whereas others, such as gender roles or the question of Austrian identity, were openly addressed in some genres and obliquely touched on in others, as the following chapters will illustrate. Looking at postwar Austrian history from the perspective of success might easily give a distorted view of Austrian society, as the historian Ernst Hanisch has pointed out. It is worth remembering that the route from the liberation from Nazi dictatorship to a stable democracy was by no means linear, and that Austria could have taken a different direction.[172] For contemporaries, the time between 1945 and 1955 was a decade marked by uncertainty and contingency as well as chance, not least due to the tensions of the Cold War and Austria's strategically important position in Central Europe. Therefore, the meanings that films held for contemporary audiences were different from those they convey to us – an important aspect to keep in mind.

Notes

1. See F. Trescher. 'Oesterreichischer Film', *Arbeiterzeitung*, 26 March 1946, 3; G. Steiner. 1987. *Die Heimat-Macher: Kino in Österreich 1946–1966*, Vienna: Verlag für Gesellschaftskritik, 47–46, 56–57.
2. Shandley, 2001, 24.
3. C. Brecht. 2005. 'Gedächtnispolitische Strategien im österreichischen Film zwischen 1945 und 1955', in K. Moser (ed.), *Besetzte Bilder. Film, Kultur und Propaganda in Österreich 1945–1955*, Vienna: Filmarchiv Austria.
4. See Heiss and Klimeš, 2003, 419–420; they rely on the numbers quoted in the journal *Film-Kunst. Zeitschrift für Filmkultur und Filmwissenschaft*. The data given by the Austrian Central Bureau of Statistics are lower, with 765 cinemas in 1936, as their records adhere to stricter specifications of what constitutes a cinema. See Österreichisches Statistisches Zentralamt. 1959b. *Beiträge zur österreichischen Statistik*, Vienna, vol. 39, 42.
5. See Verband der Wiener Lichtspieltheater und Audiovisionsveranstalter. 1986. *90 Jahre Kino in Wien. 1896–1986. Vergangenheit mit Zukunft*, Vienna: Jugend & Volk, 16.
6. See E. Bodzenta and L. Grond. 1957. 'Die soziale Wirklichkeit von heute', in O. Schulmeister, J.C. Allmayer-Beck and A. Wandruszka (eds), *Spectrum Austriae*, Vienna: Herder, 426.
7. See Österreichisches Statististisches Zentralamt. 1950. *Statistisches Handbuch für die Republik Österreich*, Vienna, vol. 1, 238.
8. See L. Gesek. 1959. 'Kleines Lexikon des österreichischen Films. Sachlexikon', *Film-Kunst. Zeitschrift für Filmkultur und Filmwissenschaft*, 22, 3.
9. E.v. Neusser. 1950. 'Die österreichischen Filmerfolge', *Film-Kunst. Zeitschrift für Filmkultur und Filmwissenschaft*, 5, 253.
10. 'Planvolle Filmwirtschaft', *Wiener Tageszeitung*, 1 May 1949.

11. In comparison, in 1937 27.5 million cinema visits were counted in Vienna; the number of visits to traditional theatre, however, had risen slightly, with 2.77 million visits. See Gesek, 1959, 2–3. For detailed data about cinemas in Vienna in 1955 see also Magistrat der Stadt Wien. 1956. 'Die Wiener Kinos und ihre Besucher. Eine statistische Analyse', *Mitteilungen aus Statistik und Verwaltung der Stadt Wien* (Sonderheft Nr. 2).

12. 'Wo bleibt der Jugendfilm?', *Wiener Zeitung*, 14 February 1954.

13. 'Fünfzehnjährige bevorzugen gute Filme', *Weltpresse*, 3 May 1955. The official survey of Amt für Kultur und Volksbildung der Stadt Wien. 1959. *Grossstadtjugend und Kino. Eine Untersuchung der Arbeitsgemeinschaft 'Jugend und Film' beim Landesjugendreferat Wien über den Kinobesuch der Kinder und Jugendlichen im Jahre 1953*, Vienna: Verlag Jugend und Volk, vol. 10, provides a very detailed investigation into the cinema-going habits of Austrian teenagers.

14. See Österreichisches Statistisches Zentralamt, 1959b, 145.

15. See Garncarz, 1994, 101–103.

16. Office of Military Government for Germany (US) Records, Record Group 260, National Archives, College Park, MD (hereafter RG 260), Entry 260 (A1), box 266.

17. Information Services Division OMGUS, 'Characteristics and Attitudes of the German Movie Audience', 23 May 1949. RG 260, Entry 260 (A1), box 288.

18. Higson and Maltby, 1999, 21.

19. See Gesek, 1959, 2; E.v. Neusser. 1950. 'Die österreichischen Filmerfolge', *Film-Kunst. Zeitschrift für Filmkultur und Filmwissenschaft*, 5, 253.

20. See '"Mariandl"-Triumphe in Holland', *Österreichische Film und Kino Zeitung*, 15 October 1949, 1.

21. At the end of the war, the US and the Soviet Forces had each confiscated copies of the film as German property. While the US Forces returned their copy to Forst, the Soviets finished the film in Prague and presented it to Viennese audiences in the Soviet Zone in February 1950 (the version had already premiered six months earlier in East Berlin). See, for example, 'Zweimal Wiener Mädeln', *Arbeiterzeitung*, 26 February 1950, 6; 'Zweimal "Wiener Mädeln" in Wiener Kinos. Russen bringen eigene Fassung zur Aufführung', *Wiener Kurier*, 22 February 1950; '"Wiener Mädeln" zwischen Ost und West', *Österreichische Allgemeine Zeitung*, 7 April 1950.

22. K. Witte. 1995. *Lachende Erben, toller Tag: Filmkomödie im Dritten Reich*, Berlin: Vorwerk, 21.

23. 'Trotzdem: grossartige "Wiener Mädeln". Eine denkwürdige Filmpremiere', *Montag Morgen*, 27 December 1949. See also Festschrift der Apollo Kino- u. Theater GmbH. 1954. '25 Jahre Kino-Theater. 50 Jahre Apollo-Theater', 1954, 16.

24. *The Thief of Baghdad* sold 820,000 tickets in fifty-one months, *The Jungle Book* 750,000 in seventeen months. E.v. Neusser. 1950. 'Die österreichischen Filmerfolge', *Film-Kunst. Zeitschrift für Filmkultur und Filmwissenschaft*, 5, 254.

25. See Festschrift der Apollo Kino- u. Theater GmbH, 1954, 16.

26. 'Polizeiaktion gegen den Schleichhandel mit Kinokarten', *Österreichische Film und Kino Zeitung*, 29 January 1949.

27. See Higson and Maltby, 1999, 22.

28. 'Wo bleibt der österreichische Mörderfilm?', *Welt am Montag*, 16 February 1948.

29. Cited by Higson and Maltby, 1999, 20.

30. See Harper, 1994.

31. *Kaiserwalzer* has 'a formidable effect on the broad audience'. *Paimanns Filmlisten*, Nr. 2002, 81, 1953. *Der Engel mit der Posaune* was attended by key figures of the Austrian government. See 'Der Engel mit der Posaune', *Wiener Tageszeitung*, 17 October 1948.

32. See Amt für Kultur, Volksbildung und Schulverwaltung der Stadt Wien, 1959, 67.

33. The melodrama *Vagabunden* was 'a noble yet highly popular film' that would appeal to both men and women, wrote the *Wiener Zeitung*. '"Vagabunden" – ein österreichischer

Glanzfilm', *Wiener Zeitung*, 20 October 1949. '*Liebe Freundin* with Vilma Degischer as heroine also pleases the sophisticated audience', *Wiener Zeitung*, 29 March 1949.

34. See P. Watson. 2003. 'Critical Approaches to Hollywood Cinema: Authorship, Genre and Stars', in J. Nelmes (ed.), *An Introduction to Film Studies*, 3rd ed., London: Routledge, 158.

35. See Amt für Kultur, Volksbildung und Schulverwaltung der Stadt Wien, 1959, 76–82.

36. See I. Bauer. 1995. 'Von den Tugenden der Weiblichkeit. Zur geschlechtsspezifischen Arbeitsteilung in der politischen Kultur', in T. Albrich, K. Eisterer, M. Gehler and R. Steininger (eds), *Österreich in den Fünfzigern*, Innsbruck: Österreichischer StudienVerlag, 36; Bundeskanzleramt. 2010. *Frauenbericht, Teil I: Statistische Analysen zur Entwicklung der Situation von Frauen in Österreich*, Vienna. http://www.bka.gv.at/studien/frauenbericht2010/Frauenbericht_Teil1_1Demografie.pdf.

37. Witte, 1995, 47.

38. See also U. Bechdolf. 1992. *Wunsch-Bilder? Frauen im nationalsozialistischen Unterhaltungsfilm*. Tübingen: Tübinger Verein für Volkskunde, 108–109; S. Lowry. 1994. 'Der Ort meiner Träume? Zur ideologischen Funktion des NS-Unterhaltungsfilms' [electronic version], *montage/av. Zeitschrift für Theorie & Geschichte audiovisueller Kommunikation*, 3(2).

39. L. Schulte-Sasse. 1996. *Entertaining the Third Reich: Illusions of Wholeness in Nazi Cinema*, Durham: Duke University Press, 202.

40. Österreichisches Statistisches Zentralamt, 1950, 238; '1950 brachte im Verleih grosse Zahlen – grosse Sorgen', *Österreichische Film und Kino Zeitung*, 23 December 1950, 15.

41. Österreichisches Statistisches Zentralamt, 1959b, 143.

42. See Österreichisches Statistisches Zentralamt, 1959b, 143. The length of exhibition (*Termintage* is the statistical term used by the Austrian Central Bureau of Statistics) is calculated as the sum of days a specific film was screened at each of the 107 Viennese cinemas in 1953. In total, these cinemas screened 876 films and counted 35,933 *Termintage* in 1953.

43. Ibid., 146.

44. Viktor Matejka, city councillor for culture in Vienna, was one of the few who encouraged Austrian emigrants to return and helped them to resettle. See Dokumentationsarchiv des österreichischen Widerstandes (ed.). *Österreicher im Exil. USA 1938–1945. Eine Dokumentation*, Vienna, vol. 2, 688–701.

45. See Dassanowsky, 2005, 114.

46. G. Tressler, 'Nur ein völlig neuer Geist kann das österreichische Filmschaffen retten. Die bewährten Rezepte sind erschöpft – Neue Ideen tun not', *Wiener Kurier*, 28 May 1949.

47. M.H., 'Debakel des österreichischen Films?' *Welt am Montag*, 8 March 1948.

48. The situation in West Germany was very similar. See K. Hickethier. 2007. 'The Restructuring of the West German Film Industry in the 1950s', in J.E. Davidson and S. Hake (eds), *Framing the Fifties: Cinema in a Divided Germany*, New York: Berghahn, 195–197.

49. L. Gesek. 'Hat Österreich eine Filmindustrie?' *Österreichische Film und Kino Zeitung*, 28 November 1953, 6.

50. See S.E. Rieser. 1995. 'Bonbonfarbene Leinwände. Filmische Strategien zur (Re-)Konstruktion der österreichischen Nation in den fünfziger Jahren', in T. Albrich, K. Eisterer, M. Gehler and R. Steininger (eds), *Österreich in den Fünfzigern*, Innsbruck: Österreichischer StudienVerlag, 127–129.

51. See W. Fritz. 1984. *Kino in Österreich 1945-1983. Film zwischen Kommerz und Avantgarde*, Wien: ÖBV, 93-95.

52. Cited in Fritz, 1984, 95.

53. See Dassanowsky, 2005, 113.

54. See C. Geraghty. 2000. *British Cinema in the Fifties: Gender, Genre and the 'New Look'*, London: Routledge, 175–195.

55. See S. Hake. 2008. *German National Cinema*, 2nd ed., London: Routledge, 105. For the ambiguous function of the 1950s war film in West Germany see J.M. Kapczynski. 2007. 'The Treatment of the Past: Géza von Radvanyi's *Der Arzt von Stalingrad* and the West

German War Film', in J.E. Davidson and S. Hake (eds), *Framing the Fifties: Cinema in a Divided Germany*, New York: Berghahn.

56. 'Der Weite Weg', *Der Aufbau*, 22 November 1946.
57. A quarter of all films shown in Austrian cinemas in 1950 were crime and gangster films. See 'Filmjahr 1950 – täglich ein neuer Streifen', *Wiener Tageszeitung*, 3 January 1951.
58. See T. Bergfelder. 2002. 'Extraterritorial Fantasies: Edgar Wallace and the German Crime Film', in T. Bergfelder, E. Carter and D. Göktürk (eds), *The German Cinema Book*, London: BFI, 41–42; T. Bergfelder. 2007. 'German Cinema and Film Noir', in A. Spicer (ed.), *European Film Noir*, Manchester: Manchester University Press, 139, 156.
59. 'Wo bleibt der österreichische Mörderfilm?', *Welt am Montag*, 16 February 1948.
60. 'Filmjahr 1950 – täglich ein neuer Streifen', *Wiener Tageszeitung*, 3 January 1951. Twenty-four per cent of all films screened in Austria fell under the category of crime film.
61. 'Österreichs Filmverleiher unterstützen "moralischen Notstand"', *Neues Österreich*, 31 September 1950.
62. See Seidl, 1987, 176.
63. See C. Dewald (ed.). 2004. *Der Wirklichkeit auf der Spur. Essays zum österreichischen Nachkriegsfilm ASPHALT*, Wien: Filmarchiv Austria; Büttner and Dewald, 1997a, 382–404.
64. See Döge, 2004, 63–74.
65. See Döge, 2004, 66, 74. Only one more social problem film was produced, *Schicksal am Lenkrad* (Fate at the Steering Wheel, 1954), by the Soviet-controlled Wien-Film am Rosenhügel, a harmless narrative of a young man who is prevented from going astray; the film went largely unnoticed.
66. G. Krenn. 1999. 'Der bewegte Mensch – Sascha Kolowrat', in F. Bono, P. Caneppele and G. Krenn (eds), *Elektrische Schatten. Beiträge zur österreichischen Stummfilmgeschichte*, Vienna: Filmarchiv Austria, 38.
67. See A. Loacker. 1999. *Anschluss im 3/4-Takt. Filmproduktion und Filmpolitik in Österreich 1930-1938*, Trier: Wissenschaftlicher Verlag Trier, 1.
68. Elsaesser, 1999, 26.
69. See Heiss and Klimeš, 2003, 421.
70. The newly created Tobis-Sascha soon gained a dominant position in the Austrian film industry, which it used to put smaller producers under pressure. Tobis-Sascha also managed Austria's film export contingents for Germany, making producers more dependent on the company. See A. Loacker. 1992. *Die ökonomischen und politischen Bedingungen der österreichischen (Ton-) Spielfilmproduktion der 30er Jahre*, unpublished master's thesis (Diplomarbeit), University of Vienna, 95–98.
71. See Heiss and Klimeš, 2003, 429–437; Tillner, 1996, 178.
72. See A. Loacker and M. Prucha. 2000. 'Die unabhängige deutschprachige Filmproduktion in Österreich, Ungarn und der Tschechoslowakei', in A. Loacker and M. Prucha (eds), *Unerwünschtes Kino: Der deutschsprachige Emigrantenfilm 1934–1937*, Vienna: Filmarchiv Austria. Amongst others, the producer Joe Pasternak, the directors Hermann Kosterlitz (Henry Koster), Richard Oswald, Kurt Gerron and Fritz Schulz (the latter two also actors), the screenwriter Felix Joachimson (Felix Jackson), the screenwriters/directors Rudolf Katscher (Rudolph Cartier) and Walter Reisch, the cinematographer Franz Planer, the composers Hans May and Hans J. Salter, and the actors Rosy Barsony, Felix Bressart, Peter Lorre, Joseph Schmidt (the famous tenor), Szöke Szakall (S.Z. Sakall) and Otto Wallburg worked in Austria from 1933 onwards, some of them continuously, others only for one film. See also C. Cargnelli and M. Omasta (eds). 1993. *Aufbruch ins Ungewisse*, Vienna: Wespennest.
73. For a detailed account see Heiss and Klimeš, 2003, 432–435.
74. In 1936, an agreement was reached between the Reich Film Chamber and the 'Österreichische Filmkonferenz', a consortium of representatives of the Austrian film industry

headed by the Ministry of Commerce, to exclude any Jews from working in productions exported to Nazi Germany. See Heiss and Klimeš, 2003, 414, 437.

75. E. Kieninger. 2000. 'Vorwort', in A. Loacker and M. Prucha (eds), *Unerwünschtes Kino: Der deutschsprachige Emigrantenfilm 1934–1937*, Vienna: Filmarchiv Austria, 7.

76. Tillner, 1996, 16.

77. See Verband der Wiener Lichtspieltheater und Audiovisionsveranstalter, 1986, 17.

78. See B. Peter. 2010. '"Wie es euch gefällt"? NS-Theaterpolitik und Theaterpraxis am Beispiel der "Josefstadt"', in G. Bauer and B. Peter (eds), *Das Theater in der Josefstadt*, Vienna: Lit Verlag, 114–115, 122.

79. See R. Dachs. 1992. *Sag beim Abschied… Wiener Publikumslieblinge in Bild & Ton. Ausstellung des Historischen Museums der Stadt Wien, 23. Jänner bis 22. März 1992*, Vienna: Eigenverlag der Museen der Stadt Wien, 115, 117. See also O. Rathkolb. 1991. *Führertreu und gottbegnadet. Künstlereliten im Dritten Reich*, Vienna: ÖBV, 56–59.

80. See K. Kreimeier. 1992. *Die Ufa-Story. Geschichte eines Filmkonzerns*, Munich: Hanser, 320; K. Kreimeier. 1996. 'Karl Hartl: Homo faber und Visionär', in R. Beckermann and C. Blümlinger (eds), *Ohne Untertitel: Fragmente einer Geschichte des österreichischen Kinos*, Vienna: Sonderzahl, 31–51.

81. The company Styria Film was incorporated into Wien-Film in 1940.

82. For the political meaning of entertainment cinema in the Third Reich see esp. Witte, 1995, 42–48.

83. See K. Witte. 1996. 'Der Violinschlüssel. Zur Produktion der Wien-Film', in R. Beckermann and C. Blümlinger (eds), *Ohne Untertitel: Fragmente einer Geschichte des österreichischen Kinos*, Vienna: Sonderzahl, 17–29.

84. See, e.g., B. Frankfurter. 1985. 'Rund um die 'Wien-Film'-Produktion. Staatsinteressen als Impulsgeber des Massenmediums eines Jahrzehnts', in L. Wächter-Böhm (ed.), *Wien 1945: davor/danach*, Vienna: C. Brandstätter, 188–189. For a discussion of the political ambiguity in Forst's operetta films see Witte, 1995, 19–21; M. Wedel. 2007. *Der deutsche Musikfilm. Archäologie eines Genres, 1914–1945*, Munich: Edition Text + Kritik, 391–441.

85. See W. Forst. 'Ich rufe nach Österreich', *Film*, 1 July 1946.

86. See RG 260, Entry E 2032 (A1), box 1; E 2018 (A1), box 15; E 260 (A1), box 286. For the conduct of actresses and actors in the Third Reich see Rathkolb, 1991, 235–265. Felix Moeller's evaluation of film artists' relations with the Nazi elite is very insightful. See, particularly, the chapter 'Der Führer mag Gustaf Gründgens nicht. Starkult und Verfolgung – Nazis und Filmkünstler in neuem Licht', in F. Moeller. 1998. *Der Filmminister. Goebbels und der Film im Dritten Reich*, Berlin: Henschel, 403–454.

87. Olden was also one of the few artists who was barred from working on stage; he was banned for one-and-a-half years and sentenced to hard labour. See RG 206, E 2018, box 15.

88. Filmwirtschaftsgesetz, 10 July 1945; Filmwirtschaftsverordnung, 7 September 1945. See Halbritter, 1993, 14–17, 49–51.

89. See E. Sieder. 1983. *Die alliierten Zensurmaßnahmen zwischen 1945–1955*, unpublished PhD thesis, University of Vienna, 120; Halbritter, 1993, 22–28; R. Wagnleitner. 1991. *Coca-Colonisation und Kalter Krieg. Die Kulturmission der USA in Österreich nach dem Zweiten Weltkrieg*, Vienna: Verlag für Gesellschaftskritik, 306–308.

90. See the memorandum of the meeting between Eugen Sharin and Major Bass from the ISB with the Soviet General Celthov. *Memorandum: Russian Protests on Film Administration*, cited by Sieder, 1983, 331.

91. The French and British only started to set up enterprises for the distribution of national films in 1946. By then, however, the USA had already gained supremacy in the Austrian distribution market. See Steiner, 1987, 49.

92. Eugen Sharin, head of the Film Section at the ISB, commented sarcastically: 'The Russians have made a great gesture by handing over to the Austrian State 160,000 meters of negative "in order to assure the start of production". Needless to say, this is a hollow gesture as no production can be started without the equipment ISB is holding at present'. *Memorandum: Sharin to Shinn, Vienna*, 7 November 1945, cited by Wagnleitner, 1991, 308–309. See also the ISB's weekly report from 15 March 1946, cited by Sieder, 1983, 125.
93. See Wagnleitner, 1991, 308–309, 314; Halbritter, 1993, 29–32.
94. See Sieder, 1983, 122.
95. See ibid., 22–23, 343–359. A list of criteria according to which a film was banned by the Allied Forces can be found on the website of the German Film Institute: http://www.filmportal.de/thema/kriterienkatalog-verbotener-ns-filme, retrieved 2 February 2011.
96. 'Volle Filmfreiheit gefordert', *Wiener Tageszeitung*, 25 June 1948; 'Wie steht es mit der alliierten Filmzensur?' *Arbeiterzeitung*, 25 June 1948. Little is known of the situation in the French Zone: the *Arbeiterzeitung* reported that the French film section had closed down in September 1947, and that French films no longer needed the approval of the military commander to be distributed in the French Zone. See 'Kunst und Kultur. Der gefährliche Film', *Arbeiterzeitung*, 13 January 1948; 'Filmzensur nur noch in Sowjet- und französischer Zone', *Wiener Kurier*, 25 June 1948.
97. See Halbritter, 1993, 37–38.
98. Memorandum: Various Matters Discussed with Wolfgang Wolf, Representative of MPEA (Austria), Inc., cited by Wagnleitner, 1991, 310.
99. Telegram Headquarters Zone Command Austria to Commanding General USFA, Salzburg, 12 January 1948, cited by Wagnleitner, 1991, 320. Amongst the films banned from screening in Austrian cinemas were, for example, *Grapes of Wrath* (1940), *Key Largo* (1948), *Casablanca* (1942), *Hunchback of Notre Dame* (1939), *Son of Dracula* (1943) and *Ghost of Frankenstein* (1942).
100. See G. Steiner. 1984. *Der Sieg der 'Natürlichkeit'. Eine Motivgeschichte des österreichischen Heimatfilms von 1946 bis 1966 mit besonderer Berücksichtigung der filmwirtschaftlichen Strukturen*, unpublished PhD thesis, University of Vienna, 119.
101. See Fritz, 1996, 214.
102. See M. Prucha. 1996. 'Agfacolor und Kalter Krieg. Die Geschichte der Wien Film am Rosenhügel 1946-1955', in R. Beckermann and C. Blümlinger (eds), *Ohne Untertitel: Fragmente einer Geschichte des österreichischen Kinos*, Vienna: Sonderzahl, 53–79.
103. See O. Möller. 2004. 'Die Pastellfarben des Proletariats', *taz* [electronic version]. http://www.taz.de/index.php?id=archivseite&dig=2004/06/08/a0228, retrieved 18 February 2011. For the ideological content in some Wien-Film productions see Prucha, 1996.
104. See O. Rathkolb. 1988. 'Die "Wien-Film"-Produktion am Rosenhügel. Österreichische Filmproduktion und Kalter Krieg', in H.H. Fabris and K. Luger (eds), *Medienkultur in Österreich*, Vienna: Böhlau, 217–219.
105. Hickethier, 2007, 196–197.
106. Johannes Hübler-Kahla; Österreichische Wochenschau- und Produktions KG; J.A. Hübler-Kahla & Co; J.-A.-Hübler-Kahla-Produktion; Géza von Cziffra: Cziffra-Film; Willi Forst: Forst-Filmproduktion; Ernst Marischka: Erma-Film; Paula Wessely: Paula-Wessely-Film.
107. Ring-Film was in business from 1948 to 1957, with nine productions in total; Nova-Film was in existence from 1950 to 1953; Vindobona-Film from 1946 to 1953; Neusser-Film from 1952 to 1955.
108. Neusser offers detailed calculations for small- and big-budget films produced in Austria. See E.v. Neusser. 1950. 'Kalkulationsfragen der Produktion', *Film-Kunst. Zeitschrift für Filmkultur und Filmwissenschaft*, 5, 248–249.
109. See Hickethier, 2007, 197–198.

110. The combined debts of film production firms amounted to 40 Mio. Austrian schillings. See Halbritter, 1993, 51–52.
111. See, for example, 'Das Ausland und der Wiener Film', *Arbeiterzeitung*, 3 August 1948; 'Die letzte Chance', *Neues Österreich*, 29 May 1949; 'Planvolle Filmwirtschaft', *Wiener Tageszeitung*, 1 May 1949.
112. See 'Der österreichische Nachkriegsfilm in den USA', *Österreichische Film und Kino Zeitung*, 21 February 1953.
113. 'Österreichischer Film – wohin?' *Neuer Kurier*, 7 December 1954.
114. See Tillner, 1996, 186; see also B. Frankfurter. 1988. 'Die Wien-Film. Ein Beitrag zur Dreieinigkeit von Staat, Film und politischer Kultur in Österreich', in H.H. Fabris and K. Luger (eds), *Medienkultur in Österreich*, Vienna: Böhlau, 104.
115. See Halbritter, 1993, 53–60.
116. The other films were *Der Engel mit der Posaune* (The Angel with the Trumpet, 1948), *Das andere Leben* (The Other Life, 1948) and *Anni* (1948). See 'Die Filmverhandlungen mit Deutschland', *Wiener Zeitung*, 25 May 1949; A. Quendler. 'Unser Film und die Welt', *Die Furche*, 20 November 1948.
117. See Halbritter, 1993, 55.
118. The earnings from Austrian film exhibition in West Germany were higher because the West German zones were much larger than Austria. See Halbritter, 1993, 59, 62.
119. See Rieser, 1995, 129.
120. Cited by Halbritter, 1993, 61.
121. See 'Kein österreichischer Grossfilm 1950?' *Wiener Tageszeitung*, 18 August 1949.
122. See 'Vom "Kleinen Schwindel" zur "Eva". Aufstieg einer österreichischen Filmgesellschaft', *Wiener Tageszeitung*, 22 September 1951.
123. See, e.g., 'Nur gute Filme sind rentabel', *Welt am Montag*, 14 February 1949; 'D-Mark Beträge für Wiener Filme frei. Drohende Sperre des Sieveringer Ateliers', *Die Presse*, 30 April 1949.
124. See Halbritter, 1993, 49–76. See also Steiner, 1987, 50.
125. 'Sanierung des österreichischen Films. Ohne Zentralisierung keine Rettung', *Die Presse*, 20 February 1949.
126. See Halbritter, 1993, 70.
127. Guenther Stapenhorst, *An Inquiry into Foreign Market Conditions*, 12 April 1949. RG 260, Entry E 260 (A1), box 283.
128. 'Der österreichische Film gesichert', *Die Presse*, 4 November 1950.
129. See Hickethier, 2007, 200–202.
130. See Wauchope, 2007, 214–15.
131. 'Die letzte Chance', *Neues Österreich*, 29 May 1949.
132. 'Folgen einer verfehlten Filmpolitik', *Österreichische Zeitung*, 22 January 1955. The newspaper was published by the Soviet Allied Forces, which explains the harshness of its criticism. Other papers, however, also criticised the growing German influence.
133. 'Das Ausland und der Wiener Film', *Arbeiterzeitung*, 3 August 1948, 4.
134. 'Österreichischer Film – wohin?', *Neuer Kurier*, 7 December 1954. The term was taken up in 'Folgen einer verfehlten Filmpolitik', *Österreichische Zeitung*, 22 January 1955.
135. 'Grosse Erwartungen', *Die Union*, 12 July 1951; M.H., 'Debakel des österreichischen Films?' *Welt am Montag*, 8 March 1948; 'Österreichischer Film – wohin?' *Neuer Kurier*, 7 December 1954.
136. See G. Enderle-Burcel. 1996. 'Die österreichischen Parteien 1945 bis 1995', in R. Sieder, H. Steinert and E. Tálos (eds), *Österreich 1945–1995: Gesellschaft, Politik, Kultur*, Vienna: Verlag für Gesellschaftskritik, 81, 86–87; P. Menasse. 1985. 'Die grosse Synthese. Bemerkungen zur Produktion des Neuen Österreich', in L. Wächter-Böhm (ed.), *Wien 1945: davor/danach*, Vienna: C. Brandstätter, 33; R. Sieder, H. Steinert and E. Tálos. 1996. 'Wirtschaft, Gesellschaft und Politik in der Zweiten Republik. Eine Einführung', in R.

Sieder, H. Steinert and E. Tálos (eds), *Österreich 1945–1995: Gesellschaft, Politik, Kultur*, Vienna: Verlag für Gesellschaftskritik, 11–12, 24–25.

137. While in 1953 female employees in Austria earned 73 per cent of the average male income, the percentage had fallen to 60 per cent in 1963. See E. Cyba. 1996. 'Modernisierung im Patriarchat? Zur Situation der Frauen in Arbeit, Bildung und privater Sphäre 1945 bis 1995', in R. Sieder, H. Steinert and E. Tálos (eds), *Österreich 1945–1995: Gesellschaft, Politik, Kultur*, Vienna: Verlag für Gesellschaftskritik, 439–440.

138. See F. Biess. 2002. 'Männer des Wiederaufbaus - Wiederaufbau der Männer. Kriegsheimkehrer in Ost- und Westdeutschland 1945–1955', in K. Hagemann and S. Schüler-Springorum (eds), *Heimat-Front: Militär und Geschlechterverhältnisse im Zeitalter der Weltkriege*, Frankfurt am Main: Campus, 349; R. Bessel. 2001. 'Was bleibt vom Krieg? Deutsche Nachkriegsgeschichte(n) aus geschlechtergeschichtlicher Perspektive', *Militärgeschichtliche Zeitschrift*, 60, 300.

139. See G. Dressel and N. Langreiter. 2002. 'Aus der Wehrmacht an die Uni – aus der Uni in die Ehe. Restaurierte Geschlechterverhältnisse nach dem Zweiten Weltkrieg', *Wiener Zeitschrift zur Geschichte der Neuzeit*, 2(2), 73–88.

140. See Mosse, 1998, 155–180; Schmale, 2003, 192–203; Hanisch, 2005, 71–88.

141. See, for example, I. Bandhauer-Schöffmann and E. Hornung. 1992. 'Trümmerfrauen – ein kurzes Heldinnenleben. Nachkriegsgesellschaft als Frauengesellschaft', in A. Graf (ed.), *Zur Politik des Weiblichen. Frauenmacht und -ohnmacht*, Vienna: Verlag für Gesellschaftskritik, 103–115; Langthaler, 1996, 41–43.

142. See Bauer and Huber, 2007, 71, 75.

143. See I. Bauer. 1996. 'Die "Ami-Braut" – Platzhalterin für das Abgespaltene? Zur (De-)Konstruktion eines Stereotyps der österreichischen Nachkriegsgeschichte 1945–1955', *L'Homme. Europäische Zeitschrift für feministische Geschichtswissenschaft*, 7(1), 115–117.

144. Sieder, Steinert and Tálos, 1996, 15–16.

145. See E. Thurner. 1995. 'Die stabile Innenseite der Politik. Geschlechterbeziehungen und Rollenverhalten', in T. Albrich, K. Eisterer, M. Gehler and R. Steininger (eds), *Österreich in den Fünfzigern*, Innsbruck: Österreichischer StudienVerlag, 1995, 54.

146. See Cyba, 1996, 437; M. Mesner. 1997. 'Die "Neugestaltung des Ehe- und Familienrechts". Re-Definitionspotentiale im Geschlechterverhältnis der Aufbau-Zeit', *Zeitgeschichte*, 5–6, 186–210.

147. These images were very similar to the iconography used by the Socialists and National Socialists. See the enlightening chapter 'Zukunftsfroh und muskelstark' in W. Kos. 1994. *Eigenheim Österreich: zu Politik, Kultur und Alltag nach 1945*, Vienna: Sonderzahl, 59–149.

148. See S. Mattl. 1992. '"Aufbau" – eine männliche Chiffre der Nachkriegszeit', in Bandhauer-Schöffmann and Hornung, 1992, 16–19.

149. See Hanisch, 2005, 102–104, 111–113.

150. In the elections of 1945, 64 per cent of the eligible voters were female. See Bauer, 1995, 36; Langthaler, 1996, 43–44.

151. H. Schissler. 2001. '"Normalization" as Project: Some Thoughts on Gender Relations in West Germany during the 1950s', in H. Schissler (ed.), *The Miracle Years: A Cultural History of West Germany, 1949–1968*, Princeton: Princeton University Press, 362–363.

152. See Thurner, 1995, 58, 62–63.

153. See K.R. Stadler. 1971. *Austria*, London: Benn, 62–81.

154. See Hanisch, 1994, 161–163; Bruckmüller, 1985, 518–520.

155. 'Official Documents: Great Britain - Soviet Union - United States. Tripartite Conference in Moscow. November 1, 1943'. 1944. *The American Journal of International Law*, 38(1), 3–8.

156. For a discussion of Austria's 'victim myth' see, in particular, W. Manoschek. 1996. 'Verschmähte Erbschaft. Österreichs Umgang mit dem Nationalsozialismus 1945 bis 1955', in R. Sieder, H. Steinert and E. Tálos (eds), *Österreich 1945–1995: Gesellschaft, Politik,*

Kultur, Vienna: Verlag für Gesellschaftskritik, 96–98; also P. Utgaard. 2003. *Remembering and Forgetting Nazism: Education, National Identity, and the Victim Myth in Postwar Austria*, New York: Berghahn.

157. C. Karner. 2005. 'The "Habsburg Dilemma" Today: Competing Discourses of National Identity in Contemporary Austria', *National Identities*, 7(4), 417.

158. See Appelt, 1999, 134–135.

159. See C. Flandera. 2000. 'Schmutz und Schund'. Die Diskussionen der sozialdemokratischen und der katholischen Lehrerschaft in Österreich, unpublished PhD thesis, University of Salzburg; A similiar moral panic arose in West Germany at the time: see W. Faulstich. 2007. 'Groschenromane, Heftchen, Comics und die Schmutz-und-Schund-Debatte', in W. Faulstich (ed.), *Die Kultur der fünfziger Jahre*, 2nd ed., Munich: Wilhelm Fink Verlag, 199–215.

160. See also 'Gefährliche Filme', *Arbeiterzeitung*, 28 December 1947; 'Die Wollzeile als verrufene Gasse', *Weltpresse*, 31 December 1947.

161. '"Mörderinflation" unter Kontrolle', *Neues Österreich*, 20 July 1948.

162. 'Zwei Gangsterfilme – 215 jugendliche Banditen', *Neues Österreich*, 18 December 1947.

163. The decisions of the Filmbegutachtungsstelle were not binding, though. See Gesek, 1959, 8, 11.

164. 'Fünfzehnjährige bevorzugen gute Filme', *Weltpresse*, 3 May 1955.

165. See 'Wo bleibt der Jugendfilm?' *Wiener Zeitung*, 14 February 1954.

166. See W.M. Schwarz. 2003. *Kino und Stadt. Wien 1945–2000*, Vienna: Löcker, 71–72; also F.X. Eder. 2007. '"The Nationalists' 'Healthy Sensuality' was followed by America's Influence": Sexuality and Media from National Socialism to the Sexual Revolution', in G. Bischof, A. Pelinka and D. Herzog (eds), *Sexuality in Austria*, New Brunswick, N.J.: Transaction Publishers, 119–122.

167. Designed specifically for the tastes of rural audiences, the *Bauernschwänke* seem also to have found an audience in the cities and suburbs, as the reviews indicate. The critics' use of negative superlatives indicates that these rustic comedies deeply disturbed the Austrian elites: *Die Verjüngungskur* (Rejuvenation Cure, 1948) was described as the 'all-time low' of Austrian film production by the *Wiener Kurier*, 9 August 1948. Another critic expressed bewilderment that the producers had used 'the silliest and most ribald jokes, coarsest gags and most feeble tastelessness' in 'Die Verjüngungskur', *Wiener Tageszeitung*, 8 August 1948. The *Wiener Kurier* lamented that *Liebesprobe* (Love Test, 1949) 'continues the series of our deepest artistic humiliations', *Wiener Kurier*, 10 November 1949. 'Why are, time and time again, Austrian filmmakers inspired by the great scenic landscape to produce oafish comedies, where farmers do absurd things?' asked the *Wiener Tageszeitung*. 'Neue Filme', *Wiener Tageszeitung*, 8 November 1949.

168. '"Die Fiakermilli" und eine Überraschung', *Weltpresse*, 22 January 1953.

169. See F. Heer. 2001 [1981]. *Der Kampf um die österreichische Identität* (3rd ed.), Vienna: Böhlau, 9.

170. See H. Uhl. 2005. 'Vergessen und Erinnern der NS-Vergangenheit in der Zweiten Republik', in Stiftung Haus der Geschichte der Bundesrepublik Deutschland (ed.), *Verfreundete Nachbarn: Deutschland - Österreich*, Bielefeld: Kerber, 185–190; Utgaard, 2003, 28–32, 71–85.

171. See Manoschek, 1996, 96–98.

172. See Hanisch, 1994, 415.

Chapter 2

THE HISTORICAL COSTUME FILM

Sissi (1955), the tragic story of the Bavarian princess Elisabeth/'Sissi', who falls in love with the young Austrian emperor Franz Joseph I and marries him, still tops the league of the most successful productions in postwar Austria.[1] It is a classic that, through frequent television screenings, has acquired a cult following across continental Europe. While *Sissi* is one of the few Austrian films known outside German-speaking countries today, it was only one of many historical costume films that were hugely profitable at the time. Why was the genre so successful? Was it because it offered an escape to a fairy-tale world through its glamorised, imperial setting and splendid costumes? Was it because it romanticised the past and thereby conveyed a sense of permanence and stability?

No other genre in postwar Austrian cinema celebrated Austria and the Austrian people more strongly than historical costume film. My argument is that historical costume films, defined as films set in the historical past but not necessarily dealing with actual historical events or personae, did not merely feed escapist desires, but played a major role in the construction of Austrian national identity.[2] The genre helped to instil a sense of national pride, and it popularised the idea that Austria was a nation in its own right – a conviction that was by no means shared by all Austrians in 1945.[3] Historical costume films thus fed into the discourse on Austrian identity, equipping it with appropriate imagery and providing 'historical evidence' for the claim that Austrians were a distinct nation; by interpreting the past in a specific way, the genre made it both 'usable' and accessible to the present. Pierre Sorlin suggests that historical costume films constitute the 'historical capital' of a society by producing 'myths' about the past.[4] The ruling elites may instrumentalise these myths to sustain their power. This, however, does not necessarily mean that historical films are always in line with the dominant discourse or serve as vehicles for national ideologies.[5] They can also act subversively; the historical genre represents an ideal forum to air displeasure, as critique can be expressed more easily when cloaked in historical costumes and placed in a bygone era.[6] Historical films therefore tell us more about the social and political context in which they were produced than the actual historical era they depict.[7]

The historical costume genre offers an interpretation of the historic past that shapes our perceptions of history and notions of identity; and as mentioned in the previous chapter, the themes and subjects that are not represented are equally important as those that are. George F. Custen's argument that 'absences ... constitute a state of symbolic annihilation ... in which a sanitised view of history is constructed eliminating problematic areas from public perusal' is insightful. It reminds us to probe deeper and look for explanations for why particular elements are omitted or marginalised, whereas others are accentuated. It is certainly no coincidence that filmmakers in postwar Austria singled out the nineteenth century for preferential treatment: the specific representation of the eras of Metternich and Kaiser Franz Joseph informed the popular discourse on Austrian identity, as this chapter will show. By analysing the images of masculinity that the genre sought to project, this book seeks to demonstrate how the formulation of national myths was interlinked with constructions of masculinity. Investigating the meaning of absences and presences in the films allows the identification of emotional currents that ran through postwar Austrian society and establishes why the genre was so appealing to contemporary audiences.

The Popular Appeal of Historical Costume Films

Domestic historical costume productions regularly topped the tables of the most frequently screened (and presumably also best-selling) films in postwar Austria. Towards the mid-1950s, the genre experienced a virtual boom: in 1953, the costume comedy *Der Feldherrnhügel* (Grandstand for General Staff) was the most successful film released; the following year, *Kaisermanöver* (The Kaiser Manoeuvres) topped the exhibitors' charts; and in 1955, *Die Deutschmeister* (The Deutschmeister) came second only to the Hollywood romantic drama *Three Coins in the Fountain* (1954).[8] The fact that these films outstripped even major Hollywood productions is evidence of their broad appeal. They offered everything that the Austrian spectator expected from a visit to the cinema, which was, according to the film producer Erich von Neusser, 'predominantly pleasure, relaxation, entertainment, preferably in a local setting, preferably set in the beautiful past'.[9]

Most Austrian costume films display a relatively high investment in the mise-en-scène, but few are visually daring. The visual language of Walter Kolm-Veltée's Beethoven film *Eroica* (1949) or G.W. Pabst's historical drama *Der Prozess* (1947/48) is sophisticated in the use of expressive camera angles and experimental lighting; in contrast, a static camera and choppy editing give Franz Antel's *Kaiserwalzer* (1953) and *Kaisermanöver* (1954) a rather wooden feel. Long and medium shots, which fix the protagonists in their (glorious imperial or beautiful rural) surroundings, as well as medium close-ups which allow for emotional identification, are the most frequently used filming techniques. The pace is usually slow, as if to fix time, and the narrative is based on character rather than on action. The narrative flow is frequently interrupted by musical interludes, such as musical-style displays of song or dance, which carry meanings that go beyond their mere entertainment value.

Contemporary critics were divided in their views on Austrian historical costume films. They lavished praise on some, such as the historical dramas *Der Engel mit der Posaune* (The Angel with the Trumpet, 1948) and *Der Prozess* (The Trial, 1948), or the costume comedy *Die Fiakermilli* (Fiakermilli, 1953). Other films, in particular those by the prolific directors Ernst Marischka and Franz Antel, were often dismissed as shallow entertainment. Critics accused these filmmakers of glorifying the past, of promoting tedious clichés and, most of all, of repeating the same formula over and over again.[10] One critic, reviewing the opening of Hans Schott-Schöbinger's costume comedy *Hofjagd in Ischl* (Royal Hunt in Ischl, 1955), remarked acidly: 'We have – thanks to the cinema – known it for a long time: it was a splendiferous time. The Kaiser Franz Josephs were sitting on benches at scenic spots, nodding benevolently. ... They did not think of war or armament, but only about how they could marry off their nephews and nieces to each other'.[11]

This ridicule, however, did not affect the films' popularity with audiences, as both the rankings and the large number of historical costume film productions demonstrate. More than one-fifth of the total output of Austrian feature films (45 out of 213) between 1946 and 1955 falls into the category of historical costume film, which is a significant number.[12] In Britain, where costume films boomed in the 1930s, their highest share only reached 13.5 per cent of total film production, which they attained in 1935.[13] In comparison, the highest proportion of film production that historical costume films garnered in Austria was a third, achieved in 1947. Considering the financial difficulties that production companies faced after the war, this figure is astonishing.[14] The film industry's severe financial crisis towards the end of the 1940s and its consequences also affected the production of historical costume films, which reached an all-time low in 1952, when only one costume film was produced. However, the lifting of trade restrictions and an increase in West German investments eventually began to take effect, and brought another dramatic rise in Austrian costume-film productions: up to one-third of all productions in 1955.

The growing influx of West German capital also resulted in an increase in production values. The Soviet-controlled Rosenhügel studio had taken the lead in producing the first costume films in colour after the war, with *Die Regimentstochter* (Daughter of the Regiment, 1953), *Eine Nacht in Venedig* (A Night in Venice, 1953) and *Franz Schubert* (1953), but the most lavish Austrian costume productions since the Ufa days in the Third Reich were produced with the support of West German distributors: *Sissi* (1955), *Die Deutschmeister* (1955) and *Der Kongress tanzt* (The Congress Dances, 1955). These films are all rich in sumptuous décor and costumes, which certainly heightened their audience appeal.

Historical costume film is a diverse genre that comprises comedies, melodramas and dramas. With nineteen biopics, biographical films make up a large share of postwar Austrian costume films. The focus on real, historical personae suggests that there was a – genuine or perceived – need for role models in postwar Austria, but it is the choice of person-ages and the manner of their depiction which is especially revealing. The fact that fifteen out of the nineteen biopics centre on national celebrities is not unusual for national cinemas. Yet, even those that tell the stories of non-Austrian figures present them in such a manner that they might easily be taken for Austrians: *Das unsterbliche Antlitz* (The Immortal Face, 1947), on the German painter Anselm Feuerbach, *Eroica*, on Ludwig van Beethoven, *Der Obersteiger* (The Mine Foreman, 1952), a fictionalised love story of the Bavarian Duke Max and Princess Luise and *Mädchenjahre einer Königin* (Victoria in Dover, 1954), about the life of a young Queen Victoria, imply Austrianness through the use of Austrian stars and settings, the Austrian mode of speaking and the foregrounding of characteristics such as sensitivity, musicality or sanguinity, which are presented as Austrian traits throughout the genre.[15]

The aristocracy and artists are important figures in postwar Austrian biographical film: while eight films portray royals and aristocrats, the others focus on the lives of artists, mostly composers such as Beethoven, Mozart, Strauss, Schubert, von Suppé or Ziehrer.[16] The genre thus high-lights musical genius, which is represented as a quintessential Austrian trait. The musical passion of these figures is usually coloured by a streak of melancholia, to emphasise the suffering these musical talents endured, although Oskar Werner's impersonation of Mozart in *Mozart* (1955) was novel for the time in that it presented Mozart as a jaunty and playful young man who composed with ease, thus reflecting the optimism of the young Austrian republic. Musicality and masculinity are closely intertwined in the narratives, making productive musical talent the domain of Austrian men. Only one of the eleven artists' biographies – Arthur Maria Rabenalt's *Die Fiakermilli* – is devoted to a woman. *Die Fiakermilli*, based on the story of the popular music-hall singer Fiakermilli, who lived in nineteenth-cen-tury Vienna, is unusual in a genre that otherwise highlights male musical genius and sidelines female talent. It stunned both critics and its audience who, according to one review, 'held its breath for a couple of minutes', be-cause it oozed eroticism and celebrated female independence – two things that are otherwise conspicuously absent from the postwar costume film.[17] The stereotype of the 'musical Austrian', promoted so vigorously in these films, had a long tradition in Austrian cinema.[18] Postwar Austrian cinema, however, reinforced popular belief in the deeply rooted musical genius of the Austrian people, and in particular Austrian men, by foregrounding the aspect of musicality in representations of masculinity, while playing down other characteristics.

The specific historical context – troubled gender relations as well as the Austrians' need to affirm their national identity – may explain why the films put so much emphasis on male musical talent. Positive images of masculinity affirmed the social status of men at a time when they were experiencing a painful diminishment of their status as 'providers, protectors and procreators'.[19] Yet, while the narratives endorse patriarchal order by underlining male superiority, they also take the edge off patriarchy by presenting the male protagonists as cultured, sensitive and creative. They thus make male authority more acceptable to the female audience, towards which the genre was, supposedly, predominantly geared.[20]

The Austrian historical costume film does not present these men as aloof geniuses, but as ordinary men with a genuine passion for music. The narratives claim that musical talent is inherently Austrian, and that every Austrian man has a potential to express it. It is perhaps for that reason that *Wien tanzt* (1951), in which Adolf Wohlbrück (Anton Walbrook) played Johann Strauss, did not quite persuade the critics. Some found that Wohlbrück's portrayal of Strauss was not folksy enough: 'very urbane, very *soigné* is this Strauss – but very un-Viennese' concluded the *Wiener Zeitung*, and the reviewer of *Neues Österreich* found Wohlbrück's Strauss simply 'too aristocratic'.[21] Musicality was for the ordinary Austrian, not the rarified genius.

At the same time that contemporary British and Hollywood historical costume films were showcasing muscular strength and physical vitality, Austrian costume films were highlighting male sensitivity, which can partly be explained by the experience of war.[22] Austrian films turned Austria's military defeat into a moral victory of music over violence, and thereby also supported Austria's claim to victim status. It seems that film producers deliberately abstained from making films about scientists, inventors or political leaders, which had been the subject of successful biopics in the Third Reich, because musicians, unlike scientists or inventors, had an air of incorruptibility (even though the experience of National Socialism had clearly proved how corruptible the arts were), and were therefore the preferred choice for biographical films after the war.[23] The narratives of postwar Austrian costume films equated musical talent with political neutrality and peacefulness, and presented them as constitutive characteristics of the new Austrian. The images are thus highly political: they serve as 'proof' of Austria's innocence but also imply that Austrian men, because of their musical sensitivity, could hardly have committed any violent acts during the war.[24]

Historical costume film employed music to define Austrian masculinity as emotional and cultured, and thus contributed to a wider cinematic discourse which presented the Austrian nation in feminine terms, contrasting it with a 'masculine Germany'. The Austrian film industry and its critics customarily referred to musicality to define Austrian cinema: 'What the foreign market expects of the Austrian film is musicality, charm, effort-lessness', stated the Austrian film journal *Film-Kunst* in 1950.[25] The film producer Erich von Neusser claimed that 'even average Austrian films are far better than the German ones' and resorted to the popular cliché of Aus-trian musicality and charm to substantiate his claim: 'maybe it is because the Austrian is musically more talented; maybe it is also due to the fact that the Germans, who are so tough, lack the light touch and deal with their subjects too seriously'.[26] Neusser's line of argument was shared by many of his contemporaries, and this contrasting of the 'soft', 'effortless', musical Austrians with the 'hard', 'profound' and tough Germans was a recurring pattern found both in the genre and in popular discourse more generally.[27]

The genre thus sought to instil a sense of pride in Austria by empha-sising the highly cultured nature of the society. For example, the central message of *Singende Engel* (Singing Angels, 1947), Gustav Ucicky's first film after the war, is the everlasting power of the Austrian male's affinity for music. The film is about the history of the Viennese Boys' Choir and presents the choirboys as a unit that survives the passage of time as well as political turmoil because their musical talent makes them endure all odds – an obvious analogy to the Austrian nation. This is best illustrated in the closing scene, set in the cathedral of St Stephen, which was badly damaged by the war: we see the choir boys singing amidst the debris, and as their crystal-clear voices rise up to where the church roof used to be, a ray of sunlight touches an old man sitting on a church bench, who watches the boys with misty eyes. It is the old master, Haydn, who has stepped down from heaven to witness the resurrection of the famous choir and, by im-plication, of Austria. While Ucicky's slow march through the times bored the critic of the *New York Times*, who complained that it 'moves like molten lead', the Austrian audience greeted the film with rapturous applause.[28]

As mentioned earlier, historical costume films offer an interpretation of the historic past that shapes our views of history. The fact that national cinemas often focus on specific historical periods while ignoring others directs us to the idea that these historical eras played a particular role in contemporary society.[29] By investigating why film producers selected some historical periods rather than others, and by analysing their visual repre-sentation, I want to illustrate how cinema participated in the construction of national myths.

Although the nineteenth century was the most popular era, a small number of films were set in other times, such as in the eighteenth century (*Maria Theresia*, 1951; *Mozart*, 1955) or in Ancient Greece (*Triumph der Liebe*, Lysistrata – Triumph of Love, 1947). The favoured historical periods were during the reign of Kaiser Franz Joseph I (1848–1916) and, to a lesser de-gree, the era of Metternich (1809–1848).[30] What was it, exactly, that made these times particularly interesting? Why did film producers, whose main interest was – after all – commercial success, believe that films set in the nineteenth century would appeal to audiences? And why, indeed, were these films so successful?

The fact that postwar Austrian film mainly dealt with these two historical periods is particularly meaningful because they occupy two opposite positions in the collective memory: while Austrians remember the governance of the German Prince Metternich – who controlled Austrian politics as foreign minister and chancellor until 1848 – mainly in terms of oppression, the reign of Kaiser Franz Joseph still evokes memories of grandeur.[31] But it was the historical costume film that played an influential role in shaping these widely held perceptions of the past, not least because the films have had many repeats on national and independent television since they were produced.

Films Set in the Era of Metternich

Metternich's control of Austrian politics in the first half of the nineteenth century forms the template for films such as *Erzherzog Johann's grosse Liebe* (Archduke Johann's Great Love, 1950), *Franz Schubert* (1953), *Einmal keine Sorgen haben* (To Be without Worries, 1953), *Der Kongress tanzt* (1955) and *Wien tanzt* (Vienna Dances, 1951). The Metternich era was a period of political oppression and censorship, a climate that gave birth to the introspective Biedermeier style in literature and architecture. A scene in *Erzherzog Johann's grosse Liebe* tangibly conveys this air of oppression by depicting country folk sitting in an inn looking fearfully at the entry of a group of men clad in dark coats and top hats. Even though the new arrivals present themselves as Viennese tourists, the locals immediately suspect them to be members of the secret police. The secret police also functions as cultural signifier in the Johann Strauss biopic *Wien tanzt*. Here, members of the secret police inform Chancellor Metternich (Erik Frey) about a new dance that has quickly attracted a large following in the Viennese music halls: the waltz. They suspect the waltz to be dangerous for arousing passionate feelings and thus sparking a revolutionary spirit. Metternich immediately calls for a covert observation and, in disguise, visits the music hall where Johann Strauss (played by Adolf Wohlbrück/Anton Walbrook) performs. Yet Strauss, having been warned in advance, switches to a traditional polka as soon as the secret police enter the music hall. The agents fail to blend into the crowd: sitting in groups, dressed in black, with their top hats on, the people quickly spot the presence of these unwelcome authority figures. Metternich feels thoroughly embarrassed by the incompetence of his subordinates, and sarcastically commends the police chief on the successful completion of the mission. Costumes, body language and the gaze function here as visual cues that identify the historical period, but also offer an interpretation of history: the representatives of power are clearly distinguishable through their demeanour and clothes and are thus isolated from the rest, who express their disapproval of the oppressors through their looks and gestures. By these visual means, the filmic texts suggest that Austrian society was divided into a few suppressors and the mass of ordinary Austrian people, who were quietly resistant to the authoritarian regime.

The fact that Metternich was not Austrian, but German, is significant, and might explain why the first half of the nineteenth century is one of the most favoured periods in postwar Austrian cinema: Metternich is often represented as a man in power who manipulates a weak Austrian Kaiser, thereby drawing parallels between Metternich's reign and Nazi dictatorship. Films such as *Wien tanzt* or *Erzherzog Johann's grosse Liebe* also demonstrate how the Austrian historical costume film functioned both as a tool of criticism and as a medium to come to terms with an uncomfortable truth: in a time when a self-critical engagement with the immediate past was largely avoided, the projection onto a different period allowed the film producers to debate the legacy of the Nazi past. Furthermore, these films did not just provide a space in which Austrians could counter the allegations about their support for the Nazi regime by emphasising that they themselves had been victims of oppression; they also played down the extent of the repression, and thus lessened the burden of the past. *Der Kongress tanzt* ridicules the overzealous secret police and thus symbolically divests it of its influence, for example, and *Wien tanzt* 'humanises' Metternich by presenting him as a man who laughs at the stupidity of his supporters and finally joins in the fun of dancing the immoral waltz.

Searching for the 'Good Old Times' in Die Welt dreht sich verkehrt

A particularly interesting example of the instrumentalisation of the past to support Austria's 'victim myth' – and therefore one worth closer analysis – is *Die Welt dreht sich verkehrt* (The World Turns Backward, 1947).[32] Even though the stated aim of the film was to show that the 'good, old times were not better than the present', the film effectively promotes the qualities of the Austrian nation.[33]

Die Welt dreht sich verkehrt not only celebrated Austria's resilience, but also marked the comeback of Austrian-born director Johannes Alexander Hübler-Kahla (1902–1965), who wrote, directed and produced the film. Hübler-Kahla started his career as a director and cinematographer in Germany in the mid-1920s, but was arrested in Berlin in April 1937 and reportedly sentenced to eight months' imprisonment for forgery of documents in attempting to hide his partly Jewish ancestry.[34] He was subsequently banned from working in the film industry and was unable to work until Nazi Germany was defeated.

Die Welt dreht sich verkehrt is a costume comedy that tells the story of the disgruntled, retired civil servant Pomeisl, played by the popular Viennese comedian Hans Moser (1880–1964), who is dissatisfied with the miserable living conditions in postwar Austria. With the help of a magic ring, he travels back in time and visits three historical periods, all of which have a constitutive place in national memory: the Congress of Vienna in 1814, the Turkish siege of Vienna in 1683 and, finally, 176 A.D., when the Roman Emperor Marcus Aurelius set up his military headquarters in Vindobona, the latter-day Vienna.

Pomeisl's yearning for the 'good old times' must have resonated strongly with audiences: when the film premiered in Vienna on 17 February 1947 the Austrians, still reeling from the effects of war, were suffering an extremely cold winter, exacerbated by coal and electricity shortages; schools had been shut since Christmas, and the city had been cut off from any coal or oil deliveries since 12 February.[35] Moser, famous for his grouchy, melancholic characters who are imperious but servile to those in power, was thus ideally cast to express the *Weltschmerz* of his fellow countrymen and women. He had first acquired stardom in the 1930s, embodying the sort of petit-bourgeois Viennese man who, 'oscillating between compliant servility and shrewd insurrection', suffers from daily injustices and fights in vain against any form of change.[36] With his mixture of compliance and obstinacy, Moser was seen as the archetypal Austrian, both at home and by the German audience, for whom he represented everything they 'expected, hoped for and feared from' the Austrians.[37]

Moser's *tour de force* – he plays five different roles – also symbolised continuity and provided reassurance: not a glamorous star, but a true man of the people, he represented 'the immortal Viennese and the immortal optimist, who, despite the hardships he faces, again and again arises anew'.[38] Like the German film star Hans Albers, whose 'reputed resistance to the Nazis lent him an authority that far exceeded that of any other actor of his stature', Moser's steadfast refusal to divorce his Jewish wife during Nazi dictatorship attested to his dignity and further increased his popularity in postwar Austria.[39]

Die Welt dreht sich verkehrt begins with a party to celebrate both New Year's Eve and Pomeisl's birthday. The frugally decorated rooms indicate that times are hard, but the guests are enjoying themselves. Their cheerfulness grows as the evening progresses, but at the same time Pomeisl's mood darkens: he complains about the mistaken optimism of the young and praises the bygone 'beautiful past'. No longer used to consuming wine, which is rationed in postwar Austria, Pomeisl eventually nods off and – in his dream – is given the ring that allows him to travel back in time. At his first stop, Pomeisl finds himself in the position of a clerk at the Congress of Vienna, suffering under an authoritarian leadership that airily decides the future of its people, and suffering also from a grumbling stomach – very much like in real life (Figure 2.1). The oppressive circumstances of the time are reflected in Moser's body language: Pomeisl continuously ducks his head and bows, making himself smaller in order to avoid being noticed.

His immediate superior, the aristocratic Polizeirat von Creutzinger (Theodor Danegger), shows little regard for his subordinate until he recognises his usefulness. Metternich has ordered Creutzinger to find somebody who can infiltrate the congress in order to gain vital information that would allow him to manipulate the outcome.

Incidentally, Pomeisl displays a striking resemblance to the short, corpulent Prince Palatzky (also played by Hans Moser). As the prince has been kidnapped by Metternich's men and is kept drunk in one of the famous Viennese wine cellars (suggestive of Austria's inherent pacifism and preference for harmless 'weapons'), Creuztinger pressures Pomeisl to go undercover as Prince Palatzky to spy on the other participants at the congress. Pomeisl is clearly unhappy about this proposition and tries to find excuses: he first presents himself as slow-witted, and stutters and gestures clumsily to show that he is not fit to play the role of a prince; when this strategy proves fruitless, he resorts to rational arguments, pointing out that 'despotism is not in my nature'. However, the hungry Pomeisl finally succumbs to the promise of roast chicken and cucumber salad, which Creutzinger describes to him in vivid colours; dressed up as Palatzky he is sent to the congress, but before he can taste the delights of the buffet he is asked to attend a meeting with other royals. It proves to be a disillusioning encounter: Pomeisl (alias Palatzky) finds himself among arrogant warmongers who care little about peace and ignore the needs of ordinary people. Upset by so much negligence, the previously servile Pomeisl becomes angry and, much to the surprise of the other royals, launches into a

Figure 2.1: Hans Moser as a dutiful clerk Pomeisl under Metternich's reign in *Die Welt dreht sich verkehrt*. Image: screenshot.

rousing, revolutionary speech, demanding peace and cucumber salad for everybody! His plea for peace, however, falls on deaf ears, and Palatzky is left behind in an empty room with a peace treaty the others have (literally) trampled on.

The narrative presents the Austrians as harmonious and peaceful; they are eternal victims of external powers – a critical nod to Austria's annexation by the Nazis and its occupation by the Allied Forces after the war. Whether set against the backdrop of European royalty, the Turks or the Romans (the latter revealing a striking resemblance to Germans in their belligerent manner), the text suggests that the Viennese/Austrians have always been the object of external aggression, but have survived thanks to their resilience, wit and diplomacy. The film thus provides 'historical evidence' for the innate pacifism of the Austrian people, and corroborates the official doctrine that Austria was a victim of Nazi aggression.

Die Welt dreht sich verkehrt also shows that filmic texts operate on a number of different levels and can easily convey contradictory messages. The scene where the officials search for a double for Prince Palatzky and finally spot Pomeisl illustrates this argument: having looked in vain for an adequate stand-in for the prince, the secretary, Windholz (Max Brod), finally draws Polizeirat von Creutzinger's attention to the clerk, Pomeisl, who sits amidst large stacks of files. Pomeisl quickly realises that he has caught the interest of his superiors, who tower high above him on a staircase, and clumsily tries to hide behind the files, pretending to be busy. At Creutzinger's triumphant outcry: 'That's him! We finally got him!' Pomeisl's head shoots up, and he responds stutteringly, with a weak voice: 'Me? Why me? Your lordship, have mercy, I have done nothing except my duty!' This remark must have produced some chuckles among 1947 audiences, as it was an unconcealed reference to the excuse presented by many Nazi collaborators after the war, who argued that they had only followed orders and fulfilled their duty. The oblique sarcasm illustrates that *Die Welt dreht sich verkehrt* also functions ambiguously; while on the one hand it heavily promotes the presiding myth of Austria as innocent victim of external aggression, on the other it hints at Austria's active support of the Nazi government and thus (tentatively) undermines this dominant discourse. The fact that later costume film productions displayed none of this ambiguity suggests that in early 1947, when the film was produced, the official 'victim myth' had not yet become absolute.

As this analysis illustrates, the context of the Metternich era also provided a forum for criticism. Whereas *Die Welt dreht sich verkehrt* took several swipes at the Germans, a recurring theme in Austrian cinema, Franz Antel's remake of the successful 1931 German costume comedy *Der Kongress tanzt* played on the Austrians' dislike of the Soviet occupation troops. Different from the original film, Antel's version portrays Uralsky, the *doppelgänger* of the Russian Czar Alexander (Rudolf Prack in both roles), as an alcoholic and kleptomaniac who likes to steal watches – a blatant allusion to the Soviet soldiers' habit of confiscating watches from the Austrians. Moreover, *Der Kongress tanzt* shows Viennese citizens expressing their disapproval about the impending arrival of the Russian Czar: Metternich, played by Karl Schönböck, orders the Austrians to display 'great enthusiasm on the scale of small, medium or great enthusiasm', but also voices concern that it might 'take ages until the Russians leave Vienna'. Contemporary audiences undoubtedly understood these jokes as criticisms directed at the Soviets and their reluctance to end their occupation of Austria. The fact that *Der Kongress tanzt* was produced after the Allied Forces had signed the state treaty that gave Austria independence in May 1945 explains the bluntness of the jokes: the producers no longer had to fear Soviet intervention, and took this opportunity to make fun of them – albeit in a very harmless manner, as anxieties about the Soviets remained strong.

The Metternich period allowed the filmmakers to express opinions on sensitive political issues. By drawing parallels between the Nazi dictatorship and the Metternich regime and playing down the severity of repression, the historical costume films trivialised the recent past and made the horrors of Nazism look less threatening. The films hence functioned as a kind of Freudian 'screen memory'. According to Sigmund Freud's theory, some individuals develop a 'screen memory' to cope with a traumatic experience, by displacing the memory of a disturbing event onto a seemingly insignificant earlier or subsequent memory, so disguising it. The 'screen memory' is therefore a compromise between the psyche's need for repression and the need to remember: it protects the subject from the disturbing memory, but also acknowledges its importance and thus tries to keep the memory alive, albeit in a concealed form.[40] Contrary to the commonly held assumption that Austrian cinema, like the Austrians themselves, repressed the unsettling memory of the Nazi past, analysis of historical costume films shows that the past was not repressed, but rather displaced to an earlier time. Screening the traumatic memory of Nazism with a past event that seemed less charged (but which still bore resemblance to it) allowed both audience and filmmakers to cope with the memory while keeping it alive. Hence, the genre smoothed over national traumas instead of working through them, thereby creating harmony between the past and the present.

Films Set in the Era of Kaiser Franz Joseph

Harmony was also a key theme in the depictions of the historical period that featured most frequently in postwar historical costume film: the era of Kaiser Franz Joseph.[41] The 'Habsburg Myth', a romanticised view of the Austrian monarchy that ignored the actual ethnic or social conflicts which brought about its downfall, was by no means a creation of the Austrian film industry.[42] Nostalgia for the Habsburg monarchy developed soon after the demise of the Austro-Hungarian Empire in 1918, predominantly among the conservative Catholic elites. After the Second World War, Austria experienced a new wave of Habsburg nostalgia, which seems understandable considering that the country had just come out of a terrible war and that society was rapidly changing; compared to the present, the era of Kaiser Franz Joseph seemed idyllic, and hence provided a 'usable' past. Where it had once been denounced as a hotbed of social conflict and as a *Völkerkerker* (prison of nations), the Austro-Hungarian monarchy was cleansed by the atrocities of the Nazi regime, allowing it to shine in new splendour, as Hanisch aptly put it.[43]

After the defeat of Nazi Germany, Austria's political and cultural elites ransacked the Austro-Hungarian Empire for symbols and clichés to provide the disoriented Austrian people with a positive historical identity. The image of the 'good, old Kaiser', demonstrations of the Empire's multi-ethnic character and the cliché of the 'musical Austrian' were presented as quintessentially Austrian.[44] The film industry quickly leapt to cash in on the revival of Habsburg nostalgia. The film directors Ernst Marischka and Franz Antel were at the forefront in creating an idyllic image of 'Austria's last happy time', as one advertisement called it.[45] Their films portrayed the last decades of the Habsburg Empire as a glorious time, with a fatherly emperor presiding over a multi-ethnic society living in harmony.

Characterisations of Kaiser Franz Joseph play a central role in these historical costume films. Often (falsely) remembered as Austria's last emperor, Franz Joseph I had already acquired mythical status during his lifetime because of his long reign (1848–1916). Postwar Austrian historical costume films turned the Kaiser into a cult figure and cemented the image of Franz Joseph as 'the good emperor'. With the exception of the trilogy *Sissi*, which shows the emperor in his youth, postwar historical costume films usually depict the Kaiser as an old man with splendid white whiskers, dressed in his characteristic slate-blue uniform. The figure of Franz Joseph is omnipresent in these films, even if he is physically absent from the filmic text: portraits, busts and statues, as well as the tunes of the 'Kaiserwalzer' or the 'Kaiserhymne', are constant reminders of his presence. Images of the imperial palaces of Schönbrunn and Hofburg, or of Bad Ischl, Franz Joseph's favoured summer retreat, underline the ubiquitous influence of the Kaiser.

Sarajevo – *The Dark Side of the Empire*

Almost all of the films set in the late Austro-Hungarian Empire portray the era in a positive light, highlighting its tranquillity and stability. A very interesting exception is the historical costume film *Sarajevo*, produced in 1955 by Wiener Mundus-Film and directed by Fritz Kortner (1892–1970), a Viennese Jew who started his career on stage in Austria and Germany before he broke into German films in the 1920s. His role as Dr Schön in *Die Büchse der Pandora* (Pandora's Box, 1929) made him internationally famous. In the early 1930s he was at the height of his film career, playing the leads in *Dreyfus* (1930), *Danton* (1931) and *Der Mörder Dimitri Karamasoff* (The Brothers Karamazov, 1931), but was soon forced to emigrate by the Nazi takeover in 1933. Kortner fled via Austria to Britain, where he played leading parts in five films, among them the comedy *Chu Chin Chow* (1934) and the historical drama *Abdul the Damned* (1935). He moved on to Hollywood, where job prospects were brighter, working as a scriptwriter and actor in anti-fascist films, such as *The Strange Death of Adolf Hitler* (1943). In late 1947, Kortner returned to Germany and successfully resumed his career on stage, but also appeared in a small number of films, among them the critical remigration drama *Der Ruf* (The Last Illusion, West Germany, 1949), for which he also wrote the script.

Kortner's historical drama *Sarajevo* is based on a script by the once successful, but nowadays almost forgotten, Austrian writer Robert Thoeren, who had co-written the story for Billy Wilder's *Some Like it Hot* (1959). *Sarajevo* follows the historical events that led up to the assassination of Archduke Franz Ferdinand, successor to the throne of the Austro-Hungarian Empire, and his wife, Sophie, in Sarajevo in June 1914, and details the last day in the lives of the royal couple. The assassins, played by Hubert Hilten, Wolfgang Lier, Michael Lenz and a young Klaus Kinski, are sympathetically portrayed as freedom fighters. The leading role of the Archduke was given to Ewald Balser, a German character actor from the classical stage, who often played serious and brooding characters. Critically acclaimed for his portrayal of the title character in *Rembrandt* (Germany, 1942), Balser continued to play great historical personalities, such as Beethoven in the Austrian biopic *Eroica* (1949) and the medic Sauerbruch in the German drama *Sauerbruch* (1954), which triggered a new boom of 'doctor' films.[46] Luise Ullrich starred alongside Balser as the Archduke's wife, Sophie; Ullrich had acquired fame in Max Ophüls's *Liebelei* (Germany, 1933). Her unaffected, jaunty style, which underlined the naturalness of her characters, made her a popular actress in the Third Reich; in the 1950s Ullrich successfully revived her stagnating career by playing devoted mothers and pragmatic middle-aged women.[47]

The warm, motherly qualities that characterised her previous roles are also evident in her portrayal of Sophie: ostracised from the Viennese court because of her relatively lowly status within the aristocracy, Sophie is presented as a down-to-earth character who is in touch with the needs of the common people and tries to find pragmatic solutions for the national conflicts that threaten to tear the empire apart. Sophie's characterisation resembles that of the young princess Sissi in Marischka's *Sissi*: both are outsiders and despise the superficiality of the court; both long for privacy and normality and love men who are burdened with heavy responsibilities. But the figure of Sophie is drafted more ambiguously, insinuating that her self-perception as a liberal and unpretentious aristocrat is misleading. The common people with whom she identifies reject her camaraderie: her chambermaid giggles in embarrassment when she hears Sophie sing

Czech folk tunes, and the assassins to whom she appeals in prison spurn her claims that she shares their goals.

The depiction of Sophie as a strong and warm-hearted woman complements the sternness of Balser's Franz Ferdinand, who is torn between his desire to gain approval from the Kaiser and his urge to rebel against tradition. Strong-willed and disciplined, with an impressive physique, he displays all the qualities of 'hard' masculinity. Yet his harshness is only a facade that conceals his powerlessness. Constantly striving to affirm his authority in public, he is kind and warm in private – an affectionate husband, grateful for Sophie's attention and motherly care, but also interested in her political judgements. Franz Ferdinand is presented as a man in crisis, who battles both his enemies at court and his inner traumas, which are directly linked to the Kaiser; his empty outbursts of anger and his recurring headaches, which repeatedly force him to lie down, are illustrative of his weakness. Caught in a tight net of social expectations and royal duties, and unable to overcome traditional ways of thinking, Franz Ferdinand is – just like the empire – doomed; his death thus also symbolises the demise of an outdated model of masculinity.

The film paints an image of Austria's imperial past that runs contrary to the nostalgic veneration of the era in postwar Austria. In *Sarajevo*, the static world of the late Austro-Hungarian Empire radiates not tranquillity, but heaviness. The film depicts the Viennese aristocracy as an elite embroiled in intrigues, clinging greedily to its endangered status and privileges, and shows the monarchy's bureaucracy to be sluggish and inflexible, incapable of adapting to changes and thus steering the empire straight towards its inevitable destruction. Everything has come to a standstill in *Sarajevo*: the dim rooms, crammed with busts and portraits of the Kaiser, appear musty. The officers and chamberlains who form Franz Ferdinand's entourage are advanced in age and display an air of complacency; leaning back in their chairs with smug smiles on their lips during Franz Ferdinand's dinner speech at the beginning of the film, these are obviously not men to be counted on for change. Their indecisiveness and reluctance to take action are symbolic of the state of the empire.

The court in Vienna is equally unwilling to take decisions, lest they might be the wrong ones. An exchange between the civil servant Pokorny (Erik Frey) and his superior (Hans Olden) wonderfully illustrates the empire's inertia. Pokorny stirs his superior from his sleep to report urgently about the precarious situation in Bosnia, which Franz Ferdinand's visit has exacerbated. Although his superior is obviously a powerful aristocrat with the authority to take decisions, he is reluctant to issue an order that would cut short Franz Ferdinand's visit to Bosnia and thus save his life. Sitting at his desk in his silken dressing gown, cutting his cigar, he muses absentmindedly about the dilemma of having to take decisive action without risking his job: 'Something should happen, but one cannot do anything'. Pokorny's reply, which is immediately taken up by his superior, is that 'one should do something, without anything happening' – an unconcealed critique of the politics of the late Austro-Hungarian Empire.

Kortner's film masterfully conveys the tensions that marked the relationship between the Kaiser and his unloved nephew Franz Ferdinand, and the national and social animosities that tore apart Austrian society. The tension is almost palpable when Franz Ferdinand walks up to his rooms after an acrid dinner speech directed at Bosnian nationalists and a clash with his advisors over a lack of guards for his planned visit to Sarajevo. The gentle tune of a waltz floats through the air. At the door, his chamberlain, Baron Rumerskirch (Hans Thimig), catches up with him, asking him to return to Vienna instead of undertaking the dangerous visit to Sarajevo. Franz Ferdinand does not reply, but picks up the melody of the waltz, hums a couple of notes and inquires about its title: 'Viennese Blood' – a name that foreshadows the coming events. Smiling, with one hand in his pocket, his upper body swaying slightly to the tune which he now recognises, but whose symbolic meaning he does not grasp, Franz Ferdinand appears suddenly at ease. For a brief moment he ponders the prospect of abandoning his duties, but then rejects the suggestion with a warm smile, pointing out that he is in Bosnia on His Majesty's order.

During this exchange with the baron, Franz Ferdinand stands in the open door, allowing the audience to catch a glimpse of his chambers. At the far end of the room, lit up by a chandelier, there is a bust of the old Kaiser, and next to it a portrait of a younger Franz Joseph. The mise-en-scène accentuates the contrast between Franz Ferdinand, who fills up the centre with his heavy frame, and the Kaiser looming in the background: clad in a simply decorated military uniform, with upturned moustache ends and a crew cut, everything about Franz Ferdinand is linear and illustrates his straightforward character; the baroque interior of the room, on the other hand, with its decorated vases, chandeliers, heavy carpets and ornamented picture frames (even the Kaiser's beard is ostentatious compared to Franz Ferdinand's), symbolises the Byzantine state of the empire.

When Franz Ferdinand closes the door on Baron Rumerskirch, gloominess returns to his face. Photographed in deep focus, we see him entering the room and slowly walking towards the camera, briefly touching his head to indicate the onset of another migraine. He starts to unbutton his uniform, but stops midway, his hand at his collar that seems to choke him, and glances reproachfully at the slightly elevated bust of his uncle, the Kaiser, now on his right (Figure 2.2). The heavy gaze and the meaningful gesture to his throat illustrate the suffocating atmosphere, accentuated by the portentous musical score that has replaced the waltz. All is suggestive of the looming danger. We follow Franz Ferdinand's laboured movements as he sinks, exhausted, into a chair while his butler helps him out of his coat; in this way the film points to his inability to throw off the heavy burden of royal duties. As if programmed, Franz Ferdinand follows the steps to his final destruction, which matches the destruction of the empire.

Figure 2.2: Franz Ferdinand (Ewald Balser) glances uneasily at the bust of the emperor in *Sarajevo*. Image: screenshot.

The slow pace of the film underlines the inertia of the Austro-Hungarian Empire and adds to the feeling of entrapment. The omnipresence of the Austrian emperor, Franz Joseph, in *Sarajevo* does not emanate reassurance but oppression: in every corner looms the Kaiser, looking down on Franz Ferdinand, who is slowly being suffocated by this dominance. The reason why Kortner's interpretation of the Austro-Hungarian Empire is so different to those of other postwar filmmakers might be explained by the director's outsider status. Kortner's experience of exile seems to have provided him with a different view of Austria's history, a view unaffected by the need to romanticise the past. The critics were full of praise for the visual style and the acting in the film, and notably pleased about this critical approach to Austria's past; nevertheless, they heavily criticised Kortner for the lack of historical accuracy in the film.[48]

The depiction of the imperial past in *Sarajevo* was an exception to the rule of the overwhelming majority of Austrian historical costume films, which typically offered a reassuring image of the Austro-Hungarian Empire with the Kaiser as the *Übervater*, the second in the holy triad of God, emperor and father.[49] Traditionally depicted as the centre point of a world that has come to a standstill, the old, white-bearded Kaiser symbolised stability. The problems of this bygone world seemed small and easily resolved – very often by the paternal emperor himself. The genre presents

Franz Joseph as an approachable father figure who is always willing to lend an ear to his subjects. The intimidating atmosphere of the imperial court and its stiff officials only accentuate Franz Joseph's kind-heartedness and understanding. In *Die Deutschmeister*, for instance, the Kaiser, played by Paul Hörbiger, listens attentively to the nervous chattering of a young sales assistant, Stanzi (Romy Schneider), who has been granted an audience. He smiles, and with a slight nod of his head reinstates her aunt to the position of a purveyor to the court and honours Stanzi's fiancé by making his composition the signature march of his royal regiment. This is similar to the depiction of the Kaiser in *Kaisermanöver* (The Kaiser Manoeuvres, 1954), in which he even-handedly distributes advice and favours and – such is his desire to be a 'people's emperor' – engages in conversation with pub owner Radler (Hans Moser) in the grounds of the Imperial Schönbrunn Palace.

Franz Joseph personifies harmony and conciliation, themes that were of paramount importance in postwar Austria.[50] The experience of war and disrupted social order fuelled a longing for stability and 'being taken care of'; the image of the fatherly emperor, almost a softer and more human *Führer* figure, seems to have answered this need. The postwar historical costume film thus juxtaposed two contrasting father images: the hard, authoritarian, German father, represented by Metternich, contrasted with the warm, kind-hearted, Austrian father, embodied by Kaiser Franz Joseph I. By promoting a national model of masculinity that was not only distinct from German masculinity, but also presented Austrian men in a more positive light, the genre corroborated the official line that Austria was a victim rather than a perpetrator; but to make this myth more credible, Austria and its men needed to be demilitarised.

Civilising the Military

Over the course of the nineteenth century, the ideal of 'hard' masculinity emerged as normative standard – and benchmark – of masculinity in large parts of Europe, born out of an increasing militarisation of society. R.W. Connell developed the concept of hegemonic masculinity to explain the enormous influence of this masculine ideal, defined by physical strength, courage, self-control, rationality and emotional restraint – characteristics that continued to be regarded as 'manly virtues' in the Western world for much of the twentieth century.[51] Considering the lasting power of this hegemonic ideal it is surprising that postwar Austrian historical costume films, populated with military men in uniforms, showcased masculinities that lacked these qualities. Instead, the genre promoted male role models that were emotional, insubordinate and hedonistic.

The narratives in *Der Feldherrnhügel*, *Die Deutschmeister* and *Kaisermanöver* imply that Austrians have an innate aversion to military discipline and remain, at heart, civilians. Indeed, the narrative in *Kaiserwalzer* suggests that the civilian's status is equal to that of an officer. Adjutant Zauner (played by the comedian Gunther Philipp) puts on an apron in the confectioner's kitchen despite the protestations of the confectioner's daughter that this role is too lowly for an officer, and answers self-assuredly: 'For a Zauner, even a baker's apron is a uniform!' While the line can be taken to mean that an officer like Zauner approaches even civilian tasks with military zeal, the film demonstrates that the opposite is the case: civilian virtues supersede military values. The postwar historical costume film thus presents the Austrian military as an institution that is preoccupied with spectacle and favours military parades over military training. Life in the army is joyful and easy, revolving around marching, singing, drinking and flirting.

In no other genre do men indulge in food and drink as much as in historical costume film. Zugsführer Radler (Walter Müller), in *Kaisermanöver*, is a pub owner's son, and has a number of girlfriends who all supply him and his comrades with delicacies; the officers Zauner, Ferry and Krallitschek (Gunther Philipp, Erik Frey and Erich Dörner) in *Kaiserwalzer* like to spend their days in confectionaries, sampling pastries; Oberst von Leuckfeld (Paul Hörbiger) in *Der Feldherrnhügel* is more interested in his goulash and beer than in doing his job; and food also features highly in *Die Deutschmeister*, in which a baker's shop plays a central role. Pubs, vineyards and even the Viennese amusement park, Prater, are filled with Austrian soldiers who indulge in their passion for food, wine and women (Figure 2.3). The Austrian officers enjoy '*Mulatság*', a bacchanal party with gypsy

Figure 2.3: Corporal Jurek (Siegfried Breuer, Jr) enjoys a date in the Prater with his new acquaintance Stanzi (Romy Schneider) in *Die Deutschmeister*. Filmarchiv Austria.

music, passionate women, Tokay wine and lots of glass smashing, under-lining the epicurean nature of the uniformed.

Despite lacking in toughness or authority, these soldiers are neverthe-less profoundly admired by the public because they represent what is dear to the Austrian: music and beauty. Marching and parading are the key military tasks in the postwar historical costume film. In *Kaisermanöver*, army units parade for several minutes at the beginning and the end of the film, watched and cheered by an excited Viennese public. Marching and music-playing soldiers also appear in less stereotyped depictions of the empire, such as in *Die Fiakermilli* or *Sarajevo*. The purpose of these military parades is simply to display the men's musical talent and elegant uniforms. The genre thus turns the Austrian military into a spectacle, and presents it as an institution whose single *raison d'être* is to entertain the public.

The figure of the male musical genius, which dominates biographical film, also reverberates in the representation of the military: every man in uniform loves music, sings or plays an instrument. Corporal Jurek (Sieg-fried Breuer, Jr) in *Die Deutschmeister* is even a talented composer. The military and music are closely connected, as if the Austro-Hungarian army was a musical society rather than a military organisation. While this showcasing of music is by no means restricted to the costume genre, it is nevertheless conspicuous how it interlinks the musical with the military, and thereby proclaims the message that soldiers who sing and play music are incapable of committing any violent act.

Historical costume film thus depoliticises the military, an act that is supported by the depiction of the uniform. The slate-blue tunic worn by infantrymen in the Austro-Hungarian army is the uniform that features most frequently in Austrian historical costume film.[52] The tunic displays little decoration or embellishment, and adornment is usually restricted to one or two medals; the uniform of German officers, such as that of Flügeladjutant von Lützelburg in *Der Feldherrnhügel*, appears frilly and flamboyant in comparison. The simplicity of the Austrian uniform serves a purpose: it attracts the gaze of the spectator and draws attention to the upper body and face through the tunic's tight cut and blue colour. Despite forcing a military posture on the wearer – after all, the uniform's function was to press the body into identical shapes to symbolise order – it does not make him appear threatening or intimidating. This is also due to the blue colour, a symbol of truth, stability and faithfulness in Western cul-ture, which radiates calmness and thus gives the wearer a certain serenity. Blue is the colour of both the Virgin Mary and the Holy Trinity and also implies innocence and chastity.[53] Presenting men in connection with the colour blue thus evokes certain associations with gentleness and pacifism and plays down the potential threat of the military uniform.

This effect is amplified by the physical appearance of the leading men, whose soft facial features, dark, wavy hair and clean-shaven cheeks un-derline their youthfulness and apparent innocence. Siegfried Breuer, Jr displays almost feminine beauty as corporal Jurek in *Die Deutschmeister*; Karlheinz Böhm as the emperor in uniform in *Sissi* and Hans Holt as lieutenant Hajós in *Der Feldherrnhügel* look smooth-faced and innocent. Despite being visibly older and more manly in appearance than the other stars of historical costume films, the heart-throb Rudolf Prack's face in *Kaisermanöver* displays no hard lines; the shape of the uniform softens his muscular body, and his sedate body language and mellow voice accentuate his gentleness (Figure 2.4).

It is important to remember that the uniform, which had been omnipresent in Austrian and German society for many years, evoked memories of violence, suppression and fear, and so the way the historical costume film utilised the uniform and divested it of any violent overtones was a significant step towards recuperating the military for contemporary audiences. The lack of weapons reinforces this sense of harmlessness evoked by the depiction of the military and the uniform. The officer's sabre merely serves a decorative purpose and is often only a vague contour at the bottom of the frame. If firearms are shown at all, they have a similarly decorative function. Generally, Austrian soldiers carry no weapons at all in the films, and often carry a musical instrument instead, which accentuates their musicality. *Maresi, Der Engel mit der Posaune* and *Kaisermanöver* are the only films that offer glimpses of war or have a shot fired in them.

Figure 2.4: Rudolf Prack as the suave Captain Eichfeld in Kaisermanöver. Filmarchiv Austria.

Postwar historical costume film thus performed two important tasks. First, it depoliticised the uniform through emphasising its decorative function and changing its meaning: the uniform no longer represented violence, war and suffering, but stood for tradition, beauty and innocence. Second, the genre exculpated the Austrian military of any wrongdoing by painting an idyllic picture of the army in which blood never sullies the uniform. The films replaced the memory of the Wehrmacht and war atrocities with a sanitised image of the Austro-Hungarian military to provide reassurance and to instil a sense of pride. This depoliticisation of the military in historical costume film was part of a wider discourse in Austrian society, as discussed above, that tried to establish Austria's status as a victim, and which went hand in hand with the formulation of new masculine ideals. To argue Austria's 'innocence' convincingly, any evidence of 'hard' military masculinity in Austrian society needed to be toned down. Popular cinema played a leading role in promoting this new conception of Austrian identity by showcasing the charming, gentle and musical soldier and presenting Austrian men as cultured and peaceful.

Sissi, undoubtedly Austria's most famous historical costume film, is a prime example of how the costume genre (literally) refashioned Austrian masculinity by foregrounding the ornamental function of the uniform, thus divesting it of associations with violence. The film successfully remodelled the image of the Austrian emperor, presenting him as gentle and peaceable, when in reality he had been a political hardliner. His reimagined character as a dashing but sensitive, gentle young man, however, makes him vulnerable to aggressive competitors – a characterisation that parallels the official portrayal of Austria as 'innocent' nation. But in the film, the love of the beautiful, self-sacrificing Princess Sissi emboldens Franz Joseph, inspiring him to wrestle control from his domineering mother – an act that signals the revival of the good old times and celebrates the victory of a softer Austrian masculinity.

Sissi – *A Fairy-tale Come True*

Sissi was a huge success both at home and in (continental) Europe.[54] Shot in Agfacolor, with splendid settings at the imperial court in Vienna and in the mountains of Bavaria and Austria, it painted an image of a depoliticised, demilitarised, demodernised Austria that proved exportable because, as Georg Seeßlen saw it, *Sissi* 'had identified a way to abolish reality and to realise a dream'.[55] The film brought international stardom to its leads: Romy Schneider (1938–1982), daughter of the German actress Magda Schneider and the Austrian actor Wolf Albach-Retty, and Karlheinz Böhm (born 1928), son of the successful Austrian conductor Karl Böhm. Their rise to fame in postwar Austria was also a consequence of an act of national purification: as children of parents who had been active supporters of the Nazis, their youthful innocence, which the film emphasised, signalled a new beginning and cleansed Austria of its sullied past.[56] Schneider had already enthralled audiences in *Die Deutschmeister*, which premiered a few months before *Sissi*, and as young Princess Victoria in *Mädchenjahre einer Königin* (1954), both directed by Marischka. With her natural charm and sprightliness, Schneider gave her role the necessary momentum and made Franz Joseph's infatuation with Sissi utterly convincing. Yet the success of the *Sissi* trilogy (sequels followed in 1956 and 1957) heavily affected the lives of Böhm and Schneider, who were typecast from then on. Both tried to escape the 'neat' image they had acquired in their home country. Böhm did so effectively – and to the horror of many – by playing the voyeuristic murderer in Michael Powell's thriller *Peeping Tom* (1960); Schneider emigrated to France, where she became an acclaimed dramatic actress whose fame was paralleled by an equally dramatic private life.

The bittersweet drama *Sissi* is the only postwar Austrian film that shows Kaiser Franz Joseph in his youth. Böhm portrays the young Kaiser Franz Joseph as soft and melancholic – a dutiful and earnest young emperor who yearns for a simple life outside the restraints of the court and the many obligations put upon him as the ruler of an empire. His sadness is aggravated by the domineering attitude of his steely mother, Sophie (Vilma Degischer), rumoured to be 'the only man at court'. That the power relations at court are askew becomes clear early on, when Franz Joseph enters his office at the imperial palace of Schönbrunn, where he is awaited by his entourage and his mother. This scene, which introduces the Kaiser, shows him in his customary light-blue uniform, whose shape and colour accentuate his soft facial features and slender figure; the tailored uniform, in combination with his mellow voice and gracious movements, underlines his elegance, but also points to his vulnerability. After he has kissed his mother's hand politely, she dismisses the Kaiser's advisors, asking to be left alone with her son. Franz Joseph accepts her request for a talk with a constrained smile that informs the spectator about the strained relationship between mother and son. Seeking refuge behind his baroque desk, he pauses for a moment, gazing pensively at his desktop; behind him is a large, framed portrait of Maria Theresia, the first (and only) female ruler of Austria and a symbol of the female dominance under which he suffers.

A cut interrupts the momentary stillness and brings his mother into focus: separated by the large desk that represents his royal duties, Franz Joseph stands very upright, with an apprehensive look on his face, and faces his mother in her grey, ruffled silk dress. Sophie beckons him away from the desk and asks him to sit down with her; her friendly tone suggests an informal chat, but Franz's apprehensive body language leaves no doubt that something serious will be debated. During the following scene it is Sophie that leads the conversation, while Franz merely responds hesitantly; the framing and the medium shot length draw attention to his passivity, showing him sitting back with his legs crossed, his slender, pale hands dangling gracefully from the armrests and the blue uniform jacket setting off the smoothness of his face. Franz looks *soigné*, almost feminine. When Sophie announces that she has decided he ought to get married, the camera moves closer to trace the pain creeping into his brown eyes. Franz Joseph, representing the glory of the Austrian Empire, averts his gaze, powerless against his domineering mother. The framing is striking here – the background shows two ornate candle-holders with white burning candles on either side of his head, lending his suffering almost religious overtones. It is a suffering that can only be relieved by fate, and which must be endured. The only resistance Franz musters is a sarcastic remark that, surely, he should be allowed to choose whom he marries; but Sophie announces that she has already decided that matter, and Franz sinks resignedly back into his chair. Only when she admits that the arranged marriage has one flaw – namely the bride's uncouth father, Franz's uncle, Duke Max of Bavaria – does his face light up. Franz feels an intimate bond with his uncle Max – a bond that will be strengthened by his fateful encounter with Max's daughter, Sissi.

The special connection between the three (Franz, Max and Sissi), which sets them apart as a trio of virtue, is symbolised by a jump cut from this conversation to the next scene, in the Bavarian forest, which shows Max (Gustav Knuth) deer hunting with his daughter. This forest scene, which promises a relief from sorrows through closeness with nature (a classic *Heimatfilm* topos) will be replicated later on, with Franz replacing Max; also, the exchange between Franz and his mother Sophie is mirrored (and reworked) in a dialogue scene between Sissi and Franz towards the end of the film, when he asks for her hand. This visual symmetry is the organising principle of *Sissi*.[57] The balanced image composition and ornamental framing, with the landscape arranged around the protagonists at the centre, emphasise harmony and balance, and can thus, as Erica Carter argues, be read as 'a nostalgic effort to fix historical time within the immobilized space of pictorial landscape'.[58] But the narrative also identifies the need for change: Max and Sophie, both set in their ways, are emblems of (positive and negative) stasis and will be replaced by the young Franz and Sissi, who set history in motion.

The tender, almost porcelain-like Franz Joseph, with his refined manners and gentle demeanour, outwardly seems to be the exact opposite of the heavy-set Max of Bavaria, whose roaring laughter fills his estate at Lake Starnberg in Bavaria. Max is an uncomplicated *paterfamilias* who enjoys the simple pleasures of life and is surrounded by a bunch of noisy kids, and so embodies a positive, strong, traditional masculinity. He feels at home in the open air and with simple village people, and detests courtly ceremonies. However, while the Duke is free to do what he pleases, his counterpart, Franz, has to shoulder the responsibilities of governing a vast empire, a burden that weighs him down and deepens his melancholic streak. Hence, it is only when Franz meets Sissi, the sister of his bride-to-be, Helene, during a chance encounter at his summer retreat in Bad Ischl that his mood lightens. Unaware of the real identity of Sissi, he is smitten by her beauty and artless charm and asks her to go hunting with him; the budding romance, however, soon comes to an abrupt end when Sissi hears that he will soon be engaged to Helene and flees the scene.

That same evening, at the ball where Franz is supposed to announce his engagement to Helene, he meets Sissi again and learns her real identity. Emboldened by this unexpected turn of events, he decides to go against the wishes of his mother and marry Sissi. Franz, dressed in a striking white and red gala uniform sporting the colours of Austria, follows Sissi into an adjacent room where she has sought refuge. He appears livelier, more assertive than before, clearly empowered by the encounter with Sissi, who has unwittingly shown him an alternative way forward. In contrast, the previously cheerful Sissi, who is now sitting opposite him on a sofa clad in a sparkling, light-blue dress, carries a doleful expression. The reversal of colours – Sissi was wearing a red riding costume with a white collar when she met Franz Josef, who was then in his light-blue uniform – marks an emotional change: the red and white colours render Franz more vivacious, with the red indicating a return of passion and the white underlining his purity; Sissi's light-blue dress, on the other hand, together with her sorrowful expression, indicate that the earnestness of stately affairs has caught up with her and that she is in a conflict of loyalty between her sister and Franz. In a replication of the earlier scene with his mother, Franz Joseph first sits opposite Sissi and declares his love for her. He ignores Sissi's fervent rejection of his offer of marriage, just as his mother ignored his own wishes, and resorts to pleading. A close-up reveals a sudden sadness creeping into his eyes; Franz averts his gaze and begs softly: 'I don't know if it is a joy to be married to me. Sure, I am Kaiser of Austria, ruler of a powerful empire. But danger lurks everywhere, rebels in Milano, revolts in Hungary...' His voice trails off, and a reverse shot to Sissi shows that his words have achieved the intended effect: Sissi looks commiseratively at the burdened Franz (Figure 2.5).

This is, however, the last time Franz Joseph readily admits weakness. With Sissi on his side he is now able to assert his masculinity; beginning with a firm rebuke of his mother in the next scene, Franz Joseph affirms his power as a man and as an emperor. The narrative thus presents the innocent, virginal Sissi as saviour of the empire. She rejuvenates the monarchy, which, as the narrative implies, has come to a standstill due to the undue influence of powerful women. By revitalising the man in power, Sissi actuates history and thus guarantees the empire's continuity.[59]

Sissi is a classic fairy-tale story, but one that resonated strongly with contemporary Austrian society. Austria had just regained its national independence when *Sissi* premiered in December 1955. The film celebrated the end of an inequitable leadership and the beginning of a new era. The new Austria, which the princess Sissi represents, is more feminine (Sophie was, after all, just a man in female dress) and more equal, but still firmly

Figure 2.5: Emperor Franz Joseph I (Karlheinz Böhm) declares his love to Sissi (Romy Schneider) in *Sissi*. Filmarchiv Austria.

based on patriarchal power relations. The narrative affirms masculine power through putting an end to a stultifying female leadership, but at the same time it underlines the need for a softer, more diplomatic approach to political affairs – a message that was fully in line with the dominant political discourse at the time. Of course, the film's success in continental Europe, and especially in West Germany, attests to the fact that *Sissi* did not speak uniquely to 'Austrian' desires. Carter argues that the *Sissi* trilogy addressed the trauma of imperial defeat experienced over the downfall of the German and Austro-Hungarian empires and aggravated by the loss of the eastern territories acquired under Nazi rule, and so points to the shared sentiments which the films tapped into.[60] *Sissi* fed imperial nostalgia and, through its melodramatic aspects, presented loss as meaningful sacrifice, which accounts for its wide, transnational appeal.

Cinematic Recycling of Austria's Multi-ethnic Past

After the Second World War, Austria's political and intellectual elites marketed the ethnic diversity of the Austro-Hungarian Empire as a constitutive feature of Austrian identity. The identity discourse wove the 'golden myth' of a harmonious, multi-ethnic, dual monarchy, (barely) held together by Kaiser Franz Joseph, who – in defiance of growing nationalism – embraced the diversity of 'My peoples'.[61] The discourse held that Austrianness was born out of the country's rich heritage – a heritage the Germans apparently did not possess. The ethnic heterogeneity of the Austrian Empire was hence used to explain the ostensible joie de vivre of the Austrian people and argue their cultural superiority over the Germans.[62] The declaration of Austria's first elected government in 1945 clearly reflects this way of thinking: with reference to Austria's multi-ethnic past, it proclaimed that the Austrians' mixed ancestry had brought them in 'natural opposition' to the Nazis, who believed in the superiority of the Aryan race. It strongly rejected equating Germans with Austrians and implied that the Austrians had always been resistant to the Nazi regime, as Nazism was 'completely contrary to the Austrian nature'.[63] References to the multi-ethnic Habsburg Empire thus served as a means to distance the Austrians from National Socialist ideology.

The fact that the elites called upon the late Habsburg Empire to provide a historical basis for this newly formulated identity may at least partly explain why the film industry took up the issue, but it does not explain why films about this historical period were so popular with audiences. Nevertheless, the sales figures speak for themselves, and they clearly indicate that these films must have tapped into powerful public sentiment. Therefore, in order to understand their popularity and the role they played in contemporary national discourse, we need to analyse the films' narrative and visual strategies.

The filmmakers used different visual and narrative means to draw attention to the ethnic diversity of the Austro-Hungarian monarchy: national stereotypes, settings in different parts of the empire, diegetic and extra-diegetic music and objects or costumes associated with a specific ethnicity served to portray the era as ethnically heterogeneous. The important question is whether the films were inclusive or exclusive: whether the narratives highlighted or toned down the differences between the nations, whom they privileged, and whom they sidelined or excluded.

Films set in the late Austro-Hungarian Empire clearly favour one nation (apart from the German-Austrian one, which was at the centre of all films): Hungary. Apart from Hungarian, Czech is the only other nationality that regularly features in the historical costume film in postwar Austria. Multi-ethnicity is therefore represented through a small number of nationalities, usually Hungarian and Czech, as well as (Prussian) German, while the full range of ethnicities actually present in the Habsburg Empire is never explored.[64] Poles, Romanians and Ukrainians are disregarded altogether, while Croats, Serbs and Bosnians can only be found in the historical drama *Sarajevo*, a film that actually debates the ethnic conflicts in the Habsburg Empire. Italians only feature in the costume melodrama *Das unsterbliche Antlitz* (The Immortal Face, 1947).

The general absence of Jewish characters is also noteworthy. Only two early films, both produced in 1948, feature Jews and even address the issues of Jewishness and anti-Semitism. Karl Hartl's melodrama *Der Engel mit der Posaune* tells the fictional story of a Jewish woman, Henriette Alt, played by Paula Wessely, who has an affair with Crown Prince Rudolf (Fred Liewehr) and commits suicide when the Nazis annex Austria. *Der Engel mit der Posaune* was a great success with both critics and audiences, and even attracted the attention of Alexander Korda, who brought the film to Britain, where Anthony Bushell directed the remake *The Angel with the Trumpet* in 1949.[65] G.W. Pabst's film *Der Prozess*, on the other hand, triggered considerable protest, especially in Hungary, where it was set. *Der Prozess* depicts the murder of a young girl that leads to an anti-Semitic show trial in nineteenth-century Hungary, and is the only film of that time that openly addressed the issue of anti-Semitism.[66] Later films avoided the depiction of Jews, perhaps because Allied pressure to face up to the Nazi past had eased off with the growing intensity of the Cold War. Only the costume comedy *Der Feldherrnhügel*, produced in 1955, features a Jewish character, and then in a minor role: an officer named Rosenstock. In the original script, the figure of the Jewish officer served as critique of the virulent anti-Semitism in the Austro-Hungarian military; the playwright's intention, however, was wholly lost in this adaptation.[67]

These absences in postwar Austrian historical costume film point to the filmmakers' unease with the representation of a specific group, as in the case of the Jews, or suggest a mere lack of interest, as with the majority of Slav ethnicities; the producers of historical costume films obviously felt that it was sufficient to include some Hungarian or Czech characters to paint a 'realistic' picture of the Austro-Hungarian past.

While Hungarians and Czechs are positioned at the margins, seemingly there only to add colour to the narrative, (German-speaking) Austrians are always at the centre of these films. True Austrianness is evoked by the use of the German language – or rather the Viennese idiom. Even though the name of Lieutenant Géza von Hajós in *Der Feldherrnhügel* or the background of Archduchess Sophie, a Bohemian aristocrat in *Sarajevo*, suggest non-Austrian origin, their Viennese accents leave little doubt about their 'true' nationality. The star images of the actors certainly helped to emphasise this message: Géza von Hajós was played by Hans Holt, who was usually typecast as the quintessential Viennese charmer, and Luise Ullrich, in the role of the Bohemian Archduchess Sophie, for many spectators always remained the 'sweet Viennese girl' she had played in Max Ophüls' *Liebelei* in 1933, which had made her famous. The narratives clearly distinguish between those who can be considered Austrians and those who cannot; yet they are more ambiguous with regard to the identities of Hungarians and Czechs. While their accents clearly demarcate them from the other characters, they are not assigned the status of the 'other'. Interestingly, it is to the Prussian German, the third prominent non-Austrian nationality in Austrian historical costume film, that the genre ascribes the function of the 'other'.

Fiery Hungarians

The figure of the Hungarian fulfils many functions in postwar Austrian historical costume film: it illustrates the multi-ethnic character of the empire but also adds an exotic touch; it serves to underline the cosmopolitan spirit of the Austrians and suggests equality between the two nations. Whether in the form of music, drink or national identity, the Hungarian is, just like the Viennese waltz or the charming officer, a key feature of any postwar costume film. The Hungarian represents passion, gaiety and beauty, and is used to draw attention to the richness of Austria's cultural heritage and to 'round off' the Austrian character. While the historical costume genre presents the Austrians as musical to the core, it also associates the Hungarian with music and complements 'Austrian' waltzes and polkas with Hungarian *Csárdás* or gypsy tunes. The couturier and bon vivant Bauer (Paul Hörbiger) in *Der alte Sünder* (The Old Sinner, 1951) usually encounters a black-moustachioed Hungarian in traditional costume on his nightly tours through Viennese cafés and night clubs, who plays sentimental tunes on his fiddle.

Hungarian characters are depicted fairly consistently. In general, Hungarians are recognisable by their distinct accent and their names, whereas their appearance and mannerisms are usually very similar to those of the Austrians. Hungarianness is primarily defined by passion: *Mulatság* and the *Csárdás* are presented as the epitome of Hungarianness. The film *Kaisermanöver* characterises the Hungarian officer Török (played by comedian Gunther Philipp) as an avid lover of young women and *Mulatság*; the erotic Frau von Lamasy (Gretl Schörg) in *Der Feldherrnhügel* bewitches all men with her sensual appearance and *Csárdás* dancing.

The brotherhood of Hungarians and Austrians is celebrated in the ball scene in *Der Feldherrnhügel*, with Austrians, Hungarians and even Germans being swept away by the rousing *Csárdás* tunes the gypsy band plays. The young Austrian countess Julia Kopsch-Grantignan (Annemarie Düringer), freshly married to Lieutenant Géza von Hajós (Hans Holt), flees with her mother to a Hungarian garrison town after discovering her husband in close embrace with his former lover, the frivolous Hungarian artist Frau von Lamasy, only minutes after the wedding. Géza, however, is also posted to this town, which is in full preparation for a ball organised to honour the visit of Archduke Karl Viktor. At the ball, Géza tries to explain to his estranged new wife, Julia, that the encounter with Frau von Lamasy was harmless, but she again rejects him and demonstratively flirts with the Archduke. As the ball proceeds, Géza withdraws to another hall and sits alone and full of self-pity at a table, drinking wine; behind him Frau von Lamasy, dressed in a sparkling black dress, makes a big entrance with a gypsy band. She is immediately surrounded by admiring officers, who were drinking at the tables; she spots Géza in the foreground, who slouches in his chair and tries to appear disinterested, and walks towards him. Lamasy puts a hand on his shoulder to console him, beckons to the gypsy band and starts to sing a song about the healing effects of Hungarian wine and music. The other Hungarians and the Austrian officers join in, and suddenly the rhythm of the tune grips Géza: he jumps up, thrusts the table aside and starts singing, circling the officers, who raise their glasses and tap their feet. Lamasy and Géza dance the *Csárdás* together, and the music sparks a *Csárdás* fever that travels fast, emphasised by the quickening pace of the music. The camera pans slowly through the large rooms to reveal that everybody has joined in the dance; quick cuts between the different couples draw attention to the jealous battle between Géza and his young wife, but simultaneously highlight the harmonious co-existence within the empire, with Hungarians, Austrians and Germans dancing merrily together.

The costume narrative highlights similarities rather than differences between Hungarians and Austrians: both share a profound love for music, wine and women. The admiration for everything that is Hungarian is particularly strong in the military, which plays a dominant role in these films. In *Kaisermanöver*, the Hungarian officer Török's love for *Mulatság* is shared by his Austrian comrades, and in particular by the Austrian officer Jurinic (Erik Frey), who is well known for his *Mulatság* parties. In *Kaiserwalzer*, Austrian officers drink with their Prussian comrade and cheer on the table-dancing Anni (Angelika Hauff), who sings, 'Let's do a *Mulatság*, *Mulatság*, *Mulatság*! Let's smash our glasses at the wall!'

The Hungarians function as agents of cultural transfer in the filmic narratives: they export Hungarian customs, which are eagerly appropriated by the Austrians as their own. Hungarians are shown to be not only spirited and warm, but also generous. In *Der Feldherrnhügel*, Colonel Esterhazy (Svet Petrovich) brings along a gypsy band and cases full of Tokay wine to the army ball; in *Der alte Sünder*, the rich pig farmer Sandor Gyöngyösházy (Fritz Imhoff) lavishes expensive presents on a beautiful woman. The dark-moustachioed Gyöngyösházy competes with the elegant, white-haired, Viennese couturier Ferdinand Bauer, a well known womaniser, for the favours of the admired Parisian singer Yvonne Farini (Susi Nicoletti). Visually, the two characters are presented as equals: they are of similar height and positioned on the same level, usually facing each other, with Farini in the middle. At their first dinner together Gyöngyösházy serves chicken paprika, a spicy Hungarian dish that leaves Bauer breathless. Gyöngyösházy belittles Bauer's 'weakness', and affirms his own masculinity by adding more paprika. This earns him Farini's applause: 'Bravo! I love men who eat spicy food!' she exclaims, which encourages Bauer to follow suit. Farini then turns to tease Gyöngyösházy by showing him her new diamond bracelet, indicating that it was Bauer who gave it to her. The competition between the two men continues, each scoring an equal number of points, until Gyöngyösházy's wealth finally decides the battle in his favour.

The relationship between Gyöngyösházy and Bauer is competitive, but restricted to verbal exchanges which remain essentially on the level of harmless mockery; and yet, even though the narratives often characterise Hungarians as amusing people, they never make them the object of ridicule. Respect for the Hungarians is further emphasised by the fact that Austrians are depicted as keen followers of Hungarian customs. The narratives and the imagery underline the equal status of Hungarians and Austrians. It may well be that this was meant to reflect the political equality of the two nations in the late Habsburg Empire. However, by depicting the Hungarians and Austrians as brothers in spirit, the films also suggest that the Austrians are equally passionate, and thus more Hungarian than German in their mentality.

The positive picture historical costume film paints of the Hungarian was by no means restricted to cinematic discourse. Social empirical research on national consciousness has shown that Austrians tend to look favourably upon Hungarians; in public opinion polls, Austrians regularly name Hungarians as the neighbours they feel most closely related to after Germans. As the first of these surveys only dates back to 1980, we can only speculate about the origins of their high regard for Hungarians. Some sources suggest that the Austrian affection for Hungarians is historically rooted; but it may also be that the positive portrayal of the Hungarian in postwar Austrian cinema and in the media contributed to this positive image.[68]

Subversive Czechs

The second ethnic group that features prominently in the costume genre is the Czechs. Their representation is more ambiguous than in the case of the Hungarians, which may be explained with the fact that Austrians have traditionally looked upon Czechs far less favourably than Hungarians. The relationship between Austrians and Czechs is complex: on the one hand, the Austrian Empire's disregard for the national rights of the Czechs in the nineteenth century, paired with a strong Czech nationalism, produced a deep rift between the two nations. On the other hand, the large-scale immigration of Czechs and Slovaks during the nineteenth century forged strong personal links between Czechs and Austrians through intermarriages and business relationships; it is a well known cliché that the Viennese telephone book displays far more Czech than German/Austrian names. In the imperial past, Austrians looked down on Czechs and Slovaks because of their lower social status, but at the same time relied on their work as servants and labourers.[69] The experience of living in close contact with Czechs, mixed with the perceived need to elevate themselves, obviously produced contradictory feelings among the Austrians; this antagonism is evident in the visual representation of Czechs in Austrian historical costume film.

At times, Czech characters merely feature to illustrate the ethnic diversity of the Austro-Hungarian Army, and are thus portrayed in a neutral way, as in the case of Officer Krallitschek (Erich Dörner) in *Kaiserwalzer*. Krallitschek is clearly distinguishable as Czech by his accent – he is a veterinary surgeon, but holds an officer's rank like his Austrian comrades Adjutant Zauner (Gunther Philipp) and Count Ferry (Erik Frey). They are stationed in Bad Ischl and enjoy themselves sampling pastries in the local confectioner's shop or having a private *Mulatság* in their accommodation. The figure of Krallitschek has seemingly no other purpose than to add colour to the narrative.

In other films, Czech characters fulfil a comic function. Making use of the distinct Czech accent and vocabulary, and drawing on the well established stereotype of the Czech as sedate, but slyly headstrong, the three soldiers Lamatsch (Heinz Conrads), Nepalek (Franz Böheim) and Kunitschek (Ernst Waldbrunn) in *Der Feldherrnhügel* are 'typical' of Czechs in Austrian film. They subvert military hierarchy with their simple-mindedness, and thus invite the audience to laugh at them. On the morning of a planned manoeuvre, Czech Sergeant Koruga (Fritz Imhoff) tries to brief his three soldiers on how to behave during the inspection by Archduke Karl Viktor. The soldiers, suffering from a heavy hangover, stand slouching with half-closed eyes in front of Koruga, who tries to fine-tune their performance. However, their blunt answers and demeanour do not please Koruga; his efforts to elicit the desired response – that everything in the military is 'excellent' – are in vain. Admitting defeat, he finally decides that 'it is best that the Archduke doesn't see you at all. Hide in the bushes and sleep off your hangover!', at which the visibly perked-up soldiers reply in unison: 'Excellent!'

Many Czech characters in postwar Austrian films, such as the kind-hearted and loyal dressmaker Pschistranek in *Der alte Sünder*, or the simple-minded soldier Kunitschek in *Der Feldherrnhügel*, were played by the popular comedian Ernst Waldbrunn. Bohemian in origin, Waldbrunn used his Czech accent effectively on stage and in his film roles, thus adding 'authenticity' to his performance as well as producing comic effect. In *Der alte Sünder*, Waldbrunn plays a dressmaker, Pschistranek, whose slight sloppiness and relaxed attitude to work enrage his immediate superior, Zirrhübel (Rudolf Carl), who demands efficiency and speed. Pschistranek accepts Zirrhübel's rebuke with a smile and with irony; hiding behind deliberately faulty German, he uses his linguistic abilities to play with the meaning of words and thus continuously undermines Zirrhübel's power, without him even noticing.

Producers of historical costume film thus employed Czech characters as a source of comic relief and of empowerment. The Czechs represent the lower-classes that make fun of the upper-classes, although this subversive criticism is delimited by turning the Czech into an object of ridicule. It is noteworthy that the filmmakers refrained from fully exploiting the negative Czech stereotype that was prevalent at the time – this would certainly have thwarted the film producers' efforts to sell the audience a harmonious image of the multi-ethnic empire.

Snappy Germans

Hanisch argues that the construction of Austrian identity after the Second World War relied heavily on the demonisation of Germany.[70] This anti-German sentiment resonates strongly in postwar Austrian cinema, in which Germans are often caricatured, even though Austrian historical costume film is by no means anti-German as a whole. In fact, the function of the German stereotype is more complex: on the one hand, it serves to distinguish the Austrians from the Germans and to present the Austrians as superior, by shifting negative characteristics onto the Germans. On the other hand, it also – though often less explicitly – integrates 'the German side' of the Austrians into the newly constructed Austrian identity.

The German protagonists we find in postwar costume films, such as *Die Deutschmeister, Kaiserwalzer, Der Feldherrnhügel, Der Obersteiger* and *Die Fiakermilli*, are usually male and from Prussia. They are distinguishable from the Austrians by their behaviour and manners, but also – and quite significantly – by their shared German language. Different pronunciations and use of words are a major source of amusement, as they create frequent misunderstandings, and these breakdowns are persistently played on in the films: in *Kaiserwalzer*, the Austrian confectioner Bachmaier (Oskar Sima) and the Prussian Hauptmann Krause (Paul Westermeier) constantly assure each other that they find it very hard to communicate because of the variations in their dialects. The depiction of the Austrian Bachmaier, who is considerably 'weightier' in stature than his shorter Prussian counterpart, leaves no doubt as to who is more powerful: Bachmaier towers over Krause, and although he is ostensibly friendly, he sneers at the Prussian officer as he tries to place an order. As Krause finds it hard to make sense of the Austrian terms for the different pastries, his companion, a charming Viennese beauty, comes to his aid and acts as translator. Bachmaier accepts the order with a smile, commenting smugly: 'How good that I speak all languages!' The narrative presents the Austrians as extraordinary cultured: whereas the Germans have only one term for coffee – as Krause's command for 'a coffee!' illustrates – the film uses the wealth of coffee specialities in Austria as a means to elevate the Austrian culture. The narrative thus claims that the Austrians are in possession of a cultural capital their German counterparts ostensibly lack.

As a rule, it is the Germans who are shown as incapable of understanding the Austrians: the Prussian Flügeladjutant von Lützelburg in *Der Feldherrnhügel*, who visits an Austro-Hungarian infantry manoeuvre, admits to his Berlin-born host, Mrs von Leuckfeld (Loni Heuser), that she is the only human being whom he is able to understand in the Hungarian garrison town, which is populated with Austrian officers. Just like the young apprentice Fritz (Wolfgang Jansen), from Berlin, in *Die Deutschmeister*, von Lützelburg derides the Austrian language as 'Chinese'. Both display a self-assured manner, but their attempts to assert themselves are fruitless and collapse before the linguistic barriers.

While the Germans seem to find it difficult to decode the Austrian language, the films portray the Austrians as more knowledgeable, implying that their inability to communicate with the Germans effectively is due to choice, not incompetence – this puts the Austrians in a position of linguistic and cultural superiority. The Viennese baker Therese Hübner in *Die Deutschmeister* gently bullies her young German apprentice, Fritz, into learning 'correct' German by teaching him to call a croissant a *Kipferl* and not a *Hörnchen*, the German word. The self-conscious Mr Stanginer (Rudolf Platte) in *Die Fiakermilli* acknowledges this Austrian superiority freely. His small stature and his demeanour suggest humility, and he habitually introduces himself in a weak voice: 'Sorry, I am from Berlin'.

The differences between Germans and Austrians become particularly evident in the realm of the military. Austrian historical costume films usually portray members of the Austrian military as suave, sedate and even a bit negligent. The German officer, on the other hand, represents the opposite: Flügeladjutant von Lützelburg in *Der Feldherrnhügel*, Hauptmann Krause in *Kaiserwalzer* and Kaiser Wilhelm II in *Sissi* display a harsh and overbearing masculinity; the Prussian officers' staccato mode of speaking and snappy movements, together with their upturned moustache-ends (particularly emphasised in the hammy performance of the German actor Wolfgang Lukschy, who plays both von Lützelburg and Kaiser Wilhelm II), represent a prime example of 'hard' masculinity, but actually caricature it.

Austrian men, even in the military, are, in contrast, presented as being civilians at heart. The encounter between the Prussian officer Krause and the Austrian confectioner Bachmaier in *Kaiserwalzer* emphasises this difference, when Bachmaier proudly proclaims that he has always been a civilian and knows nothing about the military. The Austrian officers, too, display a much less military demeanour than their Prussian comrades, indulging themselves in pastries, wallowing in delight.

The films usually present the German protagonist as a comical figure, an outsider who wants to belong in Austria and who admires the Austrians. Viewed in the context of Austria's longstanding inferiority complex towards the Germans and desire for unification with Germany after the First World War, this is an interesting reversal. In order to be admitted to the Austrian community, the Germans become eager learners of local (and Hungarian!) customs: Flügeladjutant von Lützelburg outdoes his Austrian comrades at drinking Tokay wine and dancing the *Csárdás*, and

Hauptmann Krause is so intrigued by the tradition of *Mulatság* that he wants to export the table-dancing Anni to Berlin.

But while the films caricature German mannerisms and peculiarities, often in a condescending and at times even pungent manner, they promptly downplay mockery as harmless banter. At the end of each costume film, differences between Germans and Austrians are bridged and friendship is celebrated. In one of the final scenes of *Kaiserwalzer*, the former opponents – the Austrian confectioner, Bachmaier, and the Prussian Hauptmann Krause – sit together drinking wine and strike up a conciliatory song, admitting: 'Oh well, Berlinian is difficult, but Viennese even more! Yes, Viennese is difficult, but Berlinian even more!' And in *Die Deutschmeister* the Austrian Kaiser, Franz Joseph I, and the German Kaiser, Wilhelm II, demonstrate their transnational friendship by attending a military parade, side by side on their horses. While their positioning on the same level suggests equality, their facial hair still indicates vital differences between the two nations: the old Franz Joseph, with his fluffy white whiskers, contrasts sharply with the much younger Wilhelm, with his dark, upturned moustache-ends that signify severity.

The fact that Austrian historical costume film ultimately struck a conciliatory tone with the Germans was not accidental. Although making fun of the Germans was permissible, and even increased the films' appeal for German audiences because it offered a source of identification, film producers could not afford to offend them; after all, the German market was essential for the survival of the Austrian film industry. Still, the dependency on the West German market and German financial investment in Austrian film production does not fully explain why the narratives always invite the German characters into the Austrian community at the end of the films. It seems that the negative stereotyping of the Germans also offered an opportunity to debate internal contradictions. Despite their attempts to demarcate themselves from the Germans, Austrians could not help but recognise strong similarities; by ridiculing the harsh, overbearing, 'masculine' manners which the films identified as typically German, the filmic texts made these characteristics seem less threatening, and thus more tolerable.

The genre also offered another image of the German that differed strongly from the depiction of Prussian characters: the Bavarian. Bavarians appeared from time to time in historical costume films, such as in *Sissi* or *Der Obersteiger*. The narratives emphasise the similarities between Austrians and Bavarians: they share a love for food and beer, are equally jovial and *gemütlich* and – above all – speak the same language. The aforementioned film *Sissi* implies – through its characterisations of the protagonists as well as the Alpine setting in Bavaria and the Austrian Bad Ischl – that Austrians and Bavarians are essentially the same people. The young Austrian Kaiser, Franz Joseph, and Princess Elisabeth of Bavaria/ Sissi harbour a deep love for nature and dislike the strict court ceremonial in Vienna; what is more, Franz Joseph names Sissi's down-to-earth father, Duke Max of Bavaria, as the only likeable one of his relations. *Der Ober-steiger* appropriates the Bavarian in a different way: here, the star persona, accent and mannerisms of the popular Viennese actor Hans Holt remodel the figure of Duke Max of Bavaria into an Austrian, leaving only the title as indication of the Duke's origin. Historical costume film therefore effectively rejects the Germanness of the Bavarians and affirms the popular cliché that Bavarians have more in common with Austrians than with their fellow German countrymen.

So, while the postwar Austrian costume genre claims the Bavarians as 'honorary Austrians' and uses them to aggrandise the nation, it describes the Prussian Germans as the other, against which the 'unique' Austrian character is drafted. Hungarian and Czech stereotypes, on the other hand, serve primarily to provide 'historical proof' of Austria's cosmopolitanism and multi-ethnic roots. Hungarians and Czechs thus serve as fictional ancestors: the Hungarians represent the passionate and musical side of the Austrian character, whereas the Czechs stand for the Austrians' alleged resistance to authority. The films transplant Hungarian passion and Czech subversiveness onto the Austrian character in order to emphasise the differences between Austrians and Germans, thus providing the audience with 'historical evidence' that Austrians are a distinct nationality from Germans.

Conclusion

Through its romanticised imperial setting, historical costume film offered the audience an escape to a fairy-tale world, and conveyed a sense of permanence and stability which can account for the genre's success both in Austria and abroad. However, the costume film did not just feed escapist desires; it also equipped Austria's search for a new identity with supporting imagery and historical templates, thus playing a key role in the construction of nationhood.

The promotion of Austrian identity was, as the above analysis has shown, closely intertwined with the advertisement of masculine ideals. The genre's focus on the 'male musical genius' and the gentle military man helped to remodel the militaristic masculine ideal that had been predominant in Austrian society until the end of the war. Austrian costume films stripped the male uniform and the military of any violent content, replaced 'hard' masculine attributes with more 'cultured' characteristics and thus inscribed specific ideas of nationhood onto the male body. Masculinity and nationhood were also debated through the choice of setting. The Metternich era and the reign of Kaiser Franz Joseph were the most frequently depicted historical periods in Austrian costume film; they provided a site where conflicting desires regarding the father figure could be negotiated. Metternich, usually depicted as slight and cunning, represented the authoritarian, repressive German father. The old, white-bearded Kaiser Franz Joseph, on the other hand, embodied the good, paternal Austrian father. Contrasting the 'good' (Austrian) father with the 'bad' (German) father helped to purify Austrian masculinity.

Yet, the choice of the two historical periods also served other purposes: by drawing analogies between the Metternich era and the Nazi regime, the costume genre played down the brutality of the Nazi dictatorship and amplified Austria's spirit of resistance. The period of Franz Joseph I, by contrast, drew attention to Austria's multi-ethnic past, allowing producers of costume films to present fundamental differences between Austrians and Germans; claiming a 'female', Slavic ancestry, Austrians could be set apart from the 'hard' and 'militaristic' Germans, which supported Austria's claim to victim status.

The nostalgic depiction of the Habsburg Empire provided Austrians with a positive historical identity. By replacing the memory of the Wehrmacht and the Nazis with images of a seemingly harmless Austro-Hungarian military, the costume film helped to exonerate the nation of the guilt of having enabled or actively participated in Nazi atrocities. The genre's insistence on Austria's greatness and historically rooted differences between Austrians and Germans served to rub out memories of many Austrians' fatal wish for unification with Germany. Of course, it was not only historical costume film that fulfilled a cleansing function in postwar Austrian cinema, but because the genre was able to replace a negative history with a positive history, the genre was surely successful in easing the nation's guilt. The negative past was not merely suppressed and factored out, as in some other genres, but painted over with a 'new', more 'relevant' past. The more the imperial past shone and glistened in Austrian costume film, the less visible the dark Nazi past and inter-war period became.

Notes

1. See e.g. Hake, 2008, 114.
2. Critics use the terms 'historical' and 'costume' or 'heritage' often interchangeably to categorise films that are set in what the audience perceives to be a historical milieu. The term 'costume film', as, for example, Sue Harper (1994, 2) has used it, is more open than 'historical film', which is usually used to define films that are set in the past and deal with real historical personae or events. For a discussion of the terms 'costume', 'historical' and 'heritage' film see, for example, A. Higson. 2003. *English Heritage, English Cinema: Costume Drama since 1980*, Oxford: Oxford Univeristy Press, 9–11.
3. See Hanisch, 1994, 159–163.
4. P. Sorlin. 1980. *Film in History: Restaging the Past*, Oxford: Blackwell, 21.
5. This would explain why, for example, all state-commissioned films in the Third Reich were historical films. See Hake, 2008, 77–78.
6. See F. Stern. 2005. 'Durch Clios Brille: Kino als zeit- und kulturgeschichtliche Herausforderung', *Österreichische Zeitschrift für Geschichtswissenschaften*, 16(1), 74.

7. See D. Elley. 1984. *The Epic Film: Myth and History*, London: Routledge & Kegan Paul, 6. Pierre Sorlin argues that 'nearly all films refer, if indirectly, to current events'. Sorlin, 1980, 18.

8. See Österreichisches Statistisches Zentralamt, 1959b, 145–146.

9. E.v. Neusser. 1950. 'Die österreichischen Filmerfolge', *Film-Kunst. Zeitschrift für Filmkultur und Filmwissenschaft*, 5, 253.

10. For criticisms of the costume film see, for example, the reviews for Marischka's *Verklungenes Wien*: 'Verklungenes Wien', *Wiener Kurier*, 2 November 1951; 'Die Filmpremiere von gestern abend: "Verklungenes Wien"', *Weltpresse*, 31 October 1951; '"Verklungenes Wien" im Apollo', *Wiener Tageszeitung*, 1 November 1951; 'Verklungenes Wien', *Arbeiterzeitung*, 4 November 1951; also A. Joachim, 'Offene Worte zu aktuellen Fragen: Kitschflut ohne Ende?' *Wiener Kurier*, 5 November 1951.

11. A. Bronnen. 'Hofjagd in Ischl', *Der Abend*, 9 December 1955.

12. Defining all films set in the historical past as historical costume films, I ascribe historicity to everything that lies at least one generation back, up to the end of the First World War.

13. See Harper, 1994, 10.

14. See Halbritter, 1993, 49–101.

15. I exclude the film *Sissi* here, as, even though Sissi was of Bavarian origin, she is mostly remembered as Empress of Austria.

16. The following films focus on royalty: *Erzherzog Johanns grosse Liebe* (1950) on Archduke Johann and Anna Plochl, *Maria Theresia* (1951) on Maria Theresia, *Der Obersteiger* (1952) on Duke Max von Bayern and Luise, *Kaiserwalzer* (1953) on Archduke Ludwig, *Der rote Prinz* (1954) on Archduke Johann Salvator, *Mädchenjahre einer Königin* (1954) on the English Queen Victoria and Prince Albert, *Sarajevo* (1955) on Archduke Franz Ferdinand and Sophie, and *Sissi* (1955) on Queen Elizabeth of Austria. Biopics of artists included: *Das unsterbliche Antlitz* (1947) on Anselm Feuerbach, *Singende Engel* (1947) on Johann Michael Holzer, *Eroica* (1949) on Ludwig van Beethoven, *Wiener Mädeln* (1949) on Carl Michael Ziehrer, *Wien tanzt* (1951) on Johann Strauss Vater, *Die Fiakermilli* (1953) on Milli Trampusch, *Du bist die Welt für mich* (1953) on Richard Tauber, *Franz Schubert* (1953) on Franz Schubert, *Hab ich nur deine Liebe* (1953) on Franz von Suppé, *Der Komödiant von Wien* (1954) on the actor Alexander Girardi and *Mozart* (1955) on Mozart.

17. '"Die Fiakermilli" und eine Überraschung', *Weltpresse*, 22 January 1953.

18. See Witte, 1996.

19. Fehrenbach, 1998, 109.

20. Even though there is little data available on cinema audiences in postwar Austria, research on other national cinemas has shown that costume films appealed primarily to female audiences. See, for example, Harper, 1997, 133.

21. 'Wieder ein Strauss-Film: "Wien tanzt!"', *Wiener Zeitung*, 11 September 1951; 'Wien tanzt', *Neues Österreich*, 16 September 1951.

22. See Harper, 1997, 137.

23. See Rathkolb, 1991, 80–135, 179–220.

24. The themes and images of the 'musical Austrian' in Nazi Germany were politicised too, in the way that they were used to distract the people from the war and the grim reality of their social conditions. The former Austrian production company Wien-Film was highly successful in producing seemingly apolitical 'Durchhaltefilme'; after the war, producers and actors used these films to claim their non-involvement with the Nazis or even portrayed them as acts of resistance. See B. Frankfurter and G. Scheidl. 1992. 'Die Wien-Film', in G. Ernst and G. Schedl (eds), *NAHAUFNAHMEN: zur Situation des österreichischen Kinofilms*, Vienna: Europaverlag, 188–189.

25. A. Schuchmann. 1950. 'Filmwirtschaft: Der österreichische Film im Ausland', *Film-Kunst. Zeitschrift für Filmkultur und Filmwissenschaft*, 5, 246.

26. E.v. Neusser. 1950. 'Kalkulationsfragen der Produktion', *Film-Kunst. Zeitschrift für Filmkultur und Filmwissenschaft*, 5, 249.

27. One critic noted that the foreign market demanded a combination of 'a little sentimentality, music, not too loud, nonchalance that does not turn into swashbuckling, a bit of contemplation without German profoundness', all 'effortlessly mixed'. H. Krizkovsky, 'Das Ausland und der Wiener Film', *Arbeiterzeitung*, 3 August 1948.

28. 'Singende Engel, 1949. Story about the Vienna Boys Choir', *New York Times*, 16 January 1952; 'Singende Engel, *Wiener Zeitung*, 17 December 1947.

29. See G.F. Custen. 2001. 'Making History', in M. Landy (ed.), *The Historical Film: History and Memory in Media*, New Brunswick, N.J.: Rutgers University Press, 92.

30. The German diplomat Metternich became Austrian foreign minister after Napoleon Bonaparte defeated Austria in 1809. He played a dominant role at the Congress of Vienna in 1815, which reshaped Europe after the Napoleonic wars. His reactionary politics shaped Austrian society decisively until the revolution of 1848, when he was forced to resign.

31. See Hanisch, 1994, 163, 428; Büttner and Dewald, 1997a, 182–189.

32. See, for example, Karner, 2005; also Utgaard, 2003.

33. 'Die Welt dreht sich verkehrt', *Paimann's Filmlisten*, Nr. 1611, 19 February 1947, 32.

34. See *Pem's Private Bulletins*, London, 7 April 1937 and 15 September 1937, http://deposit. ddb.de/Harvest/brokers/exil/query-glimpse.htm, retrieved 18 February 2012. I would like to thank Christian Cargnelli for this information.

35. See L. Wächter-Böhm (ed.). 1985. *Wien 1945 davor / danach*, Vienna: C. Brandstätter, appendix, n.p.

36. G. Seeßlen. 1996. 'Hans Moser oder Vom traurigen Dienstmann, dem alten Glück und der neuen Zeit', in R. Beckermann and C. Blümlinger (eds), *Ohne Untertitel: Fragmente einer Geschichte des österreichischen Kinos*, Vienna: Sonderzahl, 1996, 125.

37. Seeßlen, 1996, 137.

38. L. Simmel, 'Hans Moser', *Mein Film*, 8, 21 February 1947.

39. Shandley, 2001, 160–161.

40. According to Freud, a 'screen memory' may be 'retrogressive' and made up of 'completely indifferent' early childhood memories, or it may be 'formed from residues of memories relating to later life'. S. Freud. 1968 [1893–1899]. 'Screen Memories', in S. Freud and J. Strachey (eds), *The Standard Edition of the Complete Psychological Works of Sigmund Freud: Early Psycho-analytic Publications*, 3rd ed., London: The Hogarth Press and the Institute of Psycho-Analysis, vol. 3, 320, 307.

41. The following films are set in the Habsburg monarchy under the reign of Franz Joseph: *Das unsterbliche Antlitz* (1947); *Umwege zu dir* (1948) and *Wiener Mädeln* (1948) – both *Überläufer* (i.e. films produced during the Nazi era, but released after the war); *Anni. Eine Wiener Ballade* (1948); *Der Engel mit der Posaune* (1948); *Der Prozess* (1948); *Maresi* (1948); *Liebling der Welt* (1949); *Das vierte Gebot* (1950); *Der alte Sünder* (1950/51), *Das Tor zum Frieden* (1951); *Verklungenes Wien* (1951); *Der Feldherrnhügel* (1953); *Die Fiakermilli* (1953); *Du bist die Welt für mich* (1953); *Hab ich nur deine Liebe* (1953); *Kaisermanöver* (1953); *Der Komödiant von Wien* (1954); *Der rote Prinz* (1954); *Kaiserwalzer* (1954); *Die Deutschmeister* (1955); *Hofjagd in Ischl* (1955); *Sarajevo* (1955); *Sissi* (1955); *Spionage* (1955).

42. See Hanisch, 1994, 157–158.

43. See ibid., 163.

44. See Bruckmüller, 1997, 46–48.

45. Advertisement for the film *Verklungenes Wien* (1951), *Illustrierter Filmkurier*, 1951, Nr. 1019.

46. See M. Barthel. 1986. *So war es wirklich. Der deutsche Nachkriegsfilm*, München: Herbig, 252–253.

47. See Dassanowsky, 2005, 47; Kreimeier, 1992, 365, 387; Hake, 2008, 114.

48. See e.g. 'Um Thron und Liebe', *Das Kleine Volksblatt*, 19 October 1955; 'Betragen: 1, Geschichte: 5', *Der Abend*, 20 October 1955; 'Des Vierten Schüsse waren tödlich', *Bild-Telegraf*, 18 October 1955.
49. See Hanisch, 1994, 155.
50. Büttner and Dewald describe Franz Joseph as 'a promise of equilibrium', 'an axis where different threads converge'. Büttner and Dewald, 1997a, 187.
51. See Connell, 1996, 76–81; 185–203; Tosh, 2004, 47–51; Mosse, 1998, 40–53, 123–132; T. Kühne. 1996. 'Männergeschichte als Geschlechtergeschichte', in T. Kühne (ed.), *Männergeschichte-Geschlechtergeschichte. Männlichkeit im Wandel der Moderne*, Frankfurt am Main: Campus, 11.
52. The unit was usually referred to as 'k.u.k. Infanterie'. The abbreviation k. u. k. stands for *kaiserlich und königlich* – imperial and royal. It refers to the period of the dual Austro-Hungarian monarchy from 1867 to 1918. The Emperor of Austria was also the King of Hungary, and thus the titles of all governmental institutions and offices carried the prefix 'k. u. k.'
53. See A. De Vries. 1974. *Dictionary of Symbols and Imagery*, Amsterdam: North-Holland Publishing Co, 54–55.
54. See Barthel, 1986, 241; G. Seeßlen. 1992. 'Sissi – Ein deutsches Orgasmustrauma', in H.A. Marsiske (ed.), *Zeitmaschine Kino. Darstellungen von Geschichte im Film*, Marburg: Hitzeroth, 70.
55. Seeßlen, 1992, 68.
56. See A. Schwarzer. 1998. *Romy Schneider. Mythos und Leben*, Cologne: Kiepenheuer & Witsch, 36; J. Riedl, 'Wer war Karl Böhm?' *Die Zeit*, 17 November 2005.
57. See E. Carter. 2010. 'Sissi the Terrible: Melodrama, Victimhood, and Imperial Nostalgia in the *Sissi* Trilogy', in P. Cooke and M. Silberman (eds), *Screening War: Perspectives on German Suffering*, Rochester, N.Y.: Camden House, 84.
58. Ibid., 90.
59. See Seeßlen, 1992, 74.
60. See Carter, 2010, 82–83.
61. W. Müller-Funk. 2004. 'Lächeln, Langeweile, Zorn. Überlegungen zur österreichischen Identität' [electronic version], *Medienimpulse* (50), 14. http://www.mediamanual.at/mediamanual/themen/pdf/identitaet/50_Mueller.pdf, retrieved 18 February 2011. Kaiser Franz Joseph I addressed his subjects as 'My peoples', most famously in his Declaration of War on Serbia on 28 July 1914, 'An meine Völker!' The document can be found online at the Zeitgeschichte Informations System of the University of Innsbruck, Primary Sources of 20th Century Austrian History: http://zis.uibk.ac.at/quellen/rauch11b.htm#dok2, retrieved 10 January 2011.
62. The conservative intellectual August Maria Knoll underlined the worldliness of the Austrians by claiming: 'in Austria, political discussions were held in all European languages; but even more frequently people here thought, made poems, sang and built in all languages'. Cited by Bruckmüller, 1997, 46.
63. Declaration of the Austrian Government, 21 December 1945, cited by M. Gottschlich, O. Panagl and M. Welan. 1989. *Was die Kanzler sagten. Regierungserklärungen der Zweiten Republik 1945–1987*, Vienna: Böhlau, 93.
64. This exclusion of other nationalities obviously does not apply to those costume films where the narrative revolves around a person of different nationality, such as the French bon vivant Georges Duroy in *Bel Ami*, or Queen Victoria in *Mädchenjahre einer Königin*.
65. See K. Hartl. 1973. 'Reden Sie mit dem Karas…', in W. Kudrnofsky (ed.), *Vom Dritten Reich zum Dritten Mann. Helmut Qualtingers Welt der vierziger Jahre*, Vienna, Munich, Zürich: Molden, 266–270.
66. For *Der Engel mit der Posaune* see, for example, E. Büttner. 2007b. 'Vertraute Gesichter', *Filmhimmel Österreich. Über Ruinen zu Neuem Leben / Kontinuitäten*, 56, 8–13. The Hungar-

ian Embassy in Austria lodged a protest against G.W. Pabst's plans to make a film about this historical case. Austria's Jewish religious community also protested. The reason for their complaints was an article in a Hungarian newspaper which compared *Der Prozess* with the anti-Semitic Nazi film *Jew Süss*. As a consequence, the Austrian government issued a decree warning provincial governments and cinema operators about the film that was being produced. When the Socialist Minister of the Interior asked for clarification in parliament, the matter was resolved, with the government stressing that it had no objection to the 'artistically highly valuable' film. The Ministry of Trade also emphasised that it supported the making of the film, also for 'economic reasons'. The director G.W. Pabst took legal proceedings against the writer of the article, with the trial receiving a large amount of press coverage. The film itself was much acclaimed by the critics. See, for example, 'Keine Filmzensur', *Wiener Zeitung*, 27 February 1948; 'Zivilprozess um den Prozess', *Neues Österreich*, 1 September 1948; O. Horn. 'Wenn es einer wagt...', *Österreichisches Tagebuch*, 5 July 1947; 'Ehrenbeleidigungsklage um den Film "Der Prozess"', *Wiener Kurier*, 12 May 1948. For the attempts of the provincial governments to prohibit the screening of the film see, for example: '"Der Prozess" in Vorarlberg verboten', *Neues Österreich*, 10 January 1948.

67. The film was based on the original play written by Alexander von Roda-Roda and Carl Rössler in 1910, which was banned by the censors in the Austro-Hungarian monarchy. The play was adapted for film three times, in 1926, 1931/32, and 1953. See 'Der Feldherrenhügel', *Die Presse*, 16 October 1952.
68. See E. Bruckmüller. 2003. *The Austrian Nation: Cultural Consciousness and Socio-political Processes*, Riverside, CA.: Ariadne Press, 134–135.
69. See Bruckmüller, 2003, 147–149.
70. See Hanisch, 1994, 163.

Chapter 3

HEIMATFILM

The unexpected success of the West German film *Schwarzwaldmädel* (Black Forest Girl), which premiered in 1950, sparked a veritable *Heimatfilm* boom in Austria and West Germany.[1] Although they were often directed heavy-handedly, *Heimatfilms* frequently outdid glamorous Hollywood productions at the box office.[2] The genre's appeal was broad. One of its main selling points was certainly its visual imagery – the showcasing of nature at its most beautiful and pristine provided escape for the audience; the landscape, unspoilt by war or modernity, conveyed a sense of 'timelessness', offered security and, furthermore, promised a new *Heimat* to the millions of displaced persons.[3] The fact that the Catholic clergy, who regularly attended premieres of *Heimatfilms*, also endorsed them certainly helped to increase audience numbers in devout rural Austria.[4]

The boom of *Heimatfilm* in postwar Austria and Germany baffled the (predominantly) male critics, who, as members of the cultural elite, responded with derision to such a widespread 'lapse in taste'. *Die Sonnhofbäuerin* (The Sonnhof Farmer, 1949) 'has broken all previous records in boredom and kitsch', taunted the reviewer of the *Wiener Kurier*, adding that 'if one had to find a definition of kitsch, one would have to take this film as evidence'.[5] Faced with the heavy-handed direction and stilted dialogue of *Echo der Berge* (Echo of the Mountains, 1954), the newspaper *Die Presse* expressed the wish that the director had done without a plot at all, as it only deflected from the beautifully photographed spectacle of nature.[6] The fact that *Heimatfilms* were particularly popular with families and female audiences (as contemporary film advertisements and an Austrian survey indicate) may explain the harshness of some of the criticism.[7] The underlying concern of contemporary critics might have been that *Heimatfilm* was 'not sufficiently "masculine" in its critical faculties' in that it provided no challenges for the audience; the genre was regarded as 'feminine' because it fed emotional desires and promoted conservative values.[8]

Heimatfilm has attracted considerable scholarly attention. Most research, however, has focused on 'classics', such as the West German films

Schwarzwaldmädel and *Grün ist die Heide* (The Heath Is Green, 1951), or the Austrian *Echo der Berge*, which became famous as *Der Förster vom Silberwald* (The Forester of the Silver Forest), the title under which it was marketed in West Germany.[9] The findings of these studies are fairly consistent in their assessment: that *Heimatfilm* is an unambiguous and one-dimensional genre. Recent works, such as Johannes von Moltke's analysis of the German *Heimatfilm*, Bergfelder's book on West German cinema (which largely follows Moltke's argument) and Rachel Palfreyman's recent work on *Heimatfilm* have attempted a re-evaluation of the genre.[10] Moltke's study challenges the notion of *Heimatfilm* as anti-modern; instead, he suggests that postwar *Heimatfilms* tried to negotiate between the conflicting needs to modernise and to preserve tradition.[11] Basing his argument on detailed case studies, Moltke demonstrates how certain films, such as *Die Landärztin* (Lady Country Doctor, 1958), allowed the audience to embrace both the traditionalism of *Heimat* and the modernism and dynamism of the 1950s.

While his examples are convincing, it also needs to be pointed out that Moltke's findings are only tenable with regard to certain films; others, as he himself concedes, 'took a resolutely antimodern stance that insisted on turning back the clock'.[12] This is certainly the case with *Heimatfilms* produced in postwar Austria, which rejected modernity altogether. Bergfelder, who takes a similar line to Moltke, argues that *Heimatfilm* also eliminated the separation of urban and rural spheres. However, although some West German films may contain 'pleas for the conversation of traditional living' while promoting 'rampant consumerism', the following analysis shows that Austrian versions did not allow such a compromise, at least not before 1955.[13]

Generally, the theoretical debate on the genre has suffered from an imprecise use of the category *Heimatfilm*. By classifying both the costume trilogy *Sissi* and tourist films such as *Rendezvous im Salzkammergut* (1948) as *Heimatfilms*, for example, scholars have disregarded fundamental differences in narrative patterns, visual style and the specific aims of the films (differences that will be discussed in more detail in the next chapter, on tourist film). This has subsequently resulted in inaccurate assumptions about the genre as a whole.[14] One of the strengths of Moltke's study is that he looks at the genre from a new angle, thus giving new insights into the function of (some) *Heimatfilms*; another strength is that it moves away from the usual classics that have been the focus of previous research, and thus shows that the genre is more varied than often acknowledged. I want to avoid mere reiteration of what has already been said about the genre, by extending the usual canon while keeping to a fairly narrow definition of the term *Heimatfilm*.

The following findings are largely based on the analysis of Austrian films which have been neglected by scholarly research; by comparing the visual and narrative strategies of lesser known films to those of classics such as *Echo der Berge*, I want to highlight inconsistencies and generic developments. The analysis will focus specifically on the symbolic link between gender and landscape through which the genre formulated gender norms. *Heimatfilm* celebrated traditional masculinities and awarded men a superior status in the *Heimat* by establishing a special relationship between man and nature; at the same time, however, it expressed a profound unease about the normative ideal of 'hard' masculinity. The analysis will demonstrate that the theme of masculinity served to negotiate the national, which, though inherently present in the notion of *Heimat*, the genre tried to evade. It will show how Austrian *Heimatfilms* addressed the issues of guilt and victimhood in encoded form, and so helped to ease the conscience of the Austrians after the violent experience of the Second World War. Centring on the themes of guilt and repentance, and purity and dirt, this chapter will detail how the films used tensions within a small community or the family to negotiate larger political and social conflicts.

The *Heimatfilm* as a Genre and the Meaning of *Heimat*

The difficulties scholars have had in explaining the popularity of *Heimatfilm* might be connected to the polysemic quality of the German word *Heimat* on which the genre is based.[15] The term *Heimat* cannot really be translated into English, as it means more than its literal definition: 'home' or 'homeland'. *Heimat* describes a feeling of belonging to a nation as well as to a (usually) rural community; a sentiment which, some argue, is unique to German culture (a claim that is obviously disputable).[16] The term was introduced into everyday German language in the nineteenth century, as accelerating industrialisation and urbanisation generated feelings of loss and alienation; it was initially closely tied to the rural, but its meaning expanded over time to describe a feeling of belonging to a hometown or urban landscape. *Heimatfilm*, though, generally deploys a narrow interpretation of *Heimat* as anti-urban and politically and morally conservative. Undoubtedly, as Celia Applegate points out, the term *Heimat* is 'slippery, infinitely malleable, capable of saying many things', and thus has been used for different ideological purposes.[17] Even though the Nazis appropriated the theme for their own 'blood and soil' ideology, as illustrated by such varied films as the Luis Trenker dramas *Der verlorene Sohn* (The Prodigal Son, 1933/34) and *Der Berg ruft* (The Mountain Calls, 1937), or Gustav Ucicky's infamous anti-Semitic film, *Heimkehr* (Homecoming, 1941), they could not taint it.[18] It was *Heimat's* specific versatility and 'semantic flexibility' which secured its longevity, making it a politically acceptable motif in postwar film production.[19]

Heimat goes beyond the folkloristic; it carries emotional connotations that reverberate in the genre of *Heimatfilm* and account for much of its success with German and Austrian audiences.[20] In *Heimatfilm*, the notion of *Heimat* is intrinsically connected to the rural, which is identified as eternal and stable, as opposed to the urban, defined as unsteady and turbulent; recurring themes are the tensions that arise when the rural is confronted with the urban. In line with the narrow definition of *Heimat*, the setting of the films is rural, often Alpine. A set of emblematic characters who represent the village community, displays of folkloric customs and the celebration of tradition and traditional values are other key features.[21] These narrative and stylistic patterns originate from *Heimat* novels, poetry and folk plays that had become popular in the second half of the nineteenth century.[22]

Films with *Heimat* themes had been produced from the early twentieth century, even though *Heimatfilm* only became a recognised genre in the early 1950s. The genre's direct generic predecessors are the *Volksfilm* (folk film), which depicts the frugal life of ordinary and honest country folk in idyllic mountainous settings, and the *Bergfilm* (mountain film), which revolves around man's heroic battle against nature. The *Volksfilm's* origins go back to the beginning of cinema, whereas the *Bergfilm* emerged in the 1920s and is primarily associated with the daring and innovative German filmmaker Arnold Fanck. *Volksfilm's* positive depiction of rural life and *Bergfilm's* often misogynist glorification of virile masculinity are also found in *Heimatfilm*, even though the latter genre enunciates these elements differently.[23]

Although *Heimatfilm* shares analogies with other national genres, especially the North American western, it has often been described as uniquely German.[24] The 'Germanness' of the genre (which includes its Austrian variations) lies less in its narrative structure or use of certain topoi (these can also be found in other national genres, such as the Swedish *Landsbygdsfilm*) than in the films' emotional content – the celebration of *Heimat*.[25] Through their language, scenery, costume and display of traditions and manners, the films aim to invoke specific national or regional memories and thus instil a sense of belonging. The financial success of the genre in postwar West Germany and Austria is evidence that *Heimatfilm* struck a chord with contemporary audiences. By replacing the nation, which was tainted by Nazi ideology, with an unspoilt and seemingly apolitical *Heimat*, the films arguably answered a deep desire for stability, rekindled a sense of pride in the homeland, 'purified' the nation from the violence of war and assuaged collective guilt.

The fact that *Heimat* is not delimited by national borders, but defines an area of German culture that goes beyond the narrow confines of a nation state, also explains why postwar Austrian *Heimatfilm* avoids direct references to nationhood (unlike, for example, historical costume film, which openly celebrates Austrianness). The ambiguous national character of the cinematic *Heimat*, which, according to Hake, seems to exist 'outside all national boundaries and historical determinants', might also explain why both West German and Austrian *Heimatfilms* are often situated in generalised Alpine settings, where the country folk speak a mix of different Austrian and German dialects.[26] The protagonists, too, are stripped of their national affiliation: at the same time that the Austrian actor Rudolf Prack was being typecast as a romantic lead in contemporary dramas and historical costume films in Austria, he became a key protagonist in West German *Heimatfilm*. Geographical and national boundaries, it seems, are deliberately blurred, as if to prevent a 'nationalisation' of *Heimat*.

Another, more pragmatic explanation for the filmmakers' disregard for cultural specificities is the growing economic interdependency between the Austrian and the West German film industry after West Germany regained independence in 1949. As the *Heimatfilm* boom promised quick financial returns, West German producers were keen to make use of Austria's scenic landscape and low production costs. Austrian producers, on the other hand, increasingly relied on West German distributors to receive funding for their films, and thus had to play to their demands.[27] Claudius Seidl offers a third explanation, arguing that the avoidance of national specificity was due to feelings of confused identity and grief which both nations shared; the idealisation of landscape offered consolation and a sense of belonging to Austrians and Germans.[28] Hence, nature was one of the few places that allowed these two closely related nations, separated by the Allied prohibition from uniting once again, to dwell on their feelings of loss, thus fostering feelings of unity rather than difference. Indeed, through their similar visual and narrative style, the *Heimatfilms* produced in postwar Austria and Germany emphasised a shared cultural heritage, and thereby, at first glance, challenged the belief that Austria was a nation separate from Germany.

Yet, despite the avoidance of direct references to Austria, the Austrian *Heimatfilms* actually display a number of signifiers that imply 'Austrianness'. Dialects, costumes and the names of actual places in Austria (even if they are often a conglomeration of different settings) were meant to assure the audience that *Heimat* is a 'real', existing place that can be found on the map.[29] This was also important because these films served as promotional tools for the national tourist industry, which was keen to lure cinema-goers as tourists to Austrian villages. Audiences and critics strongly protested when filmmakers, trying to save money and time, carelessly combined disparate costumes, accents and settings, which demonstrates how much the audience identified with the depictions on screen. The cinema operators' trade journal, *Paimann's Filmlisten*, expressed disapproval for the 'agonising dialogues in high German' in *Die Sennerin von St. Kathrein* (The Dairy Maid of St. Kathrein, 1955), while the left-wing *Arbeiterzeitung* criticised the 'Babel of possible and impossible dialects' in *Bergkristall* (Rock Crystal, 1949).[30] The communist paper *Volksstimme* even queried whether the German vernacular and the deployment of German actresses in *Heimatland* (Homeland, 1955) were evidence of a lack of patriotism within the Austrian film industry.[31] This criticism shows that even though Austrian *Heimatfilm* refrained from addressing the question of nationality directly, it neverthe-less inspired the audiences to think about their national belonging.

Visual Style and Narrative Themes

Most of the twenty Austrian *Heimatfilms* produced after 1945 are visually quite different from earlier productions.[32] The visual style of postwar *Hei-matfilm* has often been described (and criticised) as 'aesthetic paralysis' and 'coloured boredom'.[33] Indeed, many post-1945 productions appear insipid in comparison to the visually much more powerful *Heimatfilms* of the 1930s and early 1940s. After 1945, daring filming techniques and expressionist traditions were largely abandoned; instead, the use of a relatively static camera, the avoidance of close-ups or expressive camera angles and the restrained acting give the films a noticeable slowness.[34] Was this apparent break in aesthetic traditions an effect of the trauma caused by the Sec-ond World War?[35] Or was the lack of expressive dramaturgy deliberate, as Manuela Fiedler argues – designed to make people forget that these films had served an ideological purpose under the Nazi reign?[36]

Fiedler's argument, though persuasive, cannot explain why the visual language of *Heimatfilm* should have changed so dramatically, while other genres displayed aesthetic continuities with the Nazi era; after all, *Hei-matfilm* was not a genre that the Nazis had particularly instrumentalised for their ideological purposes. The issue, then, is instead whether the sweeping verdict that there was a dramatic change in visual style is actu-ally true. Whilst many Austrian *Heimatfilms* do display the crude stylistic patterns that Axel Graser's and Fiedler's analyses have identified, there are also others which show distinct continuities with pre-1945 films in their use of expressive film language. In the film *Hoch vom Dachstein* (Dark Clouds over the Dachstein, 1952), for instance, dramatic weather changes herald a turn in the narrative. Footage showing dark clouds gathering behind mountain-tops, flashes of lightning in the dark night or the clearing of the sky after a heavy snow-storm presents a theatrical spectacle of the forces of nature which is typical of the mountain films of the Weimar period and the Nazi era.[37] Particularly evocative of Nazi aesthetics is the early postwar film *Bergkristall*, with its unusual number of close-ups and extreme close-ups, expressive angles and dramatic lighting. The fact that the production team of *Bergkristall* had worked with Fanck and Riefenstahl explains these stylistic continuities.[38] Even though *Bergkristall* is clearly a *Heimatfilm*, its style and imagery refer back to the older traditions of the mountain and folk film. It is therefore quite interesting that contemporary critics, clearly impressed by the film and debating whether it could be categorised as avant-garde, saw it as a new beginning in Austrian filmmaking.[39]

While some earlier postwar *Heimatfilms* display strong visual continuities with the 1930s and 1940s, the unexpected success of *Echo der Berge / Der Förster vom Silberwald* in 1954 marked a stylistic turning point. Originally designed as a documentary on hunting for an exhibition in West Germany (which explains the strong advertising character of the film), the producers later added a storyline in order to recoup some of the production costs by screening the film to mainstream cinema audiences.[40] Following the huge success of *Echo der Berge*, the film industry churned out a large number of films that more or less replicated its themes and visual style; thus, Austrian *Heimatfilm* lost the visual power some earlier films had displayed and *Heimatfilms* became virtually interchangeable.[41]

At the centre of the *Heimatfilm* is the rural community, whose stability is threatened by people who breach its rules in their search for personal fulfilment. Re-establishing order and pacifying the community are hence key narrative themes. While women in *Heimatfilm* are often the cause of a dispute, it is left to men to work through the conflict. However, although men take action, they seemingly do not possess the faculty to resolve the situation. Postwar *Heimatfilms* often present men as powerless; their actions seem empty and sometimes appear to be little more than an imitation of outworn masculine rituals. The films divest men of their power in order to test their resilience and faith – virtues that characterise 'true' men. Using the plot device of wrongful accusation, *Heimatfilm* does not allow men to redeem themselves by their own actions; they have to wait and exhibit patience until the course of nature or the actions of other people bring their innocence to light. Nowhere is this theme more vividly played out than in the early postwar film *Bergkristall*.

Guilt and Repentance in Bergkristall

The Austrian/West German co-production *Bergkristall* is based on a well known novel by the Austrian writer Adalbert Stifter (1805–1868), published as a Christmas story in 1845. Stifter's original tells the story of two mutually hostile mountain villages whose inhabitants are brought together by the disappearance of two children lost in the snow on Christmas Eve. The scriptwriter and director Harald Reinl changed the narrative considerably, adding drama by introducing Franz, a keen huntsman, who is wrongfully accused of killing the local forester (who is also his rival in love) on Christmas Eve. Although Franz pleads his innocence and is cleared in court, the village community excludes Franz, along with his wife, Sanne, and his children, because of the alleged murder. Every Christmas Eve the villagers remind Franz of his supposed crime: when darkness has fallen, the sinister-looking, long-bearded villagers knock on his door, uttering the biblical words: 'Cain, where is your brother Abel?' Slowly deteriorating under the mental torment, Franz finally renounces God and turns into an alcoholic, driving his family into ruin (Figure 3.1). Only when his children

get lost in the icy mountains one Christmas Eve does the village community put aside the conflict to search for them. Meanwhile, the children who
have lost their way come across the dead body of the forester, who has died
after falling into a crevasse, and thus clear their father of the suspicion of
murder.

Whereas Stifter put the children and their miraculous survival on an icy
winter's night at the centre of the story, Reinl's adaptation focuses on the
children's father, Franz, whose actions lead to the accidental death of the
forester, and whose family suffers from social exclusion as a consequence.
This change of narrative is highly significant in the political context of
postwar Austria, when the Austrians were confronted with the question of
(individual and collective) responsibility for their actions during the Nazi
dictatorship. Reinl's version thus functions as a parable that explores the
questions of (actual and imagined) guilt and victimhood, thereby allowing
the audience to reflect on their own past. Crucially, the narrative does not
present the hero as totally innocent, as he has sullied his hands; neither
does it side with the villagers, who are presented as vengeful and bitter
people who punish innocent children for their father's (alleged) crime.
As Büttner points out, 'guilt and innocence cannot be clearly separated'
in *Bergkristall*, and contradictions are not completely resolved.[42] The film
presents figures that echo those stereotypical examples that regularly crept
up in the discussions of Austria's involvement in Nazi crimes: on the one
hand, the essentially good Franz, who is involved in the death of his opponent, but who is not legally culpable; on the other hand, his tormenters, the
unforgiving, dark-haired villagers who resemble the negative stereotype
of the Jewish Holocaust survivors seeking justice. Yet, because the story
is played out in a seemingly ahistorical setting – the lifestyle of the rural
folk shows no traces of modernity, and even their traditional dress seems
timeless – the filmmakers disguised the topicality of the questions raised,
and thus made the film more palatable for the audience.

Another feature that distracts the audience from the loaded subject is
the impressive visual imagery of *Bergkristall*, which is very reminiscent of
the mountain-film aesthetic. The strong resemblance is not surprising considering that key members of the Austrian filmmaking crew had worked
with Arnold Fanck and Leni Riefenstahl: the director, Reinl, a brilliant
skier, had played small roles in mountain films in the early 1930s before he
worked as assistant director on Leni Riefenstahl's *Tiefland* (Lowlands, shot
1940–1944, released in 1954). The director of photography and co-producer
Josef Plesner, an international newsreel reporter, was also involved in the
making of *Tiefland*, and the executive producer, Walter Traut, acted in some
Fanck films at the beginning of his career and worked as executive producer in all major Riefenstahl productions.[43] *Bergkristall* was Reinl's first
feature film and the critical acclaim it received paved his way for a successful career in West German cinema and television; moving from *Heimatfilms*
to the adventure and crime genre, his 1960s adaptations of Edgar Wallace's

crime novels and Karl May's tales of the noble Apache warrior Winnetou became hugely popular with continental European audiences.[44]

With only a tiny budget, the crew predominantly filmed in outside locations high up in the Tyrolean Mountains. The depictions of glorious nature, weathered farmhouses and haggard mountain farmers made the film stand out, and critics from both the Left and the Right applauded the 'realism' of the picture and 'its immediacy and freshness that distinguishes it positively from the mannerisms and clichés so dominant nowadays'.[45] Expressive camera angles added suspense and heightened the appeal of the film. Particularly praised were the stunning nature shots of the snow-covered landscape and the glacial formations. Indeed, the mountains and snowy landscape take on a life of their own and dominate the film, as they do in Fanck's mountain films.[46] The narrative takes a back seat, so much so that in the view of the *Wiener Zeitung* the story seems to have been 'chosen at random', and only served as a 'pretext to film the landscape'.[47] Reinl and Plesner, with their eye for dramatic settings, used colour contrasts and natural imagery to great effect to illustrate dramatic turns and to convey symbolic meanings: mountainous landscapes covered in thick, glistening snow mirror Franz's youthful spirit and the children's innocence, and contrast with the dark interior of the old farmhouse where Franz sits brooding after the disaster.[48] Ice, snow and – most of all – the large rock crystal referenced by the film's title function as metaphors for purity and innocence (or the lack thereof). The heavy snow in *Bergkristall* does not symbolise death (even though the film team itself was almost killed by a snowstorm while filming), but purity;[49] it protects the innocent children from death and covers up the sins of the people. The rock crystal, which Franz was given by a wise man, does exactly the reverse: it functions as a moral compass by changing its colour. So, when Franz returns from the shootout in the mountains, the clear crystal has blackened, clearly contradicting Franz's belief in his own innocence. Only when Franz accepts his guilt does the crystal clear again.

The Austrian actor Franz Eichberger, who started his short acting career as the shepherd Pedro in Riefenstahl's *Tiefland*, adopted an expressionistic acting style to play Franz, the male lead. Franz is presented as a young, impetuous man who leads a slightly dissipated life; he prefers hunting and dancing to working on his father's farm. His lack of discipline, his uncontrolled passion for poaching and his vanity (he looks approvingly at his image in the mirror) designate him as immature and lacking in moral values. His outward appearance immediately sets him apart from the earnest villagers, with their worn features, rotten teeth and long, dark beards. Franz's curly, dark-blond hair and bright laughter revealing a set of shiny white teeth emphasise his youthfulness. Franz is tall, strong and full of energy, a man who easily runs up the mountain slopes to follow the game he spots. The villagers, in contrast, are presented as hard-working, God-fearing men whose life is guided by strict principles.

The gap in morals between Franz and the villagers is also underlined by the spatial distance between them. Franz lives with his father in a large farmhouse up in the mountains, away from the village. He descends to participate in the village's shooting contest, displaying a self-assured manner that indicates a haughtiness that separates him from the rural community; but Franz is essentially good at heart, and his earnest love for Sanne (Maria Stolz), a respectable girl from the neighbouring village, inspires him to change his life. Sanne is the virginal figure that promises healing, but even she cannot still his passion for hunting, which proves stronger than his promise to stop. This lack of self-control is presented as negative – it invites catastrophe and threatens to destroy the community.

As Franz sets out to cut down a Christmas tree on a beautiful Christmas Eve – an act that signifies his return to domesticity – the lure of the chamois climbing up the snowy slopes in glaring sunshine proves irresistible. Following them high up into the glacial mountains, he suddenly comes across the dark-haired, big-moustached forester, Jäger Steffl (Robert Falch), his rival in love, who tries to track down the illegal hunter; the shoot-out amidst steep rocks leaves Franz lying unconscious in the snow, while the forester, who believes he has killed Franz, flees down the slope, thereby falling into an icy crevasse. Nature punishes the crime instantly: the mountain swallows the forester who shot Franz, but, by hiding his body, it leaves Franz to face the consequences of his own immoral actions: his use of a gun against the forester and his poaching habit, which violate the rules of the community. The court acquits Franz of the killing due to lack of evidence, but this merely prevents him from acknowledging his larger, moral responsibility; moreover, the villagers remain convinced that he has murdered the forester. For them, as the village wise-man explains, 'you stay guilty' – a reference to the fact that guilt cannot be determined solely in legal terms, and that the Austrians, though perhaps not charged with participation in Nazi crimes, may still be culpable.

The analysis shows how the *Heimatfilm* narrative utilises the trope of wrongful accusation to set out the parameters of desirable behaviour and define masculine virtues. Using Franz, who seems unable to concede responsibility, as an example, the film demonstrates the need to accept one's fate. As Franz rebels against the injustice he has to endure, and as he abjures God, he increases his guilt and eventually causes a rift between himself and his family, who are the only ones left who believe in his innocence. The last scenes of *Bergkristall* vividly illustrate the effects of social exclusion on Franz and his family. Once more, it is Christmas Eve. Franz sits depressed at the table; the wall behind him still shows the shape of the large wooden cross which he tore down earlier in a fit of rage. The mark designates an absence that has taken hold of his whole life – a separation from God, family and community. His deeply religious wife, Sanne, has, like every year, sent her children to her mother to celebrate Christmas and to protect them from witnessing the gruesome ritual of the villag-

Figure 3.1: Exclusion from the community has driven Franz (Franz Eichberger) to the brink of destruction in *Der Bergkristall*. Filmarchiv Austria.

ers, who each year congregate before their house to remind Franz of his deed. Pained by the sudden emptiness of the house and the estrangement from his wife, whose quiet suffering holds a reproach, Franz finally grabs his gun to take revenge for the perceived injustice he is forced to endure. A fight ensues between Franz and his wife, who tries to wrestle the gun from Franz; he overpowers her and locks her in a room – a violent act that signals the final break of their once-loving relationship.

Meanwhile, bearded men clad in dark coats and hats are leaving their houses, carrying burning torches. They march through the dark village to Franz's house, the flames of their torches emphasising their forbidding appearance. A cut back to the inside of Franz's house shows him in the large, unrendered hallway cowering behind a chest, his gun directed at the front door and his apprehensive gaze indicative of his fragile mental state. Separated from God and the community, Franz has become a coward and lost his manly strength; but when a messenger, sent by Sanne's mother, reports that the children have gone missing, Franz regains his sanity and jumps up to free his wife. For the first time, it seems, he is looking beyond his immediate concerns.

Sanne, who has run out of the door, only to bounce into the group of men waiting in front of their house, pleads for their mercy. Filmed in shallow focus and close up, her face reveals her torment. As the villagers turn to each other, murmuring, Franz, at first only a blurred outline in the background, walks slowly towards the camera until his face is in close-up – a clear sign that he has taken control. Now Franz addresses the villagers, who stand in a semi-circle around the couple, and begs them to let him get through so he can search for his children. An extreme close-up of his face shows his desperation and signals the dramatic climax as he utters the powerful words: 'I admit it and you all shall hear it. I am guilty. I have shot the Jäger Steffl'. The impact of this confession is immediately visible, both on Franz's face and in the reaction of the villagers. The space behind his head is suddenly lit up, producing a halo-like effect that indicates a new-found virtuousness. Unlike the villagers, who are almost indistinguishable in the night because of their black dress and bearded faces, Franz is not in darkness anymore, thanks to his confession. Taken aback by Franz's admission of guilt, the group of villagers slowly parts to let Sanne and Franz through and then follows them to search for the children. When they discover the children alive, having survived the cold night in an ice cave, they also learn about the forester's accidental death.

Franz's integrity is restored the minute he admits his guilt and pledges to accept any punishment. Even though the discovery of the real reason for the forester's disappearance clears him of the allegation of murder, Franz shows earnest repentance for something that goes far beyond the disputed killing: he does penance for his previous lifestyle, his renunciation of God and his actions that brought about the death of the forester. In keeping with the strongly Catholic tone of the narrative, Franz publicly confesses and is thus healed. Sins are forgiven and the divided community is reconciled. In the final scene it is the villagers who come to Franz to ask him for forgiveness – an interesting reversal that highlights the guilt of the accusers. By distributing the blame more equally among the persons involved, *Bergkristall* essentially absolves all men from their guilt – a resolution that also helps to ease the conscience of the audience. As Palfreyman suggests, it is the 'very flexibility of the concept of *Heimat*' that allows trauma to be symbolically healed and purity to be restored; this is ultimately illustrated by the lightening of the rock crystal.[50]

As the analysis of *Bergkristall* illustrates, the *Heimatfilm* narrative emasculates men before restoring them to power. Men have to undergo a period of trial in which their faith is tested; this is a religious motif that serves to underpin *Heimatfilm*'s endorsement of traditional, Christian values. Michael, in *Das Siegel Gottes* (God's Signet, 1949), for example, has to endure two years in jail until he is set free by the deathbed confession of one of the arsonists for whose crime he has taken the blame. The theme of wrongful accusation thus provides a platform to formulate masculine virtues: patiently bearing injustice is a mark of distinction in *Heimatfilm*. Postwar *Heimatfilms* discourage masculine aggression, individual action and high-flying aspirations by illustrating the negative effects of such behaviours on the community and the individual.

The order of *Heimatfilm* is, as Claudia Beindorf points out, based on a belief in the operations of fate: those who show faithfulness, honesty and humility are rewarded.[51] The morality of the genre is simple and obligatory to everybody: to uphold and respect traditional values, to be content with one's place in society and to cherish one's *Heimat*. This ideology is perfectly illustrated in *Echo der Berge*, where the forester, Hubert, a refugee, proves his love for his new-found *Heimat* in the Austrian mountains. An upright and dutiful man, Hubert (Rudolf Lenz) catches the tourist Max Freiberg (Erik Frey) poaching a stag. The fact that Freiberg lives in the city and disrespects the rules of the rural community and the order of nature by hunting in the close season designates him as an outsider. Yet, by catching Freiberg red-handed, Hubert runs into a moral conflict. Freiberg is the lover of Liesl (Anita Gutwell), the beautiful granddaughter of Hofrat Leonhard, who is the most respected member of the village community. Suspecting that Freiberg's gun belongs to Liesl's grandfather, Hubert keeps the identity of the poacher a secret to protect the reputation of Leonhard and his daughter (whom he secretly loves), even though his stubborn silence about the identity of the poacher eventually costs him his job. In the end, the course of fate brings to light Hubert's honourable motivation, but also proves wrong his suspicions that Leonhard or his daughter were involved. Hubert is invited back into the community and marries Liesl, which seals his integration into his new *Heimat*.

What distinguishes *Echo der Berge* and other postwar *Heimatfilms* from *Bergkristall* is that the innocence of the leading characters is not called into question; unlike in *Bergkristall*, where the hero is not without guilt, the main protagonists are not forced to painstakingly search their souls to find truth in the accusations levelled against them. It seems that the question of national and individual guilt, which was still contested in the immediate postwar years, left its trace in the production of *Bergkristall*. The question of guilt did become less virulent as the official stance of 'national innocence' gained widespread acceptance in Austria, and so the discussion of guilt in *Heimatfilm*, in turn, also became more cursory. Nevertheless, it remained a key theme, as if creeping into the fabric of the films, unexpectedly cropping up amidst the beautiful scenery that tries to cover up the guilt and trauma of a nation.

Significantly, guilt is predominantly assigned to men in *Heimatfilm*, for reasons that remain obscure. That the war and the Nazi past loom on the horizon of *Heimatfilm* like dark clouds, as Kaschuba puts it, implies that the burden of guilt these men carry is connected to the dark past of their country.[52] In *Hoch vom Dachstein*, we learn that the main protagonist, Hannes, was a soldier for six years – possibly the explanation for his gloom. 'Until now, he has only learned how to survive; he hasn't found peace', hears the maid, Christl, from the wise old shepherd who encourages her to take care of Hannes. The imagery, too, draws attention to Hannes' military past. A scene where he and his co-workers dynamite and dig through a mudflow is reminiscent of newsreels from the war. *Echo der Berge*, too, alludes to the war in several instances. The artist Max Freiberg is teased by the inn-keeper's daughter that he might not know how to shoot, but insists: 'Of course I can shoot, we all had to learn it'. Even though Freiberg's outward appearance gives no indication of war-related trauma, he displays a considerable lack of sensitivity towards the natural world when he shoots the biggest stag in close season. His action might well be the result of an urban lifestyle that has distanced him from nature; it might also be an after-effect of war, which has numbed his feelings towards living creatures.

For Gerhard Bliersbach, the key to understanding *Heimatfilm* is the question: 'Why does Lüdersen poach?', referring to the compulsive hunting habit of a displaced German man named Lüdersen in the West German film *Grün ist die Heide*. Bliersbach asserts that postwar *Heimatfilm* is full of fathers who are burdened with guilt and shame, but who also feel devalued and full of bitterness. Poaching thus becomes a means to take revenge for the suffering experienced, and can be understood as the 'externalisation of an injury'.[53] The actions of the fathers have repercussions and negatively affect younger generations, who have to pay for their fathers' sins. We have seen how in *Bergkristall* Franz's two children, Sannele and Konrad, are 'quasi-ostracised' by the villager's children because their father is branded a murderer.[54] In *Hoch vom Dachstein*, the young widow Jutta is held responsible for the death of some of her mine workers, even though the collapse of a salt mine which killed them was brought about by the greed of her forefathers. In *Heimatland*, Hans Bachinger's reputation is tarnished by his father, whose alcoholism brought about the family's financial ruin and loss of status; and in *Gipfelkreuz*, Hans Leutgeber's son and daughter are shunned by the community because of their deceased father's brutish behaviour: 'Great is the guilt he put upon him through his selfish and violent manner. His name is forever tarnished with disgrace', hints the film advertisement darkly.[55] As Palfreyman points out, far from covering up the traumatic past, *Heimatfilm* narratives obliquely 'represent wartime suffering in its traumatic effects on family relationships'; the films do not brush aside guilt and suffering, but provide symbolic forgiveness by resolving the issue of perpetration 'within the family'.[56]

By detailing how the guilt of the fathers impacts on the children, *Heimatfilm* draws an analogy to the present, in which a nation has to carry the burden of guilt for the crimes committed by a (mostly) male generation during the Third Reich. It does have to be noted that the films never openly declare the men as culpable, but the fact that they are subjected to punishment points to possible misdeeds in their past. This male past, however, remains shrouded in obscurity. Hubert's reason for fleeing his estate in the East after the war and starting again as a humble forester in the 'silver forest' in *Echo der Berge* remains unexplained. What did he do on his estate during the Nazi dictatorship? Was he chased off his land because he was

German, or because he had collaborated with the Nazis? These questions also crop up in the case of the aforementioned melancholic foreman, Hannes, in *Hoch vom Dachstein*. He is a local, but he was once 'Herr Khäls von Khälsberg', a minor aristocrat who, like Hubert, has left (or lost?) his property for unknown reasons. When asked by the shepherd, Hannes refuses to explain why he did not return to his father's wealthy estate, but instead took on employment on a farm governed by a woman – the ultimate loss of power.

Nonetheless, while these allusions imply guilt, first and foremost they present men as victims. The rejection and exclusion young men face in Austrian *Heimatfilm* thus encourage empathy. Emotional release is granted when allegations turn out to be unfounded, and the men are rehabilitated and invited back into the community. Whatever guilt they carry, at the end of the films it is only their status as victims that is remembered. It is quite significant that Austrian *Heimatfilm* raises the issue of guilt, and that the confirmation of innocence and the rehabilitation of the leading man conclude each of these films. *Heimatfilms* thus do not only absolve the male protagonists, but also ease the guilty consciences of the audience. The parable-like function of the films allowed the audience to work through issues of guilt and victimhood that arose from the Nazi past, without addressing this past directly. *Heimatfilm* grants absolution to the faithful who believe that their guiltlessness will be proven – a reward that might explain the genre's particular popularity in the postwar era.

It's a Man's World: Gender Norms in Austrian *Heimatfilm*

The world of *Heimatfilm* is dichotomous; divided into rural and urban, good and bad, male and female. The genre prescribes clear-cut gender roles and promotes specific gender ideals by presenting positive and negative examples of masculinity and femininity. The positive masculine ideal is generally embodied by a forester, or sometimes a squire or manager of an estate; his display of self-control, rectitude, fairness and humility designate him as exemplary. The forester's opponent is traditionally the poacher, who is in many ways equal to the forester, as he is positioned in the same surroundings. As long as a poacher does not shoot game in close season, does not openly brag about poaching and avoids encounters with the forester on duty, he remains an accepted member of the community.[57] Yet, the poacher often violates these rules because he is unable to discipline his desires; this lack of self-control turns him into an example of negative masculinity. The poacher's urge to go hunting is often accompanied by aggressive sexual behaviour that brings him into conflict with other men, who consider their territory invaded. The community in *Heimatfilm* is founded on conservative moral principles and a hierarchical distribution of power, and therefore cannot accept the poacher's trespassing; he needs to be reprimanded or excluded from the community. When the figure of the poacher merges with the character of the stranger, another key figure in postwar *Heimatfilm*, he becomes the ultimate outsider, whose (physical) elimination is necessary to assert the values and rules of community. The stranger is at the lowest end of the masculine hierarchy because he is a *Heimatloser*: a person without *Heimat*. Often he is a city dweller, like the artist Max Freiberg in *Echo der Berge*; a person without known origin, such as Franz in *Die Sennerin von St. Kathrein*; or a vagabond, like Hans Bachinger in *Heimatland*, who is already tainted by the bad reputation of his father. *Echo der Berge* is an exception in this regard: here, the exact origin of the main protagonist, the forester Hubert, is unknown, but he gains acceptance because he fully identifies with his new *Heimat*: he protects the 'silver forest' against intruders and fights for its preservation when lumberjacks start cutting down the trees. Moreover, he 'fits in' because he wears the same clothes and speaks the same language as the villagers.

Heimatfilm assigns men clearly defined social roles that allow them to act and take decisions. Even negative male figures are independent and self-sufficient: the artist Freiberg in *Echo der Berge* works in his own studio, and the carver Franz in *Die Sennerin von St. Kathrein* roams the country and is his own boss. Women, on the other hand, are confined to the role of passive bystanders, with the exceptions of *Der Weibsteufel* (A Devil of a Woman, 1951) and *Hoch vom Dachstein*, where strong, self-confident women play the leading parts. The latter heroine's quest for independence and self-fulfilment, however, is stifled, illustrating that a virtuous woman needs to be humble and submissive. Although postwar *Heimatfilm* features a number of seemingly modern women who have a profession and are self-confident and independent-minded, these women still yearn to return to a more traditional gender set-up. Even Liesl in *Echo der Berge*, who is perhaps the most 'modern' woman in Austrian *Heimatfilm* because she works as an artist and cohabits with another artist in the city, submits easily to the patriarchal rule of her grandfather and seems unsure whether she actually wants to be independent. Fehrenbach's claim that the pretty young women populating postwar *Heimatfilms* embody a new femininity is thus disputable.[58] The truly independent women, like Jutta in *Hoch vom Dachstein* or Marei in *Der Weibsteufel*, are punished; those who appear outwardly modern through their dress and hairstyle, however, never truly challenge traditional gender order.

What is striking in *Heimatfilm* is the absence of mothers and older women.[59] The Austrian films feature a large number of fathers or paternal figures, partly in very dominant roles, such as Hofrat Leonhard and his servant, Kajetan, in *Echo der Berge*, Passegger in *Das Siegel Gottes* or Maylechner in *Der Sonnblick ruft*, but mothers are rare. Considering the specific context of postwar Austria, where many women had to bring up their children on their own because men had died or were imprisoned, this is an interesting reversal. Was the abundance of available men and father figures in *Heimatfilm* perhaps meant to reassure the audience? Both men and women may have found the projected illusion of an intact society in which men act as heads of families appealing. Moreover, the genre assigns men a crucial role in protecting the *Heimat* – hence the importance of restoring 'patrilinear harmony'.[60]

However, Fiedler offers another interesting explanation for the absence of mothers in *Heimatfilm*, detecting an 'oedipal idealisation of mother images': the real mother is replaced with a purer and eternal image of motherhood – nature itself.[61] Because the *Heimat*, as Fiedler suggests, signifies the intimate bond between infant and mother, *Heimatfilm* invites the audience to re-experience that sense of lost 'wholeness' with the mother.[62] Consequently, representations of real mothers or elderly women must be avoided, as they would reveal the artificiality of this imagined paradise.

In narrative and imagery, Austrian *Heimatfilm* endorses clear-cut gender roles and unambiguous sexual identities. Unlike the tourist film, which emphasises similarities between men and women, *Heimatfilm* stresses the differences: masculinity is characterised by a distinct body language and costume, and by exclusive access to certain objects and spaces. In a very archaic way, *Heimatfilm* measures masculinity by a man's ability to hunt, barring women from touching a gun and thereby protecting this male domain from female intrusion. The city-dwelling artist, Max Freiberg, in *Echo der Berge*, criticises the villagers for assigning so much importance to hunting as proof of masculinity by remarking ironically to the innkeeper's daughter, Vroni: 'Strange people here. Amongst you a man is only considered to be a man if he is a hunter'. Vroni adroitly retorts that Freiberg's girlfriend, Liesl, seems to be rather fond of 'a certain hunter', thus indicating that hunting is a proof of the virility that Freiberg might lack. The sexual undertones are evident: when a local forester in *Heimatland* repeatedly misses the targeted game, he has to endure his mates' ridicule, as his failure suggests impotence and weakness.

But hunting in *Heimatfilm* also functions as a controlled outlet for male aggression, which has no place in a civilised, postwar society. The need to repress male aggression in order to civilise men who had fought in the war was also highlighted in other national cinemas.[63] In postwar Austrian cinema, however, this avoidance of violence and aggression seems to be particularly salient, as illustrated by the absence of war and crime films and the presentation of Austrian men as cultured and harmonious. *Heimatfilm* is thus an exception, as it is the only genre where weapons are frequently used and blood is on display. Importantly, though, shootings or other violent acts are conducted in a restrained manner. Men who cannot control their lust and aggression, such as poachers, are disciplined by authority: the gun is taken away and the men are symbolically castrated. The films thus prescribe self-control as a crucial masculine virtue – a characteristic that is emphasised by the particular demeanour of the male characters.

Typically, men in postwar Austrian *Heimatfilm* display a striking 'stiff-ness': they gesticulate very little, move in a rigidly controlled manner, take long, purposeful strides and stand upright with both feet firmly rooted in the ground. They are often shown in typical 'masculine' postures, with hands folded behind their backs or buried in their pockets, with the el-bows claiming space, all as if to affirm their manhood.[64] Physical contact with other men is strictly limited, and confined to fighting or supporting the injured. Physical contact with women is similarly constrained: men usually touch women in a staccato and hesitant way, giving the impression that they not only fear rejection but are also unsure of themselves and their own feelings. Due to the strict moral code of the *Heimat* narratives, the films usually avoid showing passionate embraces or kisses, or the touching of sexually connoted female body parts. This display of pronounced physical restraint has given postwar *Heimatfilms* a reputation for being particularly prudish. Moreover, in postwar Austrian cinema, *Heimatfilm* stands out as the genre in which men show the greatest emotional restraint. Men seldom laugh, or express their happiness through uncontrolled body movements or sounds. The only exception is Franz in *Bergkristall*, who is presented as a child of nature at the beginning of the film, unable to discipline his desires and being all smiles. Negative emotions are equally unacceptable: men are not hot-tempered, bad or violent; even a negatively portrayed character such as Hans in *Heimatland* only resorts to violence because he is provoked (Figure 3.2). The *Heimatfilm* narratives thus set certain norms: men 'bite their lip', suffer in silence and do not rebel against the injustice

Figure 3.2: The outsider Hans Bachinger (Adrian Hoven), left, and his opponent, the forester Thomas Heimberg (Rudolf Prack), in *Heimatland*. Filmarchiv Austria.

they experience. Surprisingly, this restraint does not emanate 'coolness' (as it does with heroes in westerns, for example), but instead conveys a sense of defeat and submissiveness; thus, even though the men in *Heimatfilm* appear to embody the traditional ideal of 'hard' masculinity, they have lost their strength.

An unwillingness – or rather inability – to voice their feelings characterises men in *Heimatfilm*. Even when Liesl in *Echo der Berge* implores Hubert to explain why he avoids her, Hubert replies curtly: 'I cannot. It is just not possible'.[65] The forester Thomas Heimberg in *Heimatland* also finds it hard to declare his love for Helga, who has fallen for the more passionate outsider, Hans, in his stylish leather jacket. Thomas only reveals his feelings in a covert way, by telling Helga that his house and his dog, Waldi, are waiting for her. Importantly, *Heimatfilm* does not problematise this inability to express emotions, but instead turns it into a positive feature; only women, who are allowed a certain emotional expressivity, or unruly male outsiders express their emotions spontaneously. However, by demonstrating that female gossip and uncontrolled passion drive a wedge into the community, the films underline the need for controlling one's emotions.

By presenting emotional restraint as masculine virtue – or, indeed, a masculine norm – postwar *Heimatfilm* keeps within generic traditions. However, in the postwar context, the propagated imperative of emotional self-restraint acquires a particular significance because self-control is directly linked to male power. Because men hold the power in the idealised *Heimat*, outbursts of male emotion can easily disturb the social equilibrium and thus cause damage. The war had shown just how much destruction displays of unbridled enthusiasm or aggression could cause. Thus, the *Heimat* can only be sustained if the people who populate it adhere to strict rules.

Self-control and Purity of Character in Hoch vom Dachstein

The film *Hoch vom Dachstein* addresses the issue of emotional self-control in the context of conflicted gender relations. Here, the Alpine scenery does not merely serve as a backdrop for a gripping drama of passion, rejection and struggle for power; it also triggers conflicts and illustrates emotional climaxes. What differentiates *Hoch vom Dachstein* from other postwar Austrian *Heimatfilms* is the level of emotional expressivity of the leading characters, whose acting style is forceful without being hammy, as in *Bergkristall*.

Hoch vom Dachstein was jointly produced by Austrian Telos-Film and the West German Süddeutsche Filmproduktion in 1952. It premiered in early 1953 and was marketed under several different titles, which suggests that its success with audiences was limited.[66] The scriptwriter and director, German-born Anton Kutter, was a trained mechanical engineer with a keen interest in filming and astronomy. He joined the Bavaria Filmkunst in 1931, producing a number of shorts, most notably a science-fiction film about a moon landing in 1937 entitled *Weltraumschiff 1 startet…* (Space Ship No 1 Takes Off…). During and after the war, Kutter concentrated on developing a new astronomic telescope, which became widely known among astronomers.[67] He directed only four feature-length films; all of them were produced between 1952 and 1955, and all had a *Heimat* theme. After his last production, *Das Lied der Hohen Tauern* (The Song of the Hohe Tauern, 1955), which was set against the backdrop of the building of the Kaprun Dam, Kutter ended his career and opened a cinema with an observatory in his native town of Biberach.

Hoch vom Dachstein tells the story of a beautiful widow, Jutta (Gisela Fackeldey), who is the self-assured mistress of the rich Salzer estate high up in the Styrian mountains. Because she anxiously guards her independence, her relationship with her foreman, Hannes (Pero Alexander), who is clearly in love with her, is complex. After a storm has cut off the water supply and the local government has cordoned off parts of her land due to danger of collapse, the two get into a fight, during which Jutta sacks Hannes in a bout of temper. Before leaving, Hannes dutifully restores the water supply and then retreats to an Alpine hut, where he re-encounters a pretty young maid, Christl (Marianne Koch), who has admired him from afar for a long time. Kind, humble and caring, Christl is the exact opposite of the resolute and passionate Jutta, and therefore the ideal wife for Hannes.

The scene is set with establishing shots of beautiful Alpine scenery: impressive shots of a snow-covered mountain range, a shepherd's boy playing his flute among grazing goats on a meadow and the reflection of a snow-capped mountain in a pristine Alpine lake. From a slow pan over the lake, the camera cuts abruptly to a scene that presents the setting for the unfolding drama. The underlying musical score suddenly takes on a dramatic tone, highlighting the momentousness of the place: a wide shot filmed from a low angle shows a large, wooden farm building, with a massive stone wall running down parts of the slope that fortifies its front. Just behind the building towers a snow-covered mountain that seems to be split by a ravine – suggestive of the forces that threaten to break the estate apart. The camera cuts to a weathered coat of arms made of stone and bearing the words, 'My house. My legacy. My right', then moves slowly downwards, passing a stone plate that details that the house was built in 1653, and finally stopping at a large, arched doorway made out of stone, into which a young woman (Jutta) steps. The camera's movement establishes a connection between the inscription and the self-confident appearance of the woman.

Clad in a black, long-sleeved, high-cut blouse that accentuates her prominent golden crucifix and her carefully coiffed light hair, the woman rests her right arm on her hip and looks into the sunshine, her chin slightly turned upwards, her lips showing traces of a smirk. Her posture and expression give her an air of pride, even arrogance. Indeed, Jutta reigns with a firm hand. Her volatile character and gruff tone, used against servants and unwelcome visitors alike, contrast sharply with her beauty. Only her bubbly kitchen maid, Cilly (Jutta Bornemann), and the wise old shepherd, played by the seasoned Austrian *Heimatfilm* actor Eduard Köck, are allowed to see a different, friendlier side of her. Her behaviour towards her foreman, the handsome, black-haired Hannes, on whom she relies for his expert opinion in all practical matters, is ambiguous: she longs for his affection but alienates him by behaving coldly, even condescendingly towards him, afraid to lose her independence.

The German actress Gisela Fackeldey, who initially worked mostly in theatre before appearing in a number of *Heimatfilms* in the 1950s, portrays the volatile heroine convincingly by sensitively accentuating the complexity of the character. A strong-willed but sensitive woman, Jutta is afraid of being taken advantage of, and thus behaves coolly towards the people around her. The price she pays is loneliness. Desperate to take charge of her life after six months of enforced mourning for her dead but unloved husband, Jutta exchanges her widow's dress for a low-cut, tight-fitting dirndl dress and an ornate necklace that draws all eyes. The old shepherd, fully aware that Jutta has her eye on Hannes, disapproves of this improper gesture.

The German actor Pero Alexander, who plays Hannes, was also at the beginning of his film career. Jutta's hot temper contrasts with Hannes' calmness. He is portrayed as a brooding, serious character who seldom smiles. With his shiny black hair and upright posture he attracts the gaze of the women around him; but Hannes is immune to female banter or the admiring looks of the young maid, Christl, because his attention is fully on his mistress. Although they behave formally in front of others, everyone working at the estate is fully aware that their relationship is more than purely professional. Yet their relation is an unequal one: even though Jutta relies on Hannes' advice and judgement, he is still her employee and forced into passivity by her; this is underlined by the fact that it is usually Jutta who comes to him or sends for him.

As in other *Heimatfilms*, a man's difficulty in reining in his feelings significantly reduces his masculine power. The disconcerting effect of Hannes' love for Jutta is shown very early in the film when Jutta receives a visit from the district's governor, who warns her of the erosion threatening her land. When they step out on the terrace to inspect her land, Jutta asks Hannes to be present to give his advice. As the governor explains the problem, though, Hannes can only focus on Jutta. He is no longer the level-headed foreman, but a man consumed by passion. As the camera cuts from Hannes, who is shown from the front in a medium shot, to Jutta's profile in extreme close-up, the governor's voice becomes an indistinct blur and is replaced by a sweet, melodic score. The camera lingers on Jutta's face, allowing the spectator to study her beautiful features in detail. The image reflects Hannes' concentration; he seems spellbound, and awakens only when Jutta turns abruptly towards him, posing a question.

The logic of *Heimatfilm* suggests that men who follow their feelings become more like women, and thus lose their position of power. Hannes is aware of the need to control his feelings, as his unbridled passion is in danger of emasculating him. He even warns Jutta that 'feelings are deceptive', and that it is important to yield to reason, but finds it hard to follow the advice himself. By mastering his feelings for Jutta, Hannes eventually reasserts his position of power, and is thus able to re-establish the traditional gender hierarchy that was presented as being askew at the beginning of the film. However, it takes a natural catastrophe (a whole house is swallowed up by the earth during a violent storm, and a landslide cuts the water supply to the farm) to make Hannes realise that there is no future in his relationship with his 'erratic-sensitive' mistress;[68] even then, it is she who angrily ends the relationship and sends him away. Only after he has spent several days in the mountains is Hannes able to reassert his masculine identity, by choosing a more submissive and, importantly, 'purer' partner. By mirroring emotions with natural catastrophes, the film underlines the need for self-control and the dangers of emotional excess.

Through a highly metaphoric language that utilises symbols of water and salt, the film expresses specific codes of behaviour and gendered norms. It also debates the issues of guilt and purity.[69] In *Hoch vom Dachstein*, impurity of character is not indicated by dirt, but by the absence of elements associated with purity. A heavy storm has brought about the collapse of a salt mine, leaving six people dead. Crucially, it has also cut off the water supply to the Salzer estate, which casts a damning light on Jutta. Her overbearing behaviour and unseemly relationship with Hannes would appear to have invited this catastrophe. The lack of water is presented as an omen. It does not just bring hardship because the water has to be brought in from elsewhere; it suggests impurity, as water is needed for cleaning and the fight against dirt and sin. Furthermore, the loss of water, a symbol of fertility, highlights Jutta's childlessness. Childless from her first marriage, Jutta toys with the idea of having a child with Hannes, but her confidant, the old shepherd, warns her that 'this is not right'. It is unclear whether he disapproves of the relationship because they are not married or because Jutta is too powerful, and thus forces Hannes into submission. The fact that the loss of the water supply is preceded by the first passionate kiss between Hannes and Jutta the night before indicates a logical connection between the two events. 'The mountain has taken the water away', remarks the old shepherd sagely when Jutta inquires about the reason for the sudden drought. Jutta is under double pressure: she has to restore the water supply and find alternative watering holes for her cattle; at the same time, the district's governor has cordoned off parts of her land due to danger of collapse. Jutta feels disempowered by external forces.

The fight that ensues between Hannes and Jutta following the catastrophe and culminates in their separation is interesting because it exemplifies gender 'disorder', and ultimately divests Jutta of her femininity. Hannes comes to look for Jutta and finds her at the bottom of a meadow, looking at a sign that warns of danger. Significantly, Jutta is far away from her house, her allocated place, which makes her vulnerable, but also gives her a distorted view of things. Hannes approaches Jutta from behind, putting his arms protectively around her shoulder. The next shot shows the couple from the front, with Jutta leaning against Hannes; she relinquishes her superiority for a moment, and asks him to stand by her and help her fight the governor. However, when Hannes questions her attitude, she turns towards him, an action suggestive of the growing rift. Jutta passionately defends her point, while Hannes presents himself as level-headed – finally even he erupts in an exasperated cry, telling her to be reasonable. She furiously turns against him, accusing him that he is using reason only to conceal his cowardice. A reverse cut reveals Hannes' shock; his lips pressed together in an attempt to control his feelings, he stands rigid, slightly higher up the slope, which indicates his moral superiority (Figure 3.3). His demeanour contrasts with Jutta's, who shouts abuse at him. A close-up of her face highlights her uncontrolled temper, catching the fury in her eyes as she taunts him as 'noble Khäls von Khälsberg', who in her eyes is nothing but a menial worker who wants to find an easy way to become master of an estate. Hannes breaks his silence to protest against the accusation, but Jutta turns her head away, demanding that he leave for good. Hannes' stiffness and frozen facial expression demonstrate his effort to control his temper, but he agrees to do so, although only after he has restored the water supply to the Salzer estate. He starts walking up the hill, but halfway

Figure 3.3: Hannes (Pero Alexander), rejected by his erratic lover, Jutta (Gisela Fackeldey), in *Hoch vom Dachstein*. Image: screenshot.

up he turns around, looks down on Jutta and tells her in a firm voice: 'I pity you. You are no longer a woman'. His words, which make Jutta cringe, seal the verdict that the Salzerhof and its mistress have run 'dry', and are thus impure. As promised, Hannes restores the water supply to the farm, but leaves 'selfish' Jutta for her young and innocent maid, Christl.[70]

It is no coincidence that our first encounter with Christl in the film is at a well, where she is collecting water. Christl is presented as virginal, and the *Heimatfilm's* narrative logic suggests that she, and not the self-assured widow Jutta, will gain Hannes' love. Yet, *Hoch vom Dachstein* does not leave it there, but underscores the message through the metaphor of salt. Even though salt serves as symbol of purification, it can take a contrary meaning, as it can turn soil barren and water bitter. With the water run dry and her relationship destroyed, all that is left to Jutta is the salt of the salt mines. Marrying the old Salzer made her rich, but left her without child and without motherly feelings. Jutta, however, just like Liesl in *Echo der Berge*, undergoes a process of purification. After she has sent Christl away in foul weather to punish her for winning Hannes' affection, Jutta repents and rescues Christl in a snowstorm. The snow implies her redemption – the whiteness cleanses her of sin. In the last scene, Jutta is shown sitting by the riverside, weeping tears of remorse. Her closeness to the water emphasises the positive change. Because Jutta repents and accepts her traditional female role, she is rewarded with an orphaned child, whom the wise shepherd sends for her consolation. Natural events have thus re-established traditional gender order, which is the guarantor of purity in the *Heimat*. Hannes, 'noble Khäls von Khälsberg', becomes his own master again and marries a dutiful, loving wife, who is in turn rewarded for her patience and kindness. Jutta, in exchange for celibacy, is allowed to remain in her position of power, and is given a child to foster her motherly qualities. The powerful message that *Heimatfilm* proclaims, and that resonated with audiences, is that purity is something that can be regained through acceptance of fate and acquiescence to and trust in nature.

Gendered Space: Nature and Masculinity

Nature is the main protagonist in *Heimatfilm*. Whereas in mountain film men prove their virility by fighting hostile nature, in *Heimatfilm* nature is generally not wild and erratic, but a cultured landscape that chiefly functions as narrative backdrop.[71] Nature needs to be inhabited and shaped by human beings in order to be considered *Heimat*, and therefore the films are populated by farmers, foresters, farm labourers and squires. However, the work of cultivating and tending the landscape is usually not shown. With a few exceptions, such as in the film *Bergkristall*, where Franz ploughs the fields and makes hay, or in *Das Jahr des Herrn* and *Die Sonnhofbäuerin*, we hardly ever see people 'working' the land. It is significant that the land in *Heimatfilm* does not provide food for the people; neither does hunting – this lack of food-gathering is a generic theme. The fact that the landscape is not productive – and perhaps need not be, as the people are seldom seen eating – demonstrates that the function of landscape is only symbolic.[72] Thus, the professions of the forester, foreman or squire act as signifiers of the symbiotic relationship between the people and the landscape; they suggest self-sufficiency and permanence. *Heimat* and the landscape represent a closed system that undergoes seasonal revolutions but remains essentially unchanged, making it particularly appealing to audiences in postwar Austria and West Germany, whose existence had been considerably disrupted by the war. Thus, like the historical costume film, Austrian *Heimatfilm* 'celebrates standstill as the best condition possible', as Steiner notes.[73]

Moltke has suggested that the emphasis on the visual and the beauty of the landscape accounts for the success of the genre.[74] The fact that reviewers who were very critical of postwar *Heimatfilm* as a whole praised the visual representation of Austria's landscape confirms 'the spectacular role of nature in the visual fabric of the *Heimatfilm*'.[75] The film *Bergkristall*, for example, was hailed for the 'pure, grand beauty' of its images of glaciers and meadows.[76] Critics complimented the makers of *Echo der Berge* for letting 'only mountains, forest and animals speak' and for presenting 'admirable' imagery of nature and animals.[77] 'Masterly', 'gracious' and 'exceedingly charming' are the terms frequently used by reviewers to describe the depictions of nature in Austrian *Heimatfilm*.[78]

The scenery in the films is varied, ranging from the impressive glaciers and snowy landscapes of *Bergkristall*, or the typical Alpine mountain pastures and forests populated by all sorts of wild animals as in *Echo der Berge*, to the charming, non-threatening foothills of the Alps in *Das Siegel Gottes* and *Das Jahr des Herrn*. The way nature is represented changes over time: in the earlier films, such as *Bergkristall*, *Hoch vom Dachstein* or *Der Sonnblick ruft*, the filmmakers assigned nature a more dominant role, as dramatically changing weather conditions herald the turn of events or underscore emotional climaxes. Towards the mid-1950s, as the advertising character of the genre became more important, nature turned increasingly into a scenic backdrop.[79] *Heimatfilms* came to represent 'Austria's calling cards', as a critic from the newspaper *Die Presse* described it, whose main aim was to sell the Austrian landscape to potential tourists.[80]

With their glorification of Austria's Alpine scenery, the films, as the reviews above demonstrate, provided a source of identification for Austrian people. After all, the beauty of the landscape was one of the few things the Austrians could take pride in after the war, especially because most of it had not been touched by military action. *Heimatfilm*, Büttner suggests, provided assurance that 'fashions or historic events may come and go, but the beauty of the country is timeless and invulnerable'.[81]

Figure 3.4: The forester (Rudolf Lenz) as a guardian of nature in *Echo der Berge*. Filmarchiv Austria.

Unlike tourist film, where nature is open to everyone, access to nature in *Heimatfilm* is strongly regulated according to gender. The genre depicts an intimate connection between man and nature, and uses the symbolic figure of the forester to affirm – and police – this claim (Figure 3.4). The forester acts as protector of the landscape; he patrols the forests and mountains and protects the deer against unauthorised hunting. The foresters and their adversaries, the poachers, are free to move everywhere – they enter forests, climb rocks and walk over mountain pastures and meadows. This 'freedom to roam' applies in principle to all men, even though older men make less use of this privilege. The virility which the genre ascribes to the foresters and poachers stems from their ability to explore the different forms of natural spaces.

In certain cases, children and virginal women are permitted to enter the various rural spaces, but, unlike men, their access is restricted and circumscribed. Generally, women remain in close proximity to their homes and villages, and are only allowed to explore different landscapes when accompanied by a male chaperon; if women ignore this rule, they are reprimanded. This happens to Liesl in *Echo der Berge*, when she skis down a mountain slope. She is stopped by the angry forester, Hubert, who tells her that it is forbidden to ski in the area as it might disturb the game; it is clearly not only concern for the deer that causes so much indignation, though, but also the fact that a woman has dared to trespass in the forester's territory.[82] However, peace is restored when Liesl apologises and promises to enter the mountains only in his company from then on. There are other occasions in *Heimatfilm* when women leave their surroundings and enter spaces which are usually reserved for men. These movements are usually justified by a specific goal: Sanna in *Bergkristall* repeatedly crosses a mountain pass to meet her lover from another valley, for example. Later on, her mother undertakes the same journey to visit Sanna and her children in their new home. The women's destination is clear, and they do not stray from the path. So, while the narrative may permit women to enter different landscapes, they are not allowed to wander around for simple enjoyment, as men are.

Women are typically confined to the garden and meadow; the forests and the mountains can only be accessed by men, or by women in the company of men. The forest can be seen as a symbol of the womb, a place where many animals breed, and where people meet for sexual encounters.[83] It is a place full of secrets and therefore perilous and frightening. This dark side, however, is not explored in postwar Austrian *Heimatfilm*. In fact, the forest features less prominently in Austrian than in German *Heimatfilms*, perhaps because the forest is first and foremost a symbol of German identity.[84] Nevertheless, it is always present in the background, and its absence from the immediate landscape is remarked upon, as in *Das Siegel Gottes*, where the wedding guests, marvelling at the beautiful landscape, suddenly stop at the sight of a barren slope; the emptiness, the result of a forest fire, causes interest and concern. The barren land is like a scar, arousing fears of castration and violation.

Mountains, like forests, are realms of masculinity in *Heimatfilm*. Mountains and rocks symbolise solitude, meditation and closeness to heaven.[85] The phallic shape of mountains is emblematic of the male, indicating strength and power, but the mountainous landscape also contains female elements: with the birth of Alpinism in the nineteenth century, the once-feared, inhospitable mountains became playgrounds for male heroism, and the Alpinists and skiing teachers prime examples of virile masculinity.[86] The sport of conquering 'virgin' mountain tops and skiing down untouched mountainsides gave mountains a female connotation. The mountain films of the 1920s and 1930s glorify male heroism, comradeship and rivalry, but also have a strong misogynist and elitist undercurrent.[87] In *Heimatfilm*, the themes of comradeship and male heroism play a minor role, but both mountain film and *Heimatfilm* stress the view that the further men venture and the higher they climb, the more masculine (in the traditional sense) they are. In both genres the mountains serve as the stage where male rivalry is played out, but the mountain film foregrounds the battle between nature and Alpinists. In *Heimatfilm*, on the other hand, the mountains are a backdrop to conflict resolution between men. The classic shoot-out between forester and poacher, as depicted in *Heimatland, Berg-*

kristall and *Echo der Berge*, usually takes place between steep rocks that indicate male territory.

However, the mountains, especially the mountain tops, are also a place for inner reflection and catharsis. In *Gipfelkreuz* (1948), Fritz erects a cross on a mountain top to expiate the sins of his brutal father; Hannes in *Hoch vom Dachstein* finds inner peace on the top of a snow-capped mountain, where he decides to declare his love for Christl and leave Jutta; and the film *Der Sonnblick ruft* focuses on the wise old Maylechner, who lives a lonely but fulfilled life at an observatory on Austria's highest mountain, highlighting his sense of duty and virtue.[88]

But why are forests and mountains generally forbidden territories for women in *Heimatfilm*? A straightforward explanation would be that women, unlike the forester or shepherd, have no professional purpose in the forests or mountains. We could also argue that because the forest symbolises maternity and mountains virginity, there is no need for women to enter these territories. However, a psychoanalytic reading would suggest that women are prevented from entering them unguarded because they are perceived as carriers of impurity, and are thus in danger of polluting them. Men's role is to guard the forest and mountains and control access to them. Their intimate relationship with nature legitimises men's superior position of power in the gender hierarchy. Men's closeness to nature is also suggested by their outward appearance. Unlike the colourful dirndl dress worn by the women, the men's clothes are very earthy. The green, brown and grey shades of the men's loden jackets and leather trousers reflect the colours of nature and function like protective mimicry, enabling men to reunite with nature, the symbol of the idealised mother (Figure 3.4).[89] The rather thick and stiff fabrics of traditional clothing – milled wool and leather – and the cut of the costumes give men a sturdy appearance, suggesting physical strength and power; a stiff felt hat, often decorated with chamois hair, adds height.

In *Heimatfilm*, a close connection with nature often denotes a virtuous character: all positively portrayed men work not just in open nature but also in harmony with it. In *Das Siegel Gottes*, Michael's love for animals marks him as a morally upright man, as does his positioning in the landscape. Michael (Alexander Trojan) bridles horses, walks across the fields and even spends his spare time outside. Michael's special relationship with nature draws him to open spaces and earns him the love of the squire's daughter (Figure 3.5). His boots are emblematic of his freedom to wander the fields, meadows and forests. His rival in love, Stefan von Mansfeld (Robert Lindner), on the other hand, usually enters the countryside on horseback, an indication of his higher social status, but also of his alienation from nature. Mansfeld's lack of empathy with nature is disclosed when he forces his foreman, who has accidentally dropped a burning lantern in the forest, to move on, causing a forest fire. Mansfeld is often depicted inside the house or in the groomed garden: territories

Figure 3.5: The priest (Josef Meinrad) blesses the union between Andrea (Hilde Mikulicz) and Michael (Alexander Trojan) in *Das Siegel Gottes*. Filmarchiv Austria.

that generic tradition assigns to women and old men. The stone terrace on which he proposes to Andrea (Hilde Mikulicz) reflects his gloomy character and coldness; it comes as no surprise that Andrea rejects his offer and runs to Michael, who, tellingly, is waiting in a blooming meadow nearby.[90]

Michael and Andrea share a love for nature and for animals; she greets his gift of a little puppy dog with much joy, whereas she refuses the (cold) bracelet that Mansfeld wants to give her. The degree of closeness to nature is thus indicative of masculine status in the order of the *Heimat*: the closer to nature a man is, the higher are his masculine faculties, and hence the higher he is positioned in the male hierarchy, which makes him more attractive to women.

Conclusion

Austrian *Heimatfilm* showcases law-abiding men who are principled and who adhere to moral values. However, as Fehrenbach has pointed out, this 'moral masculinity' in postwar *Heimatfilm* is essentially humanitarian, and thus distinctly different from the Nazi civil servant who 'just followed orders'.[91] Austrian *Heimatfilm* redeems men of their guilt and reintegrates them into the community, a message that must have been of fundamental appeal to postwar Austrian audiences mired in guilt and recrimination. Blame is usually assigned to an outsider who disrespects the laws of the community – usually a poacher or stranger; the perpetrator is designated as the 'other' who, if he fails to repent, is 'accidentally' killed or expelled from the *Heimat*.

By granting only men full access to the different landscapes, and by presenting them as guardians of nature, Austrian *Heimatfilm* claims a strong and intimate connection between masculinity and nature. This relationship constitutes men's superior status in the *Heimat* and suggests that it is not only tradition but nature itself that supports patriarchy and traditional gender relations. It is not charm, musicality or beauty that characterises the masculine ideal in *Heimatfilm*, but physical and mental strength, rationality and emotional control. However, while postwar Austrian *Heimatfilm* outwardly affirms the hitherto hegemonic standard of 'hard' masculinity, a closer analysis reveals a much more ambiguous stance towards this masculine ideal. Even though postwar *Heimatfilm* highlights male strength and virility, it is also suspicious of traditional masculinity, expressing fear of its inherent aggression and violence. As a result, *Heimatfilm* narratives force men into passivity to test their ability to repress aggression and conquer their emotions. Self-control and a willingness to sacrifice personal happiness are defining elements of *Heimatfilm*'s masculine ideal. At the same time, however, *Heimatfilm* presents empathy and amicability as desirable masculine attributes, softening the previously venerated 'hard' masculinity in order to make it more fitting for postwar society, and more acceptable to women. Postwar Austrian *Heimatfilm* could thus be described as the masculine form of melodrama minus the emotional outbursts. Perhaps this is what made it particularly appealing to female audiences: men fighting inner turmoil while retaining the appearance of strong masculinity.

Notes

1. See G. Koch, K. Konz, W. Öhrle, G. Schmidt, and B. Wilczek. l. 1989. 'Die Fünfziger Jahre. Heide und Silberwald', in W. Kaschuba and D. Bahlinger (eds), *Der deutsche Heimatfilm. Bildwelten und Weltbilder. Bilder, Texte, Analysen zu 70 Jahren deutscher Filmgeschichte*, Tübingen: Tübinger Vereinigung für Volkskunde, 72.
2. See W. Kaschuba. 1989. 'Bildwelten als Weltbilder', in W. Kaschuba and D. Bahlinger (eds), *Der deutsche Heimatfilm. Bildwelten und Weltbilder. Bilder, Texte, Analysen zu 70 Jahren deutscher Filmgeschichte*, Tübingen: Tübinger Vereinigung für Volkskunde, 7.
3. See Seidl, 1987, 64–66.
4. The Archbishop of Vienna attended the premieres of *Das Siegel Gottes* (1949) and *Das Jahr des Herrn* (1950), the latter was also attended by Austria's chancellor and vice-chancellor.
5. 'Die Sonnhofbäuerin', *Wiener Kurier*, 24 January 1949.
6. R. Weys, R., 'Die Berge leben', *Die Presse*, 28 November 1954.
7. In a sociological survey of the cinema-going habits of Viennese children and teenagers from 1953, girls under fourteen named the genre of 'mountain film' (here obviously a synonym for *Heimatfilm*) as their favourite, while boys ranked it seventh. However, the majority of girls went to the cinema accompanied by a parent, so this choice partly reflects the preferences of the parents. See Amt für Kultur, Volksbildung und Schulverwaltung der Stadt Wien, 1959, 67. The trade journal *Paimann's Filmlisten* recommended the films *Dein Herz ist meine Heimat* and *Hoch vom Dachstein* explicitly for a family audience, while *Das Mädchen vom Pfarrhof* was thought to appeal to 'friends of emotional entertainment'. See 'Dein Herz ist meine Heimat', *Paimann's Filmlisten*, 2 December 1953, Nr. 2016, 109; 'Hoch vom Dachstein', *Paimann's Filmlisten*, 17 March 1953, Nr. 1970, 17; 'Das Mädchen vom Pfarrhof ', *Paimann's Filmlisten*, 5 October 1955, Nr. 2155, 109.
8. See H. Fehrenbach. 1995. *Cinema in Democratizing Germany: Reconstructing National Identity after Hitler*, Chapel Hill: University of North Carolina Press, 149. According to Fehrenbach, young men, who accounted for a considerable part of the audiences in the mid-1950s, preferred active American heroes, and found male characters in *Heimatfilm* too passive. See ibid., 165–166.
9. I use the original Austrian title. See particularly Bliersbach's excellent case study of *Grün ist die Heide* and *Förster vom Silberwald*: G. Bliersbach. 1985. *So grün war die Heide... Der deutsche Nachkriegsfilm in neuer Sicht*, Weinheim, Basel: Beltz Verlag; see also M. Fiedler. 1995. *Heimat im deutschen Film: Ein Mythos zwischen Regression und Utopie*, Coppengrave: Coppi Verlag; W. Kaschuba and D. Bahlinger (eds). 1989. *Der deutsche Heimatfilm. Bildwelten und Weltbilder. Bilder, Texte, Analysen zu 70 Jahren deutscher Filmgeschichte*, Tübingen: Tübinger Vereinigung für Volkskunde; J.v. Moltke. 2005. *No Place Like Home: Locations of Heimat in German Cinema*, Berkeley: University of California Press, 52–102; J. Trimborn. 1998. *Der deutsche Heimatfilm der fünfziger Jahre: Motive, Symbole und Handlungsmuster*, Cologne: Teiresias.
10. See Moltke, 2005; Bergfelder, 2006, 40–43. R. Palfreyman. 2010. 'Links and Chains: Trauma between the Generations in the Heimat Mode', in P. Cooke and M. Silberman (eds), *Screening War: Perspectives on German Suffering*, Rochester, N.Y.: Camden House.

11. See Moltke, 2005, 117.
12. Ibid., 123.
13. Bergfelder, 2006, 43, also 42.
14. See Steiner, 1987; Bergfelder, 2006, 40; Moltke, 2005, 22, 124; Palfreyman, 2010, 154, 159.
15. For the nuanced meanings of the term *Heimat* and the important role the notion of *Heimat* has played in the formation of German cultural identity see the informative study by C. Applegate. 1990. *A Nation of Provincials: The German Idea of Heimat*, Berkeley: University of California Press.
16. See Applegate, 1990, 4; Moltke, 2005, 9.
17. Applegate, 1990, 5.
18. According to Fiedler, films depicting *Heimat* were not used more frequently for propagandistic purposes than other genres; however, like other genres in Nazi cinema, they often featured negative Jewish or Polish stereotypes, or illustrated the necessity for subordination to a leader. See Fiedler, 1995, 22.
19. Moltke, 2005, 8.
20. See Bliersbach, 1985, 45.
21. See I. Reicher and S. Schachinger. 1999. 'Heimat Film and Mountain Films', in T. Elsaesser (ed.), *The BFI Companion to German Cinema*, London: BFI, 133; Bliersbach, 1985, 45.
22. See Kaschuba, 1989, 9.
23. See Fiedler, 1995, 17–19; also Kaschuba, 1989, 9–10.
24. Reicher and Schachinger claim that *Heimatfilm* is 'unique to Germany'. Reicher and Schachinger, 1999, 133; see also Kaschuba, 1989, 9.
25. See C. Beindorf. 2001. *Terror des Idylls. Die kulturelle Konstruktion von Gemeinschaften im Heimatfilm und Landsbygdsfilm 1930–1960*, Baden-Baden: Nomos Verlag.
26. Hake, 2008, 119.
27. According to Seidl, West German companies produced significantly more *Heimatfilms* in Austria than films of other genres. See Seidl, 1987, 66.
28. See ibid., 66–67.
29. See Fiedler, 1995, 12.
30. 'Die Sennerin von St. Kathrein', *Paimann's Filmlisten*, 1955; 'Bergkristall', *Arbeiterzeitung*, 30 October 1949.
31. 'Heimatland', *Die Volksstimme*, 27 August 1955.
32. This number includes two *Überläufer*.
33. Fiedler, 1995, 36; A. Graser. 1989. 'Filmtechnik und Filmsprache im *Heimatfilm*', in W. Kaschuba and D. Bahlinger (eds), *Der deutsche Heimatfilm. Bildwelten und Weltbilder. Bilder, Texte, Analysen zu 70 Jahren deutscher Filmgeschichte*, Tübingen: Tübinger Vereinigung für Volkskunde, 227.
34. See Fiedler, 1995, 36; Graser, 1989, 226.
35. See Brecht, 2005, 159.
36. See Fiedler, 1995, 36.
37. For example Arnold Fanck's *Stürme über dem Montblanc* (Avalanche, 1930) or Leni Riefenstahl's *Das blaue Licht* (The Blue Light, 1932). See Kracauer, S. 1984 [1947]. *Von Caligari zu Hitler: Eine psychologische Geschichte des deutschen Films*, Frankfurt am Main: Suhrkamp Verlag, 271–272.
38. E. Riederer, 'Das Abenteuer vom "Bergkristall". Österreichische Bergfilm-Avantgarde in Tirol', *Die Presse*, 16 October 1949.
39. For the discussion see the article above as well as 'Zaghafte Vorhut. Zu dem österreichischen Film "Bergkristall"', *Montag Ausgabe*, 31 October 1949; '"Bergkristall" – österreichischer Avantgarde-Film', *Wiener Zeitung*, 25 October 1949.
40. For a detailed outline of the production of *Echo der Berge* see Steiner, 1987, 160–170.
41. The films *Die Sennerin von St. Kathrein* (1955) and the German *Försterliesel* (1956), both directed by Herbert B. Fredersdorf, have an almost identical cast and display a very

similar use of images of nature and wild animals – clearly an attempt to buy into the success of *Echo der Berge*.

42. E. Büttner. 2007a. 'Angriff auf die Ordnung', *Filmhimmel Österreich*, 55, 8.
43. See E. Riederer, 'Das Abenteuer vom "Bergkristall". Österreichische Bergfilm-Avantgarde in Tirol', *Die Presse*, 16 October 1949.
44. See Barthel, 1986, 163; Bergfelder, 2005, 65.
45. 'Bergkristall', *Arbeiterzeitung*, 30 October 1949. For the production see E. Riederer, 'Das Abenteuer vom "Bergkristall". Österreichische Bergfilm-Avantgarde in Tirol', *Die Presse*, 16 October 1949.
46. See B. Balázs. 1984. 'Der Fall Dr. Fanck. Vorwort zu Arnold Fancks Filmbuch "Stürme über dem Montblanc" (1931)', in H.H. Diederichs, W. Gersch and M. Nagy (eds), *Béla Balázs. Schriften zum Film*, Berlin: Henschel, vol. 2, 288.
47. 'Bergkristall – österreichischer Avantgarde-Film', *Wiener Zeitung*, 25 October 1949.
48. See 'Mitautor Adalbert Stifter: Bergkristall', *Weltpresse*, 25 October 1949.
49. See E. Riederer, 'Das Abenteuer vom "Bergkristall". Österreichische Bergfilm-Avantgarde in Tirol', *Die Presse*, 16 October 1949.
50. Palfreyman, 2010, 150.
51. See Beindorf, 2001, 236.
52. See Kaschuba, 1989, 11.
53. See Bliersbach, 1985, 39.
54. 'Bergkristall', *Illustrierter Filmkurier*, 1949, Nr. 704.
55. 'Gipfelkreuz', *Illustrierter Filmkurier*, 1948, Nr. 513.
56. Palfreyman, 2010, 149, 150.
57. For an analysis of the figure of the poacher and its position inside the Alpine community see the interesting socio-historical study by R. Girtler. 2000. *Wilderer. Rebellen in den Bergen*, Vienna: Böhlau.
58. See Fehrenbach, 1995, 161.
59. With the exception of *Bergkristall* or *Die Sonnhofbäuerin*.
60. Palfreyman, 2010, 149.
61. Fiedler, 1995, 40.
62. See also Bliersbach, 1985, 45.
63. See, for example, the very informative analysis by Steven Cohan on how Hollywood film dealt with male aggression after the Second World War. S. Cohan. 1997. *Masked Men: Masculinity and the Movies in the Fifties*, Bloomington: Indiana University Press.
64. An informative analysis of gendered body language is provided by G. Mühlen-Achs. 2003. *Wer führt? Körpersprache und die Ordnung der Geschlechter*, Munich: Verlag Frauenoffensive. See also the inspiring book by M. Wex. 1979. *'Let's Take Back Our Space': 'Female' and 'Male' Body Language as a Result of Patriarchal Structures*, Berlin: Frauenliteraturverlag Hermine Fees.
65. Critics noted the 'stiffness' and 'stiltedness' of the dialogue in *Echo der Berge*. See, for example, R. Weys, 'Die Berge leben', *Die Presse*, 18 November 1954.
66. Alternative titles were *Wetterleuchten vom Dachstein*, *Die Herrin vom Salzerhof* and *Die Hochzeit vom Salzerhof*.
67. See G.D. Roth. 1985. 'Nachrufe: "Anton Kutter"', *Mitteilungen der Astronomischen Gesellschaft*, 64, 9–10.
68. 'Hoch vom Dachstein', *Paimann's Filmlisten*, 17 March 1953, Nr. 1970, 17.
69. The following analysis is inspired by D. Trotter. 2000. *Cooking with Mud: The Idea of Mess in Nineteenth-century Art and Fiction*, Oxford: Oxford University Press.
70. 'Hoch vom Dachstein', *Paimann's Filmlisten*, 17 March 1953, Nr. 1970, 17.
71. See Seidl, 1987, 60.
72. A critic described *Die Sonnhofbäuerin* as 'a good Austrian farmer's film', praising the 'healthy, hefty' dialogues and the 'strong symbolic power of the visual language', which were perceived to be sufficient to give a realistic picture of rural Austria. See 'Uebelrie-

chender [*sic*] Wochenaufruf für Film-Normalverbraucher', *Montag Ausgabe*, 31 January 1948.

73. I. Steiner. 2005. 'Österreich-Bilder im Film der Besatzungszeit', in K. Moser (ed.), *Besetzte Bilder. Film, Kultur und Propaganda in Österreich 1945–1955*, Vienna: Filmarchiv Austria Steiner, 206.

74. See Moltke, 2005, 83.

75. Ibid., 83

76. 'Bergkristall', *Arbeiterzeitung*, 30 October 1949.

77. 'Aus der Filmwelt "Echo der Berge"', *Wiener Montag*, 29 November 1954.

78. 'Weihnachtsgeschenk des österreichischen Films "Das Jahr des Herrn"', *Die Union*, 28 December 1950; 'Das Siegel Gottes, *Weltpresse*, 10 February 1949; 'Das Siegel Gottes', *Wiener Tageszeitung*, 10 February 1949; '"Das Siegel Gottes". Ein österreichischer Film aus katholischem Geist', *Die Furche*, 19 February 1949.

79. See Steiner, 2005, 206.

80. 'Die Berge leben', *Die Presse*, 28 November 1954. See Beindorf, 2001, 231–234.

81. See E. Büttner. 2005. 'Harmonie, die Zündstoff birgt – *Der Heimatfilm* der 1950er Jahre', in G. Matzner-Holzer (ed.), *Verfreundete Nachbarn: Österreich-Deutschland. Ein Verhältnis*, Vienna, 135.

82. 'The hunter has to be first and foremost a gamekeeper', noted one critic, emphasising the protective element of the hunter's profession. 'Ferner liefen: "Echo der Berge"', *Der Abend*, 30 November 1954.

83. See De Vries, 1974, 199.

84. See A. Lehmann. 1999. *Von Menschen und Bäumen. Die Deutschen und ihr Wald*, Reinbek: Rowohlt.

85. See De Vries, 1974, 329–330.

86. Skiing and mountain climbing received their chauvinist and sexist connotations through Alpinism and, especially, the militarisation of Alpine sports in the First World War. See G. Strohmeier. 1999. 'Schneelandschaften. Alltag, romantische Bilder und politsche Ladungen' [electronic version], in R. Grossmann (ed.), *Kulturlandschaftsforschung*, vol. 5, Vienna: Springer. http://www.iff.ac.at/oe/ifftexte/band5gs.htm, retrieved 12 April 2012.

87. See Fiedler, 1995, 17.

88. See Steiner, 1987, 110.

89. For a psychoanalytic reading of nature in *Heimatfilm* see Bliersbach, 1985, and Fiedler, 1995.

90. According to the review in the *Weltpresse*, Robert Lindner, 'who plays the knavish Stephan von Mansfeld a bit too chillingly … looks pale in comparison' to Alexander Trojan as Michael. See 'Das Siegel Gottes', *Weltpresse*, 10 February 1949.

91. Fehrenbach, 1995, 155.

Chapter 4

Tourist Film

Tourist film has a long tradition in Austrian cinema. The film adaptation of the musical *Im Weissen Rössl* (The White Horse Inn, 1926), directed by Richard Oswald, is certainly one of the most famous, and was remade four times between 1935 and 1960.[1] However, 'tourist film' is not a recognised genre or industrial category, but a term I apply retrospectively to describe a specific type of film that deals with the holiday experiences of urban tourists. Film scholars have customarily considered these light-hearted comedies about people spending holidays in the countryside as a simple variation of the *Heimatfilm* genre, as both types of films lend particular importance to the landscape.[2] Yet tourist film and *Heimatfilm* display crucial differences in narrative patterns and visual style, as well as in the way they deal with modernity and tradition. Even though Johannes von Moltke has convincingly shown how specific *Heimatfilms* negotiate 'peace between restoration and modernity', the genre is still essentially retrospective, whereas tourist film is forward looking.[3] *Heimatfilm* promotes conservative values and patriarchal order, and gives a rather static view of community and society. Tourist film, on the other hand, embraces modernity and promotes change and mobility. In *Heimatfilm*, the focus is on a local, rural community that looks upon non-locals with suspicion, whereas in tourist film urban citizens take centre stage as holiday makers, and are portrayed in a positive light. In tourist film the urban is not a threat to the rural community, as it is in *Heimatfilm*, but a herald of a new and better world. The crucial differences between *Heimatfilm* and tourist film have been dismissed by scholars such as Steiner, Moltke and Bergfelder, who classify tourist film merely as a variation of *Heimatfilm*. Yet there *are* differences between the two genres, which close analysis of the film texts reveals, and this means that looking at tourist film as a critical category in its own right is warranted.

While tourist film and *Heimatfilm* may have had a shared purpose, namely to sell the Austrian landscape to potential tourists, each of them fulfilled specific and unique functions. This chapter will discuss the role tourist film played in popular cinema and investigate its popular appeal.

It will demonstrate that tourist film, perhaps because it is not a genre with long historical roots, was very responsive to social shifts, and therefore much quicker to incorporate new attitudes than other genres. This is especially noticeable in the representations of gender and gender relations, which show that tourist film functioned as a kind of sensor of societal developments. At a time when the old social order seemed in tatters, these films promoted female independence and gender equality, even though those participating in their production were mostly male; it even hinted, however obliquely, at the possibility of alternative, non-heterosexual sexualities. Nevertheless, tourist film was also quick to revive traditional gender models when Austria's economic recovery fuelled a reversal in gender relations.

The Attraction of Tourist Film

The number of tourist films produced between 1945 and 1955 is relatively small: only twelve films – that is, approximately 6 per cent of total film output – produced in this ten-year period fall into this category. Still, their influence on other genres was considerable: many visual or narrative topoi typical of tourist film can be found in other Austrian films from the same period. Tourist film has much in common with romantic comedies, and most directors of postwar tourist film were seasoned filmmakers who had a professional background in light-hearted entertainment cinema; for others, such as the two young filmmakers Franz Antel and Rudolf Nussgruber (for whom tourist film would become their trademark), it was the entry-ticket into commercial filmmaking.

The first Austrian film produced after the war was a tourist film: *Glaube an mich* (Believe in Me, 1946). Tourist film suited the difficult conditions of production in postwar Austria, and *Glaube an mich* was no exception. Mostly shot in outside locations, the film was cheap to produce and, in addition, aimed at providing escapist entertainment for a disillusioned and hungry audience. The film's title can be read as a plea to put faith in the rebirth of Austria and its film industry. This is precisely the effect it did *not* achieve, according to the left-wing *Arbeiterzeitung*, which critically commented that the film's moronic story line 'makes it difficult to believe in a rebirth of Austrian film art'.[4] *Glaube an mich* was followed by a number of more successful tourist films in the early postwar years, among which *Der Hofrat Geiger* (Privy Councillor Geiger, 1947) remained the most popular for some time, attracting large audiences in Austria and abroad and inspiring two remakes.[5] The genre's popularity after the war can be explained by the optimistic mood and light-hearted humour of the films, which contrasted with the rather grim postwar reality.[6] In addition, the fact that (early) postwar tourist film was progressive in its depiction of gender, presenting men and women as essentially equal and subscribing to the idea of female independence, might have made it especially attractive for women. After all, women constituted a large proportion of cinema audiences in the first years after the war, as many Austrian men had died or had not yet returned from imprisonment; but it is safe to assume that the beautiful settings accounted for much of the genre's popularity with a broad audience. The films offered a kind of 'ersatz holiday' for the urban citizens of the war-damaged cities, who simply could not afford to go on holiday for a change of scenery, but went to the cinema instead.

Indeed, the main purpose of tourist film was, and had always been, to sell beautiful landscapes to the cinema-going public. The genre's modernity and optimistic outlook are directly related to, and probably arise from, this objective. The producers of *Glaube an mich* explicitly drew attention to the film's advertising function: an image of Austria was to be sold, at this point not so much to attract foreign tourists, but to rehabilitate Austria as a nation by deflecting attention from political issues to the beautiful countryside.[7] Unscathed by war, the beauty of the landscape reflected positively on the nation, and attested to its innocence and that of its inhabitants – a view that was not only implied in tourist film, but also expressed in contemporary media and political discourse.

There are noticeable differences between earlier and later tourist films: those produced in the immediate postwar era, from 1946 to 1949, such as *Der Hofrat Geiger, Der Herr Kanzleirat* (Sir Kanzleirat, 1948) or *Rendezvous im Salzkammergut* (Rendezvous at the Salzkammergut, 1948), convey a feeling of pride in one's country. The urban tourists in these films are Austrians and show a strong connection to *their* countryside, either because they have holidayed there before or because they have come to visit a friend or relative. These films established continuity between the present and the pre-war past; they plugged into the memories of the audience in order to increase the films' appeal – and they did so quite successfully, as the reviews indicate. The critic of the *Wiener Zeitung* marvelled that 'so many generations of couples have enjoyed happiness for one or more summers' at the shores of Lake Wolfgang, citing this personal resonance as a key selling point of the film *Kleiner Schwindel am Wolfgangsee* (Little Swindle at Lake Wolfgang, 1949).[8] There was another reason for their popularity: due to strict export restrictions, these early tourist films first and foremost targeted a national audience, providing reassurance that the war had left their beautiful countryside intact.

Büttner and Dewald suggest that around 1950 the meaning of the imagery changed: in the new decade, the landscape was increasingly turned into a commodity that profited the tourist industry and national economy.[9] In *Eva erbt das Paradies* (Eva Inherits Paradise, 1951), the fight for the paying customer is already on, and Eva and her female team have to resort to all sorts of manipulations to lure the paying guest into their grandly named Hotel Paradise.[10] The Austrian holidaymaker had by then been largely replaced by the German tourist who looked differently at the Austrian landscape. The films' perspective shifted to that of a consumer who does not identify with the country he is visiting. An explanation for this change in the meaning of the landscape can be found in economic development: by the beginning of the 1950s, export and travel restrictions between West Germany and Austria had largely been removed; by this time, West Germany's 1948 monetary reform had sparked a remarkable economic boom that turned the West Germans (once again) into attractive customers for Austria's tourist industry.[11] Furthermore, aid received through the Marshall Plan helped to revive Austria's tourist industry in the western and southern regions. The film industry jumped at the opportunity to earn money by promoting Austria's scenic beauty to the German audience.[12]

Probably because tourist film openly addressed potential West German tourists from the early 1950s onwards, it was the first genre to show signs of 'Germanisation': an increasing deployment of German actors, the inclusion of German characters and locations in the narrative and a growing standardisation of dialects spoken in the films. Aesthetically, the postwar Austrian tourist film marked no break with the visual style of the Ufa entertainment cinema of the Third Reich. Indeed, the makers of the early winter-tourist films attempted to reproduce Ufa's polished style with lavish decorations and costumes; yet, due to the material and financial constraints of the immediate postwar period, the mise en scène in these films is lacklustre and the overall quality is poor.

However, continuities with Third Reich cinema are not only apparent on stylistic or personal levels: rarely did the Nazi past shine through as literally as in the first postwar Austrian tourist film, *Glaube an mich*. Its Austro-Hungarian director, Géza von Cziffra, faced with severe lack of film stock when he started filming in January 1946, bought raw film material on the black market. When Cziffra and his team inspected the negatives after the on-location shooting in the Arlberg mountains, they were shocked to see Wehrmacht troops with swastika flags marching through the skiing scenes they had filmed. The film stock, showing traces of earlier filming, had obviously been exposed before.[13] Cziffra's team had unintentionally created a work of art with a strong symbolic message. Their efforts to efface all traces of the Nazi past by producing a cheerful winter comedy had failed; instead, remnants of the Nazi era sneaked their way into the ostensibly apolitical tourist film, serving as symbolic reminder of the strong continuities between past and present. Sadly, the doubly exposed scenes were discarded by Cziffra.

Tourist film is a very coherent genre, which can be divided into summer and winter films. The latter, with images of daring skiers racing down steep slopes and glistening snow covering the landscape, bear some resemblance to mountain films, but the emphasis is on the social aspect of skiing and holidaying rather than on the struggle between man and nature. Winter holidays in tourist films are still exclusive to the upper-classes, an issue that is taken up by *Drei Männer im Schnee* (Three Men in the Snow,

1955), which makes fun of the snobbishness of hoteliers and hotel guests.[14] Summer tourist films, on the other hand, are much more democratic. They carry the message that summer holidays are for all people, rich and poor alike.

Visually, medium-long shots and medium close-ups dominate Austrian tourist film, while extreme close-ups and high and low angle shots are used sparsely, and usually only for the few emotional climaxes, with the exception of the film *Wintermelodie* (Winter Melody, 1947), a skiing film that bears close resemblance to the mountain films of the 1920s and 1930s. In tourist film, male and female characters are usually positioned at the same height and shot at eye level to imply their equality. Deep-focus cinematography draws attention to the landscape, which mainly serves as illustrative background.

The majority of tourist films produced between 1945 and 1955 were summer tourist films – the ability to shoot in outside locations meant that they were cheap to produce, as no studios were needed.[15] In addition, summer was still the most important season for Austrian tourism.[16] The summer tourist films are mostly set in the Austrian lake districts of the Salzkammergut or Carinthia, i.e., in western and southern Austria respectively. *Zwei in einem Auto* (Two in a Car, 1951) is the only production in which the protagonists venture further afield, travelling to the Italian Riviera.[17] In reality, however, Italy did not replace Austria as a prime destination for Austrian (and German) holiday makers until the 1960s, when travelling abroad became more affordable.[18] In the 1940s and 1950s, Austrian tourists largely remained within the borders of their own country, travelling from the East to the more scenic and – importantly – more affluent West.

Travelling towards a Better Future

Mirroring the increased (physical and social) mobility of postwar society, mobility is a key theme in summer tourist films, which thus convey a strong sense of adventure and freedom. The growth in motorised travel in the 1950s changed the way people spent their holidays: a contemporary analyst of tourism described the modern motor tourist as 'restless', only staying for short periods and always venturing further.[19] Postwar tourist film promoted this modern way of holidaying. *Eva erbt das Paradies* and *Verliebter Sommer* (Loving Couples, 1954) both advertise the joys of camping, which was rapidly gaining in popularity, especially among younger people. With the caravan as 'home on wheels' and the camping cooker as symbol of the hearth, travelling became an 'extension of the domestic zone'.[20] Camping in open nature, as the films illustrate, facilitates the breakdown of barriers between the private and public spheres, which partly accounts for its pleasure – what is usually hidden, be it housework or family routines, comes into the open and is visible to everyone.

The summer tourist films attribute as much importance to the journey as to the final destination. Travelling is fun because the traveller is freed from the habitual; it is also worthwhile because travelling often ends with finding a husband or wife, a new home, a job or all of these combined, as in *Rendezvous im Salzkammergut* or *Eva erbt das Paradies*. Thus, at a time when the state could provide little in terms of material support or jobs, the tourist film encouraged people to take matters in their own hands, promising fortunes to those who ventured on a journey. The films implied that summer holidays and travelling are not just for the rich, but for everybody, a message that is particularly stressed in the tourist films produced in the early postwar period: you may be poor or even broke, but this is no reason to stay at home.[21] The two young female office workers in *Rendezvous im Salzkammergut*, Fritzi and Gretl, who lose their meagre earnings at the races, tramp happily along a dusty country road towards their holiday destination, carefree and optimistic. The two friends Brösecke and Walzl in *Zwei in einem Auto* also gamble, but are luckier. They invest their small winnings in an old car to travel to Italy. Fortune – coming from an unexpected inheritance, or a win or loss on the pools – is clearly a recurring motif in tourist films; however, it does not determine the protagonists' actions. Indeed, tourist narratives clearly show that luck is fickle: what may seem like a stroke of luck (the inheritance of a hotel in *Eva erbt das Paradies*, for example) turns out to be a nightmare (the hotel is in dire need of expensive restoration) and vice versa.

The protagonists in tourist films succeed because they are optimistic and make the best of a situation. The fact that money is lost or won is ultimately of little importance, because the key message of tourist film is that the essential things are free. Transport is provided by generous fellow countrymen, home-made sandwiches satisfy hunger and camping by the road is inexpensive and, above all, a good way to meet like-minded people (as in *Verliebter Sommer*). Crucially, it is the landscape – the sun, the valley with the blue lake, the snow-capped mountain, the green forest – that is 'Alles kostenlos', all for free, as Fritzi and Gretl sing jubilantly on their way to the 'golden' West in *Rendezvous im Salzkammergut* (Figure 4.1)

Economic constraints informed the production of these early films, although on-location reports convey the same air of blithe unconcern as the films themselves. When *Der Herr Kanzleirat* was shot in Carinthia, members of the crew had to spend their first night in empty rail carriages, due to a lack of accommodation.[22] The production team of *Rendezvous im Salzkammergut* faced a similar problem, and some actors were forced to find accommodation in the local prison, as one journalist cheerfully reported.[23]

Celebration of Female Independence in Rendezvous im Salzkammergut

No other tourist film conveys these feelings of optimism, carefree spirit and female independence more strongly than *Rendezvous im Salzkammer-*

gut. The critics complained about the superficial plot, a lack of artistic ambition and too many musical interludes. Yet, as the *Weltpresse* had to admit, Alfred Stöger, the director and producer of the film, had not set out to revolutionise Austrian cinema, but to produce a successful entertainment movie.[24] And popular it was, as the attendance figures show.[25] It was one of many genres Stöger tried his hand at in postwar Austria. He had started off as a stage actor in Germany in the 1920s before moving into the film business in the 1930s, when he predominantly directed short features as well as some feature-length films. His career never really took off during the Third Reich, but he became a productive director and producer in postwar Austria. The peppy script of *Rendezvous im Salzkammergut* was written by the Italian Aldo von Pinelli, a prolific writer of lyrics and scripts for German film since the 1930s. Among Pinelli's successes were the lyrics for the popular Ufa musical comedies *Wir machen Musik* (We Play Music, Germany, 1942) and *Der weiße Traum* (The White Dream, Germany, 1943). The fact that the admired Austrian composer Robert Stolz wrote the musical score for *Rendezvous im Salzkammergut* counted in its favour in the eyes of the Austrian critics. The leading parts were given to young Austrian actors at the beginning of their careers, with the exception of Hans Holt, who had already played some leading dramatic and comical roles.

Rendezvous im Salzkammergut tells the story of two young, female office workers in Vienna, Gretl Wiesinger (Inge Konradi) and Fritzi Werner (Herta Mayen). They plan to spend their three-week holiday in St. Gilgen, a village in the lake district of the Salzkammergut. Gretl is loosely engaged to the boyish Peter Baumkirchner, played by Josef Meinrad, whom she met briefly in Vienna the previous winter and who is to inherit the hotel Seehotel in St. Gilgen. Because of a lack of funds, she and her friend Fritzi make their way to their destination on foot and by hitching rides (Figure 4.1). As progress is slow and Fritzi suffers from blisters, they eventually separate. Fritzi manages to get a ride with a travelling salesman to St. Gilgen, where she is mistaken for the new waitress of the Seehotel. She grabs the unexpected chance of employment and starts working at the hotel, much to the delight of Peter, who soon forgets about Gretl. While Fritzi conquers the heart of Peter with her banter and new-found mastery of the hotel trade, Gretl is still a long way from St. Gilgen. In fact, she is in no hurry to arrive, as she has met suave Thomas Brand, played by Hans Holt, who travels the country in his car. Thomas is initially rather cold towards the self-confident Gretl, but soon succumbs to her hearty charms. The couple drive through the Austrian countryside and experience unexpected adventures. At the end, the two couples reunite in St. Gilgen, happy that fate (in the case of the men) and entrepreneurship (in the case of the women) have brought them love and happiness.

Figure 4.1: Gretl (Inge Konradi) and Fritzi (Herta Mayen) tramp happily towards their future in *Rendezvous im Salzkammergut*. Filmarchiv Austria.

What distinguishes *Rendezvous im Salzkammergut* and early tourist film in general (with the notable exception of *Der Hofrat Geiger*) from other Austrian films is their rather progressive treatment of gender. The films present men and women more or less as equals, and emphasise similarities rather than differences between the sexes. The two main protagonists in *Rendezvous im Salzkammergut*, Gretl and Fritzi, are depicted as witty, intelligent, adventurous and brimming with self-confidence. They demonstrate that they are capable of fending for themselves when they hitch a ride to Lake Wolfgang. They not only escape their importunate male colleague,

Harry (Harry Fuss), who wants to accompany them on their holiday, but are also resourceful in persuading male drivers to give them a lift. These women are determined to get what they want, and neither lack of money nor any commitment to their employers or families hold them back from undertaking a journey.

It is significant that the narrative does not question the women's independence or the fact that they travel the country roads alone, without a male guardian. Indeed, from the very beginning, the initiative lies with the women, in practical as well as in erotic matters. Unlike *Heimatfilm*, which continually confronts women with traditional expectations about gender and consequently curbs their movements, these tourist narratives do not challenge the women's desire to travel independently. Obviously, the holiday trope plays a big part in freeing the female protagonists from the constraints of gender norms. The following scene tellingly illustrates how *Rendezvous* depicts modern gender relations through characterisation, narrative, framing and editing.

Having left Vienna and covered a considerable distance in a lorry, on a hay cart and on foot, the two friends tramp tiredly along a winding, dusty road, arm in arm, whistling a cheery tune. Despite the glaring sunshine, they wear thick loden costumes and heavy shoes; they also carry a knapsack and a suitcase – all indicators that modernity, with its loose-fitting, stylish clothes, has not quite arrived yet. While their outward appearance and their heavy footsteps might have reminded the contemporary audience of the refugee treks that had populated the roads not too long ago, their cheerful demeanour indicates that their journey is pleasant. The women are determined to enjoy themselves, and their readiness to improvise and jump at every chance that presents itself is rewarded. When they hear a car approaching, the women grab a stop sign from the road works to block the path of the car. Once the car has been forced to a stop, they start negotiating for a lift with the reluctant driver. His protestations that he has no room in the car are ignored. Gretl shoves her friend onto the passenger seat of the stranger's car, leaving the exasperated travelling salesman no choice but to accept her. The scene is an amusing commentary on the shake-up of traditional gender relations in early postwar Austria: while the male car driver is outwardly still in command, in reality he is locked behind his steering wheel and no longer in a position of power. He is unable to move in the confined space of his crammed car, or to defend himself against the verbal female onslaught. He has no option but to surrender to the women, who have taken command. At breathtaking speed he leaves the scene of his defeat, delivering Fritzi in no time to her destination, glad to regain his freedom.

Gretl is left behind to continue the journey on her own, and she does so with confidence. The next scene shows her waiting at a closed rail-crossing barrier, when an old black car approaches. In a reversal of the classic filmic introductory scene, in which the male character usually holds the gaze to observe the arrival of the female, we witness (from Gretl's perspective) a tall, dark-haired man in a white shirt, Thomas Brand (Hans Holt), stepping out of his car. The melodic violin score that accompanies this scene underlines his erotic attractiveness. In the next shot, Gretl rushes to his side, thanking him profusely for stopping for her, but he remains indifferent to her attempts at making conversation. Gretl's agitated face and gestures contrast vividly with Thomas' sedate body language, which suggests that he feels in control of the situation. As the camera lingers on Thomas, showing him carefully refilling the water tank while the wind tousles his hair, he is clearly the object of erotic attraction. When Gretl enters the frame and, undeterred by his rebuffs, appeals to him to give her a lift, he simply closes his door on her, thus asserting his masculine power. A cut to the train passing by briefly leaves the audience in suspense about the outcome of this battle of strength, but the next shot shows Gretl sitting with a complacent smile next to a stony-faced Thomas, who is visibly displeased about his defeat. Gretl has prevailed and successfully claimed her equal share of power. Her bubbly, cheerful manner has succeeded in cutting through his resistance, so that Thomas finally abandons his old-fashioned masculine behaviour to become a comradely partner. The film emphasises that both sides profit from leaving behind traditional gender roles; women who dare to reject them acquire independence and freedom of movement; men who relinquish some of their power to women are no longer bound to strict norms of conduct and become more youthful and sprightly, finding new freedom in equal relationships.

From Pragmatism to Romance: Changing Views on Marriage

Compared to later tourist films, then, these early narratives display a surprisingly liberal attitude to sexual relations. The fight for available bachelors, a theme that dominated contemporary popular discourse, is an open one, without manipulations or feelings of jealousy. Finding a mate is, the films suggest, a practical matter. Even though neither women nor men in *Rendezvous* are without romantic aspirations, they look first and foremost for practical qualities in the opposite sex. Thomas proves his suitability by showing creativity when he and Gretl get stranded in a small town without petrol or a free room for the night. Thomas pretends to be the missing guest speaker at a local pigeon-breeding conference and, with a fabulous fictitious report about recent successes in pigeon breeding, secures room and board as well as Gretl's heart. She has found a soulmate, one who is adventurous and does not expect a submissive wife. Men, too, like their partners hands-on: while they like their women pretty, they also wish them to be professionally competent and able to work. Peter, as he admits later on in the film, had invited Gretl first and foremost to see whether she would make a good landlady. When he notices that Fritzi excels as a waitress, he transfers his affections from Gretl to Fritzi without any hesitation.

Early postwar tourist film does not romanticise marriage. Matrimony is presented as a sensible choice rather than an ultimate goal or inevitable trajectory in a woman's life. *Rendezvous im Salzkammergut* humorously discusses the problems of marriage in a dialogue scene between Gretl and Fritzi: Gretl is shown to be a romantic who is reluctant to even entertain the thought of marrying Peter, whereas Fritzi is presented as the pragmatist. She looks upon Gretl's romantic aspirations with scepticism, jestingly reminding her that 'these days you must not be too demanding. After all, he owns a hotel'. Her practical view, which was probably shared by many women in postwar Austria, is rewarded. She gets engaged to the hotelier, while Gretl finds somebody to satisfy her own romantic inclinations.

Women are the driving forces in early tourist film, and in response the leading men are presented as comradely and cheerful, willing to be conquered by women. The fact that men are portrayed as passive in erotic matters is certainly connected to the specific postwar context, where women outnumbered men and thus had to actively court them. Available men, especially attractive ones, were scarce in postwar Austria, and war-time casualties had drastically reduced the male population, as noted earlier. Indeed, the shortage of men (which was often discussed in terms of a 'surplus of women', implying that women had lost value) was a much debated issue all over postwar Europe. Contemporary commentators, as Dagmar Herzog notes, tended both to 'pity the involuntarily single woman and to aggravate every already married woman's sense of anxiety that she was about to lose her man'.[26]

There were certainly strong voices deploring the fate of women forced into spinsterhood in postwar Austria, but there were also alternative discourses which discussed the issue more optimistically.[27] Tourist film was one of these discourses. It offered a positive view of female singledom by celebrating female independence and showcasing young women who were not at all desperate to get married. By promoting self-confident, independent women, the genre created role models for young women at a time when traditional gender structures had become unworkable. The industry thus catered to the desires of the female audience, suggesting that women had a choice when in reality they had very little opportunity to choose.[28]

However, these role models were short-lived, and soon gave way to representations of women who, while outwardly modern, were anxious for male protection – characterisations that strongly resembled those in comedy and *Heimatfilm*. The tourist film *Eva erbt das Paradies*, directed by Franz Antel, is situated at the crossroads of these developments; while it celebrates female independence, it also suggests that a return to traditional gender roles, albeit superficially modernised, was inevitable. *Eva erbt das Paradies* features self-confident, modern women who set out to live independently, but have to realise that they cannot live without the support of men. The film tells the story of Eva (Maria Andergast), a frustrated secretary from Munich who inherits a hotel by an Austrian lake. She quits her job and travels to Austria with her best friend, Daisy (Susi Nicoletti), full of dreams of an exciting life as a wealthy landlady. These dreams are shattered when they find the hotel derelict and without any guests. Undeterred, the two friends and a group of newly acquainted female holidaymakers optimistically set out to renovate and promote the hotel. The women's enterprise initially looks promising: new guests arrive in large numbers, and male admirers, intrigued by the women's confidence, willingly submit to female rule. However, behind the scenes, and unknown to Eva, it is her new fiancé, Hans Holzinger (Josef Meinrad), who ensures that her hotel business survives; as the son of the owner of the large Grand Hotel he possesses the financial power to pay the bills that the young women lack. This discrepancy between appearances and reality is significant. Just as the derelict Hotel Paradies is superficially redecorated in order to attract customers, concepts of gender are only outwardly updated to meet the audience's expectations of a modernised society in which women earn their own money and make independent decisions. The core of the hotel remains unchanged, as does (if we want to follow the analogy) the patriarchal order. Behind the scenes, it is still the man who holds power, while the women in the foreground give in to the illusion that society has become more equal.

In contrast to later tourist films, productions like *Eva* are still decisively more modern in their representation of the sexes. These early films promote companionable, practical relationships in which men and women are comrades rather than lovers. In *Eva erbt das Paradies*, Hans Holzinger proposes to Eva under the full moon, but in prosaic financial terms: 'Eva, let me pay all your electricity bills from now on!' His financial power (combined with ownership of the rival hotel) is clearly an incentive for her to agree to marry him. In *Der Hofrat Geiger*, Geiger's rival immediately suspects that the marriage between Mr Geiger and Marianne is devoid of romantic feelings: Marianne agrees to marry Geiger in order to gain Austrian citizenship and, in return, allows him access to his daughter.

By depicting gender relations as guided by pragmatism, the tourist genre captured the mood of the time: like a seismograph, it identified and responded to shifts in Austrian society. So, when Austria's economic recovery and social stabilisation precipitated a reversal in gender relations, noticeable by an increasing idealisation of marriage and the marketing of the role of the housewife in the media, tourist film responded quickly and started to revive traditional gender models that were only outwardly modernised.[29] The tourist film *Zwei in einem Auto*, directed by Ernst Marischka, demonstrates the changing attitude towards matrimony in Austrian society. While *Eva erbt das Paradies*, which was produced in the same year, still promotes a kind of female independence, *Zwei in einem Auto* heavily romanticises marriage and ascribes fairly traditional roles to men and women, which is evidence of competing discourses. Here, young Lisa Krüger (the first role of the nineteen-year-old Austrian actress Johanna Matz) falls in love with her visibly older travelling companion, Georg (the Ufa heart-throb Wolf Albach-Retty), whom she met through an advertisement she placed in a newspaper. Lisa is led by romantic considerations, and thus takes him for a poor teacher when in fact he is a famous racing driver. Even though all the facts, from his sleek sports car and stylish dress to his lavish presents, contradict the idea that Georg is poor, she must hold on to this illusion to prove her innocence and purity to the man she loves.

During the mid-1950s, the pragmatic views on marriage displayed in earlier tourist films became socially less acceptable. Tourist films were now full of protestations of romantic love, as in *Drei Männer im Schnee* (1955) or *Verliebter Sommer* (1954). Only *Sonnenschein und Wolkenbruch* (Sunshine and Cloudburst, 1955) is more ambiguous in this regard; while it celebrates the romantic love between a poor pianist and a millionaire's daughter, it is also full of male and female crooks, who want to trick others into marriage to gain money or status. The change in the portrayal of marriage was accompanied by a quite remarkable shift in the representation of gender. The fact that there was a two-year gap in the production of tourist films in the early 1950s makes the transformation even more noticeable. In *Verliebter Sommer, Sonnenschein und Wolkenbruch* and *Drei Männer im Schnee*, all produced in 1954/55, women no longer have any need (or desire) to work. Female interests, once varied, are now solely focused on finding a husband. Representations of masculinity, too, have changed significantly. Men seem to have lost their sense of companionship and the ability to communicate with women on an equal level, qualities which were so characteristic of the male protagonists in *Eva erbt das Paradies* or *Rendezvous im Salzkammergut*. Where they were once playful and sprightly, men behave more formally in these later tourist films – as potential providers rather than friends. These narratives present men as polite charmers who adore women but do not take them seriously; women, on the other hand, are infantilised or characterised as greedy. Overall, the films spotlight hierarchical differences between men and women and accentuate gender-specific characteristics.

What were the reasons for this palpable change? Had the producers of tourist film gone too far in advocating gender equality and female independence in the early postwar years, and did they now feel obliged to pull back? There is no doubt that the progressive views on gender in the early films were a result of the massive disruptions Austrian society had experienced. The light-hearted mood of tourist film, and particularly the tropes of mobility and holidays, allowed filmmakers to venture further and to experiment with new concepts of gender, until the stabilisation of society prompted a reorientation of their approach.

The Road to Happiness – Key Themes in Tourist Film

Tourist film tempts the audience to venture out by taking the protagonists into the blooming countryside because, as Inglis notes, 'the good holiday relieves us of the grubby city and restores us to the fresh bosom of nature'.[30] The Austrian landscape in these films is cultivated, but it shows no traces of the war or Nazi dictatorship. By utilising the discursive theme of mobility, the genre offers the promise of a new beginning: the tourist narrative suggests that ties of (personal and national) history can be easily shed, making holidays profoundly liberating. At the same time, it divested travel of the negative connotations it had acquired through the enforced movements during and shortly after the war.

Mobility was a central issue in postwar Austria. Free movement between the different Austrian provinces was restricted because the four Allied powers had divided Austria into separate zones of power. Yet, despite these imposed restrictions, people were constantly on the move: the large number of refugees which had populated the streets in the first months after the war had largely gone, but city dwellers continued to roam the countryside in desperate search of food, trying to exchange their valuables for vegetables, meat, milk or butter. These so-called 'hamster trips' aggravated relations between the rural and urban populations. Farmers saw themselves as incapable of meeting the demands of the hungry city dwellers, who, in return, held a grudge against the peasants, accusing them of greed and meanness.[31] No wonder that the majority of Austrians regarded travelling as a tiresome and frustrating experience. The people forced to roam the countryside in search of something edible, experiencing humiliation and disappointment as they did so, had little interest in the beauty of the landscape. Tourist film sought to blot out these negative experiences by presenting mobility as a joyful experience and conjuring up an image of perfect harmony between urban and rural people. The film *Der Hofrat Geiger* is different in that it offers a rare glimpse into this postwar reality by showing how Mr Lechner, a Viennese tourist with bourgeois airs, has to haggle for his allowance of meat at his holiday destination, a small village by the Danube. The local butcher, who also owns the largest hotel and is mayor of the village, is the new master and behaves condescendingly towards his customer, letting him feel that the relations of power between country and city have been reversed. Thus Mr Lechner, equipped with food stamps and obscure *objets d'art* as means of payment, finds his social status suddenly and painfully diminished – an experience he would have shared with many urban contemporaries in real life.

Taking the particular historical context into consideration is vital to
fully understand the meanings these films carried for contemporary audiences. Postwar tourist films were popular because they spread optimism;
they gave travelling and mobility a new connotation, or rather, reinstated
their old meaning. As people perceived tourism to be a 'measure of normality', resumption of travel for enjoyment was taken as indicator that
society was recovering.[32] In *Rendezvous im Salzkammergut*, hiking on the
road is no longer reminiscent of the treks of refugees who fled the East,
or the strenuous trips of hungry townsfolk to obtain food in the country;
on the contrary, it is a joyful experience that leaves no desire unfulfilled.
These wayfarers are no longer beggars, but eagerly awaited guests who
bring modernity and culture to the countryside. In tourist film, the power
relations between the urban and rural populations once again shift in favour of the urban citizens: while the protagonists in earlier tourist films
are hardly ever wealthy, they are still treated with respect and welcomed
as if they were. Unlike in *Heimatfilm*, the urban tourist as messenger of
modernity is not an outsider, but the centre of attention.

It is worth pointing out that in reality travelling and holidaymaking
were still the preserve of the middle-class in postwar Austria. Neither the
Nazis, with their popular organised holidays, 'Kraft durch Freude' (KdF,
Strength through Joy), nor tourist films were able to change this quickly.
After all, holidays were costly, and working-class families could not afford them. However, as Alon Confino has shown in his insightful analysis
of tourist rhetoric in postwar West Germany, the National Socialist travel
programme, KdF, had strengthened the idea, especially among workers, that holidays were an entitlement and not a luxury.[33] Therefore, even
though the majority of people did not actually travel in postwar Austria,
travelling for pleasure was, Confino argues, nevertheless perceived as an
established right 'that reflects the ability of the system to keep the promise
of a better life'.[34] In tourist film, only the grumpy Viennese truck driver
(convincingly portrayed by the Viennese actor Hugo Gottschlich) in *Rendezvous im Salzkammergut*, who gives the two female protagonists a lift in
his lorry, seems to be ignorant of the joys of holidaymaking. 'What are you
looking for in the Salzkammergut?' he inquires disapprovingly, showing
himself clearly resistant to the idea that travelling could be fun. For him,
as he cheerfully admits, relaxation means staying at home, watching his
wife doing her chores.

Closely linked to the theme of mobility is the metaphor of the road.
Roads play a key role in the tourist genre, as they connect the urban with
the rural. The road is also the point from which travellers gaze at the countryside: the landscape becomes a fleeting image that constantly changes,
very much like a film. Whereas in *Heimatfilm* it is gender divisions that
prohibit women from entering the landscape without a male guardian,
the urban holiday-makers in tourist film hardly ever venture away from
the road into the countryside, regardless of gender, because the landscape

functions only as imagery. The protagonists – just like the cinema audience – marvel at the landscape but do not really experience it, as, for example, men do in *Heimatfilm*, when they go hunting in the mountains.

The pictorial camera frame that presents postcard-like images of the picturesque landscape is frequently used in Austrian cinema.[35] However, unlike in *Heimatfilm* or historical costume film, tourist film demonstrates awareness of the artificiality of these images. In *Kleiner Schwindel am Wolfgangsee*, an unemployed painter (Hans Holt) wins first prize for a painting of his holiday resort which is commercially used for a tourism advertisement. In *Rendezvous im Salzkammergut*, the main protagonist, Gretl, sighs when her travel companion stops to take a picture of a mountain lake: 'Yet another lake. You could do this much cheaper. Buy postcards!' Gretl exclaims when she gets out of the car to stretch her stiff legs, demonstrating that the gaze at the landscape can become tedious once it is commercialised.

The holiday experience in tourist film is structured by the country road, which opens up specific destinations to the tourists and channels their gaze. The striking lack of traffic also makes the road itself part of the enjoyment: in *Zwei in einem Auto*, Georg can use the deserted road to teach his young companion, Lisa, how to drive. In *Rendezvous im Salzkammergut*, it takes the two friends, Gretl and Fritzi, a long time to hitch their way from Vienna to their holiday destination in the Salzkammergut because of the lack of cars on the road; the enforced slowness is part of the holiday experience and adds to the enjoyment. Even the German *Autobahn*, the pride of the Nazis who built it, lies deserted in the film *Verliebter Sommer*; a few cars, a bus with tourists and a small number of girls on their scooters and bicycles designate the motorway as route of pleasure, offering opportunities for flirtation and charming encounters. With little traffic and therefore few exhaust fumes to pollute the fresh air, travelling on the road becomes an essential part of the holiday excitement.

Just like the urban street, country roads promise adventure and escape, but these roads are the antithesis of the dangerous, dark and erotic streets of the city, as depicted in the 'street films' of the *Weimar* era, the social problem films produced after the war or contemporary American crime films. In German films such as Karl Grune's *Die Strasse* (The Street, 1923), G.W. Pabst's *Die freudlose Gasse* (Joyless Street, 1925) or, to give an example of a postwar Austrian film, Harald Röbbeling's film *Asphalt* (1951), the street belongs to the poor and squalid lower-classes, an underworld milieu that is both threatening and appealing to bourgeois men who seek 'relief from both the ennui and the moral confinement of bourgeois existence'.[36] The country road, in contrast, is clean and safe, and the men on the road are trustworthy and helpful. The road that winds through the countryside under a blue sky and brilliant sunshine belongs to the carefree, jolly and brave people who travel towards their happiness.[37]

The road as symbol of (regained) freedom performs another crucial function in tourist film, as mentioned above: it connects the town with the country and brings people together. On the road, travelling companions are found, and lasting love relationships are sealed. Differences of class, political views and nationalities are (temporarily) suspended, and antagonisms between the urban and the rural population suppressed. As drivers of the cars, men's powers are reinstated; as navigators, women are given the choice of direction. Men and women access the road on equal terms: together they travel in the same direction, towards the future. The country road thus unites people in harmony and kindles communal spirit, if only for the duration of the holiday.

With very few exceptions where elderly men take centre stage, such as *Der Hofrat Geiger* or *Der Herr Kanzleirat*, Austrian tourist films feature urban, young men and women in their twenties, who find happiness and love during their holidays. In this regard, the Austrian films are quite different from holiday films of other countries, such as the British *Holiday Camp* (1947) or the French *Les Vacances de Monsieur Hulot* (Mr Hulot's Holiday, 1953), which centre on family life and offer a much broader range of characters of all ages. The focus on young people and the increased showcasing of popular music and modern fashion indicate that Austrian tourist films targeted urban spectators and younger audiences.[38] Yet the fact that Austrian tourist films showcase young people has symbolic implications that go beyond the profit considerations of the film industry. Seemingly unburdened by the past, the young protagonists stand for a new beginning, in economic as well as ideological terms. Still teenagers in the Nazi era, they have entered the adult world in postwar tourist films. With their optimistic outlook, they carry the message of change and modernity to the countryside. The genre thus promotes the myth of a fresh start, a message conveyed through the characters as well as through the narratives. In *Eva erbt das Paradies* and *Verliebter Sommer*, women break away from their ordinary world completely to start a new life. They follow an impulse, and quit their mundane jobs as sales assistants or telephonists, fuelled by optimism and the certainty that the future will hold a reward. Men, in contrast, are presented as steadier, but they, too, are given a new chance, allowed to restart their lives and recommence relationships that they were forced to break off in the past. Thus, Mr Geiger in *Der Hofrat Geiger* not only reconnects with his lost love, but is also ceremonially restored to his office post, from which he resigned in 1938 to protest against Austria's annexation by Nazi Germany.

The genre's emphasis lies firmly on the here and now, but in its vitality and sense of freedom it anticipates a brighter future. Unlike the British *Holiday Camp*, where tourists suffer from loneliness, lovesickness or financial worries, the protagonists in Austrian tourist films are surprisingly carefree, confident and healthy. The films hence present a vivid contrast to social reality: although many Austrian men had sustained physical or mental injuries during the war, the bodies (and thus souls) of the male characters in tourist films are unharmed. Because tourist films are closely related to comedies, the mood is necessarily upbeat. Consistent with the spirited characters of the protagonists, frustrations do not go deep and affections are easily transferred from one person to the next. Hence, tourist films sell the capitalist dream of holidays as an imitation of paradise: by presenting protagonists whose cheerfulness is spoilt neither by loss of love nor financial hardship, the narratives emulate a capitalist lifestyle that is based on the 'pleasure of infinite anticipation, smoothly replacing disappointment with the promise of another, future satisfaction'.[39] It is this mood of unconcern and carefree enjoyment in particular which distinguishes the tourist genre sharply from *Heimatfilm*, whose protagonists seem constantly in agony, suffering from societal restraints and inner turmoil.

Negative emotions such as anger, frustration or even grief are almost absent and only displayed by older women, such as the hard-hearted Mrs Holzinger in *Eva erbt das Paradies*. Men, in contrast, hardly ever harbour negative feelings of that kind: they may be greedy or deceitful, but their behaviour is a result of business considerations and is not founded on emotion. In fact, tourist film is full of avaricious and two-faced men in minor roles – predominantly hoteliers or concierges – who are solely interested in profit. The hotelier in *Sonnenschein und Wolkenbruch* is a crook; the concierges in *Glaube an mich* and *Drei Männer im Schnee* are two-faced; and the waiter in *Rendezvous im Salzkammergut* behaves condescendingly towards the guests and his female colleagues. Yet, their negative characteristics are displayed in such a manner that they amuse rather than disturb, encouraging the audience to laugh at the tourists or the tourist industry.

The leading men, in contrast, are always kind-hearted, sanguine and carefree. In a way, the main male protagonists in tourist film bear close resemblance to the cultured, non-aggressive masculine ideals of historical costume film, even though generic conventions demanded that men in tourist film be sprightlier and more energetic. Being neither gutsy nor ambitious, they lack the attributes of the then-dominant ideal of 'hard' masculinity. Instead, the films show them as emphatetic and harmonious, striving for reconciliation. Hans in *Eva erbt das Paradies* acts as mediator between his girlfriend, Eva, and his possessive mother, and is sympathetic towards the needs of both. In *Kleiner Schwindel am Wolfgangsee*, Walter (Hans Holt) cannot bring himself to tell his hotelier uncle that he has studied fine arts instead of medicine, and therefore does everything to make his uncle believe he is a medical doctor – which leads to considerable comic turmoil. Mr Geiger in *Der Hofrat Geiger* wants to make amends to Marianne for leaving her eighteen years previously by finally offering her marriage as a form of compensation for the hardships she has experienced.[40] By characterising Austrian masculinity as non-confrontational and harmonious, tourist film was in line with the dogma of compromise and balance that dominated Austrian politics and society after the Second World War.[41]

Although tourist film celebrates mobility, it presents men as more root-ed than women, longing for stability and a home. The three male friends in *Verliebter Sommer* essentially never leave home when they travel, as their caravan serves as their home on wheels. Mr Bachmayer in *Der Herr Kanzleirat* shows consistency in his choice of holiday destinations, having spent all his holidays at the Wörthersee. Other men, such as Hans in *Eva erbt das Paradies* or Peter in *Rendezvous im Salzkammergut*, do not merely stay, but actually live in a hotel. This portrayal of men as rooted and stable references the fact that the majority of Austrian men had been on the move for years – as soldiers, as labourers and as prisoners of war. In this way, by celebrating the joys of movement while at the same time holding out the promise of a steady home, tourist film fed two conflicting desires: the in-tense longing to settle down after the turmoil of the war and the desire to see more of the world and to move forward.[42] By presenting men as embed-ded in society, tourist film affirmed their importance as formative elements of the nation state. This must have been an attractive proposition, both to men who found it difficult to settle down after the war and to women, who were hoping for some stability and easing of their workload.[43] These representations of gender can be understood as responses to the collective feelings of rootlessness and disorientation that the increase in social and geographical mobility in Austrian society triggered. The films helped to ease these anxieties by emphasising the positive side of mobility, while at the same time underlining the need for men to settle down.

The Heterosexual Norm and Alternative Masculinities

The genre's emphasis on men's search for stability is underlined by their appetite for marriage. Men's eagerness to get married in tourist film is clearly meant as a display of moral virtue and seriousness, rather than evi-dence of a genuine romantic disposition or of overwhelming sexual desire, which, due to the strict moral codes of the staunchly Catholic Austrian so-ciety, could only be satisfied within the bounds of marriage. However, this might not be the only explanation. If we look at European or US societies after the war, we find that marriage and sexuality were intensely debated issues. Herzog's insightful analysis of sexuality and fascism shows that in postwar West Germany concerns about marriage and heterosexuality were widespread: the experience of war and military defeat had undermined the dominant masculine norm and complicated relations between men and women.[44] Steven Cohan gives a similar verdict on the US, suggesting that society grappled with troubled gender relations.[45] As in postwar Eu-rope, divorce rates rose sharply in the US after the war, causing consider-able alarm among the political and professional elites, who saw the nuclear American family and American society as endangered.[46] A sociological study on postwar Austrian society published in 1957 concluded that the

Austrian family and the population as a whole were threatened by growing individualism as well as the 'passive behaviour of men within their
families'.[47] What is more, US research findings revealed that a surprisingly
high number of US soldiers had had homosexual encounters during their
military service, which fed anxieties about traditional heterosexual masculinity and the dangerous feminisation of modern America that marked
masculinity's 'incipient decline'.[48] Hence, uneasiness about shifting gender
relations, combined with an often unspoken fear of a rise in male homosexuality and loss of male power, fuelled the postwar discourses on family
and matrimony on both sides of the Atlantic.[49]

In their attempt to overcome the 'sexual' and 'marital' crises that
seemed to unsettle society, considerable attempts were made to enforce
heterosexuality as the absolute norm.[50] Political and religious elites and
medical and legal experts saw in matrimony and the nuclear family the
remedy for all kinds of social ills. Marriage was considered to be a means
to strengthen masculine identity and provide ultimate proof of (heterosexual) masculinity. Cohan has shown how the US media and Hollywood
cinema tried to boost the appeal of marriage by advertising the new ideal
of 'domesticated' masculinity, which served to counter the hitherto hegemonic ideal of heroic, 'hard' masculinity. The new ideal of a professionally
successful man who provides for the family and has a companionate, loving relationship with his wife and children very quickly spilled over to
Europe, where it was disseminated by the media.[51] Considering the genre's
openness to modernity, it is perhaps no coincidence that representations of
masculinity in Austrian tourist film very much resemble this ideal of the
domesticated male.

Ideas about masculinity or sexuality are constantly shifting, and the
makers of postwar tourist films seem to have taken note of this and responded by offering views that captured the mood of the time. *Glaube
an mich*, the first tourist film produced after the Second World War, still
shows traces of the comparatively liberal views on sex found in films
produced during the war. In *Glaube an mich*, the middle-aged professor
Franz Wiesinger (Ewald Balser) and his nephew want to test the faithfulness of Wiesinger's young fiancée, Irene (Marte Harell). The young
nephew is supposed to tempt Irene into an affair, but because of a mix-up
she does not end up with the nephew, but with handsome Hans (Rudolf Prack). The night she spends with Hans in a mountain hut leaves
her in emotional confusion. Both ashamed and excited, she confesses
to her best friend, Gertie (Senta Wengraf), that for the first time in her
life she has experienced a 'real' man. Both her elderly fiancé, Franz, and
Gertie's admirer, Dr Moll (Erik Frey), who are intellectuals by profession,
obviously do not fall into the category of 'real men'. They have brains,
but are clumsy on skis, suggesting similar clumsiness in their sexual
skills. Hans, on the other hand, although not much of a talker, is athletic
and handsome; above all, he takes the initiative in erotic matters. Even

though the narrative underlines Hans' earnestness and faithfulness, it is his erotic attractiveness that singles him out as the embodiment of ideal masculinity. Still, *Glaube an mich* is a film that points backwards to an earlier tradition of sexual freedom. In the films that follow, men can no longer prove their virility in extramarital sexual encounters, but have to affirm their heterosexual masculinity through marriage.

The fact that Austrian cinema prescribes the heterosexual norm seems to leave no room for alternative lifestyles, in particular homosexual masculinities; even more so given that until 1971 homosexuality was illegal in Austria, thus forcing homosexuals into secrecy.[52] However, although popular Austrian cinema avoided the subject of homosexuality, tourist film represents a notable exception. Although it is not immediately evident to the unsuspecting audience, postwar tourist film (even though it does not openly endorse homosexuality) offers glimpses of alternative sexualities. On their journey to Italy in the tourist film *Zwei in einem Auto*, the male friends Brösecke and Walzl, played by the comedians Leopold Rudolf and Hans Moser, burst into a suggestive song: 'Everyone one has his pleasures, one does this, one does that, whether openly and often, or quietly and in silence'. Brösecke and Walzl are not only colleagues, but very close friends who have invested the money they won on the pools in an old car to travel to the Italian holiday resort of Portofino. What distinguishes them from other male friends is that they are surprisingly physical in demonstrating their affection for each other. On arrival at a luxurious hotel in the Italian Riviera, Brösecke is mistaken for a famous racing driver who is travelling in disguise under the same name; through this coincidence, the two men are offered a spacious suite at a bargain price. Walzl and Brösecke are particularly excited about the size of the bed, exclaiming: 'What freedom of movement!' They immediately try it out, rolling about on the mattress and cuddling close together. Their excitement has no end, and Brösecke starts to perform gymnastic exercises on the bed with Walzl cheering him on. Staff members, raised by the racket, enter the room. The camera zooms in on their faces, revealing their awe and disgust as they peek at the male pair enjoying themselves on the bed. Their reaction suggests that they are witnessing something the heterosexual gaze would not perceive: two homosexuals having fun together.

Keeping Up Appearances: Der Hofrat Geiger

Even though Walzl and Brösecke are not openly presented as homosexuals, the filmmakers did surprisingly little to suggest the opposite. In an earlier film, *Der Hofrat Geiger*, the homosexual subtext is much more concealed. While the story of *Der Hofrat Geiger* celebrates the return to traditional gender relations, this dominant narrative is repeatedly disrupted and subverted by another narrative. The covert celebration of homosexual relationships in this film, and the filmmakers' efforts to suppress such readings, warrant a closer analysis that will reveal the limits of permissible representations of sexuality in postwar Austrian cinema.

As a tourist film, *Der Hofrat Geiger* is atypical in several ways: even though amusing, it is less light-hearted than other works of the genre; it touches on problematic issues, such as the Nazi past or the power struggle between men and women; it does not advocate radical change, but a return to 'normality' in the shape of traditional patriarchy; and, lastly, its main protagonists are of advanced age and entangled in the past. In that respect, *Der Hofrat Geiger* displays many similarities with *Heimatfilm*. Yet, despite these affinities, *Der Hofrat Geiger* is clearly a tourist film, as shown by the important fact that it does not pit the rural against the urban. What is more, the role of the landscape is different from that in *Heimatfilm*: it is not pure and eternal, but a culturally shaped landscape whose main purpose is to attract tourists.[53]

Der Hofrat Geiger was German-born Hans Wolff's directorial debut. Wolff, who had worked as Willi Forst's cutter and assistant director, directed and edited the film. Forst, the famous director, produced the film, and it was largely due to Forst's prominent status in Austrian cultural life that the film was eagerly awaited by the film press; the critics held high expectations of Forst's first production after the war and, as the reviews illustrate, they were very pleased with the result. Forst and Wolff chose a text by Martin Costa that had already proven popular on stage. First premiered in Prague in 1942, it was restaged by the Viennese Theater an der Josefstadt immediately after the end of the war in May 1945. The play benefited from the fact that it could be turned into a film 'without those massive expenditures, which we still have to deny ourselves these days'.[54] With war-damaged Vienna and a village by the Danube as its setting, the film was inexpensive to produce. The writers changed the narrative to the postwar present, which involved, amongst other things, making the female lead more assertive, 'as befits these times'.[55] Maria Andergast was cast in the role of the feisty, independent Marianne Mühlhuber, the single mother of a teenage daughter and the landlady of a crisis-ridden country inn. The unexpected success of *Der Hofrat Geiger* revived Andergast's flagging career, but also saw the breakthrough of young Waltraud Haas (playing Andergast's daughter Mariandl). The popular comic pairing of Paul Hörbiger (as Franz Geiger) and Hans Moser (as his servant, Ferdinand Lechner) was chosen for the male leads.

Der Hofrat Geiger tells the story of a middle-aged privy councillor, Geiger, who lives with his former clerk, Lechner, in his villa in Vienna. Geiger, we learn, was forced out of office in 1938 because he did not want to serve under Nazi leadership. His long-serving clerk, Lechner, accompanied him, and has worked as his servant ever since, looking after his physical and mental well-being and desperately trying to keep up the lifestyle of a middle-class household. In order to give Geiger a sense of purpose, Lechner secretly borrows old court files from his former office, pretending that Geiger's input is still much needed. Lechner thus creates a false reality for Geiger that is interrupted by an unexpected turn of events: in studying one of these old files Geiger discovers that he fathered a child eighteen years ago while on holiday in the small village of Spitz, in the rolling hills of the Wachau, by the Danube. Excited about this news, and obviously yearning for a new purpose in life, he decides to search for his daughter and reconnect with his former lover, Marianne, who now runs an inn in the very same village where they met. Having first sent Lechner to Spitz to gain some background information, Geiger eventually presents himself to an unsuspecting Marianne, offering to accept the responsibilities of a father and marry her as an act of 'compensation' (*Wiedergutmachung*). To his surprise, Marianne coldly rejects him: she points out that she suffered humiliation and poverty as a single mother, and is not prepared to give up her daughter or her independence as an innkeeper.[56] However, once she realises that she has lost her Austrian citizenship through the redrawing of borders after the war, she agrees to marry Geiger, granting him access to his daughter in return for citizenship. But her efforts to retain her independence after she is married fail, as Geiger, who has in the meantime been ceremoniously called back into office, forces her into submission. At the end, she loses not only her daughter, who marries her waiter, but also her inn – and thus her economic independence. She also forfeits her sexual attractiveness by being made a grandmother by her daughter Mariandl who, unlike Marianne, has married before getting pregnant. Thus, by the end of the film, 'normality' has been restored: Marianne has become a reputable wife and acquired a comfortable living, but has lost her freedom. Geiger and the waiter, on the other hand, have regained social and economic control and affirmed their position of power – to the disadvantage of the women, who are locked into the position of housewives and mothers.

Like other tourist films, *Der Hofrat Geiger* showcases a strong and independent woman who speaks her mind. Beautiful Marianne Mühlhuber is the person in command at the country inn Blaue Gans; her upright posture, emphasised by a tight-fitting dirndl dress, and her clipped voice lend her authority. The men, on the other hand, are depicted as weak: the old inn owner, Windischgruber (Josef Egger), often seen sitting snoozing on a bench or mumbling incoherently in the local vernacular, is half-senile; the young waiter, Hans (Louis Soldan), who is in love with Marianne's daughter, Mariandl, and has big plans for modernising the inn, is continuously rebuffed by Marianne. However, Marianne's position of power is fragile: the old inn she manages is verging on bankruptcy, making her vulnerable to the aggressive approaches of the rich Mr Pfüller, played by Hermann Erhardt, the influential mayor and owner of the prosperous hotel Goldener Ochse, who is keen to marry her.

At the beginning, the narrative clearly sympathises with Marianne, honouring her for raising her child single-handedly and for keeping the inn afloat. Marianne's depiction as a vibrant, hands-on woman who is unfazed by the problems she faces contrasts with that of Councillor Geiger, who is shown sitting in his darkened chambers, huddled in his dressing gown, constantly whining to his servant about trivial things (Figure 4.2). Geiger is emasculated by the loss of his position and wealth through the war, a fact underlined by the soft dressing gown he wears and his constant squabbling with Lechner. However, the journey to Spitz rejuvenates Geiger and strengthens his masculinity, and the sympathies shift in his favour. He not only gains a daughter and a wife, but also experiences his professional rehabilitation. Yet, the more Geiger gains in assertiveness – and thus in masculine power – the more Marianne loses influence. The narrative disapproves of her rebellion against this development: because she does not succumb easily to subservience, Marianne is punished. The film displays a distinct misogynist outlook in the last scenes, when Councillor Geiger, back in power as a magistrate, and his servant, Lechner, anonymously direct Marianne on frustrating errands from one magistrate to the next, until finally giving her a humiliating rebuke in Geiger's office.

Der Hofrat Geiger hence does not advocate equality between the genders, as other early tourist films do. Yet its discussion of heterosexual relations is ambiguous: while it endorses a return to traditional patriarchy, it also, albeit covertly, alludes to the possibility of homosexual relationships. Geiger and Lechner's relationship is more than that of a servant and master. They have been together for over twenty-five years, and spend all their days and evenings together. As Lechner points out to the new maid at the beginning of the film: 'We tend to live a very private life. We have no friends and no relatives. The councillor has only me'. The following scene illustrates this life: Geiger stands shivering behind his desk, clutching his dressing gown with both hands and scolding Lechner for leaving the window open. Geiger nags grumpily about the disorder on his desk, the missing cushion for his back, the sunshine in his study. The small, corpulent Lechner scurries around, busily trying to appease him and put things right. To what lengths Lechner is prepared to go to keep his friend and master happy is illustrated in the next scenes, in which Lechner desperately tries to barter some bric-a-brac for fresh eggs – a difficult task at a time when food was scarce due to rationing. He calls on a number of different people, and crosses half the city to lay his hands on those rare goods – only to hear that the scrambled eggs he has so painstakingly produced are not really to Geiger's liking. Lechner assumes the caring part in the relationship: he looks after Geiger's well-being and jealously guards his master from any disturbance and company. Geiger, on the other hand, even though constantly complaining, is totally dependent on Lechner. The evenings they spend together, reminiscing about their past, attest to their mutual emotional attachment.

Unsurprisingly, the resurfacing of Marianne, Geiger's former lover, produces a rift between the two men. However, harmony is restored when Geiger marries Marianne, but leaves her to continue his life with Lech-

Figure 4.2: The servant, Lechner (Hans Moser), and his master (Paul Hörbiger) live a secluded life in *Der Hofrat Geiger*. Filmarchiv Austria.

ner in Vienna. The wedding is not only a sham because both Marianne and Geiger agree to it out of practical considerations; it also seems bogus because Geiger's interests lie elsewhere: with his daughter, his job and, not least, with his friend Lechner. Geiger having been called back to office immediately after the wedding, he and Lechner return to their home in Vienna and continue their previous life together; but now Geiger has changed. Once a nagging, ailing man, he appears visibly revived, despite having forgone the consummation of the marriage. Geiger's ceremonial reinstatement into office, which immediately follows his wedding, is symbolic on various levels. He not only regains his lost professional and social status, but also is rehabilitated as having been an upright Austrian citizen during Nazi occupation. His professional vindication is paralleled by the private one. The suddenly emerging evidence that he has fathered a child in the past secures Geiger's heterosexuality. In addition, Geiger gains in social power through his newly acquired position as a husband and father.

Hence, the visible happiness Geiger and Lechner display after their return to Vienna may not only be due to their return to office and the elevated social status that results from it; it may just as well be triggered by the fact that Geiger's marriage dispels any doubts about his sexual orientation. The scene that follows his official welcome as a magistrate is meaningful: Councillor Geiger, who always preferred darkened rooms in the past, now complains about the solemn atmosphere of his office. Opening the shutters, he orders the bewildered Lechner to open the other window to let in the sunshine: light which he once found too intrusive. He laughingly brushes aside Lechner's objection ('But we are in the office!'), explaining that the office could do with a breath of fresh air. Geiger wants to be seen, and to demonstrate that he has nothing to hide. As the sunlight streams through the tall windows, it lends more prominence to the bric-a-brac on Geiger's rococo desk and the details on his large, embroidered velvet chair from which he conducts his affairs. The baroque interior reflects Austria's bygone imperial past, but it also hints at Geiger's and Lechner's sensuality. The opening of the windows in Geiger's office can be read as a celebration of their coming-out. They have exchanged the intimacy of their dark villa for the light-flooded 'official' space. Their being together in public is safe because Geiger's heterosexuality is officially certified through his marriage and fatherhood.

Der Hofrat Geiger and other tourist films confirm the heterosexual norm. However, as we have seen, some tourist films, such as *Zwei in einem Auto*, accommodate deviations from the norm, although in a concealed manner, which lends them a certain permissive flair. The representations of masculinity in *Der Hofrat Geiger* and *Zwei in einem Auto* also show that popular cinema is rarely as one-dimensional as it may seem at first glance; sometimes, competing discourses and alternative representations – of masculinity or of sexuality – break through the surface of the dominant narrative. However, as Cohan has pointed out, these deviations 'still occurred with reference to the formidable ideal of the middle-class breadwinner', and therefore also confirm the dominant norm.[57]

The question is: why does tourist film provide the space for alternative masculinities when other genres do not? It may well be that the genre's topoi of holidaying and mobility supplied the right stimulus for the expression of alternative masculinities. According to Inglis' insightful analysis, holidays are meant to enable people to express their individuality as well as release them from the restraints of everyday life; a good holiday, Inglis suggests, 'must be licentious' and 'at the edge of things', tempting the holidaymakers to fulfil their desires and to live in excess.[58] Tourist films met these expectations. They promised new opportunities and (sexual) freedoms which were usually not open to the audience.

Permanent sunshine and lakeside settings provide the protagonists with the opportunity to shed their clothes and expose their bodies. Swimming trunks and bikinis play an essential role in summer tourist films. In *Eva erbt das Paradies*, the tourists admire the beautiful landscape before turning their gaze to the bodies of the female holidaymakers. A telescope installed in the garden of the Grand Hotel to allow guests to inspect the mountain range suddenly becomes popular among the men when a group of young women start performing gymnastics in bikinis across the lake; looking at beautiful bodies is on a par with looking at the beauties of nature. Just like the landscape, the bodies are on display to be admired. The scantily dressed young women that parade in *Eva erbt das Paradies* became the trademark of the Austrian director Franz Antel, who specialised in tourist film and comedies before moving on to sex films in the 1970s. These 'Antel-Bees', as Büttner and Dewald describe the female protagonists, served little more than decorative purposes; their main function was to attract male audiences and thus increase ticket sales.[59] Yet, there is little eroticism or even lasciviousness about Antel's bikini girls: despite their revealing garments they look neat and 'clean', consistent with the harmless tone of the genre.

Male bodies are also on display in the tourist film. It was usually the well-built comedian and former professional swimmer Gunther Philipp who had to parade his body in swimming trunks. Aware of the gaze of the onlookers, Philipp, in the role of Peter Kurz, walks self-confidently across the lawns and drapes himself next to his admired Trixi in *Kleiner Schwindel am Wolfgangsee*. Here, the male body has been turned into an object of the (male and female) gaze and has become a potential target of erotic interest; but, as with the female protagonists, the male body is de-eroticised to downplay its sexual appeal. Philipp's comical antics make sure that his eroticism does not win the upper hand. Still, it is hard to overlook his well-built body. It obviously had a disconcerting effect on some reviewers, who repeatedly brought up Philipp's previous success as a professional swimmer, as well as his medical degree, as if to rationalise the alluring presence of his bare body.[60]

The presentation of Gunther Philipp's stripped body touches on not only the issue of the desiring gaze, but also that of gender as performance. In *Eva erbt das Paradies*, Philipp plays Bill Wokulek, who struts half-naked in front of the girls to win their attention (Figure 4.3). Bill is a performer in more than one sense: he entertains the hotel guests as a musician in a band, but he also puts his body on display and tries to impress his audience with his physique and swimming skills. Bill easily slips from one role into the next, and is difficult to pin down; he changes smoothly from musician to chef, from gigolo to comradely friend. With his obvious expertise and

Figure 4.3: Bill Wokulek (Gunther Philipp) shows off his toned body in Eva erbt das Paradies. Image: screenshot.

love of cooking, he is associated with talents mostly attributed to women at the time. However, these 'female' attributes are clearly contrasted with references to his virility. Bill is fit: he swims across the lake, shows off his toned body at the beach and, above all, chases women constantly, as if to counteract any suspicion of homosexuality.

Eva erbt das Paradies thus tries to confirm Bill's manliness by showcasing his muscular body. This was against the trend in the postwar era, when, alarmed by the extent of homosexual encounters between 'manly' American GIs, society became suspicious of the masculine body as proof of (heterosexual) masculinity.[61] Mainstream Hollywood cinema in the 1950s, as Cohan shows, played a key role in raising suspicion 'about the authenticity of the male body itself as a "natural" guarantee of heterosexuality'.[62] As the muscular body and 'masculine behaviour' lost some of their significance in determining masculinity, the 'object choice' – exclusive sexual interest in women – became the defining factor of modern normative masculinity in the US and postwar Europe.[63] In postwar Austrian cinema, however, a toned, muscular, male body together with a professed interest in women seemed sufficient to deflect suspicions of homosexuality.

Conclusion

The fact that postwar tourist film embraces modern models of masculinity more readily than other genres can be explained by the genre's optimistic outlook on the future. Austrian tourist film does not completely discard the masculine body or traditional masculine norms, but complements them with more feminine elements. Men and women are presented as more alike than in other genres. The genre's dominant topoi – the landscape, the road, mobility and modernity – reverberate in the representations of gender. The road in tourist film denotes change, and it is in the representation of gender where this change is most evident. While the landscape traditionally represents conservative values, and *Heimatfilm* clearly regulates access to the rural according to gender, tourist film ties modernity to the landscape and thereby bridges the gap between men and women.

For a brief span of about five years – from around 1946 to 1951 – men and women stood on a more equal footing in tourist film. The leading men, again with the notable exception of Geiger in *Der Hofrat Geiger*, are mostly presented as companionable, cheerful, energetic and carefree; importantly, they communicate with women on an equal level. This type of masculinity in early Austrian tourist film closely resembles the 1950s US model of the 'domesticated male', best portrayed by stars like Jack Lemmon. However, even though the Austrian version of domesticated masculinity shares some essential traits with its US counterpart, such as a strong family orientation and camaraderie with women, it is presented as less ambitious or materialistic. Instead, the films underline the harmonious and modest traits of the men, and thereby feed into the popular discourse that promoted Austrian masculinity as gentle and cultured.

Early postwar tourist film subverted the existing, though destabilised, social system, in that the narratives suspended capitalism for a limited period of time and insisted on pleasures and freedom without money. It was this new-found freedom that temporarily liberated men and women from the constraints of traditional gender roles. Tourist film thus kindled a spirit of optimism and community that was needed to rebuild the shattered Austrian economy and society. However, once Austria's economy was in upswing, these ideas were revoked and replaced with more traditional concepts of gender. Still, the fact remains that Austrian tourist film temporarily challenged the patriarchal order and offered an alternative view of society in which men and women are equal.

Eva, in *Eva erbt das Paradies*, does indeed, as the title suggests, inherit paradise, starting out without money and on an equal footing with her male friends; but the mountain of debt soon weighs her down, giving her new lover, Hans, the opportunity to step in with his assets. The reward for his financial support is marriage and, as a predictable consequence, the reinstatement of patriarchal order. Austria's relatively fast economic recovery went hand in hand with a reversal in gender relations and the consolidation of patriarchy. The significant changes in characterisation and narrative show that the filmmakers watched social trends closely and responded by promoting views that seemed to capture the dominant mood of the time. Tourist film, which had once advocated comparatively radical ideas on gender and society as a whole, offering a glimpse of a world in which gender or class differences have become irrelevant, pulled back from these visions in the early 1950s. Perhaps the producers of tourist film felt that – in view of the economic upswing and stabilisation of society – audiences no longer demanded uplifting messages or promises of a new, more equal society, but looked for inspiration about what their hard-earned money could buy: a holiday in beautiful surroundings that promised temporary escape from everyday routine and gave confirmation that one's standards of living had markedly improved.

Notes

1. The first film version of *Im Weissen Rössl* was based on a comedy by Oskar Blumenthal und Gustav Kadelburg. Ralph Benatzky turned the play into a musical, which formed the basis for the subsequent film adaptations.
2. See Steiner, 1987, 46, 55; Moltke, 2005, 22, 132; Bergfelder, 2006, 42; G. Heiss. 1990. 'Ein Reich von Künstlern und Kellnern', in O. Rathkolb, G. Schmid and G. Heiss (eds), *Österreich und Deutschlands Grösse. Ein schlampiges Verhältnis*, Salzburg: O. Müller, 120.
3. Moltke, 2005, 133.
4. 'Glaube an mich!', *Arbeiterzeitung*, 24 November 1946, 5.

5. E.v. Neusser. 1950. 'Die österreichischen Filmerfolge', *Film-Kunst. Zeitschrift für Filmkultur und Filmwissenschaft*, 5, 253. According to *Film-Kunst*, *Hofrat Geiger* was the bestselling Austrian film in the period from 1947 to 1950 with 2.9 million visitors; by 1950, every third Austrian had seen the film, and its theme song, 'Mariandl', had become a musical hit in both Austria and Germany. The two sequels were produced in 1961 (*Mariandl*) and 1962 (*Mariandls Heimkehr*), both directed by Werner Jacobs.

6. The financial success of the tourist film *Rendezvous im Salzkammergut*, for example, was above average, with 710,000 spectators over a period of fourteen months. See .v. Neusser. 1950. 'Die österreichischen Filmerfolge', *Film-Kunst. Zeitschrift für Filmkultur und Filmwissenschaft*, 5, 253.

7. 'Wiederaufnahme der österreichischen Filmproduktion', *Arbeiterzeitung*, 12 January 1946, 3.

8. 'Österreichischer Lustspielfilm: "Kleiner Schwindel am Wolfgangsee"', *Wiener Zeitung*, 4 January 1950.

9. See Büttner and Dewald, 1997a, 306–310.

10. With the title 'The Making of Home and Abroad', one review explicitly refers to the constructedness of Austria. See 'Konfektion des In- und Auslandes', *Wiener Kurier*, 22 September 1951.

11. See H. Spode. 2005. 'Deutsch-österreichischer Tourismus und nationale Identität', in Stiftung Haus der Geschichte der Bundesrepublik Deutschland (ed.), *Verfreundete Nachbarn: Deutschland-Österreich*, Bielefeld: Kerber.

12. Marshall Plan aid went primarily to the western Austrian provinces, further disadvantaging the east, which was largely occupied by Soviet Forces and was hit hardest by the war. See Weber, 1996, 76–78. See also A. Hofstätter-Schmidt. 1994. 'Die Entwicklung des Salzburger Fremdenverkehrs in der Zweiten Republik', in H. Haas, R. Hoffmann and K. Luger (eds), *Weltbühne und Naturkulisse. Zwei Jahrhunderte Salzburg-Tourismus*, Salzburg: Verlag Anton Pustet, 135–134. See also G. Kerschbaumer. 1994. 'Die Wiederbelebung der Glanzzeiten in den Nachkriegsjahren', in H. Haas, R. Hoffmann and K. Luger (eds), *Weltbühne und Naturkulisse. Zwei Jahrhunderte Salzburg-Tourismus*, Salzburg: Verlag Anton Pustet, 132. According to Kerschbaumer, four million Germans entered Austria alone in August 1951.

13. See Steiner, 1987, 56.

14. The film is based on a novel with the same title by the German author Erich Kästner, who also wrote the script for the film. Kästner's novel was published in Switzerland in 1934 because his popular works, mainly children's books, were banned by the Nazis, who denounced his writings as 'Bolshevist'. *Drei Männer im Schnee* was adapted for the screen four times: in Sweden in 1936 (*Stackars miljonärer*), in the US in 1938 (*Paradise for Three*), in Austria in 1955 and in West Germany in 1974. The 1955 adaptation was an Austrian production, but the leading roles were all played by German actors.

15. *Kleiner Schwindel am Wolfgangsee* (1949) was considered to be one of the cheapest productions at the time, with a budget of only 800,000 Austrian schillings, which would be around 40,000 British pounds today. In comparison, a cinema ticket cost 2.50 schillings on average in 1949. See 'Vom "Kleinen Schwindel" zur "Eva". Aufstieg einer österreichischen Filmgesellschaft', *Wiener Tageszeitung*, 22 September 1951.

16. See P. East and K. Luger. 2002. 'Living in Paradise: Youth Culture and Tourism Development in the Mountains of Austria', in R.N. Voase (ed.), *Tourism in Western Europe: A Collection of Case Histories*, Wallingford, UK: CABI, 232.

17. The film is a remake of a German-French film with the same title, directed by Joe May in 1931/32; Ernst Marischka, the director and screenwriter of the 1951 film, co-authored the script. The narrative in the later version closely follows the earlier one; only the location has changed (from the French to the Italian Riviera), and Lisa Krüger's mysterious travel companion, a British lord, has been replaced by a racing driver.

18. See Kos, 1994, 168; also Sieder, Steinert and Tálos, 1996, 19.

19. P. Bernecker. 1955. *Der moderne Fremdenverkehr. Markt- und betriebswirtschaftliche Probleme in Einzeldarstellung*, cited by Kos, 1994, 166.

20. Kos, 1994, 167. It is not only *Verliebter Sommer* that depicts men with their caravans, but also films closely related to tourist film, such as *Liebe Freundin* (1949) and *Auf der grünen Wiese* (1953). The caravans serve to highlight the owners' suitability as future husbands and providers.

21. Nevertheless, in Austria, travelling for pleasure remained largely a privilege of the urban middle-class well into the 1970s. In 1972, only 30 per cent of Austrians had gone on holiday. See, for example, I. Karazman-Morawetz. 1996. 'Arbeit, Konsum, Freizeit. Veränderungen im Verhältnis von Arbeit und Reproduktion', in R. Sieder, H. Steinert and E. Tálos (eds), *Österreich 1945–1995: Gesellschaft, Politik, Kultur*, Vienna: Verlag für Gesellschaftskritik, 414.

22. See M. Füringk, 'Aus österreichischen Ateliers. Hans Moser verliebt sich', *Mein Film*, 38, 19 September 1947.

23. See M. Füringk, 'Aus der österreichischen Produktion: Hertha Mayen und Theodor Danegger lernen servieren', *Mein Film*, 39, 26 September 1947.

24. See 'Plätschern wir weiter', *Welt am Abend*, 26 March 1948; 'Aus der Filmwelt', *Weltpresse*, 30 March 1948.

25. See E.v. Neusser. 1950. 'Die österreichischen Filmerfolge', *Film-Kunst. Zeitschrift für Filmkultur und Filmwissenschaft*, 5, 253.

26. D. Herzog. 2003. 'Desperately Seeking Normality: Sex and Marriage in the Wake of War', in R. Bessel and D. Schumann (eds), *Life after Death: Approaches to a Cultural and Social History of Europe during the 1940s and 1950s*, Washington: German Historical Institute, 162.

27. See Bodzenta and Grond, 1957, 232.

28. See, for example, E. Thurner. 1992. 'Frauen-Nachkriegsleben in Österreich – im Zentrum und in der Provinz', in I. Bandhauer-Schöffmann and E. Hornung (eds). 1992. *Wiederaufbau weiblich. Dokumentation der Tagung 'Frauen in der Österreichischen und Deutschen Nachkriegszeit'*, Vienna: Geyer-Ed, 9–13; Bandhauer-Schöffmann and Hornung, 1992, 113.

29. The dominant discourse that promoted traditional gender relations nevertheless stood in contrast to a rise in female employment in the 1950s. Both Heineman and Schissler offer insightful analyses of these contradictory positions in West Germany. See E.D. Heineman. 2003. *What Difference Does a Husband Make? Women and Marital Status in Nazi and Postwar Germany*, Berkeley: University of California Press, 217–223; Schissler, 2001, 365–369.

30. F. Inglis. 2000. *Delicious History of the Holiday*, London: Routledge, 11.

31. See Sieder, Steinert and Tálos, 1996, 15.

32. A. Confino. 2003. 'Dissonance, Normality and the Historical Method: Why Did Some Germans Think of Tourism after May 8, 1945?' in R. Bessel and D. Schumann (eds), *Life after Death: Approaches to a Cultural and Social History of Europe during the 1940s and 1950s*, Washington: German Historical Institute, 332–333.

33. See ibid., 331.

34. Ibid., 334. According to Alon Confino, only one-third of the population of West Germany travelled in 1960, despite the onset of mass tourism.

35. See Carter, 2010, 90.

36. J. Munby. 1999. 'Strassenfilme', in T. Elsaesser (ed.), *The BFI Companion to German Cinema*, London: BFI, 230.

37. See Büttner and Dewald, 1997a, 325–326.

38. See Heiss, 1990, 120.

39. Inglis, 2000, 8.

40. Geiger's use of the heavily loaded term *Wiedergutmachung* (reparation or compensation) is an undisguised reference to the contemporary political discussion on paying compensation to the victims of Nazi crimes, a demand of which the majority of Austrians disapproved. See also Brecht, 2005, 169–171.

41. See A. Pelinka. 1985. 'Zur Gründung der Zweiten Republik. Neue Ergebnisse trotz personeller und struktureller Kontinuität', in L. Wächter-Böhm (ed.), *Wien 1945 davor/ danach*, Vienna: Christian Brandstätter, n.p.

42. See Kos, 1994, 151–172.

43. See Hanisch, 2005, 99.

44. See Herzog, 2003, 161–164.

45. See Cohan, 1997, 45–49; also J.T. Patterson. 1996. *Grand Expectations: The United States, 1945–1974*, New York: Oxford University Press, 32–38.

46. See E.K. Pavalko and G.H. Elder, Jr. 1990. 'World War II and Divorce: A Life-Course Perspective', *The American Journal of Sociology*, 5(March), 12–14; for postwar Austria, see Österreichisches Statististisches Zentralamt, 1959a, 21–27.

47. Bodzenta and Grond, 1957, 438.

48. J.B. Gilbert. 2005. *Men in the Middle: Searching for Masculinity in the 1950s*, Chicago: University of Chicago Press, 67.

49. Ibid., 77.

50. Cohan, 1997, ix–xxi.

51. According to Cohan, the masculine ideal of the domesticated male of the 1950s was seen as the family's 'moral and psychological leader'. Cohan, 1997, 49–56.

52. See A. Pilgram. 1996. 'Die Zweite Republik in der Kriminalpolitik', in R. Sieder, H. Steinert and E. Tálos (eds), *Österreich 1945–1995: Gesellschaft, Politik, Kultur*, Vienna: Verlag für Gesellschaftskritik, 491. After the Allied Forces had liberated Austria, the penal law of 1852 was reinstated, which made the exercise of male and female homosexuality illegal and penalised it with imprisonment for between one and five years. See W. Wilhelm. 2005. *Dossier zum Hintergrund der Verfolgung wegen sexueller Orientierung in der Zeit des Nationalsozialismus und danach*, http://www.publicartvienna.at/downloads/ Dossier_morzinplatz_d.pdf, retrieved 18 February 2011.

53. See Sonja Schachinger's penetrative analysis: Schachinger, 1993, 96–98.

54. 'Bühnenstück wird Drehbuch', *Mein Film*, 23, 5 June 1947.

55. Ibid.

56. See Brecht, 2005, 169.

57. Cohan, 1997, 38.

58. See Inglis, 2000, 12.

59. Büttner and Dewald, 1997a, 240.

60. See, for example, 'Österreichischer Lustspielfilm: "Kleiner Schwindel am Wolfgangsee"', *Wiener Zeitung*, 4 January 1950; 'Komikerstelldichein am Mondsee', *Weltpresse*, 26 July 1951.

61. Up to the Second World War, 'an energetic and vigorous homosexual was beyond imagination', at least in dominant discourse. Mosse, 1998, 139.

62. Cohan, 1997, 292.

63. Ibid., xii–xiii.

Chapter 5

COMEDY

With around sixty-five films, comedy was the largest genre in postwar Austria. About one-quarter of the yearly film output between 1945 and 1955 was comedy, making it one of the most popular genres in Austrian cinema.[1] Comedies provided light-hearted, escapist entertainment, albeit a form of escapism that differed from that of other genres. Historical costume film, for instance, invited the spectator to relive a glorious past, thereby instilling a sense of national pride. *Heimatfilm* provided escape to an unspoilt, rural world in which those faithful to traditional values were rewarded. The pleasures that audiences derived from watching comedy were different: the genre made light of the problems that arose from social transformations, thus helping the audience to embrace change.

Because comedy is a very diverse and fluid genre, there are many overlaps with other types of film; some critics even argue that comedy should not be considered a genre at all, but rather a mode of dealing with a subject.[2] There is an ongoing academic debate about what actually defines a film comedy: whether a happy ending or the generation of laughter are essential elements; and whether it is primarily the narrative which constitutes a comedy, as Gerald Mast argues, or rather the 'comic units' of gags and jokes.[3] More important for the purposes of this book is the idea that comedy animates the audience to question social standards and rules. Because comedy's mockery exposes existing norms, it can also give us insights into contemporary views on gender and gender relations; in particular, we should ask whether masculinity is an object of laughter in Austrian comedy or not. If so, which forms of masculinities are ridiculed? In what ways are they mocked, and to what effect? And, crucially, does parody undermine men's position of power, or does it actually affirm it? In order to be able to decode representations of gender in comedy, we first need to understand how it actually creates comic effect.

According to Geoff King, comedies are perceived as funny because they often involve departures from what are generally considered 'normal' routines of life. To make these digressions comical, the actions or events presented have to remain very close to reality; often they require only a slight exaggeration or disproportional representation.[4] Stephen Neale and Frank Krutnik suggest that a constitutive element of the genre is the violation of 'decorum' and 'verisimilitude', which allows characters to transgress traditional gender roles or display behaviour that in reality would be considered unacceptable.[5] Obviously, as Mast emphasises, the audience has to remain reassured that what they see is not true, as only the 'disbelief in comedy's reality' can provide the necessary emotional release for the audience.[6]

Because comedy mainly creates laughter through the transgression of rules or conventions, it is generally viewed as subversive and even empowering.[7] In our case, comedy may confront the audience with views on gender relations opposed to the dominant norm, and thus encourage the audience to challenge the existing order. Some critics, however, have questioned comedy's subversive potential and its ability to undermine authority: Neale and Krutnik, for example, deny that comedy is 'inherently subversive', arguing that deviation from norms is the essence of comedy and, indeed, its key function.[8] They argue that deviation is playful, not subversive, a point of view shared by Mast, who insists that 'the enjoyable silliness' of many comedies tempts the audience 'to indulge their own antisocial urges without damaging the social fabric'.[9] A Foucauldian view would go even further and argue that comedy merely dupes the spectator into believing that norms and rules are undermined, when in fact they are actually reasserted through comedy's controlled, sanctioned transgression. Comedy therefore may *appear* subversive, but actually reaffirms social order by acknowledging its norms.[10]

Still, as Mikhail Bakhtin's classic study of the 'carnivalesque' in the Middle Ages and the Renaissance has shown, humour can also get out of hand and end in actual riots.[11] We can conclude that comedy creates subversive potential by exposing and playing with the rules, although whether this potential can effectively unfold its power depends very much on the specific context in which comedy is produced and seen.[12] Its ability to be critical is inevitably restricted by generic rules and the producers' economic interests as well as by the wider socio-political context. The question as to whether postwar Austrian comedy was inherently affirmative of the established order or tried to subvert it is important insofar as it allows us to determine the role of popular cinema in society. Did Austrian comedy expose the seemingly 'natural' gender order as manmade, or did it mock those that challenged it? Did it make fun of men who embodied the masculine ideal, or those who tried to achieve it? Keeping these questions in mind will help us to decode the double meaning of comedy and its response to contemporary discourses.

The Attraction of Comedy

As noted above, comedies were very successful with Austrian audiences. Statistics show that the ten most screened films in 1953 include seven comedies, four of them produced in Austria: *Pünktchen und Anton* (Anna Louise and Anton, 1953), *Ich und meine Frau* (Me and My Wife, 1953), *1. April 2000* (April 1, 2000, 1952) and *Hannerl* (Hannerl, 1952). The first two were only superseded in popularity by the Austrian historical costume comedy *Der Feldherrnhügel* and the Italian comedy *Don Camillo und Peppone* (The Little World of Don Camillo, 1952).[13] For the film industry, comedy was an economically 'safe' genre: always popular with audiences, comedies were also comparatively cheap and fast to produce, as no expensive décor and settings were needed.[14] Antel's comedy *Der Mann in der Wanne* (The Man in the Bathtub, 1953), for example, took only six weeks to film, earning the director praise for his 'fast', 'precise' and 'economical' filmmaking.[15]

It was not only domestic audiences that loved Austrian comedies – they sold well in West Germany, too.[16] This raises the question of the exportability of humour. Jean-Pierre Jeancolas famously postulated that humour, or at least a certain kind of humour, is 'inexportable' because audiences need to be familiar with the traditions and contexts the films allude to in order to find them funny. Jeancolas used this claim to explain why national film industries in Europe produced a certain quota of films solely directed at a national or even regional audience, films he described as 'too insignificant and/or unintelligible to be appreciated by spectators outside'.[17] In his view, it is not so much the language per se, but the missing intertextuality that makes a film incomprehensible to a foreign audience.

The fact that Austrian comedies were popular with German audiences suggests, then, that these comedies plugged into the 'cultural capital' both nations shared. Austrian filmmakers were able to take full advantage of the long tradition of exchange between the two film industries. German audiences knew and loved the stars of Austrian comedy, such as Hans Moser, Paul Hörbiger and Wolf Albach-Retty, and they were familiar with the characteristics of Austrian comedy: the Viennese vernacular, adapted to make it intelligible for German ears; the operetta or musical theme that featured in many Austrian films; and the stereotypical protagonists, such as the 'sweet' Viennese girl, the charming philanderer and the seemingly misanthropic but good-hearted Viennese everyman.[18] Last but not least, Austrian comedies featured a growing number of German actors in key roles to increase their appeal to West German audiences. We can certainly suggest that the shared language and traditions facilitated the export of Austrian comedies to Germany, and by the same token it is questionable whether their dialogue-based humour would have been successful in other, non-German speaking countries.[19]

Comedy is a multi-faceted form that can be divided into a number of sub-genres.[20] The Austrian film industry's preference for romantic comedies and so-called 'domestic comedies' and 'children's films', which depict family life or the problems of children and teenagers in a humorous light, catered to the tastes of Austrian audiences, who liked light-hearted entertainment without too much action. According to the conservative newspaper *Die Presse*, Austrian audiences favoured films that provided 'relaxation, cheeriness, a respite from everyday life, without putting any demands on the cinema-goer'. Therefore, to be successful a comedy had to be 'cheerful, not too droll and entertaining without being irritating'.[21] A romantic comedy, such as *Ein bezaubernder Schwindler* (A Charming Fraud, 1949), that 'makes up for the lack of new ideas with charm' was therefore, in the view of the left-wing *Weltpresse*, judged as good entertainment.[22] As these quotations indicate, the Austrian audience found too much agitation or turbulence unsettling, which might explain why masquerade, slapstick and physical humour are almost entirely absent from postwar Austrian comedy.

An exception is the sub-genre called the *Bauernschwank* – a burlesque form of entertainment set in the rural community.[23] The ribald humour and trite sexual innuendos of the nine *Bauernschwänke* produced between 1946 and 1955 caused much outrage, among both middle-class critics and the rural population. While the critics damned the films for their 'artistic failure' and lack of originality, rural audiences were offended by the sexual allusions and the depiction of farmers as backward and dumb. The negative response suggests that these rustic comedies deeply disturbed Austria's cultural elites: the *Wiener Tageszeitung* criticised *Die Verjüngungskur* (Rejuvenation Cure, 1948) for 'the silliest and most ribald jokes, coarsest gags and most feeble tastelessness', whereas the *Wiener Kurier* lamented that *Liebesprobe* (Love Test, 1949) 'continues the series of our deepest artistic humiliations'.[24] Some provincial governments, following demonstrations by outraged Catholics, even banned the comedies *Die Verjüngungskur* and *Der Leberfleck* (The Freckle, 1948) for violation of morality and the suggested debasement of the rural community.[25] The fact that these *Bauernschwänke* triggered so much criticism from the Catholic Church, provincial authorities and the cultured bourgeoisie points to their subversive potential. However, they were by no means politically subversive, but rather subversive in a moral sense: in a society so preoccupied with 'cleanliness' and the repression of 'loose' moral behaviour, the sexual humour of the rustic comedies must have caused considerable offence as it ran counter to the official (self-)image of Austria as a nation of culture and innocence.

Visual Style and the Object of Humour

The most successful comedies, however, were those that featured popular stars and generated humour through dialogue and narrative. As with other Austrian genres, comedy displayed strong continuities with the cinema of the Third Reich and beyond. E.W. Emo, Eduard von Borsody and Géza von Cziffra, all experts in creating musical comedies and operetta films, continued to produce similar films after the war, albeit in a slightly modernised but less lavish form. Newcomers such as Antel, who became one of the most prolific directors of comedies in postwar Austria, brought little innovation to the genre. His trademark was simply structured comedies of mistaken identities, garnished with scantily clad women – films that were cheap to produce and directed at a mass audience.

The visual style of most Austrian postwar comedies is fairly conventional: balanced, 'natural' lighting, eye-level shooting and a shot scale ranging from medium shots to medium close-ups are typical. Editing is relatively slow – fast or trick editing are seldom used. Cinematography and montage clearly take a back seat in Austrian comedy so as not to distract from the dialogue as the comedy is primarily verbal, not visual. Some of the earlier postwar comedies do stand out as visually more original, however: *Der himmlische Walzer* (Heavenly Waltz, 1948) is framed by a story in which the scriptwriter discusses his film with the producer and the sponsor of the film project. When the latter, having seen the end product, disapproves of the ending, the film is rewound and an alternative ending is presented. Von Cziffra, the director, thus deliberately breaks the illusion of cinema and draws attention to the film's fictionality, thereby increasing audience satisfaction by giving viewers credit for their familiarity with the modes of filmmaking.[26] Hans Wolff used a different method to get the attention of the audience in *Ein bezaubernder Schwindler*. Here, the film begins with the male lead, played by Wolf Albach-Retty, opening a window and addressing the audience directly by asking the 'Ladies and Gentlemen in the audience' whether they have ever been in love. Such innovative devices, however, would soon disappear from Austrian comedy; filmmakers who were perhaps still unsure about which direction to take in the early postwar era returned to tried and tested methods after society had recovered from the turmoil.

Generally, then, the producers of comedies prioritised the narrative and verbal over the visual. Puns, verbal misunderstandings and the mispronunciation of non-German or difficult words, combined with facial expressions and gestures that underline this miscommunication, provide the main source of laughter. Emphasis on dialogue has a long tradition in Austrian comedy due to the country's strong and very influential cabaret tradition, which focused on deft wordplay and the game of coding and decoding rather than physical humour.[27] Prime examples are the films featuring the popular comedian Hans Moser. One of Moser's trademarks was his mumbling speech and creative use of the Viennese vernacular. He seemed continuously at war with the formal German language, a conflict which led him to pronounce words wrongly or produce fabulous word creations that were (seemingly unintentionally) funny. Moser's broad appeal guaranteed packed houses, which, unfortunately, led to him being typecast in his later career, in roles that did not make full use of his extraordinary talents. Marketed as 'Moser-films', these postwar comedies functioned as mere star vehicles.

The Function of the Star in Hallo Dienstmann

Moser usually played the ordinary everyman who desperately tries to gain attention and thus produces all kinds of trouble. Like his characters, Moser had to fight hard to win recognition. Born in 1880, he was already in his fifties when he had his film breakthrough in the 1930s. Before that, he had played provincial stages and cabarets for many years before finding engagements in Viennese theatres. One of his most famous roles was that of a porter, a character he had created in the 1920s and which he re-enacted successfully in the comedy *Hallo Dienstmann* (Hello Porter!, 1951). The film was a big success, and became a classic that experienced many reruns on national television. Directed by Antel and written by Lilian Belmont and Rudolf Österreicher, the film's popularity was largely a result of clever casting. The leads were played by Hans Moser and Paul Hörbiger, a popular comic pairing who had acted alongside each other in many films. The conservative newspaper *Die Presse* summed up the chief attraction of the film as involving 'two of our most popular comedians, side by side in friendship and quarrel'.[28] The left-wing *Arbeiterzeitung*, too, showered praise on Moser for being 'captivatingly funny'.[29] Only the trade journal *Paimann's Filmlisten* was slightly more restrained, conceding that the film was 'remarkably entertaining', largely because of the 'delicious interplay between Hörbiger and Moser, neither of whom strains himself excessively'.[30]

Hallo Dienstmann was one of many comedies directed by Antel, who specialised in light entertainment, but who lacked the effortless touch of a Géza von Cziffra or E.W. Emo. Antel's self-proclaimed motto was that films should do nothing else but 'give pleasure to the people', but his presumed knowledge of what the audience craved often resulted in run-of-the-mill productions that made him one of the most taunted filmmakers in postwar Austria.[31] Yet, his films usually sold well, a fact one contemporary film critic acidly ascribed to Antel's ability to 'extort a maximum of joy and suffering from the audience'.[32]

Hallo Dienstmann, a comedy of mistaken identity, tells the story of Professor Godai (Paul Hörbiger), a much admired teacher of music at the academy in Vienna, who dresses up as a porter for a carnival ball. A real porter, Anton Lischka (Hans Moser), then mistakes him for a colleague, and demands his assistance in transporting the luggage of a new arrival, Miss Brandstätter (Maria Andergast), from the station to her home. Godai, who is drunk, willingly plays along, and makes a fool of himself when moving her goods into her flat (Figure 5.1). The next day he discovers that Miss Brandstätter is his new colleague and, having fallen for her, he desperately

Figure 5.1: The two porters (Paul Hörbiger, left, and Hans Moser) enjoy a drink with Miss Brandstätter (Maria Andergast) in *Hallo Dienstmann*. Filmarchiv Austria.

tries to conceal his 'other identity'. Miss Brandstätter soon discovers the truth, and uses her knowledge to play a few tricks on Godai; meanwhile the porter, Lischka, believes Godai to be a crook and tries to expose him. In the end, all misunderstandings are resolved and Godai and Brandstätter emerge as a happy couple.

The most famous part of the film is the so-called 'suitcase scene', which is based on a comedy sketch Moser himself had developed and played on stage in the 1920s. It shows the clownish attempts of two porters trying to get a big suitcase (or, in the case of the film *Hallo Dienstmann*, a wooden box) upstairs; yet, true to the Austrian comedy tradition, the humour of the scene results not so much from physical action as from the verbal exchange between the two porters.[33]

Despite the emphasis on the verbal, a key element of Moser's star image was his bodily appearance. He was of advanced age when he started his film career, and was small and corpulent. Because his physical appearance was that of a man who is easily overlooked, he had to act himself into the foreground: Moser's characters are notable for their empty outbursts of frustration, their vigorous attempts to create order, their rebellion against a system that threatens to crush the individual and their strong sentimental streak, which always makes them side with young lovers and dogs.[34] His animated gestures and vigorous movements, which defy the inertia of his small, overweight, aging body, amplify his verbal expressions. Moser is not a modern man; he usually plays the *paterfamilias* who claims absolute power in the family; even though he is a kind-hearted father, he strongly disapproves of female independence and rebuffs any attempts by women to interfere with his decision-making. Moser displays an interesting mix of positive and negative characteristics: he is quick-tempered, but easily conciliated; servile and even hypocritical when confronted with authority, but never ruthless or overly ambitious.

With his penchant for music and wine, his kind-hearted nature and lack of ambition, Moser expresses many traits that postwar cinema displayed as masculine virtues. Yet, at the same time, he embodies characteristics that stand in opposition to this masculine ideal: his characters lack the optimism or cultured behaviour of those played by Paul Hörbiger, for example; neither is he harmonious, but quarrelsome and grumbling. These apparent contradictions can only be explained by his star image: star figures, Christine Gledhill argues, not only 'personify' the values and imperatives of the genre, they also condense the social and ideological values of a specific society and era.[35] Hans Moser thus did not represent an ideal that people should emulate; instead, he embodied the inconsistency of the traditions and aspirations of contemporary society. He not only played men who seemed to have been taken directly from the street, but actually was such a man - Moser was the incarnation of real rather than ideal masculinity. Numerous stories about Moser's frugal lifestyle, his stinginess, his domineering wife and his love of good wines resonated in the characters he played on screen. Moser bridged the gap between reality and fiction and, in his function as star, acted as 'mediator between the real and the imaginary'.[36]

Significantly, his image withstood the test of time and hardly changed over the course of his long career, making Moser an emblem of continuity from the 1930s to the 1960s.[37] Nevertheless, the figures he played were remnants of the past.[38] They were, in the words of the porter Lischka in *Hallo Dienstmann*, 'threatened with extinction'. 'Once we were two thousand licensed porters, two thousand! Now we have dwindled – to a nonentity', Lischka laments, and his diagnosis also holds true for the masculine type he embodies, which is doomed to vanish as it offers no potential for modernisation. Moser's famous porter role is nostalgic, recalling an idealised Austrian past, and thus serves to inspire patriotism as it reaches back to its origins in the inter-war years, when Austrian culture flourished on the stages of cabarets and theatres.

Hallo Dienstmann is fairly untypical of Austrian comedy in that it does not address contemporary issues or display many time-specific codes in narrative or in mise en scène. The great majority of comedies commented on dominant discourses or otherwise connected to social reality. *Kleine Melodie aus Wien* (Little Melody from Vienna, 1948), for example, uses the massive problem of the housing shortage to deal with the prejudices of people who are forced to take in lodgers. Alfred Stöger's *Triumph der Liebe*

(Triumph of Love, 1947), an adaptation of Aristophanes' anti-war comedy *Lysistrata*, ironically alludes to the experience of the Second World War, mocking men's preoccupation with war and their willingness to follow orders. Later postwar comedies responded to the modernisation of society and the influx of US culture and consumer products by commenting humorously on conflicted marriages, career issues or the damaging effects of money.

By engaging with these issues in an ironic way, comedy could have realised a subversive potential, but in fact the humour in these comedies remained mostly apolitical. Satires were scarce, which can be explained by the absence of Jewish comedians, who had shaped Austria's political cabaret and film scene until they were forced into emigration or murdered by the Nazis. Another reason for the absence of satirical comedies was the brutal suppression of any form of criticism during the Nazi regime, which made people wary of expressing discontent openly.[39] During the Allied occupation, Austria's film industry sustained a form of pre-emptive self-censorship that it had grown accustomed to in the previous years. Taking all this into account, it is not really surprising that the humour of postwar Austrian comedies was usually harmless and that the jokes were often trite.[40]

Even the political sarcasm in the few satirical comedies produced in postwar Austria – *Die Welt dreht sich verkehrt*, *1. April 2000* and *Hin und her* (To and Fro, 1948) – was fairly tame. The former two films are strongly nationalistic, and thus represent an interesting combination of subversion and affirmation. *1. April 2000*, for example, was commissioned by the Austrian government to bolster Austria's call for national independence and the withdrawal of the foreign troops, but in order not to offend the Allied Forces, the demand was to be presented in comical form.[41] *1. April 2000* depicts the Allies as alien intruders who occupy Austria and accuse the Austrians of being compulsive warmongers; the Austrians, however, manage to 'prove' their innocence by providing historical evidence of Austria's innate pacifism.[42] Contemporary reviews indicate that the audience understood the film in the way intended by the filmmakers: as criticism of the Allies' political claims, which were viewed as unjustified.[43]

Mistaken Identities and the Chance of a New Beginning

The vast majority of Austrian postwar comedies revolve around the theme of mistaken identity and follow a similar pattern. At the centre of these stories are characters who either deliberately assume a false identity or who are mistaken for somebody else. They all adapt to their new self with surprising ease: the artist Mühlmeier (Wolf Albach-Retty) in Antel's *Der Mann in der Wanne*, for instance, is mistaken for a burglar in a friend's apartment, but accepts his arrest as a convenient way of escaping marriage.[44]

After much confusion and many narrative twists and surprises, the 'real' identities are revealed and everything falls into place. The pleasure for the audience lies in anticipating the revelation rather than in comic surprise.

The high frequency with which the theme of mistaken identity occurs in Austrian comedy suggests that it had a particular resonance with the audience. This was an audience unsure about its national identity, as the experience of Nazi rule and defeat of Germany had made it impossible for most Austrians to describe themselves as Germans.[45] The Austrian elites made great efforts to promote a new national identity, both to orient its people and to receive favourable treatment from the victorious Allied Forces. Popular cinema engaged with this political discourse and took up the issue through the theme of mistaken identity; it tapped into the 'collective fears, hopes and hidden anxieties' of the Austrians and offered reassurance by depicting how joyful and rewarding it is to assume a different self.[46]

The play with identities was not limited by gender, age or class; yet, while everybody could become somebody else, Austrian comedy drew a strict line when it came to sexual identities. So the theme of gender ambiguity through cross-dressing, which was such a prominent feature of British comedy at the time, is absent from postwar Austrian cinema. The absence of female and male transvestites is also surprising when one considers the long tradition of cross-dressing in neighbouring German cinema, both before the war (*Viktor und Viktoria*, Viktor and Viktoria, 1933) and after it (*Fanfaren der Liebe*, Fanfares of Love, 1951; *Tante Jutta aus Kalkutta*, Aunt Jutta from Calcutta, 1953; *Charleys Tante*, Charley's Aunt, 1955). In Austrian comedy, on the other hand, it was not until the early 1960s that the first male character dressed up as a woman appeared (from then on usually played by the Austrian actor Peter Alexander); this did then trigger a brief boom in this trope, with the release of *Die Abenteuer des Grafen Bobby* (The Adventures of Count Bobby, 1961), *Das süße Leben des Grafen Bobby* (The Sweet Life of Count Bobby, 1962) and a remake of a British stage comedy, *Charleys Tante* (1963).

It is quite difficult to establish the exact reasons for the lack of cross-gendering in Austrian comedy. What remains important is that up to 1960 Austrian comedy presented gendered identities and sexual orientation in an unambiguous light: the films clearly demarcate masculinity from femininity through distinct body language and costume. Unlike historical costume film or tourist film, which occasionally allude to homosexuality, postwar comedy neither silently undermines nor openly questions the heterosexual norm. It deliberately eschews gender ambiguity, even as it blurs distinctions of class, regional identity or age – all to produce the illusion of a homogeneous society. It was this obscuring of differences in response to the erosion of class distinctions and the process of national reorientation that required gender as an anchor point. With a society in flux, gender seemed to remain the only constant; if gendered identities had been depicted as just as unstable, comedy would have threatened this last pillar of society. Of course, the fact that it did not challenge gender roles demonstrates that comedy essentially affirmed the positions of the ruling elites, who aimed to stabilise society by glossing over class differences, promoting an Austrian identity and postulating the 'naturalness' of traditional gender roles.

One key message of Austrian comedy is that a change of identity provides you with the things you long for, be it love, a job or money. In the hugely successful comedy *Hannerl*, for example, the heroine, Hannerl (Johanna Matz), who struggles to find employment as a dancer, approaches a stage producer with the lie that she is his illegitimate daughter – and is promptly given a contract. Narratives such as this suggest that acquiring a new identity is a worthwhile and, above all, straightforward process: all it takes is a lie and perhaps a change in appearance or manners. Hence, in *Glück muss man haben* (Strike it Lucky, 1953), unemployed Robert Wiesinger (German actor Wolfgang Lukschy), who has been unsuccessful in his job hunt, simply sets himself up in an empty office in a large company; by displaying an air of bustling activity he makes people believe he actually works there. His 'entrepreneurial spirit' is rewarded, and Wiesinger is given the job of manager. How easy (if exhausting) it is to slip from one role to another can be observed in the Austrian screwball comedy *Ein bezaubernder Schwindler*, where the male lead, Martin Palmer (Wolf Albach-Retty), switches from athlete to percussionist to intellectual (Figure 5.2). Making

Figure 5.2: Martin Palmer (Wolf Albach Retty), exhausted from switching roles in *Ein bezaubernder Schwindler* (here with Inge Konradi). Filmarchiv Austria.

a young, female philosophy student believe he is a French existentialist is not difficult: black-rimmed glasses, a couple of journals on existentialism, a slightly condescending manner and the furrowing of his brow turn him into the intellectual the young woman is pining for. Critics loved the 'exhilarating airiness' of *Ein bezaubernder Schwindler,* and praised 'the highly unlikely story of the swindle of three unemployed bank clerks' in *Glück muss man haben* for radiating 'so much optimism ... that the audience is much delighted by this clean and nice film'.[47]

By celebrating such metamorphoses, comedy draws attention to the performativity of social identities – the fact that 'people ... "present" themselves rather than just be'.[48] This emphasis on performance hints at the deceptiveness of appearances. Nothing is as it seems in Austrian comedy, and identities appear constantly in flux. Crucially, this volatility is not presented as unsettling, but liberating. Postwar comedies convey the impression that just by dressing or speaking like one of the upper-classes, one can become a member. However, the ease with which protagonists slip into a different social field, usually from lower class to middle-class, also underlines the necessity to comply with existing (middle-class) rules. Whilst members of the working-class are not excluded in comedy as they are in other genres, they are positioned within middle-class surroundings whose standards are presented as the norm.

Thus, contrary to other national cinemas in postwar Europe, Austrian comedy marginalises the working-class, suggesting that its members must give way to middle-class norms if they are to proceed. These efforts to omit the working-class could be a response to the decline of the old proletariat, or perhaps to the attempts of the political elites to bridge the class divide with a policy of consensus.[49] Presenting the middle-class as the only viable lifestyle, these comedies therefore affirm rather than subvert bourgeois values, albeit to varying degrees. To be sure, Austrian comedy sometimes ridicules these values and conventions, as, for instance, in *Das Kuckucksei* (The Cuckoo's Egg, 1949), where the snobbish, bourgeois groom, Dr Kurt Walla (Curd Jürgens), checks the social background of his bride before marrying her. Walla is presented as a negative character because he is a firm believer in biological heredity, a school of thought closely connected to National Socialist eugenic politics. The film inspires a feeling of *Schadenfreude* when shallow Kurt finds out that his bride has been adopted, and that her biological mother, Marie (Käthe Dorsch), is a prostitute and kleptomaniac – and thus the worst mother-in-law he could imagine. Yet, Marie, though loud, amoral and unruly, is the most likeable character in the rather stiff and dusty middle-class setting she is thrown into. Even so, Marie has been tamed into an (almost) presentable middle-class woman by the end of the film and, through her (socially sanctioned) business, has gained acceptance even in the conservative circles of Salzburg. *Das Kuckucksei* is quite ambiguous in its presentation of middle-class values: while affirmative of bourgeois standards, it also shows how enjoyable it is to violate these rules. As a whole, then, Austrian comedies emphasise that class barriers are not rigid, but that the middle-class is open to everyone willing to accept its rules.

These examples serve to illustrate where the pleasure for the audience lies: the spectators are invited to identify with the characters on screen, who dare to do something they would not do themselves. The comedies offer a mixture of suspense – we expect the true identity of the protagonist to be revealed at any moment and fear or await the punishment – and relief, when the revelation brings the turmoil to an end and resolves all problems without any negative consequences. The message that old identities burdened by the past can so easily be shed was surely an optimistic prospect for an audience that was only too glad to move on from its travails during the war. One reviewer explicitly drew the connection between fiction and social practice when he concluded, referring to the comedy *Ein bezaubernder Schwindler*: 'he who finagles, thrives and prospers is not only the motto of our times, but also the basis for this new comedy'.[50] Although Austrian comedy avoids any direct reference to the Nazi past, it suggests that it is acceptable and even necessary to lie about one's past to be successful.

Despite the films' emphasis on untruthfulness, it would be incorrect to deduce that postwar comedy presents truth as entirely dispensable;[51] rather, it is presented as relative and subjective. This goes particularly for those comedies in which people are taken for somebody else by mistake. When a man (Walter Giller) rescues the heroine, Irene (Bruni Löbel), from the street where she has fainted in Emo's comedy *Irene in Nöten* (Irene in Trouble, 1953), he uses the name in her address book to establish her identity. The fact that the address book is not her own, and that she is consequently put into the bed of a man unknown to her, triggers an avalanche of misunderstandings. All the protagonists in *Irene in Nöten* take their individual interpretations of facts as objective truth, which then results in false assumptions. The comic narrative thus suggests that no fault can be ascribed to the individual for believing in a different truth than the others. This was obviously a message loaded with meaning in postwar Austria, where people quickly turned from collaborators to victims of Nazi aggression. In postwar comedy, people are always better – or at least, less guilty – than they appear at first. In *Es schlägt dreizehn* (That's the Limit! 1950), a butler and his successor, played by the popular comic pairing of Theo Lingen and Hans Moser, suspect each other to be murderers. The harmless tourist Otto Liebling (Walter Müller) in *Auf der grünen Wiese* (In the Green Meadow, 1953) is wrongly imprisoned as a poacher; and the chaotic Bimbi (Hannelore Schroth) in *Fräulein Bimbi* (Miss Bimbi, 1951) is mistaken for a dangerous lunatic. These fictions could function as what Anton Kaes describes as a 'form of communal self-reflection'.[52] In a country whose citizens were preoccupied with denial of their actions during the Nazi occupation, the comic resolution that everything was just a misunderstanding could provide welcome relief.

The Pleasures of a New Identity in Der himmlische Walzer

Austrian comedy presents the past as a burden. What better state, then, than to have no past at all, like the naïve angel, Angelika, in *Der himmlische Walzer*, whose lack of a personal past allows her to adapt almost effortlessly to a life on Earth? *Der himmlische Walzer*, produced in 1948, was one of the most successful comedies in early postwar Austria. *Die Presse* complimented the producers on a charming comedy that offered a successful mixture of 'music, charm, wit and humour', pointing out that it contained all the elements that the Austrian audience and the export market would expect from such a film: 'the plot unfolds swiftly. Each scene is filled with pep and spirit. Each part has been cast perfectly'.[53] Other reviewers were less gushing, but conceded that the director had delivered an effective comedy.[54] So well received was the film that it was exported not only to West Germany but also to the US, France and Italy, where it was banned in 1951 for violating religious feelings.[55]

Der himmlische Walzer was directed, produced and written by the Hungarian-born Géza von Cziffra, a talented producer of light-hearted entertainment cinema.[56] Cziffra had written a large number of successful screenplays in the 1930s, before making his breakthrough as director with the ice-skating revue *Der weiße Traum* (The White Dream, 1943), one of the most expensive and successful films produced in the Third Reich.[57] Briefly imprisoned by the Nazis in spring 1945, Cziffra continued his successful career after the war with musical comedies, first in Austria and then, from 1950, in West Germany.

Der himmlische Walzer starts out with an angels' rebellion in heaven: the female angels, unhappy about their 'old look', are keen to dress in a more modern style, and thus demand that one of their fellow angels is sent to Earth to acquire new dresses from Vienna's foremost fashion designer. The angels' committee agrees, and sends Angelika (Elfie Mayerhofer) to the studio of fashion designer Clemens Maria Weidenauer (Curd Jürgens). Angelika is chosen because she is the most naïve angel, and so thought to be immune to the temptations of the city. Blissfully ignorant of all worldly things, she soon finds herself without her magic wings and thus cut off from heavenly assistance. In Weidenauer's fashion studio she is mistaken for a chorus girl who has to be fitted with an angel costume for the new musical revue. Angelika quickly adapts to her new role by copying the behaviour of the people around her, but this brings her into conflict with the good-looking young composer Hans Lieven (Paul Hubschmid), whose car she enters self-confidently. Hans feels manipulated when she answers his questions with remarkable naivety, and so remarks, sarcastically: 'Say, Fräulein, do you live on the moon?' 'Not quite, but close by', she responds forthrightly. By showing how Angelika's ingenuous account of having no home, no family and no clothes is met with disbelief, the comic narrative suggests that the truth is hard to accept, whereas lies are readily believed.

Hans is first offended, then intrigued by Angelika's unusual directness, and finally falls for her when he hears her singing at an audition. In the end, the two become a couple and Angelika remains on Earth, leaving the angels in heaven still pining for the 'New Look' that conquered Europe in the late 1940s.

Cziffra added colour to the narrative by casting a set of well-known Austrian actors in supporting roles, who deliver most of the punchlines: the formidable comedian Fritz Imhoff plays an unperturbed porter, Hans Olden gives a rather hammy performance as an exasperated theatre manager and Theodor Danegger impersonates an ironic Saint Peter, who knows more about the things going on in heaven and Earth than he lets on. By switching between the two settings, the story gains momentum. While Angelika tries to live the life of a human in Vienna, the astute angel Beate (Inge Konradi) and her progressive colleague Archangel Raphael (Harry Fuss) comment on her earthly adventures from the clouds above. The angels are presented as worldly figures in touch with the times: they complain about the backwardness of heaven, express their desire to modernise and quietly subvert heavenly regulations. Their detached analysis of human behaviour produces comic effect, and turns the angels into accomplices of the audience.

Cziffra gave his film an additional satirical touch by framing the main narrative with a story that mocks the film industry. The film thus begins with a scriptwriter who wants to sell his story, but who is warned that he will encounter difficulties when trying to reconcile the diverse interests of producer, director and sponsor; and indeed, the sponsor is the first to object to the setting in heaven: in his view the audience wants to see pretty secretaries who marry their bosses and listen to sentimental Viennese tunes. His objections, however, are overruled. At the end, the film cuts once again from the 'fictional' setting to the 'real' one: a projector's room where the production team has just seen the finished film. The sponsor protests vigorously against the ending, which shows the angel leaving Hans and returning to heaven, and demands a happy resolution. As the film is duly rewound, the director complains in a whisper to his scenario editor: 'for once in my life I would like to make a film without a happy ending'.

The use of the framing device and the humorous commentaries on the newest fashion craze and conflicted gender relations give the film a contemporary feel; Cziffra was clearly an accomplished filmmaker who knew his audience and applied his technical expertise skilfully. The depictions of gender in *Der himmlische Walzer* reveal a great deal about the historical context in which the film was produced. Here, gender models seem less rigid and more varied than in later productions, and are thus representative of a more liberal period of Austrian filmmaking. The two leading men express two different types of masculinity: young Hans Lieven is played by Paul Hubschmid, who, with his tall, dark looks and elegant appearance, bears a resemblance to the Hollywood icon Cary Grant. Swiss-born Hubschmid started his career as a stage actor in Vienna, embarked on a successful film career in Switzerland and Nazi Germany from the late 1930s, and later also appeared in several Austrian postwar productions and international films, including a stint in Hollywood around 1950. Hans is presented as a kind and sensitive man whose musical genius remains unacknowledged because he is not very assertive. He treats women as equals, and willingly takes a back seat to let Angelika shine. His counterpart is the self-confident, slightly arrogant fashion designer Weidenauer (Curd Jürgens), whose many affairs attest to his virility. Jürgens, whose impressive physique does not quite match that of a stereotypical fashion designer, was probably cast to contrast with Hubschmid's 'soft' masculinity. Weidenauer is a much-admired macho man who exploits women; his professional interest in fabrics and shapes expresses his superficiality, whereas Hans' profession as composer and his love for music imply a deep, artistic mindset. Hans thus embodies an ideal of national masculinity that resembles those in tourist film and historical costume film. Even so, Weidenauer is not presented as a diametrical opposite; after all, his appeal even extends to heaven, where he is admired by angels. Instead, he simply represents a differently accentuated form of masculinity: virile and self-assured, but still charming and artistic. Most importantly, he displays seriousness by proposing marriage to his loyal assistant, who has been pining for him in secret. *Der himmlische Walzer* thus proposes two masculine ideals that are identical in their love for culture and beauty – an essential characteristic of the Austrian ideal that popular cinema propagated so consistently.

Conflicted Gender Relations and Female Rebellion

Sexual identity may have been beyond controversy, but conflicted gender relations were a popular theme of Austrian comedies. Conflicts mainly revolve around women, who fight for entitlements while men defend the status quo; what changed in the period from 1946 to 1955, however, was the way these conflicts were resolved. Early postwar comedies feature self-confident and independent women who insist on their rights and who are sometimes even rebellious, as in *Der himmlische Walzer*. Women shut men out of their homes in Alfred Stöger's anti-war comedy *Triumph der Liebe*, to punish them for constantly going to war; and in *Ein bezaubernder Schwindler*, four female friends, dissatisfied with men, swear an oath not to talk to any male who is between twelve and sixty years old. Crucially, the women are able to maintain their revolutionary verve for most of the film, although their resistance is broken down in the end.

In the early 1950s there occurred a noticeable break in this narrative convention. Comedy changed tack by widening the gap between men and women and by advocating male superiority. Women, characterised as practical and matter-of-fact in early postwar comedies, increasingly resort to tears or erotic flattery in these later films. Moreover, they become financially dependent on men, and therefore have to resort to emotional manipulation to obtain money. In *Irene in Nöten*, Mrs Cirman (Susi Nicoletti) discovers another woman in her matrimonial bed, and is coaxed by her mother to take advantage of her husband's dilemma and demand an expensive present in exchange for reconciliation. In these comedies, suspected or real moral misconduct seem to be the only options for putting legitimate pressure on men: Lilli (Hilde Berndt), in Emo's *Schäm dich, Brigitte!* (Shame on You, Brigitte! 1952), throws a jealous tantrum when she finds a love letter addressed to her husband; he instantly buys her an expensive hat to appease her. By suggesting that women need to be creative to elicit money from their husbands, the narrative rewards (and defines) female 'genius': rather than celebrating their talents or practical skills, as in earlier comedies, their manipulative powers are highlighted. The comedies are quite open about the fact that inequality between the sexes is based on the uneven distribution of economic assets. Seen from a Marxist-feminist perspective, one could argue that the narratives actually highlight the expropriation of married women by their husbands.[58] Yet, the knowledge of economic inequality is not used to challenge the patriarchal system. Rather, it serves to affirm the gap between men and women by presenting men as the exploited sex, who can easily become victims of 'greedy' and even predatory women who want money, which 'rightfully' belongs to men; hence the misogynistic touch evident in many later postwar comedies.

Women who manipulate their husbands, and men who let themselves be 'exploited', are made objects of mockery. By deriding the female quest for economic security, Austrian comedies affirm the norm of unequal distribution of power between men and women. Georg Seeßlen has shown how this relationship of norm and counter-norm shapes the critical potential of comedies: 'the more the counter-norm (the outsider or negative mirror image) is turned into the subject of ridicule, the more humour works as a stabilizing factor of the dominant norm. Comedy can thus function in quite a reactionary way'.[59]

As women's behaviour towards men shifts from sober reasoning to manipulation and tears, men's conduct also changes: in earlier postwar comedies, men usually meet women at eye-level. Often, they go through considerable trouble to prove their worthiness as partners. Martin Palmer in *Ein bezaubernder Schwindler* dresses up as an intellectual, pretends to be a sportsman and learns to play percussion instruments just to impress the girlfriends of the woman he adores. The swift change between identities puts him under considerable pressure – and produces comic effect. Significantly, Martin does not flash his wealth or celebrity status as a popular singer, but engages with the women and their interests. *Mein Freund Leopold* (My Friend Who Can't Say No, 1949) depicts the undesirable consequences of being too accommodating to the needs of women.[60]

Leopold, the title character played by Josef Meinrad, is funny because he is unable to refuse any requests from women, and thus finds himself in all sorts of predicaments – and even gets engaged against his will. Instead of clearing up the misunderstanding, he tries to comply with the demands of his future mother-in-law, who orders him to split up with his many girlfriends – a task that proves difficult because they have a habit of not listening to him. The comedy ridicules Leopold as a weak character who is overpowered by female confidence through his exaggerated efforts to preserve harmony. Quite interestingly, Leopold's lack of traditional masculine qualities, such as assertiveness or willpower, contrasts with his evident popularity with women. Indeed, the last laugh is on Leopold when his best friend, Hans (Hans Olden), who has always been amused by Leopold's inability 'to be a man' and put his foot down, falls into the same trap: feeling unable to make himself heard, Hans is forced to marry Leopold's prospective mother-in-law. Crucially, these early comedies do not ridicule or punish women, nor do they present men as unhappy victims, even though they have to play to the wishes of women. By showcasing self-assured, powerful women, they give satisfaction to the female audience, but at the same time the comic structure reassures the male spectator that what they are seeing is just a fantasy.

However, the depiction of gender relations gradually changed. From the early 1950s onwards, male characters become increasingly dominant in relationships and play out their power against women. Yet, true to the character of comedy, these positions of power are continually undermined: wives, children and staff continually subvert men's power, so that although they pay lip service to male authority, they disregard men's orders. Unlike in Austrian melodrama, where men disrupt the female sphere of the home, in postwar comedy men try to maintain order and harmony in the house, fighting in vain against female unruliness. In *Schäm dich, Brigitte!* the rich and successful cosmetic surgeon Felix Schneider (played by the German actor Heinz Rühmann) complains that his instructions are consistently ignored; his daughter Brigitte comes late for lunch, his wife displays no interest in his tales from the office and his female housekeeper follows his orders only reluctantly (Figure 5.3). Felix is surrounded by female disobedience, which is blown out of proportion when a mix-up of letters presents him as an adulterer and causes outrage. His efforts to sort out the misunderstanding only lead to further discord and outbursts of female hysteria. As in other genres, Austrian comedy features men who are striving for harmony; ironically, though, they are unable to establish peace at home, and hence have to hand out material comforts to appease their (mostly female) opponents.

The representation of gender relations in these later postwar comedies helps to explain the hegemonic functions of Austrian cinema, which, especially from the early 1950s, sought to affirm the set standards of masculinity and femininity. To foster consent, cinema had to render the patriarchal

Figure 5.3: Felix Schneider (Heinz Rühmann) fails to make himself heard in his home in *Schäm dich, Brigitte!* (here with Hilde Berndt as his wife Lilli). Screenshot.

system attractive, especially to women. Comedy did so by covering up gender inequality, and by presenting men as easy-going and charming. Women, on the other hand, are not presented as powerless victims in the films, but as ingenious actors who successfully manipulate their gullible partners. Comedy thus glossed over the unequal distribution of power, and thereby played down the crucial fact that women, as in *Schäm dich, Brigitte!*, end up with a fashionable hat while men have control over the family income.

As gender relations in Europe have been predominantly defined through the separation of spheres, analysing where men and women are positioned within the comic narrative and how the two spheres of public and private life are connected can provide valuable insights into the representation of gender relationships.[61] Most postwar comedy plots revolve around the workplace and home, and thus address the issue of how modern man can meet the demands of work and family. Unlike melodrama, where the division between the separate spheres of work and home is presented as a source of conflict, the two spaces seem more compatible in comedy. In early postwar comedies, the two spheres often melt into each other: in *Hannerl*, the home of stage director Bergmeister is constantly invaded by employees; *Mein Freund Leopold* features two male friends who share a flat but also work in the same ministry. Although work is presented as an integral part of masculinity and defines a man's social standing, the fact that men and women are depicted in both the work and private spheres implies an equal distribution of power between the sexes.

In later postwar comedies the gap between the two spheres widens, at least for the female protagonists. In *Schäm dich, Brigitte!* Felix's office is quite close to his home, so he can commute on almost an hourly basis to sort out his domestic problems, but his wife and daughter have already been excluded from the professional realm. This obviously does not apply to all female characters, but women's access to the public sphere decreases noticeably from the early 1950s onwards: young and single women are in employment, but the comedies ban married women from the workplace. Proclaiming the man as the sole breadwinner and head of the household as the norm, the narratives endorse dominant discourses which prescribe a clear division between realms of influence.[62] To be sure, the family model advertised by Austrian comedies bore little relation to postwar reality; but as many women worked only out of necessity, rather than choice, and then in menial and low-paid jobs, the valorised model of housewife-mother seemed liberating rather than suffocating to many women.[63] Thus, postwar comedy's depiction of the middle-class family, even though it focused on familial conflict, conveyed the promise of a better life. It provided an aspirational model of living that seemed entirely feasible considering the economic boom of the 1950s. Consequently, it would be too simplistic to interpret the relegation of women to the role of 'consumer-housewives' in later postwar comedy (as well as in political and media discourses) simply as an act of suppression. Austrian comedy depicted marriage as a means of upward mobility, and thus gave housewives a higher social status than their working counterparts. As Erica Carter argues, the modern, middle-class-family model of the female housewife and male breadwinner offered many women 'a specifically feminine form of historical agency', both on screen and in reality.[64]

Modernising Masculinity: In Search of a New Father

Even though Austrian postwar comedy endorsed patriarchal gender relations, then, it embraced modernity and responded positively to the challenges modern society presented to families and to men. Of particular interest with regard to representations of masculinity is the fact that comedy gives more attention to the father figure than any other genre in Austrian cinema. The father was not an entirely new theme in German-language comedy: *Hurra! Ich bin Papa!* (Hurrah! I am a Dad!), produced in Nazi Germany in 1939, presents a young man (Heinz Rühmann) who is put in charge of a little boy who is supposedly his son. The issue of fatherhood is taken up much more frequently in postwar comedies – interestingly, in West Germany even more so than in Austria. A whole sub-genre of father comedies developed in West Germany in the 1950s, which revolved around the father and the challenges he faced in modern Germany. The stars Heinz Rühmann and Heinz Erhardt were typecast as the quintessential, ordinary, middle-class man, who was a modern and devoted father.[65] One might suspect that this preoccupation with the modern father figure had to do with the need to establish a clear distance from the dominant, 'hard' ideal of masculinity, and the negative image of a militaristic 'fatherland' – a need that seems to have been greater in West Germany than in Austria.[66] After all, the Austrians could fall back on the 'softer' national stereotypes of the musical and charming Austrian. Nevertheless, a new father type also emerged in Austrian cinema, first of all in comedy, because of the comedy writer's keen sense for contemporary debates. As in West Germany, it was military and political defeat as well as socio-economic transformation which gave rise to this new father figure. The experience of war and Nazi dictatorship had undermined the hegemonic position of the hitherto dominant ideal of 'hard', militaristic masculinity, which was now held accountable for the brutalisation of men.[67] The downfall of Hitler brought about the destruction of the father *imago*, just as the death of the old Kaiser and the demise of the Austro-Hungarian Empire had given way to a short-lived 'fatherless' society after the First World War.[68]

In postwar Austria, people were looking for orientation and guidance, but were wary of *Führer* figures. Senior politicians, untainted by the Nazi regime, represented positive, fatherly role-models: Karl Renner, who was born in 1870 and had already been Austria's first chancellor in the First Republic, took over the provisional chancellorship after Austria's liberation and also acted as the country's president from 1945 until his death in 1950. Renner, with his white beard, was the embodiment of the old, kind-hearted patriarch. So was his successor, Theodor Körner, another bald man with a white beard, who was seventy-eight years old when he became Austrian president in 1951. Paternal figures dominated the highest political level, as well as public and private institutions. The Church and the unions, too, were headed by elderly patriarchs, and paternalism remained the dominant practice for governing companies and society.[69] Whereas historical costume film celebrated the paternal figure in the shape of the old Kaiser Franz Joseph, postwar comedy presented elderly gentlemen as kind-hearted fathers of teenage daughters.

There are obvious reasons for this predominance of older men, both in postwar cinema and in Austrian society: the rejection of militaristic masculinity, the longing to be taken care of in a time of turmoil, the absence of younger men due to war casualties and imprisonment and, last but not least, the fact that old men were under less suspicion of having collaborated with the Nazis.[70] Towards the mid-1950s, a shift occurred, and the elderly father figures in cinema were replaced by younger and more dynamic ones. These new fathers show an interest in their children, but are also professionally successful and sexually attractive, such as Wolf Albach-Retty as Max in *Seine Tochter ist der Peter* (His Daughter Is Called Peter, 1955) or Curd Jürgens as Stefan Selby in *Du bist die Richtige* (You Are the Right One, 1954).

Social and economic changes spurred on the demand for new masculinities. The decrease of hard labour, particularly in agriculture, as well as the growth of the service sector, demanded different skills and attitudes from men. Hanisch argues that these developments in the economic sector 'eased the proletarian and farmer's *habitus*', and made room for new behavioural standards.[71] But analysis of contemporary discourse also reveals growing fears about the Austrian family, sparked by the rapid decline in birth rates. Social experts identified lack of female interest in a 'cosy home' as causal, but also saw a 'patriarchal tendency' amongst men and their passive behaviour within the family as roots of the problem.[72]

Postwar comedy took note of these discourses: by advertising images of affectionate and permissive fathers, attractive men who are successful in their jobs and admired by well bred children and pretty women, it 'sold' the concept of the modern family to Austrian men and women. Interestingly, postwar comedy also downplayed the importance of biological fatherhood, although the nuclear family remained the norm. A father was now defined by his degree of emotional investment, and not by biological parenthood. This new development can be read as a critique of National Socialist notions of race and blood, as well as an attempt to disassociate Austria from Nazi Germany. One could also argue that postwar comedy responded to the large number of single-parent families and stepfamilies the war had produced, promoting stepfathering as a positive alternative to biological fatherhood.

The issue of biological linkage is directly addressed in the children's comedy *Maxie* (Maxie, 1954). Maxie (Sabine Eggerth) has been adopted from an orphanage by a rich couple. Her adoptive mother soon becomes jealous of the growing emotional attachment between her husband and the child, and sends Maxie to boarding school. All problems seem resolved when the biological parents of Maxie are found; they are poor but honest working-class people with many sons. However, since Maxie's adoptive father misses his daughter, he visits her biological father's shop in disguise, to check if she is in good hands. Maxie, although she is quite happy with her biological family, 'recognises' her adoptive father in the double sense of the word: she identifies him, but also acknowledges him as her 'real' father, even though he is not her biological father. It is significant that this comedy depicts both the biological and the adoptive father as kind-hearted and affectionate. The biological father proves his love for his daughter by letting her go into a better future with her new father, and the adoptive father shows his worth by demonstrating concern about the well-being of his child.[73] The fact that the film does not privilege one father over the other suggests that popular cinema identified a widespread 'hunger' for new father figures that had to be fed generously.

The lack of fathers was indeed a topic of heated debate in Austria (and other European societies) after the war: 247,000 of Austria's 1.2 million soldiers had died during the Second World War, and 480,000 were held in captivity in 1945; in addition, a large number of men had been killed by the Nazis.[74] Political and media discourses linked the rise in youth crime and the (alleged) moral decline in postwar Austrian society to the absence of fathers.[75] The media, depending on their ideological orientation, also cited other explanations for the rise in juvenile delinquency: some pointed to the experience of violence during the war, while others ascribed it to the influence of American culture, such as comics or gangster films. Journalists from both the Left and the Right agreed, though, that the absence of fathers and the 'moral failure' of a whole generation of fathers were at the root of the problem.[76]

Asphalt (1951), *Wienerinnen* (Viennese Women, 1952) and *Schicksal am Lenkrad* (Fate at the Steering Wheel, 1954), the only social problem films produced in postwar Austria, directly addressed the issue of missing or negative father figures.[77] Yet, these films triggered much criticism and failed at the box office, which suggests that the Austrian public did not want to be confronted too directly with the uncomfortable truth of neglectful or abusive fathers. Perhaps as a result of the growing debate on the lack of 'wholesome' films for the young, the film industry produced a number of films specifically directed at younger audiences in the mid-1950s. Whereas in West Germany producers targeted teenagers with 'youth films' that celebrated youth culture and rebellion, such as *Die Halbstarken* (Teenage Wolfpack, 1956) or *Endstation Liebe* (Last Stop Love, 1957), both directed by the Austrian Georg Tressler, popular Austrian cinema avoided such themes; instead, it produced comedies such as *Der erste Kuss* (The First Kiss, 1954), *Ihr erstes Rendezvous* (Her First Date, 1955) or the aforementioned *Pünktchen und Anton*, *Maxie* and *Seine Tochter ist der Peter*, which emphasised harmonious relations between the generations.

Contemporary discourse lamented the absence of positive father figures, but also expressed concern about single mothers. Austrian and West German media described the large number of fatherless families as 'incomplete' or 'unhealthy', and suggested that children raised by single mothers would turn out to be anti-social and problematic. In an attempt to provide a remedy for these problematic developments, the political elite, together with the media, drew on medical and psychological debates to formulate a family ideal that positioned both parents, with their gender-specific qualities, as indispensable for successful child-rearing.[78]

It is crucial to situate comedy in this discursive context in order to comprehend the cinematic representation of the father. The father figure in comedy fiction differed from social reality in three principal ways: first, the father is present in comedy; second, he is not an authoritarian patriarch, but engages with his child; and third, he is unaffected by the traumas of war and violence, unlike so many men in postwar Austria. The films offer a positive and light-hearted image of the paternal parent, whose status is underlined by the fact that he is often the most cherished member of the family. Even though a small number of Austrian comedies feature single fathers or stepfathers, the presented goal is that they will marry and thus form 'whole' families again. In the early postwar comedy

Kleine Melodie aus Wien (Little Melody from Vienna, 1948), highly praised by critics as 'very pretty, very clean, and very entertaining', the retired Professor Griesbichler (Paul Hörbiger) falls in love with his lodger, a young widow (Maria Andergast) with three children; the children rejuvenate Griesbichler, who consequently marries the widow.[79] Another comedy, *Das Herz einer Frau* (Heart of a Woman, 1951), depicts a widowed father (Stefan Skodler) whose little boy sets out to find a mother, but this film was much less welcomed by the critics: the *Arbeiterzeitung* described it as 'pathetic and unimaginative … a crushing defeat', whereas *Die Presse* found that the colours were appealing, at least, but expressed disdain for the 'staggering lack of inspiration in storyline and dialogue'.[80] The fact that the film, produced at the Soviet-controlled studio Rosenhügel, also had an ideologically tinged subplot of exploited workers might explain the harshness of some critics, who may have sensed communist propaganda.

Austrian postwar comedies often feature liberal fathers who treat their children like grown-ups and interfere little with their lives. Sure enough, there is little childishness about these children: almost like miniature adults, they seem very much in control and even 'wise'. The only 'childish' child in Austrian postwar comedy is a 21-year-old woman impersonating a 12-year-old girl in order to conceal the fact that she was conceived out of wedlock from her conservative but financially generous aunt. The film *Ein tolles Früchtchen* (A Great Rascal, 1953), 'a story of mistaken identities with a pseudo-children's role', is all the more interesting because it presents the prototype of a progressive father (Fritz Schulz): being a free-spirited artist, he even shares a smoke and a drink with his daughter in a café.[81] The audience knows that the pigtailed girl, Eva (Ingrid Pan), emptying a glass of brandy, is of drinking age, but the outraged woman from social services (Annie Rosar), who witnesses this incident, reports the father for neglecting his parental duties, an accusation he simply shrugs off.

The Modern Father in Seine Tochter ist der Peter

The children's comedy *Seine Tochter ist der Peter*, produced in 1955, features another liberal father: Max, a single father who brings up his daughter in the idyllic countryside and leaves the tomboyish girl to roam freely. The comedy was directed and scripted by Gustav Fröhlich, a German actor who had played one of his first film roles in Fritz Lang's *Metropolis* (1927) and became a hugely popular actor in German films.[82] Highly active in Nazi cinema, he continued his career after the war, most notably as the male lead opposite Hildegard Knef in the controversial drama *Die Sünderin* (The Sinner, 1951), but he also directed a few films.

Seine Tochter ist der Peter (1955) is a remake of the Austrian comedy of the same name directed by Heinz Helbig in 1936. A big success at the box office, the original had been censored by the Austrian Ministry of Education because of the tomboyish behaviour of the girl and the way divorce was presented.[83] In postwar Austria, however, these issues no longer caused offence among the authorities. The title role was played by the twelve-year-old German actress Sabine Eggerth, already an established child star following her roles in the Erich Kästner adaptation *Pünktchen und Anton*, a Austrian-West German co-production, and the German film *Das Mäd-chen mit den Schwefelhölzern* (The Little Match Girl, 1953). Fröhlich chose Austria's former heart-throb Wolf Albach-Retty, in real life the father of the young, emerging star Romy Schneider, for the role of the single father, Max. Albach-Retty, who represented the archetypal Viennese charmer in many romantic comedies, but whose popularity had begun to fade after the war, was almost fifty years old when he accepted the role of a supposedly younger father. His suave appearance and frequent changes of dress from smart, white, linen suits to classy tuxedos reflected Albach-Retty's star persona. He approached his role very much like that of a romantic lead, with the result that he seems more interested in attracting the attention of grown-up women than in the harmless mischief of his daughter, which he tolerates liberally.

Handsome Max is an engineer, working mostly from his home in the beautiful lake district of the Salzkammergut. Divorced from his wife, Nora (Gretl Schörg), a popular singer, he lives with his eleven-year-old daughter, Elisabeth, whose nickname, Peter, reflects her 'boyish' behaviour. Max and his best friend, Felix (Josef Meinrad), who is a psychiatrist and thus has the medical expertise to support Max's opinion, see no problem in Peter's upbringing; Max's female housekeeper, Kathi (Lucie Englisch), though, who is always worried about Peter's well-being, insists that a father cannot bring up a child on his own, especially not a girl (Figure 5.4). The story takes a dramatic turn when the girl's mother turns up unexpectedly on the doorstep, and a battle for the child ensues. Peter eagerly follows her newly found mother into the city, but is soon disappointed because her career-oriented mum has little time for her. Consequently, she exchanges her expensive dresses and dolls for the masculine lederhosen and her dachshund, and returns to her father. Max, as the narrative implies, has proven to be a better parent because he has been with his daughter throughout her childhood, and has thus provided the necessary stability. This is a significant point, as the film clearly draws on contemporary discourses that accentuated the psychological needs of children and the involvement of both parents in child-rearing. Women were considered to be providers of the essential *Nestwärme*, the love and security a child needs, and should thus refrain from working outside the home.[84] The comedy's negative presentation of Max's divorced wife, who pursues a career, supports that notion, as does the positive portrayal of the father, who is always pictured in or near the house. Linking Nora to the urban sphere, connoted as superficial and erratic, and Max to the rural sphere, which stands for stability and

Figure 5.4: The single father Max (Wolf Albach-Retty, second from right) admonishes his daughter (Sabine Eggerth) under the watchful eyes of his housekeeper and his best friend in *Seine Tochter ist der Peter*. Filmarchiv Austria.

harmony, the narrative leaves no doubt which surroundings are better for the child; but the film also contradicts these dominant views on parenting by suggesting that one parent might actually be sufficient to raise a happy child. Admittedly, this message is put forward tentatively, and extenuated through the introduction of a female protagonist who might be a prospective stepmother; but it is presented as a possible alternative to the normative family.

Max displays an air of unconcern that is presented as a masculine quality, and which contrasts sharply with the housekeeper's female hysteria. Max is modern and tolerant, and thus allows his daughter to address him by his first name and dress and behave like a boy. Like a traditional father, Max is not overly affectionate, but he shows that he cares by being present and by communicating with his daughter eye-to-eye. The reason why he was awarded custody of his daughter is not quite clear. It seems that the judge disapproved of Nora's career and thus gave Max custody; however, as such a view could be seen as outdated, the narrative implies that the real reason was that Max cares more for the child than his wife. This issue is first brought up in a scene towards the beginning of the film when Max reads in the newspaper that his ex-wife will spend her holidays in the

Salzkammergut. He wakes his best friend, Felix, a frequent visitor, who is napping in the living room, to express his indignation about the news. The two friends are shown from the side, sitting next to each other, their armchairs separated by a small table, which forces Max to lean to the right to speak to Felix. The friends do not face each other during their talk, but gaze off in the same direction, which underlines the relaxed intimacy of their relationship. Max is every inch the gentleman, with a silk neck-scarf, a gold wristwatch and a signet ring on his little finger. Smoking a cigarette, he tells his friend that he is thinking of leaving his home for a while, so that his ex-wife cannot find the child. His friend, slouching in his chair, is unperturbed by the news and responds quizzically: 'Are you worried?' Max looks at Felix, and after a brief moment of silence answers in the affirmative; clearly this is a modern man not afraid to admit his fears for his daughter. He then goes on to explain that after the divorce trial his ex-wife had told him that their daughter would eventually come to her mother because 'a daughter belongs with her mother'. Might this be a reason why he raises his daughter like a boy? The director avoids any close-ups, which would have added drama to the narrative by highlighting Felix's emotional turmoil. Instead, the scene depicts a level-headed discussion between two men trying to solve a problem. To lighten the mood, Max jokingly accuses Felix of being the source of conflict, as it was he who first introduced Nora to Max.

The narrative repeatedly touches on issues of gender and the power of biological imperatives. It contrasts the housekeeper's view that Peter needs a mother to correct her wild, boyish behaviour that will result in her 'never finding a husband' with Max's liberal attitude. Max brushes off her concerns, insisting that his daughter is growing up in a simple and natural way and that her upbringing is thus 'exactly right'. The narrative proves him right. While Peter cannot resist the lure of her newly found mother, who turns her into a pretty girl, she soon feels uncomfortable in her new life and returns to her former identity. Max has proven his strength, not by imposing strict rules but by giving his daughter the necessary leeway. He is thus by no means one of the weak fathers that Fritz Göttler found to be ubiquitous in West German cinema.[85] It is worth pointing out that this softened, liberal concept of fatherhood does not question the gendered division of work: Max is still the sole breadwinner and head of the household, whereas the female housekeeper does the actual housework and takes care of the physical needs of the child. But the film depicts an important shift in parental roles: the father who becomes emotionally involved in the upbringing of his daughter gains in social status and sex appeal, while the mother who pursues a career is rejected, as her interest in work creates an emotional distance between her and her child.

These comedies suggest that children in postwar Austria need fatherly love and not authority, and thus challenge or undermine any attempts by fathers to exert their authority. Overly authoritarian fathers are openly ridiculed: in *Hannerl*, the father, Eberhard Moeller (Richard Romanowsky), whose sole interest in dinosaur skeletons symbolises his backwardness, is accused by his wife (Adrienne Gessner) of being a tyrant because he forbids his daughter to become a dancer. *Ich und meine Frau*, a vehicle for the prominent star couple Paula Wessely and Attila Hörbiger, was so successful that it even outdid *Gone with the Wind* (1939, released in Austria in 1953) at the box office, and presents the male lead, Hermann Naglmüller (Hörbiger), as an authoritarian, old-fashioned patriarch.[86] His wife, Sophie (Wessely), and the teenage children have to adhere to his strict rules, which include eating raw vegetables for breakfast, and bedtime for everybody at ten. Hermann, who works in a music shop, disapproves of everything modern, and dismisses jazz and rock 'n' roll as 'negro music'; moreover, Hermann is convinced that showing affection for his wife or his children would undermine his authority. He is, as the conservative newspaper *Die Presse* noted, 'indeed not a pleasant figure'.[87] Sophie shields her children from his strictness and bears her lot patiently, channelling her frustration into secretly writing a book about modern marriage, which becomes a bestseller. The film presents Hermann as the anti-father who is out of touch with the times because he still insists that 'there has to be someone who dictates what we have to do; who gives permission and who prohibits'. The tyrannical Hermann clearly bears resemblance to the outdated *Führer* image, and his family and friends not only undermine his authority, but question it openly.[88] What is more, Hermann's dislike for 'negro-music' is not criticised because it is racist, but because his attitude is anti-modern and inflexible. At the end of the film, Hermann (suddenly and unconvincingly) reconciles himself both with modernity and his wife: putting on a jazz record and dancing wildly, he virtually shakes off his former, stiff self and reveals a new, visibly more flexible masculinity which is more suitable for modern Austria.

Conclusion

Film comedy performed an important social task in postwar Austrian society. While melodrama, for instance, allowed Austrian audiences to work through the traumas of war and Nazism by providing catharsis, comedy reassured them of their innocence, suggesting that everything might just have been a silly misunderstanding. Through the theme of mistaken identity, a key narrative in Austrian comedy, it presented the truth as relative and appearances as deceptive. The genre thus advertised the pleasures of inventing new identities, and suggested that shedding one's past is easy, and necessary to succeed in life. Narratives such as these also appealed to West German audiences, who were just as eager to leave their burdened past behind as the Austrians. However, the popularity of Austrian comedy

in West Germany was not merely a result of these themes. The traditionally close relationship between the two film industries meant that the German audience had grown accustomed to the stylistic formulas of Austrian
comedy; moreover, the growing deployment of German actors, which was
higher in comedy than in any other genre, helped to broaden the films'
appeal.

Much of the comic effect of postwar comedy was produced by the
currency of its themes. Through exaggeration and caricature, the comic
genre made economic and social transformations appear less threatening, and encouraged the audience to embrace change. Postwar comedy
underlined its apparent modernity by advertising images of new fathers
that contrasted with the model of the old, authoritarian father still dominant in large parts of society. It thus did not just engage with powerful
social discourses, but anticipated the transition from the authoritarian to
the liberal father which occurred around the late 1960s.[89] Yet, while the
comedies brought father and child closer together by promoting the ideal
of the liberal father who is emotionally attached to his children, it pulled
women and men further apart. Even though the films' protagonists cross
class barriers easily, boundaries of gender remain impenetrable. In Austrian comedy, the gap between genders increasingly widens from 1945
onwards; in later postwar comedies, men are assigned 'natural' positions
of power that allow them to force women into submission, thereby turning into objects of ridicule those women who try to 'play the game' to
their own advantage or men who are unable to assert their authority.
The advertisement of the new, liberal father figure can thus be seen as an
attempt to smooth the hard edges of masculinity that became more noticeable in the films over time. The genre promoted an image of modern
Austrian masculinity as charming, harmonious and cultured. Professionally successful, open-minded and optimistic, the apparent progressiveness of the ideal Austrian man did, however, go hand-in-hand with
a fairly traditional stance on gender roles and increasingly intolerant
views on female independence. Film comedies' representations of gender
are generally consistent with the normative standard of the time, which
means that their subversive potential can at best be described as limited.
The fact that the Austrian government chose a comedy as its 'national'
film (*1. April 2000*), intended to support the call for national independence and the withdrawal of the Allied troops, is especially significant
in this regard. It draws attention to the overall tendency of the domestic
film industry to work for rather than against official policies. Comedy's
stance towards modern Austrian society can be described as ambiguous:
while it promoted change on certain levels, for example with regard to
consumerism and mobility, it was quite reactionary in its depictions of
gender relations, and thus bolstered contemporary social discourse that
endorsed the male-breadwinner model.

Notes

1. I use Geoff King's criterion that a film 'should be dominated to a substantial extent by the comic dimension' to be considered as comedy. See G. King. 2002. *Film Comedy*, London: Wallflower, 1.
2. See ibid., 2–3.
3. See G. Mast. 1979. *The Comic Mind: Comedy and the Movies*, 2nd ed., Chicago: University of Chicago, 199–200; S. Neale. 2000. *Genre and Hollywood*, London: Routledge, 59–60.
4. See King, 2002, 5–7.
5. S. Neale and F. Krutnik. 1990. *Popular Film and Television Comedy*, London: Routledge, 84–91.
6. See Mast, 1979, 15.
7. See D. Sutton. 2000. *A Chorus of Raspberries: British Film Comedy 1929–1939*, Exeter: University of Exeter Press, 58.
8. Neale and Krutnik, 1990, 92–94.
9. Mast, 1979, 21.
10. Though Susan Purdie follows this argument, she also points out that joking (in a wider sense) constructs discursive power that can counter dominant discourses and so potentially undermine authority. See S. Purdie. 1993. *Comedy: The Mastery of Discourse*, Hemel Hempstead: Harvester Wheatsheaf, 126–127.
11. See P. Morris (ed.). 1994. *The Bakhtin Reader: Selected Writings of Bakhtin, Medvedev and Voloshinov*, London: Arnold, 197.
12. See, e.g., Frank Stern's interesting analysis of subversion in Third Reich cinema, which perhaps overrates the subversive content of some films. F. Stern. 2003. 'Tanz auf dem Vulkan. Das Kino Nazi-Deutschlands in der heutigen Filmkultur', in J. Distelmeyer (ed.), *Tonfilmfrieden, Tonfilmkrieg. Die Geschichte der Tobis vom Technik-Syndikat zum Staatskonzern*, Munich: Edition Text + Kritik, 12–19. Eric Rentschler has criticised scholarly endeavours that highlight the 'resistant energy' of Nazi cinema. See E. Rentschler. 1996. *The Ministry of Illusion: Nazi Cinema and its Afterlife*, Cambridge, MA: Harvard University Press, 11–12.
13. See Österreichisches Statistisches Zentralamt, 1959b, 146.
14. See King, 2002, 1.
15. 'In Rekordzeit fertiggestellt. "Der Mann in der Wanne"', *Der Abend*, 28 April 1952.
16. See, e.g., 'Der österreichische Film seit 1945', *Österreichische Film und Kinozeitung*, 9 May 1953.
17. Jeancolas, 1992, 141.
18. See Elsaesser, 1999, 26–28.
19. A few comedies were exported to the US via the Casino Film Exchange, but they were presumably aimed at expatriates, as they were usually not dubbed or subtitled. See 'Der österreichische Nachkriegsfilm in den USA', *Österreichische Film und Kino Zeitung*, 21 February 1951, 6.
20. See Mast, 1979, 14–27.
21. 'Neue Filme "Hallo, Dienstmann!"', *Die Presse*, 10 February 1952.
22. 'Ein bezaubernder Schwindler', *Weltpresse*, 20 December 1949.
23. Designed specifically for the tastes of rural audiences, the *Bauernschwänke* seem also to have found an audience in the cities and suburbs. See 'Neuer Lustspielschlager', *Welt am Abend*, 8 August 1948; 'Die Verjüngungskur', *Wiener Tageszeitung*, 8 August 1948.
24. 'Die Verjüngungskur', *Wiener Tageszeitung*, 8 August 1948; 'Liebesprobe', *Wiener Kurier*, 10 November 1949.
25. See 'Verjüngungskur beim Verfassungsgericht', *Die Presse*, 26 June 1949; 'Gerichtstag über die "Verjüngungskur"', *Weltpresse*, 1 July 1949; 'Demonstrationen Jugendlicher gegen den Film "Der Leberfleck" in Salzburg', *Wiener Kurier*, 21 November 1949; 'Jugend

demonstriert wieder gegen einen Schmutzfilm', *Das Kleine Volksblatt*, 22 November 1949; 'Deutsche Filmselbstkontrolle lehnt "Leberfleck"-Film ab', *Wiener Kurier*, 3 October 1949.

26. Mast compares these distancing devices to Brecht's *Verfremdungseffekt* (distancing effect). See Mast, 1979, 15.

27. See A. Lang. 1999. 'Comedy: Austria', in T. Elsaesser (ed.), *The BFI Companion to German Cinema*, London: BFI, 55.

28. 'Neue Filme: "Hallo Dienstmann"', *Die Presse*, 10 February 1952.

29. 'Filme der Woche', *Arbeiterzeitung*, 10 February 1952.

30. 'Hallo Dienstmann', *Paimann's Filmlisten*, 1952.

31. 'Filmregisseur Franz Antel ist tot', *Wiener Zeitung*, 12 August 2007 (obituary). See also Büttner and Dewald, 1997a, 244.

32. *Weltpresse*, 21 August 1957.

33. See G. Seeßlen. 2004. 'Triumph des Scheiterns', *Filmarchiv Filmprogramm*, 19(11–12), 12.

34. See Seeßlen, 1996, 123–128.

35. C. Gledhill. 1991. 'Signs of Melodrama', in C. Gledhill (ed.), *Stardom: Industry of Desire*, London: Routledge, 215.

36. S. Hayward. 2000. *Cinema Studies: The Key Concepts*, London: Routledge, 354.

37. See E. Büttner and C. Dewald. 1997b. 'Gespräch mit Christa Blümlinger, Oliver Rathkolb, Gottfried Schlemmer und Maria Steiner', in E. Büttner and C. Dewald. 1997a. *Anschluß an Morgen. Eine Geschichte des österreichischen Films von 1945 bis zur Gegenwart*, Salzburg: Residenz, 145.

38. See Seeßlen, 2004, 13.

39. See, for example, M. Fritsche. 2003. '"Goebbels ist ein großer Tepp." Wehrkraftzersetzende Äußerungen in der Deutschen Wehrmacht', in W. Manoschek (ed.), *Opfer der NS-Militärjustiz. Urteilspraxis, Strafvollzug, Entschädigungspolitik in Österreich*, Vienna: Mandelbaum; R. Gellately. 1996. 'Denunciations in Twentieth Century Germany: Aspects of Self-policing in the Third Reich and the German Democratic Republic', *Journal of Modern History*, 4(68).

40. See, for example, Hanisch, 1994, 42–43, 443–444.

41. It is interesting that the Austrian government did not choose an Austrian director for this celebratory film, but a German one: Wolfgang Liebeneiner. Neither his function as head of production at the Ufa from 1942 onwards nor his infamous euthanasia propaganda film *Ich klage an* (1941) were considered obstacles to his assignment. Instead, his expertise in modern colour-film technology was given as the reason for this choice. See G. Heiss. 2006. 'Österreich am 1. April 2000 – das Bild von Gegenwart und Vergangenheit im Zukunftsraum von 1952', in E. Bruckmüller (ed.), *Wiederaufbau in Österreich, 1945–1955: Rekonstruktion oder Neubeginn?* Vienna: Verlag für Geschichte und Politik, 108.

42. For a detailed analysis see Heiss, 2006; also B. Fremuth-Kronreif. 1999. *1. April 2000. Die Produktionsgeschichte eines im Auftrag der österreichischen Bundesregierung hergestellten Filmes*, unpublished master's thesis (Diplomarbeit), University of Salzburg; E. Kieninger (ed.). 2000. *1. April 2000*, Vienna: Filmarchiv Austria.

43. See, for example, 'Der Österreicher und sein Film. Volksbefragung vor dem Kinoausgang', *Arbeiterzeitung*, 30 November 1952; 'Der Österreich-Film "1. April 2000" im ganzen Land bejubelt', *Wiener Zeitung*, 30 November 1952; 'Überall Jubel um den Österreich-Film', *Wiener Zeitung*, 14 December 1952.

44. Interestingly, critics considered the comedy *Der Mann in der Wanne* as 'too turbulent' and 'burlesque' to be good entertainment, which highlights the Austrians' dislike for slapstick or swift pace. See 'Der Mann in der Wanne', *Tagblatt am Montag*, 18 August 1952; 'Filmspiegel der Woche', *Volksstimme*, 19 August 1952.

45. See Bruckmüller, 2003, 382–385.

46. Kaes, 1995, 51.

47. 'Ein bezaubernder Schwindler', *Weltpresse*, 20 December 1948; 'Glück muss man haben', *Wiener Tageszeitung*, 9 January 1954.

48. R. Schechner. 1973. 'Performance & the Social Sciences: Introduction', *The Drama Review*, 17(3), 3.

49. See, for example, Hanisch, 1994.

50. 'Ein bezaubernder Schwindler', *Wiener Tageszeitung*, 18 December 1948.

51. The film titles already refer to the theme of lies and impostors: for example *Ein bezaubernder Schwindler* (A Charming Fraud), *Alles Lüge* (All Lies) and *Knall und Fall als Hochstapler* (Knall and Fall as Impostors).

52. Kaes, 1995, 51.

53. 'Ein Lustspielerfolg', *Die Presse*, 10 December 1948.

54. 'Walzerfilm und englische Groteske', *Wiener Kurier*, 6 December 1948; 'Der himmlische Walzer', *Weltpresse*, 6 December 1948.

55. '"Himmlischer Walzer"– italienisch und französisch', *Weltpresse*, 7 January 1949; 'Der "Himmlische Walzer" in Italien verboten', *Neues Österreich*, 16 September 1951;

56. See Kreimeier, 1992, 390.

57. See Dassanowsky, 2005, 98.

58. See S. Walby. 1995. *Theorizing Patriarchy*, 6th ed., Oxford: Blackwell, 21.

59. G. Seeßlen. 1982. *Klassiker der Filmkomik. Geschichte und Mythologie des komischen Films*, Reinbek bei Hamburg: Rowohlt, 22.

60. Reviews criticised this comedy for its storyline and its lack of tempo, imagination or innovative humour. The audience's positive reaction displeased one critic: 'At the opening night the audience made ample use of the opportunity to laugh. It loves the lowbrow cinema entertainment [and] shies away from the minimum of intellectual activity'. 'Österreichischer Lustspielfilm', *Wiener Zeitung*, 22 December 1949.

61. See Schissler, 2001, 364–365.

62. See, for example, Mesner, 1997; Moeller, 1997, 122–123, 129–131.

63. In 1951, the overall labour-force participation rate was 47.6 per cent, and the female labour-force participation rate 35 per cent. See R. Sandgruber. 1995. *Ökonomie und Politik. Österreichische Wirtschaftsgeschichte vom Mittelalter bis zur Gegenwart*, Vienna: Ueberreuter, 498–500; Cyba, 1996, 438–439. According to Bandhauer-Schöffmann and Hornung, the need to earn wages resulted in overwork rather than female emancipation. See Bandhauer-Schöffmann and Hornung, 1996, 230. See also Thurner, 1992, 9–10; Heineman, 2003, 216–219.

64. E. Carter. 1997. *How German Is She? Postwar West German Reconstruction and the Consuming Woman*, Ann Arbor: University of Michigan Press, 7.

65. See Seidl, 1987, 256–257.

66. Fehrenbach, 1998, 117.

67. See Herzog, 2003, 187–188.

68. See Hanisch, 2005, 291–293.

69. See ibid., 293–294.

70. Their age was one reason why the Allies confirmed these politicians in their position. See W.B. Bader. 1966. *Austria between East and West 1945–1955*, Stanford: Stanford University Press, 21–22. Schwarz has shown how the German chancellor, Adenauer, countered the anxieties of the 'fatherless' society by being portrayed as a patriarchal but caring father of Germany in newsreels. See U. Schwarz. 2002. *Wochenschau, westdeutsche Identität und Geschlecht in den fünfziger Jahren*, Frankfurt am Main: Campus, 206.

71. See Hanisch, 2005, 294. For economic changes in West Germany see J. Mooser. 1998. 'Arbeiter, Angestellte und Frauen in der "nivellierten Mittelstandsgesellschaft". Thesen', in A. Schildt and A. Sywottek (eds), *Modernisierung im Wiederaufbau. Die westdeutsche Gesellschaft der 50er Jahre*, Bonn: Dietz.

72. This was an interesting claim considering the Catholic-Conservative editorship of this particular study. See Bodzenta and Grond, 1957, 438. According to statistics, the birth

rate in Vienna was one of the lowest worldwide during the first half of the 1950s, ranging between 6.5 and 7.5 births per thousand people; see ibid., 432.

73. It is interesting to compare *Maxie* with the popular West German children's film *Toxi* (1952) – the similarity between the films' titles suggests that the producers wanted to cash in on the success of *Toxi*, which tells the story of the mixed-race girl Toxi, daughter of a German mother and an African-American GI. For an in-depth analysis of the film and the discourse surrounding it see Fehrenbach, 1998, 119–125.

74. See E. Bruckmüller (ed.). 2006. *Wiederaufbau in Österreich, 1945–1955: Rekonstruktion oder Neubeginn?* Vienna: Verlag für Geschichte und Politik, 12.

75. See M. Varga. 1953. *Die Jugendkriminalität in ihrer Behandlung durch die Wiener Tagespresse in den Jahren 1946–1950*, unpublished PhD thesis, University of Vienna; H. Veigl. 2004. Geplantes Glück im Alltag. Der kulturelle Wandel der 50er und 60er Jahre aus der Sicht der Illustrierten. http://www.alltagskultur.at/veigl01.doc, retrieved 7 December 2010.

76. W.M. Schwarz. 2004. 'ASPHALT und die Jugend- und Schulddiskurse in der österreichischen Nachkriegszeit', in C. Dewald (ed.), *Der Wirklichkeit auf der Spur. Essays zum österreichischen Nachkriegsfilm ASPHALT*, Vienna: Filmarchiv Austria, 13–14. For Germany, see, for example, Fehrenbach, 1998, 117–119.

77. See V. Öhner. 2004. 'ASPHALT und der Diskurs über "Jugendverwahrlosung" und "Jugendkriminalität"', in C. Dewald (ed.), *Der Wirklichkeit auf der Spur. Essays zum österreichischen Nachkriegsfilm ASPHALT*, Vienna: Filmarchiv Austria, 30.

78. See Heineman, 2003, 221–222.

79. 'Kleine Melodie aus Wien', *Arbeiterzeitung*, 30 October 1948; 'Kleine Melodie aus Wien', *Weltpresse*, 30 October 1948.

80. 'Das Herz einer Frau', *Arbeiterzeitung*, 19 August 1951; 'Neue Filme', *Die Presse*, 24 August 1951.

81. 'Ein tolles Früchtchen', *Paimann's Filmlisten*, 14 October 1953.

82. See Hake, 2008, 48, 83.

83. K. Moser. 2002. 'Die Bilderwelt der ÖSTERREICH IN BILD UND TON – Die konstruierte Realität eines ständestaatlichen Propagandainstruments', in M. Achenbach and K. Moser (eds), *Österreich in Bild und Ton– Die Filmwochenschau des austrofaschistischen Ständestaates*, Vienna: Eigenverlag, 21–22.

84. See, for example, Moeller, 1997, 121.

85. See F. Göttler. 1993. 'Westdeutscher Nachkriegsfilm. Land der Väter', in W. Jacobson, A. Kaes and H.H. Prinzler (eds), *Geschichte des deutschen Films*, Stuttgart: Metzler, 190.

86. *Ich und meine Frau* was ranked fourth on the list of the most popular films in 1953; *Gone with the Wind* came sixth. See Österreichisches Statistisches Zentralamt, 1959b, 146. The Catholic newspaper *Die Furche* hailed the film as a continuation of the famous 1930s romantic comedies *Maskerade* (1934) and *Episode* (1935). See 'Anschluss an "Maskerade"', *Die Furche*, 5 September 1953.

87. 'Ehekrise – durchs Objektiv betrachtet', *Die Presse*, 27 March 1953.

88. 'Ich und meine Frau', *Die Union*, 3 September 1953.

89. See Hanisch, 2005, 320.

CONCLUSION

A major reason why cinema – and particularly domestic cinema – was so popular in postwar Austria was that the films provided reassurance to the audience. Struggling for economic survival, burdened with the trauma of war and dictatorship and apprehensive about the country's uncertain future, people looked for reassurance as well as escape. Popular cinema's seemingly apolitical stance offered encouragement and comfort to an audience wary of politics. Like other postwar cinemas, it helped audiences to manage their suffering or unacknowledged guilt, to cope with rapid social transformations and to embrace change. But Austrian cinema was unique: it did not just bolster the flagging morale of the Austrian people – it also played a specific, active role in the 'invention' of the Austrian nation. By formulating concepts of national identity and selling them to a mass audience, cinema was instrumental in fostering identification with the new Austria at a time when many Austrians still felt insecure about their national identity.

And it was masculinity, as this book has demonstrated, that constituted a prime site for the inscription of national values, due to the historical intertwining of masculinity, nationhood and citizenship. In postwar Austria, concepts of national masculinity needed to be redefined and strengthened, both to buttress the new nation state and to stabilise the social patriarchal order, which had come under threat through shifts in gender relations. The hitherto dominant ideal of hard masculinity, discredited by the experiences of Nazi dictatorship and war, had come under pressure and needed to be reformed, not least because rapid economic and political transformations called for new skills and attitudes. The remodelled masculine ideals needed to appeal to both men and women, facilitate the integration of veterans into a modernised economy and, at the same time, affirm men's superior status in society.

In a social context in which both nationhood and masculine norm had become unstable, popular cinema acquired a key role in formulating and selling notions of national masculinity. Seeking to reach large audiences, commercial cinema engaged with and fuelled popular discourse; it responded to the desires and anxieties of the audience and took note of social and economic shifts, but sometimes also anticipated developments and took the lead by proposing new ideas. By engaging with or glossing over sensitive issues, such as troubled gender relations, the quest for national independence or the problematic question of Nazi collaboration, popular cinema shaped public discourse decisively, and provided orientation for society. Yet, popular cinema, as this book has shown, offered a variety of responses to issues of public concern in order to appeal to as many people as possible. This analysis of a large number of Austrian films has revealed considerable differences in the way the genres dealt with the issue of gender or addressed pressing social issues, according to the kind of emotional release each genre offers.

Historical costume film most overtly promoted a *national* masculine ideal, by using Austria's imperial past as a background on which to create a historical template of Austrian masculinity. Historical costume film did not evade the uncomfortable memory of National Socialism completely, but addressed the experience of Nazi dictatorship in loosely disguised form in a small number of films set in the repressive regime under Metternich in the first half of the nineteenth century. This displacement onto another historical period functioned as a screen memory that enabled both filmmakers and spectators to deal with traumas of the past. These films drew parallels between Hitler's and Metternich's rule, but trivialised the repression people suffered under the authoritarian chancellorship of Prince Metternich, and exaggerated the anti-authoritarian stance of the Austrians – a method that aimed to ease the burden of the Nazi past. The majority of historical costume films, however, were set in the last decades of the Austro-Hungarian Empire, and disavowed the recent Nazi past completely through the celebration of 'Austria's last happy time'.[1] Presenting the imperial past in glorious colours, with a fatherly emperor ruling over a happy and diverse people living together peacefully, the films furnished Austria's political elite with adequate imagery to promote the new national identity; the empire's multi-ethnic past was instrumentalised to present the Austrians as harmonious people who, in contrast to the 'nationalist' Germans, had always lived in peace with other cultures. Through its popular appeal, the costume genre thus took the lead in inventing a nation and a national masculinity not tainted by the Nazi past. By depicting Austrian men primarily as sensitive musical geniuses or charming officers, and by divesting the army (which occupied a central role in these films) of any connection to violence, the genre softened masculinity and depoliticised the military; historical costume film depicted the Austrian army as musical and hedonistic, and thus cleverly disconnected the Austrian military from acts of violence. Furthermore, despite toning down 'hard' masculine characteristics, the genre did not feminise men. Instead, it subtly underlined male power by equipping men with a special musical gift, a higher social status or, if nothing else, a dashing uniform. The genre's showcasing of a cultured masculinity served several purposes. First, it helped to smooth tense gender relations by making male superiority appealing to women.

Furthermore, it substantiated the claim that Austria was a nation in its own right by providing evidence for deep-rooted historical differences between Austrians and Germans. Finally, the cultured, non-aggressive masculinity the genre advertised served as proof of the nation's 'innocence' – a fiction that was also used by the governing elites to successfully promote the view that the Austrians had been victims of Nazi aggression; a myth which became a pillar of the new Austrian nation state. It is easy to see why historical costume film was popular with Austrian as well as West German audiences: the films' high production values (beautiful costumes and spectacular settings), together with the light-hearted or melodramatic narratives and star-studded casts, satisfied the appetite for spectacle and, in addition, provided access to an uncomplicated, positively connoted past that glossed over the painful memory of more recent history.

While the costume genre offered a fairly hedonistic image of masculinity, the genre of *Heimatfilm* did quite the opposite. Austrian *Heimatfilm* highlighted male suffering, and advocated self-control and renunciation as masculine virtues. On the surface, the stiff and restrained men that populated *Heimatfilms* bore close resemblance to the traditional ideal of hard masculinity. Unlike some of its West German counterparts, Austrian *Heimatfilm* took an anti-modernist stance; set against the backdrop of a rural lifestyle immersed in tradition that signified stability and order, it endorsed traditional gender roles. The *Heimatfilm* narrative legitimised men's superior status within the *Heimat* by fabricating an intimate relationship between men and nature. Eternal nature itself, which occupied a key role in *Heimatfilm* and usually took the shape of a pristine Alpine setting, did not allow departure from traditional patriarchal order, so the underlying message.

Despite affirming traditional masculine virtues such as self-control, rationality and determination, however, the genre's stance towards traditional masculinity was ambiguous. The fact that the *Heimatfilm* narratives subjected men to great injustices, and thereby forced the male protagonists to suppress their emotions and demonstrate self-discipline, suggests a considerable fear of men's seemingly innate aggression. *Heimatfilm* insists that masculinity needs to be contained and pacified to safeguard the *Heimat* from destruction. Although the genre painstakingly avoided references to the Nazi past, it engaged with its traumatic repercussions in enigmatic form on a symbolic and metaphoric level, as the analysis of *Bergkristall* and *Hoch vom Dachstein* has shown. Apart from melodrama, *Heimatfilm* was thus the only genre in Austrian cinema that compelled men to face up to their guilt. This guilt, which burdens the young (particularly, young men) in *Heimatfilm*, is representative of the guilt of the whole nation. By subjecting men to punishment, *Heimatfilm* not only purified the dominant masculine norm that had been tainted by the war, but also provided absolution for the audience – and thus for the nation as a whole. Because the genre offered catharsis, and promised stability and harmony in a familiar rural landscape, it appealed to both Austrian and West German audiences, who felt just as uneasy about the past and a rapidly transforming society. Even though the genre avoided an outright nationalisation of the *Heimat* – it tried to generate national pride by evoking a sense of belonging with a seemingly apolitical, regional *Heimat* that was not delimited by national borders – nationality and masculinity were closely entangled in *Heimatfilm*. The genre addressed the question of national guilt and attempted to cleanse traditional masculinity of the taint of its dark past, thereby presenting a future that could resist modernity.

Nature was also a prominent feature of postwar tourist film, but in tourist film nature did not dominate or control the narrative, nor did it signify conservatism as in *Heimatfilm*. On the contrary, the landscape in Austrian tourist film served as a backdrop to the celebration of movement and freedom. The optimistic feeling the genre emanated was largely due to its key themes of mobility, travel and leisure. The films, in which urban people took centre stage, embraced change, which explains the (comparatively) progressive views on gender that the genre promoted. The earlier tourist film, at least, allowed women considerable freedom, highlighting similarities rather than differences between men and women and promoting gender equality. Like *Heimatfilm*, tourist film advocated harmony and the values of community, but it was much more inclusive, and relatively effortlessly bridged the gap between urban and rural, male and female, rich and poor. The road, a key feature in tourist film, brought people together, broke down class barriers and elided gender differences. Austrian tourist film accommodated alternative lifestyles and even offered a glimpse of male homosexuality, as the queer reading of films such as *Der Hofrat Geiger* and *Zwei in einem Auto* has revealed. Though the presence of homosexual masculinities was obscured (homosexual relationships were, after all, illegal in Austria until 1971), some tourist films hinted, if ever so slightly, at the possibility of alternative sexualities, which suggests that the genre's inclusivity and the themes of mobility and pleasure invited a certain permissiveness.

The narratives and characterisations of early tourist films convey a strong immediacy and show a society in flux. At a time when economic survival was paramount, the tourist films presented relationships in which practical thinking superseded romanticism, and companionship replaced erotic attraction. Tourist film promoted models of masculinity that very much resembled what Cohan described as the 1950s US American ideal of the 'domesticated male', though adjusted to national traditions and thus less consumption- and career-oriented than their Hollywood counterparts.[2] However, with the economic upturn and the Austrian film industry's recovery, the genre lost some of the momentum evident in earlier productions; after 1950, a growing emphasis on consumption increasingly replaced the previously dominant themes of frugality and female entrepreneurship. The celebration of female independence, which had been strong in earlier films, became superficial, and was undercut by an accentuation of differences between men and women and an affirmation of traditional gender roles. The changes in the economy and the transformation into a consumer society clearly affected the function of the genre, which became an advertising vehicle for the Austrian tourist industry and a modern consumer lifestyle.

While tourist film met social change with optimism, postwar comedy dealt with modernity slightly differently. Its key function was to provide emotional release by turning the challenges of modernity into a source of humour and thus to make them seem less threatening. Like the future-oriented tourist film, Austrian postwar comedy was receptive to current trends; however, it was not politically or aesthetically progressive, but responded to the economic and social changes with a capitalist fantasy of a comfortable, middle-class life. While the display of modern household gadgets or the trendy clothing and haircuts of the actors aimed at demonstrating modernity, the comedy narratives and aesthetics were more or less traditional. Unlike early postwar tourist film, which did advertise change and propose a more equal society, postwar comedy's professed progressiveness remained superficial (albeit more genuine in earlier comedies), and never really challenged the existing social or political order. Furthermore, although comedy advertised a modern, consumption-oriented lifestyle, it exhibited rather conservative views on gender, presenting the idea that there were insurmountable differences between men and women, and endorsing fairly traditional gender roles. By championing the new, middle-class family ideal of male breadwinner and female housewife as a norm without alternatives, Austrian comedy set the nuclear family as standard, and thereby bolstered the public discourse of the 1950s that called upon women to leave employment and devote themselves to domestic issues and childrearing. One might have expected that comedy would ridicule gender standards or subvert them, especially as transgressing norms and challenging established notions of gender or class are generic traits of comedy. But Austrian comedies displayed little subversiveness, although the theme of mistaken identity, a key theme in Austrian comedy, would have lent itself to the critique of social norms. Filmmakers could have utilised the topic to satirise the constructedness of gender roles or to question Austria's political opportunism, but only a few films, such as J.A. Hübler-Kahla's 1947 costume comedy *Die Welt dreht sich verkehrt*, offered a glimmer of ideological rebellion, albeit in the disguise of historical costume.

The masculine ideals comedy promoted were outwardly modernised, but not original. What *was* new, though, was the emphasis these films placed on paternity. The father figure became a popular theme of comedy – a response to contemporary anxieties about fatherless families and the hotly debated problem of delinquent youth that came as a result of absent or overly strict fathers. Austrian comedy either mocked strict patriarchs or replaced the outmoded authoritarian father with progressive and warm-hearted dads. Yet, while comedy called for the modernisation of men, it ridiculed 'modern' career women or mothers who did not devote themselves entirely to their children. Comedy emphasised the fatherly aptitude of men, and insisted that fathers needed to get involved to compensate for past neglect and the shortcomings of modern women. So, although it showcased seemingly self-confident, independent young women, it called for their retreat into the private sphere once they got married, and thus endorsed female submission. Importantly, though, it disguised the severity of this message by making these propositions in a very light-hearted, humorous manner, as well as by stressing the comforts of a modern, middle-class home and the status it would bring to women. Comedy thus made traditional gender roles appealing, not least by glossing over the women's lack of political influence by underlining their power as consumers.

Cultural transformations, as this analysis of cinematic genres has demonstrated, are closely connected to social transformations, but often have a different momentum. Some genres show an immediate engagement with social change, whereas others precede social transformations, or lag behind them. Tourist film, for example, changed quite radically over the short course of ten years: in the immediate postwar era, when there was widespread uncertainty about the direction society and cinema would take, tourist film pressed ahead, advertising progressive views on gender and a vision of a more equal, non-materialistic society, but by the mid-1950s it had lost all of its initial political momentum. The producers of tourist films now answered different needs, and turned the films into advertising vehicles for pop stars and regional holiday destinations that sought to exploit the increase in leisure time and purchasing power, especially among the young. The success of these new *Schlagerfilme* was short-lived. In the early 1960s, remakes of the early postwar film *Der Hofrat Geiger*, now promoted as *Mariandl* (1961), and the popular and often adapted musical *Im weissen Rössl* (At the White Horse Inn, 1960), which went on to spark several spin-offs, were the last commercially successful tourist films. They marked the end of a film mode that would only live on in television. Unlike tourist film, representations of gender changed little in *Heimatfilm*; however, its dramatic visual tone gradually wore off as the rural theme became, as in tourist film, a commodity that had to be sold to potential tourists. It was the endless repetition of once-successful visual and narrative formulae through a series of remakes and sequels which brought about the genre's demise in the late-1950s. Although some filmmakers made attempts to rescue the genre from 'comedic or trendy dilution' with films such as Georg Tressler's critically acclaimed *Der Weibsteufel* (The She-Devil, 1966), they failed.[3]

Other genres, such as historical costume film, melodrama and, partly, comedy, remained more stable. During the first postwar decade, historical costume productions became more lavish, thanks to the influx of German capital and the competition from Hollywood and television. The genre reached the height of its commercial success in the mid-1950s with Ernst Marischka's *Sissi* trilogy (1955–1957), which inspired a new wave of imperial-era costume films that took the form of romantic love stories or musical comedies; but the audience, whose appetite for a romanticised imperial past diminished with their growing prosperity and (arguably) a stronger identification with the new nation, eventually grew tired of imperial clichés. When Marischka retired in 1958, the decline of the genre had already set in.

Comedy seemed the most resilient of all genres, not least because the producers tried to make their films more appealing by responding to short-lived fashion trends and by borrowing heavily from other genres. In the early 1960s there were a series of cross-dressing comedies (for example *Charleys Tante*/Charley's Aunt, 1963) and crime spoofs (*Kriminaltango*/ Criminal Tango, 1960 or *Die Abenteuer des Grafen Bobby*/The Adventures of Count Bobby, 1961), many directed by the seasoned filmmaker Géza von Cziffra and featuring the handsome Peter Alexander as the new comedy star, and these temporarily breathed new life into the genre. The master of shallow entertainment, Franz Antel, whose 1950s comedies and tourist films had once been populated by neat bikini girls, started to spice up his films with sexual innuendos and more naked skin to attract jaded audiences. In the end, none of these attempts could stop the demise of comedy or, indeed, Austrian cinema as a whole.

The Austrian film industry, however, was not the only one to suffer a sharp decline in audience numbers. Internationally, large cinema production companies had been struggling with falling box office returns since the mid-1950s, largely due to the competition from television; Hollywood experimented with new film techniques, such as cinemascope and 3-D, and epic spectacles to hold its ground. But the Austrian film industry, which was firmly focused on the West German market and spoiled by its commercial success in the mid-1950s, failed to take the competition from television seriously (the first regular public broadcast started in West Germany in 1952; in Austria in 1955). The mostly commercially oriented Austrian filmmakers also ignored new aesthetic trends in European cinema. Whereas in the late 1950s the *Nouvelle Vague* successfully challenged traditional French cinema, and British filmmakers produced impressive social-realist dramas centred on the British working-class, Austrian cinema continued in the traditional mould. In the 1960s, Austria's film industry mostly churned out tourist film-*Heimatfilm*-musical comedy blends, such as Rolf Olsen's *Hochzeit am Neusiedlersee* (Wedding at the Neusiedlersee, 1963), Hans Hollmann's *Happy-End am Attersee* (1964) or Antel's James Bond spoof *00Sex am Wolfgangsee* (Double-O-Sex at the Wolfgangsee, 1966), whose titles were symptomatic of an overall lack of originality. There were some serious attempts at creativity, such as Arthur Maria Rabenalt's crime film *Mann im Schatten* (Man in the Shadow, 1961), featuring the comedian Helmut Qualtinger, whose enigmatic humour exposed the ambiguity of the famed Viennese charm, but these were exceptions and did not mark a turning point. Clearly, the industry had been too complacent about audiences, and failed to analyse why cinema attendance fell from 122 million visitors in 1958 to 84 million in 1963.[4] The decreasing interest in popular cinema was also reflected in the stagnation of sales of Austrian film journals: the fan magazine *Mein Film* was discontinued in 1957, followed by *Funk und Film* in 1961. Cinemas closed on a large scale. As the films failed to recoup expenses, the number of productions dwindled, falling from twenty-three productions in 1958 to sixteen in 1963, and reaching a low of four feature films premiering in 1969. Thus, after having experienced a surprising boom in the mid-1950s, commercial Austrian cinema was virtually dead by the mid-1960s.

It would take many years until Austrian cinema would once again become a household name, and even then only on a much smaller scale. Its slow recovery in the 1980s was helped by modest film funding provided by the municipality of Vienna from 1977 onwards; on the national level, financial support for filmmakers was finally introduced in 1980 with the *Filmförderungsgesetz* (Film Promotion Act). The first signs of a new, innovative cinema had already appeared in the mid-1970s, when a generation of new filmmakers started to make small, low-budget films. Interestingly, it was Austrian television, through the national broadcasting company, Österreichischer Rundfunk ORF, which played an influential role in furthering new talent, by giving filmmakers room to experiment. From the scatterings of small-scale, often avant-gardeish productions that dominated in the 1970s and early 1980s, Austrian cinema slowly moved towards more traditional narrative forms and commercially viable films. Some films even attracted substantial audiences, such as Niki List's *Müllers Büro* (Mueller's Office, 1986), attracting 439,000 spectators, or Harald Sicheritz's cabaret film *Hinterholz 8* (1998) with over 600,000 tickets sold in Austria[5] – still small fry compared with previous smash hits such as Forst's *Wiener Mädeln*, which had sold 300,000 tickets in one cinema alone during its first eleven weeks of screening in 1950.[6] Austrian cinema would never again be as lucrative as it had been in the 1940s and 1950s. However, with the old guard of Austrian directors having left the scene in the 1960s due to death, retirement or reorientation towards television (only the unflinching Antel tried to revive cinema attendance with a number of soft-porn *Heimatfilms* in the 1970s), the way was now open for young, experimental filmmakers, who brought with them new ideas and a more critical view of Austrian society.

The new Austrian cinema, which took its first hesitant steps in the 1970s and found its footing in the 1990s, marked a clear break with the aesthetic and narrative formulae of traditional cinema.[7] It engaged with social reality more directly than postwar cinema had done, and also tackled issues that had largely been glossed over before (or provided with pleasing alternatives): class conflict, the uncomfortable memory of the Nazi past or troubled gender relations, which had again come to the fore with the strengthening of the feminist movement in the late 1960s. Axel Corti was one of the first filmmakers to engage critically with Austrian complicity with the Nazis in his documentary-style television film *Der Fall Jägerstätter* (The Case of Jägerstätter, 1972), which contrasted the story of the steadfast Catholic farmer, Franz Jägerstätter, who was executed for his refusal to fight in Hitler's army, with the narrow-mindedness of his former neighbours, who showed little sympathy for the symbolic importance of Jägerstätter's stance. From the 1980s onwards more films emerged that reflected critically on the role the Austrians played during the Nazi dictatorship; even Antel tried his hand at this political subject with *Der Bockerer* (Bockerer, 1981) – a film that engaged seriously with Austria's Nazi past, but still exculpated the majority of Austrians. Much more nuanced was Andreas Gruber's outstanding *Hasenjagd* (The Quality of Mercy, 1994), about the escape of Soviet prisoners from the Austrian concentration camp Mauthausen, which convincingly illustrated the broad range of Austrian attitudes, ranging from willing support for the Nazis to cases of quiet resistance.

Thus, new Austrian cinema did precisely the opposite of 1940s and 1950s Austrian cinema in that it showed a more realist, sometimes very critical, counter-traditionalist engagement with Austrian society that made no direct references to cinematic traditions. Some genres, such as tourist film or musical revues, disappeared entirely. An almost similar fate befell historical costume film; once a defining genre of Austrian cinema, it was now reduced to a few co-productions, such as the drama *Oberst Redl* (Colonel Redl, 1985), directed by the Hungarian filmmaker István Szabó and starring the Austrian actor Klaus Maria Brandauer.[8] Although comedy remained a popular genre in Austrian cinema, the new comedies bore little resemblance to the 1950s musical comedies and the theme of mistaken identity. Having been proclaimed dead, however, the surprisingly resilient genre of *Heimatfilm* received critical treatment in the six-part television series *Alpensaga* (1976–1980) and was also revived by Stefan Ruzowitzky in his *Die Siebtelbauern* (The Inheritors, 1998). Overall, though, the New Austrian Cinema showed few traces of the Austrian cinematic tradition. Many Austrian filmmakers who had started to make films in the 1970s and 1980s, and who had witnessed cinema's aesthetic decline first-hand, did not look to traditional Austrian cinema for orientation, but turned for inspiration elsewhere – to avant-garde film or to US cinema of the late 1960s, as the filmmaker Peter Patzak did.

For many years the Austrian film industry had been in the grip of a generation of established filmmakers and producers, who warded off any newcomers who attempted to challenge cinematic tradition. Consequently, early postwar Austrian cinema remained conservative in its outlook; this was also reflected in its representations of gender. Only in the late 1970s would Austrian cinema adopt a more proactive role by challenging the establishment and projecting more radical visions, not least because women finally gained a foothold as filmmakers and producers.

Even so, the fact that postwar Austrian cinema eventually manoeuvred itself into obscurity and seemingly had little to offer to subsequent generations should not obscure its enormous influence on the process of nation building. Through the many reruns of Austrian films on national television since the 1970s, postwar cinema's images of Austria and Austrian masculinity were perpetuated and advertised to a new generation. Postwar cinematic discourse successfully redefined what Connell describes as the hegemonic standard of hard masculinity – that powerful ideal that had held generations in its sway.[9] The masculine ideals that cinema proposed were not entirely new, but modified versions of existing norms and generic types; these cinematic concepts of masculinity were broad enough to invoke identification from different men, and flexible enough to adapt to generic and social developments. By attributing traditionally feminine characteristics to men, rather than masculine ones, popular cinema in a certain way 'feminised' national archetypes of masculinity; this remodelling of masculine ideals assisted the government's effort to present Austria as a passive victim of Nazi aggression and thus exculpate the Austrians from involvement in Nazi crimes – a reminder of the immanent political meaning of gender constructions.

Hence, the construction of the musical, charming, peaceable Austrian man was very much the result of cinematic traditions and the revival of cliché, but was also driven by political necessity. Yet, even though the masculine ideals promoted by popular cinema were highly influential, and reverberated in the media and in political discourse on Austrian independence or the war, for example, they were always in competition with other discourses and traditions. The traditional ideal of hard masculinity retained considerable influence in both public and private spheres. Public spaces in postwar Austria were dominated by images of vigorous, muscular masculinity that called on 'real' men to rebuild their country, as Kos has detailed in his analysis of public iconography.[10] Attempts by women's groups and the Socialists to reform family and matrimonial law to give married women equal rights were repeatedly thwarted by the conservative elites up to the 1970s.[11] Many men also continued to hold on to the traditional masculine values that had been the dominating influence in their youth – many autobiographical accounts illustrate that the discursive construction of a softer Austrian masculinity had yet to be appropriated by individual men in the 1950s, especially in rural areas.

Even cinematic representations of masculinity were ambiguous: while postwar cinema promoted sensitive, democratic and non-aggressive masculine ideals, few films challenged the unequal distribution of power between men and women; the bulk of films affirmed male superiority by prescribing the middle-class ideal of the nuclear family as the norm while omitting alternative representations. Again, there were exceptions, since

Austrian cinema produced some films that ran counter to these images, or that were ambiguous, as the analysis of the comedy *Seine Tochter ist der Peter* illustrated. Within a relatively short time span, during the immediate postwar years, Austrian cinema did express more liberal views on gender, especially in the genres of tourist film, comedy and melodrama; but once society had stabilised and the economy started to recover, cinema swiftly adjusted to the changed circumstances: it not only responded to the backlash against female independence in the late 1940s and early 1950s, but actually helped to induce this reaction. It did so by promoting outwardly modernised ideals of masculinity whose claim to superiority was obscured by male charm and passiveness, by presenting traditional gender relations as the only form of socially acceptable relationships and by depicting gender inequality as natural. Thus, the cinematic representations of masculinity, which toned down the hard aspects of the hitherto dominant ideal and promoted a less authoritarian, softer masculinity (not least to make films more appealing to women), merely masked cinema's patriarchal core. Only the strengthening of the feminist movement and the student revolutions of the late 1960s would radically challenge these views on gender. By then, commercial cinema was dead.

This study of a large number of films has established that popular cinema performed important functions in postwar Austria by remodelling masculine stereotypes it equipped the national quest for a new identity with adequate imagery, and helped to homogenise disparate identities; it adjusted masculine norms to meet the demands of a modernised capitalist economy and consumer culture; it absolved men from responsibility for their actions during the war, transforming brutalised soldiers into domesticated citizens; and, lastly, it sought to maintain patriarchy and secure the social order – which had become destabilised by the shifts in power relations between men and women – by promoting outwardly modernised masculine ideals. In these ways, cinema responded to the experience of the war and to Austria's economic and political transformations that demanded new attitudes and skills from its citizens. Austrian cinema's popularity with West German audiences shows that many of the concerns it dealt with were not uniquely Austrian, but were shared by the Germans – who faced very similar challenges.

This analysis of postwar Austrian cinema has been able to show empirically that masculinity, due to its historical intertwining with nationhood, was a key site for the reformulation and inscription of national values. It has demonstrated that popular cinema not only responded to social transformations by catering to the desires of the audience, but sometimes also took the lead by projecting visions of a glorious past or a prosperous future. Cinema, I argue, intervened directly in popular discourse – and shaped and modified it – by giving widespread publicity to specific views on gender and the nation, while marginalising or obscuring other views. Obviously, the scope of such a study is limited, and therefore this book could not tackle all the questions that arise when analysing the role and influence of popular cinema in a given society. One could, for example, ask whether Austrian cinema produced uniquely national ideals of masculinities, or whether the proposed concepts of masculinity were responses to the larger social and cultural transformations that occurred across different countries and thus displayed similarities with those of other national cinemas. The concept of cultural transfer would be a promising tool to analyse cross-cultural influences between different national cinemas in the postwar context. A question that also begs investigation is the dominant influence of Hollywood on the representations of masculinity in postwar Austrian and other national cinemas. Austrian audiences, despite their overall preference for domestic productions, liked to watch a variety of films, and Hollywood cinema, together with other cultural imports from the US, had a considerable impact on Austrian society in the 1950s.

Domestic cinema, however, was a potent cultural force in postwar Austrian society. Its ability to exert considerable influence on society was not merely down to its mass appeal; rather, it was, on the one hand, the specific constellation of a society undergoing rapid social, economic and – most importantly – national transformations and, on the other, the popularity of a cinema to which audiences looked for comfort and reassurance. This lent cinematic discourse such power that it was able to shape popular views on gender and help to instil a new sense of national identity in the Austrian people.

Notes

1. Advertisement for the film *Verklungenes Wien* (Vienna as it Used to Be, 1951), directed by Ernst Marischka. *Illustrierter Filmkurier* (1951), Nr. 1019.
2. Cohan, 1997, 49–56.
3. Dassanowsky, 2005, 174.
4. Fritz, 1984, 123.
5. See R. Standún. 2011. 'National Box-office Hits or International "Arthouse"? The New Austrokomödie', in R. Dassanowsky and O.C. Speck (eds), *New Austrian Film*, New York: Berghahn Books, 320–331.
6. Festschrift der Apollo Kino- u. Theater GmbH, 1954, 16.
7. For the 'New Austrian Film' see R. Dassanowsky and O.C. Speck (eds). 2011. *New Austrian Film*, New York: Berghahn Books.
8. See Dassanowsky, 2005, 214–225.
9. See Connell, 1996.
10. See Kos, 1994, 59–149.
11. See Cyba, 1996, 437; for a detailed account of the struggle for a reform of matrimonial law see Mesner, 1997, 186–210.

BIBLIOGRAPHY AND SOURCES

Archival Records

National Archives College Park, Maryland, USA
RG 260, Office of Military Government for Germany (US) (OMGUS):
   Records of the Information Control Division, Records re: Motion Picture Production and Dist., 1945–49, E 260 (A1)
   US Allied Command Austria, Film Section, General Records, 1945–50, E 2032
   US Allied Command Austria, Information Services Branch, Operations Section, General Records, 1945–50, E 2018

Newspapers and Periodicals

Arbeiterzeitung
Beiträge zur österreichischen Statistik
Bild-Telegraf
Das kleine Volksblatt
Der Abend
Der Aufbau
Die Furche
Die Presse
Die Union
Film
Film-Kunst. Zeitschrift für Filmkultur und Filmwissenschaft
Frankfurter Allemeine Illustrierter Filmkurier
Mein Film
Montag Morgen
Neuer Kurier
Neues Österreich
New York Times
Österreichische Allgemeine Zeitung
Österreichische Film und Kino Zeitung
Österreichische Zeitung
Österreichisches Tagebuch
Paimann's Filmlisten
Pem's Private Bulletins
Volksstimme
Welt am Abend

Welt am Montag
Weltpresse
Wiener Kurier
Wiener Tageszeitung
Wiener Zeitung

Government Publications

Amt für Kultur und Volksbildung der Stadt Wien. 1959. *Grossstadtjugend und Kino. Eine Untersuchung der Arbeitsgemeinschaft 'Jugend und Film' beim Landesjugendreferat Wien über den Kinobesuch der Kinder und Jugendlichen im Jahre 1953*, Vienna: Verlag Jugend und Volk, vol. 10.

Bundeskanzleramt. 2010. *Frauenbericht, Teil I: Statistische Analysen zur Entwicklung der Situation von Frauen in Österreich*, Vienna. http://www.bka.gv.at/studien/frauenbericht2010/Frauenbericht_Teil1_1Demografie.pdf.

Magistrat der Stadt Wien. 1956. 'Die Wiener Kinos und ihre Besucher. Eine statistische Analyse', *Mitteilungen aus Statistik und Verwaltung der Stadt Wien* (Sonderheft Nr. 2).

Österreichisches Statistisches Zentralamt. 1950. *Statistisches Handbuch für die Republik Österreich*, Vienna, vol. 1.

Österreichisches Statistisches Zentralamt. 1953. *Statistisches Handbuch für die Republik Österreich*, Vienna, vol. 4.

Österreichisches Statistisches Zentralamt. 1959a. *Die Ehescheidung. Eine statistisch-soziologische Untersuchung*, Vienna.

Österreichisches Statistisches Zentralamt. 1959b. *Beiträge zur österreichischen Statistik*, Vienna, vol. 39.

Literature

'Official Documents: Great Britain – Soviet Union – United States. Tripartite Conference in Moscow. November 1, 1943'. 1944. *The American Journal of International Law*, 38(1), 3–8.

Allen, R.C. and D. Gomery. 1985. *Film History: Theory and Practice*, New York: McGraw-Hill.

Anderson, B. 2006. *Imagined Communities: Reflections on the Origin and Spread of Nationalism*, rev. ed., London: Verso.

Antel, F. and C.F. Winkler. 1991. *Hollywood an der Donau. Geschichte der Wien-Film in Sievering*, Vienna: Edition S.

Appelt, E. 1999. *Geschlecht - Staatsbürgerschaft - Nation. Politische Konstruktionen des Geschlechterverhältnisses in Europa*, Frankfurt am Main: Campus.

Applegate, C. 1990. *A Nation of Provincials: The German Idea of Heimat*, Berkeley: University of California Press.

Ashby, J. and A. Higson. 2000. 'Re-framing British Cinema Studies', in J. Ashby and A. Higson (eds), *British Cinema, Past and Present, London*, New York: Routledge, 19–20.

Bader, W.B. 1966. *Austria between East and West 1945–1955*, Stanford: Stanford University Press.

Baer, H. 2007. *'Film und Frau* and the Female Spectator in 1950s West German Cinema', in J.E. Davidson and S. Hake (eds), *Framing the Fifties: Cinema in a Divided Germany*, New York: Berghahn Books, 151–165.

Balázs, B. 1984. 'Der Fall Dr. Fanck. Vorwort zu Arnold Fancks Filmbuch „Stürme über dem Montblanc" (1931)', in H.H. Diederichs, W. Gersch and M. Nagy (eds), *Béla Balázs. Schriften zum Film*, Berlin: Henschel, vol. 2, 288–289.

Bandhauer-Schöffmann, I. and E. Hornung. 1992. 'Trümmerfrauen - ein kurzes Heldinnenleben. Nachkriegsgesellschaft als Frauengesellschaft', in A. Graf (ed.), *Zur Politik des Weiblichen. Frauenmacht und -ohmnacht*, Vienna: Verlag für Gesellschaftskritik, 93–120.

Bandhauer-Schöffmann, I. and E. Hornung (eds). 1992. *Wiederaufbau weiblich. Dokumentation der Tagung 'Frauen in der Österreichischen und Deutschen Nachkriegszeit'*, Vienna: Geyer-Ed.

Bandhauer-Schöffmann, I. and E. Hornung. 1996. 'War and Gender Identity: The Experience of Austrian Women, 1945–1950', in D.F. Good, M. Grandner and M.J. Maynes (eds), *Austrian Women in the Nineteenth and Twentieth Centuries*, Providence: Berghahn, 213–233.

Barthel, M. 1986. *So war es wirklich. Der deutsche Nachkriegsfilm*, Munich: Herbig.

Bauer, I. 1995. 'Von den Tugenden der Weiblichkeit. Zur geschlechtsspezifischen Arbeitsteilung in der politischen Kultur', in T. Albrich, K. Eisterer, M. Gehler and R. Steininger (eds), *Österreich in den Fünfzigern*, Innsbruck: Österreichischer StudienVerlag, 35–52.

Bauer, I. 1996. 'Die "Ami-Braut" – Platzhalterin für das Abgespaltene? Zur (De-) Konstruktion eines Stereotyps der österreichischen Nachkriegsgeschichte 1945–1955', *L'Homme. Europäische Zeitschrift für feministische Geschichtswissenschaft*, 7(1), 107–121.

Bauer, I. and R. Huber. 2007. 'Sexual Encounters across (Former) Enemy Borderlines', in G. Bischof, A. Pelinka and D. Herzog (eds), *Sexuality in Austria*, New Brunswick, N.J.: Transaction Publishers, 65–101.

Bechdolf, U. 1992. *Wunsch-Bilder? Frauen im nationalsozialistischen Unterhaltungsfilm*, Tübingen: Tübinger Verein für Volkskunde.

Beckermann, R. and C. Blümlinger (eds). 1996. *Ohne Untertitel: Fragmente einer Geschichte des österreichischen Kinos*, Vienna: Sonderzahl.

Beindorf, C. 2001. *Terror des Idylls. Die kulturelle Konstruktion von Gemeinschaften im Heimatfilm und Landsbygdsfilm 1930–1960*, Baden-Baden: Nomos Verlag.

Bergfelder, T. 2002. 'Extraterritorial Fantasies: Edgar Wallace and the German Crime Film', in T. Bergfelder, E. Carter and D. Göktürk (eds), *The German Cinema Book*, London: BFI, 39–47.

Bergfelder, T. 2005. 'National, Transnational or Supranational Cinema? Rethinking European Film Studies', *Media, Culture & Society*, 27(3), 315–331.

Bergfelder, T. 2006. *International Adventures. German Popular Cinema and European Co-productions in the 1960s*, New York: Berghahn Books.

Bergfelder, T. 2007. 'German Cinema and Film Noir', in A. Spicer (ed.), *European Film Noir*, Manchester: Manchester University Press, 138–163.

Bergfelder, T. and C. Cargnelli. 2008. *Destination London: German-speaking Emigrés and British Cinema, 1925–1950*, New York: Berghahn Books.

Bergmeister, J. 1971. *Die Lichtspieltheater in Vorarlberg*, Innsbruck: Wagnersche Universitätsbuchhandlung.

Bessel, R. 2001. 'Was bleibt vom Krieg? Deutsche Nachkriegsgeschichte(n) aus geschlechtergeschichtlicher Perspektive', *Militärgeschichtliche Zeitschrift*, 60, 297–305.

Biess, F. 2002. 'Männer des Wiederaufbaus - Wiederaufbau der Männer. Kriegsheimkehrer in Ost- und Westdeutschland 1945–1955', in K. Hagemann and S. Schüler-Springorum (eds), *Heimat-Front: Militär und Geschlechterverhältnisse im Zeitalter der Weltkriege*, Frankfurt am Main: Campus, 345–365.

Biess, F. 2006. *Homecomings: Returning POWs and the Legacies of Defeat in Postwar Germany*, Princeton, N.J.: Princeton University Press.

Bliersbach, G. 1985. *So grün war die Heide... Der deutsche Nachkriegsfilm in neuer Sicht*, Weinheim: Beltz Verlag.

Bock, H.M. and M. Töteberg. 2002. 'A History of Ufa', in T. Bergfelder, E. Carter and D. Göktürk (eds), *The German Cinema Book*, London: BFI, 129–138.

Bodzenta, E. and L. Grond. 1957. 'Die soziale Wirklichkeit von heute', in O. Schulmeister, J.C. Allmayer-Beck and A. Wandruszka (eds), *Spectrum Austriae*, Vienna: Herder, 423–477.

Bordwell, D. 1996. 'Convention, Construction, and Cinematic Vision', in D. Bordwell and N. Carroll (eds), *Post-theory: Reconstructing Film Studies*, Madison: University of Wisconsin Press, 87–107.

Brecht, C. 2005. 'Gedächtnispolitische Strategien im österreichischen Film zwischen 1945 und 1955', in K. Moser (ed.), *Besetzte Bilder. Film, Kultur und Propaganda in Österreich 1945–1955*, Vienna: Filmarchiv Austria, 157–201.

Brix, E. 1988. 'Zur Frage der österreichischen Identität am Beginn der Zweiten Republik', in G. Bischof and J. Leidenfrost (eds), *Die bevormundete Nation. Österreich und die Alliierten 1945–1949*, Innsbruck: Haymon, 93–104.

Bruckmüller, E. 1985. *Sozialgeschichte Österreichs*, Vienna: Herold.

Bruckmüller, E. 1997. *Symbole österreichischer Identität zwischen 'Kakanien' und 'Europa'*, Vienna: Picus Verlag.

Bruckmüller, E. 2003. *The Austrian Nation: Cultural Consciousness and Socio-political Processes*, Riverside, CA: Ariadne Press.

Bruckmüller, E. 2006. 'Von der Unabhängigkeitserklärung zum zweiten Kontrollabkommen', in E. Bruckmüller (ed.), *Wiederaufbau in Österreich, 1945–1955: Rekonstruktion oder Neubeginn?*, Vienna: Verlag für Geschichte und Politik, 10–27.

Büttner, E. 2005. 'Harmonie, die Zündstoff birgt – Der *Heimatfilm* der 1950er Jahre', in G. Matzner-Holzer (ed.), *Verfreundete Nachbarn: Österreich - Deutschland. Ein Verhältnis*, Vienna: Ed. Atelier, 132–139.

Büttner, E. 2007a. 'Angriff auf die Ordnung', *Filmhimmel Österreich*, 55, 3–9.

Büttner, E. 2007b. 'Vertraute Gesichter', *Filmhimmel Österreich*, 56, 8–13.

Büttner, E. and C. Dewald. 1997a. *Anschluß an Morgen. Eine Geschichte des österreichischen Films von 1945 bis zur Gegenwart*, Salzburg: Residenz.

Büttner, E. and C. Dewald. 1997b. 'Gespräch mit Christa Blümlinger, Oliver Rathkolb, Gottfried Schlemmer und Maria Steiner', in E. Büttner and C. Dewald (eds), *Anschluß an Morgen. Eine Geschichte des österreichischen Films von 1945 bis zur Gegenwart*, Salzburg: Residenz, 140–153.

Büttner, E. and C. Dewald. 2002. *Das tägliche Brennen. Eine Geschichte des österreichischen Films von den Anfängen bis 1945*, Salzburg: Residenz.

Butler, J. 1993. *Bodies that Matter: On the Discursive Limits of 'Sex'*, New York, London: Routledge.

Cargnelli, C. 2006. 'Austrian Cinema: A History. Review', *Historical Journal of Film, Radio and Television*, 26, 628–631.

Cargnelli, C. and M. Omasta (ed.). 1993. *Aufbruch ins Ungewisse*, Vienna: Wespennest.

Carter, E. 1997. *How German Is She? Postwar West German Reconstruction and the Consuming Woman*, Ann Arbor: University of Michigan Press.

Carter, E. 2000. 'Sweeping up the Past: Gender and History in the Postwar German 'Rubble' Film', in U. Sieglohr (ed.), *Heroines without Heroes: Reconstructing Female and National Identities in European Cinema*, 1945–51, London: Continuum International Publishing Group, 91–110.

Carter, E. 2010. 'Sissi the Terrible: Melodrama, Victimhood, and Imperial Nostalgia in the Sissi Trilogy', in P. Cooke and M. Silberman (eds), *Screening War: Perspectives on German Suffering*, Rochester, N.Y.: Camden House, 81–101.

Church Gibson, P. 1998. 'Film Costume', in J. Hill and P. Church Gibson (eds), *Oxford Guide to Film Studies*, Oxford: Oxford University Press.

Cohan, S. 1997. *Masked Men: Masculinity and the Movies in the Fifties*, Bloomington: Indiana University Press.

Cohan, S. and I.R. Hark (eds). 1993. *Screening the Male: Exploring Masculinities in Hollywood Cinema*, London: Routledge.

Confino, A. 2003. 'Dissonance, Normality and the Historical Method: Why Did Some Germans Think of Tourism after May 8, 1945?' in R. Bessel and D. Schumann (eds), *Life after Death: Approaches to a Cultural and Social History of Europe during the 1940s and 1950s*, Washington: German Historical Institute, 323–347.

Connell, R.W. 1987. *Gender and Power: Society, the Person, and Sexual Politics*, Cambridge, UK: Polity Press.

Connell, R.W. 1993. 'The Big Picture: Masculinities in Recent World History', *Theory and Society*, 22(5), 597–623.

Connell, R.W. 1996. *Masculinities*, Cambridge: Polity Press.

Cook, P. 1996. *Fashioning the Nation: Costume and Identity in British Cinema*, London: BFI.

Crofts, S. 1998. 'Concepts of National Cinema', in J. Hill and P. Church Gibson (eds), *Oxford Guide to Film Studies*, Oxford: Oxford University Press, 385–394.

Custen, G.F. 2001. 'Making History', in M. Landy (ed.), *The Historical Film: History and Memory in Media*, New Brunswick, N.J.: Rutgers University Press, 66–97.

Cyba, E. 1996. 'Modernisierung im Patriarchat? Zur Situation der Frauen in Arbeit, Bildung und privater Sphäre 1945 bis 1995', in R. Sieder, H. Steinert and E. Tálos (eds), *Österreich 1945–1995: Gesellschaft, Politik, Kultur*, Vienna: Verlag für Gesellschaftskritik, 435–457.

Dachs, R. 1992. *Sag beim Abschied… Wiener Publikumslieblinge in Bild & Ton. Ausstellung des Historischen Museums der Stadt Wien, 23. Jänner bis 22. März 1992*, Vienna: Eigenverlag der Museen der Stadt Wien.

Danielczyk, J. 2001. '"Unternehmen Eroica" – Entstehungs- und produktionsgeschichtliche Aspekte', *Maske und Kothurn. Internationale Beiträge zur Theaterwissenschaft*, 46(1), 91–98.

Dassanowsky, R. 2001. '"Märchen vom Glück". Postwar Austrian Cinema's Iconoclastic Missing Link', *Maske und Kothurn. Internationale Beiträge zur Theaterwissenschaft*, 46(1), 61–68.

Dassanowsky, R. 2005. *Austrian Cinema: A History*, Jefferson, N.C.: McFarland & Co.

Dassanowsky, R. and O.C. Speck. 2011. *New Austrian Film*. New York: Berghahn Books.

Davidson, J.E. and S. Hake (eds). 2007. *Take Two: Fifties Cinema in a Divided Germany*, New York: Berghahn Books.

De Vries, A. 1974. *Dictionary of Symbols and Imagery*, Amsterdam: North-Holland Publishing Co.

Dewald, C. (ed.). 2004. *Der Wirklichkeit auf der Spur. Essays zum österreichischen Nachkriegsfilm ASPHALT*, Vienna: Filmarchiv Austria.

Dinges, M. 2005. '"Hegemoniale Männlichkeit"– Ein Konzept auf dem Prüfstand', in M. Dinges (ed.), *Männer-Macht-Körper. Hegemoniale Männlichkeiten vom Mittelalter bis heute*, Frankfurt am Main: Campus, 7–33.

Döge, U. 2004. 'ASPHALT 1951–1953 in Österreich, Frankreich und der Schweiz', in C. Dewald (ed.), *Der Wirklichkeit auf der Spur. Essays zum österreichischen Nachkriegsfilm ASPHALT*, Vienna: Filmarchiv Austria, 61–77.

Dokumentationsarchiv des österreichischen Widerstandes (ed.). 1995. *Österreicher im Exil. USA 1938–1945. Eine Dokumentation*, Vienna: Dokumentationsarchiv des österreichischen Widerstandes, vol. 2.

Dollhofer, C. 1990. *Dunkle Lust – Gelenkte Schaulust. Frauen im Männerkino als Rezipientinnen ihres Objektstatus. Aufgezeigt anhand deutschsprachiger Filme der 50er Jahre*, unpublished master's thesis (Diplomarbeit), University of Vienna.

Dressel, G. and N. Langreiter. 2002. 'Aus der Wehrmacht an die Uni – aus der Uni in die Ehe. Restaurierte Geschlechterverhältnisse nach dem Zweiten Weltkrieg', *Wiener Zeitschrift zur Geschichte der Neuzeit*, 2(2), 73–88.

Dudink, S., K. Hagemann and J. Tosh (eds). 2004. *Masculinities in Politics and War: Gendering Modern History*, Manchester: Manchester University Press.

Dyer, R. and G. Vincendeau (eds). 1992. *Popular European Cinema*, London: Routledge.

East, P. and K. Luger. 2002. 'Living in Paradise: Youth Culture and Tourism Development in the Mountains of Austria', in R.N. Voase (ed.), *Tourism in Western Europe: A Collection of Case Histories*, Wallingford, UK: CABI Pub., 227–242.

Eder, F.X. 2007. '"The Nationalists' 'Healthy Sensuality' was followed by America's Influence": Sexuality and Media from National Socialism to the Sexual Revolution', in G. Bischof, A. Pelinka and D. Herzog (eds), *Sexuality in Austria*, New Brunswick, N.J.: Transaction Publishers, 102–130.

Elley, D. 1984. *The Epic Film: Myth and History*, London: Routledge & Kegan Paul.

Elsaesser, T. 1999. 'Austria', in T. Elsaesser (ed.), *The BFI Companion to German Cinema*, London: BFI, 25–31.

Enderle-Burcel, G. 1996. 'Die österreichischen Parteien 1945 bis 1995', in R. Sieder, H. Steinert and E. Tálos (eds), *Österreich 1945–1995: Gesellschaft, Politik, Kultur*, Vienna: Verlag für Gesellschaftskritik, 80–93.

Faulstich, W. 2007. 'Groschenromane, Heftchen, Comics und die Schmutz-und-Schund-Debatte', in W. Faulstich (ed.), *Die Kultur der fünfziger Jahre*, 2nd ed., Munich: Wilhelm Fink Verlag, 199–215.

Fehrenbach, H. 1995. *Cinema in Democratizing Germany: Reconstructing National Identity after Hitler*, Chapel Hill: University of North Carolina Press.

Fehrenbach, H. 1998. 'Rehabilitating Fatherland: Race and German Remasculinisation', *Signs*, 24(1), 107–127.

Fehrenbach, H. 2000. 'Persistent Myths of Americanization: German Reconstruction and the Renationalization of Postwar Cinema 1945–1965', in H. Fehrenbach and U. Poiger (eds), *Transactions, Transgressions, Transformations: American Culture in Western Europe and Japan*, Oxford: Berghahn, 81–108.

Fehrenbach, H. 2001. '"Ami-Liebchen" und "Mischlingskinder". Rasse, Geschlecht und Kultur in der deutsch-amerikanischen Begegnung', in K. Naumann (ed.), *Nachkrieg in Deutschland*, Hamburg: Hamburger Edition, 178–205.

Fehrenbach, H. 2005. *Race after Hitler: Black Occupation Children in Postwar Germany and America*, Princeton, N.J.: Princeton University Press.

Ferro, M. 1973. 'Le film, une contre-analyse de la société?', *Annales*, 28(1), 109–124.

Festschrift der Apollo Kino- u. Theater GmbH. 1954. *25 Jahre Kino-Theater. 50 Jahre Apollo-Theater*, Vienna.

Fiedler, M. 1995. *Heimat im deutschen Film: Ein Mythos zwischen Regression und Utopie*, Coppengrave: Coppi Verlag.

Flandera, C. 2000. *'Schmutz und Schund'. Die Diskussionen der sozialdemokratischen und der katholischen Lehrerschaft in Österreich*, unpublished PhD thesis, University of Salzburg.

Forbes, J. and S. Street. 2000. *European Cinema: An Introduction*, Basingstoke: Palgrave.

Forrest, A. 2007. 'Citizenship and Masculinity: The Revolutionary Citizen-Soldier and his Legacy', in S. Dudink, K. Hagemann and A. Clark (eds), *Representing Masculinity: Male Citizenship in Modern Western Culture*, New York: Palgrave Macmillan, 111–130.

Foucault, M. 1967. *Madness and Civilization: A History of Insanity in the Age of Reason*, London: Tavistock.

Foucault, M. 1981. *Archäologie des Wissens*, Frankfurt am Main: Suhrkamp.

Fowler, C. (ed.). 2002. *The European Cinema Reader*, London: Routledge.

Frankfurter, B. 1985. 'Rund um die "Wien-Film"-Produktion. Staatsinteressen als Impulsgeber des Massenmediums eines Jahrzehnts', in L. Wächter-Böhm (ed.), *Wien 1945: davor/danach*, Vienna: C. Brandstätter, 186–195.

Frankfurter, B. 1988. 'Die Wien-Film. Ein Beitrag zur Dreieinigkeit von Staat, Film und politischer Kultur in Österreich', in H.H. Fabris and K. Luger (eds), *Medienkultur in Österreich*, Vienna: Böhlau, 104–116.

Frankfurter, B. and G. Scheidl. 1992. 'Die Wien-Film', in G. Ernst and G. Schedl (eds), *NAHAUFNAHMEN: zur Situation des österreichischen Kinofilms*, Vienna: Europaverlag, 20–27.

Fremuth-Kronreif, B. 1999. *1. April 2000. Die Produktionsgeschichte eines im Auftrag der österreichischen Bundesregierung hergestellten Filmes*, unpublished master's thesis (Diplomarbeit), University of Salzburg.

Freud, S. 1968. 'Screen Memories', in S. Freud and J. Strachey (eds), *The Standard Edition of the Complete Psychological Works of Sigmund Freud: Early Psycho-Analytic Publications*, 3rd ed., 1893–1899, London: The Hogarth Press and the Institute of Psycho-Analysis, vol. 3, 303–322.

Frevert, U. 1996. 'Soldaten, Staatsbürger. Überlegungen zur historischen Konstruktion von Männlichkeit', in T. Kühne (ed.), *Männergeschichte - Geschlechtergeschichte. Männlichkeit im Wandel der Moderne*, Frankfurt am Main: Campus, 69–87.

Frevert, U. 2004. *A Nation in Barracks: Modern Germany, Military Conscription and Civil Society*, Oxford: Berg Publishers.

Fritsche, M. 2003. '"Goebbels ist ein großer Tepp." Wehrkraftzersetzende Äußerungen in der Deutschen Wehrmacht', in W. Manoschek (ed.), *Opfer der NS-Militärjustiz. Urteilspraxis, Strafvollzug, Entschädigungspolitik in Österreich*, Vienna: Mandelbaum, 215–237.

Fritsche, M. 2004. *Entziehungen. Österreichische Deserteure und Selbstverstümmler in der Deutschen Wehrmacht*, Vienna: Böhlau.

Fritsche, M. 2005. 'Feige Männer? Fremd- und Selbstbilder von Wehrmachtsdeserteuren', *Ariadne. Forum für Frauen- und Geschlechtergeschichte*, 54–60.

Fritz, W. 1984. *Kino in Österreich 1945–1983. Film zwischen Kommerz und Avantgarde*, Vienna: ÖBV.

Fritz, W. 1991. *Kino in Österreich 1929–1945. Der Tonfilm*, Vienna: ÖBV.

Fritz, W. 1996. *Im Kino erlebe ich die Welt. 100 Jahre Kino und Film in Österreich*, Vienna: Verlag Christian Brandstätter.

Gaines, J. 1988. 'White Privilege and Looking Relations', *Screen*, 29(4), 12–27.

Garncarz, J. 1994. 'Hollywood in Germany: The Role of American Films in Germany, 1925–1990', in D.W. Ellwood and R. Kroes (eds), *Hollywood in Europe: Experiences of a Cultural Hegemony*, Amsterdam: VU University Press, 94–135.

Gedye, G.E.R. 1939. *Fallen Bastions: The Central European Tragedy*, London: Victor Gollancz.

Gellately, R. 1996. 'Denunciations in Twentieth Century Germany: Aspects of Self-policing in the Third Reich and the German Democratic Republic', *Journal of Modern History*, 4(68), 931–967.

Gesek, L. 1959. 'Kleines Lexikon des österreichischen Films. Sachlexikon', *Film-Kunst. Zeitschrift für Filmkultur und Filmwissenschaft*, 22, 1–19.

Geraghty, C. 2000. *British Cinema in the Fifties: Gender, Genre and the 'New Look'*, London: Routledge.

Gilbert, J.B. 2005. *Men in the Middle: Searching for Masculinity in the 1950s*, Chicago: University of Chicago Press.

Girtler, R. 2000. *Wilderer. Rebellen in den Bergen*, Vienna: Böhlau.

Gledhill, C. 1991. 'Signs of Melodrama', in C. Gledhill (ed.), *Stardom: Industry of Desire*, London: Routledge, 210–233.

Gledhill, C. 2007. 'History of Genre Criticism: Introduction', in P. Cook (ed.), *The Cinema Book*, 3rd ed., London: BFI, 252–259.

Göttler, F. 1993. 'Westdeutscher Nachkriegsfilm. Land der Väter', in W. Jacobson, A. Kaes and H.H. Prinzler (eds), *Geschichte des deutschen Films*, Stuttgart: Metzler, 171–210.

Goltermann, S. 2000. 'Die Beherrschung der Männlichkeit. Zur Deutung psychischer Leiden bei den Heimkehrern des Zweiten Weltkrieges 1945–1956', *Feministische Studien*, 18(2), 7–19.

Gottschlich, M., O. Panagl and M. Welan. 1989. *Was die Kanzler sagten. Regierungserklärungen der Zweiten Republik 1945–1987*, Vienna: Böhlau.

Gramsci, A. 1971 [1935]. 'Notes on Italian History', in A. Gramsci, Q. Hoare and G. Nowell-Smith (eds), *Selections from the Prison Notebooks of Antonio Gramsci*, London: Lawrence and Wishart, 52–120.

Graser, A. 1989. 'Filmtechnik und Filmsprache im *Heimatfilm*', in W. Kaschuba and D. Bahlinger (eds), *Der deutsche Heimatfilm. Bildwelten und Weltbilder. Bilder, Texte, Analysen zu 70 Jahren deutscher Filmgeschichte*, Tübingen: Tübinger Vereinigung für Volkskunde, 221–233.

Gripsrud, J. 1998. 'Film Audiences', in J. Hill and P. Church Gibson (eds), *Oxford Guide to Film Studies*, Oxford: Oxford University Press, 202–211.

Hämmerle, C. 2005. 'Zur Relevanz des Connell'schen Konzepts hegemonialer Männlichkeit für Militär und Männlichkeit/en in der Habsburgermonarchie (1868–1914/18)', in M. Dinges (ed.), *Männer-Macht-Körper. Hegemoniale Männlichkeiten vom Mittelalter bis heute*, Frankfurt am Main: Campus, 103–121.

Hämmerle, C. 2007. 'Back to the Monarchy's Glorified Past? Military Discourses on Male Citizenship and Universal Conscription in the Austrian Empire, 1858–1914', in S. Dudink, K. Hagemann and A. Clark (eds), *Representing Masculinity: Male Citizenship in Modern Western Culture*, New York: Palgrave Macmillan, 151–168.

Hagemann, K. 2002. 'Home/Front: The Military, Violence and Gender Relations in the Age of the World Wars', in K. Hagemann and S. Schüler-Springorum (eds), *Heimat-Front. Militär und Geschlechterverhältnisse im Zeitalter der Weltkriege*, Frankfurt am Main: Campus, 1–41.

Hake, S. 2008. *German National Cinema*, 2nd ed., London: Routledge.

Halbritter, U. 1993. *Der Einfluss der Alliierten Besatzungsmächte auf die österreichische Filmwirtschaft und Spielfilmproduktion in den Jahren 1945 bis 1955*, unpublished master's thesis (Diplomarbeit), University of Vienna.

Hall, S. (ed.). 1997. *Representation: Cultural Representations and Signifying Practices*, London: Sage.

Hanisch, E. 1994. *Der lange Schatten des Staates. Österreichische Gesellschaftsgeschichte im 20. Jahrhundert*, Vienna: Ueberreuter.

Hanisch, E. 2005. *Männlichkeiten*, Vienna: Böhlau.

Harper, S. 1994. *Picturing the Past: The Rise and Fall of the British Costume Film*, London: BFI.

Harper, S. 1997. 'Bonnie Prince Charlie Revisited: British Costume Film in the 1950s', in R. Murphy (ed.), *The British Cinema Book*, London: BFI, 133–143.

Harper, S. 2001. 'Historical Pleasures: Gainsborough Costume Melodrama', in M. Landy (ed.), *The Historical Film: History and Memory in Media*, New Brunswick: Rutgers University Press, 98–122.

Harper, S. 2006. 'Fragmentation and Crisis: 1940s Admissions Figures at the Regent Cinema, Portsmouth, UK', *Historical Journal of Film, Radio and Television*, 26(3), 361–394.

Harper, S. and V. Porter. 2003. *British Cinema of the 1950s*, Oxford: Oxford University Press.

Hartl, K. 1973. '"Reden Sie mit dem Karas…"', in W. Kudrnofsky (ed.), *Vom Dritten Reich zum Dritten Mann. Helmut Qualtingers Welt der vierziger Jahre*, Vienna: Molden, 257–272.

Hayward, S. 2000. *Cinema Studies: The Key Concepts*, London: Routledge.

Heer, F. 2001. *Der Kampf um die österreichische Identität*, 3rd ed., Vienna: Böhlau.

Heineman, E.D. 2003. *What Difference Does a Husband Make? Women and Marital Status in Nazi and Postwar Germany*, Berkeley: University of California Press.

Heiss, G. 1990. '"Ein Reich von Künstlern und Kellnern"', in O. Rathkolb, G. Schmid and G. Heiss (eds), *Österreich und Deutschlands Grösse. Ein schlampiges Verhältnis*, Salzburg: O. Müller, 118–126.

Heiss, G. 2006. 'Österreich am 1. April 2000 – das Bild von Gegenwart und Vergangenheit im Zukunftsraum von 1952', in E. Bruckmüller (ed.), *Wiederaufbau in Österreich, 1945–1955: Rekonstruktion oder Neubeginn?*, Vienna: Verlag für Geschichte und Politik, 102–124.

Heiss, G. and I. Klimeš. 2003. *Obrazy Času / Bilder der Zeit. Tschechischer und österreichischer Film der 30er Jahre*, Prague: Národní Filmový Archiv, VPS.

Herzog, D. 2003. 'Desperately Seeking Normality. Sex and Marriage in the Wake of War', in R. Bessel and D. Schumann (eds), *Life after Death: Approaches to a Cultural and Social History of Europe during the 1940s and 1950s*, Washington: German Historical Institute, 161–192.

Hickethier, K. 2007. 'The Restructuring of the West German Film Industry in the 1950s', in J. E. Davidson and S. Hake (eds), *Framing the Fifties: Cinema in a Divided Germany*, New York: Berghahn, 194–209.

Higson, A. 2002 [1989]. 'The Concept of National Cinema', in C. Fowler (ed.), *The European Cinema Reader*, London: Routledge, 132–142.

Higson, A. 2000. 'The Limiting Imagination of National Cinema', in M. Hjort and S. MacKenzie (eds), *Cinema and Nation*, London, New York: Routledge, 63–74.

Higson, A. 2003. *English Heritage, English Cinema: Costume Drama Since 1980*, Oxford: Oxford University Press.

Higson, A. and R. Maltby. 1999. "'Film Europe" and "Film America": An Introduction', in A. Higson and R. Maltby (eds), *'Film Europe' and 'Film America': Cinema, Commerce and Cultural Exchange 1920–1939*, Exeter: University of Exeter Press, 1–31.

Hochholdinger-Reiterer, B. 2001. "'Das Lied hat Wunder gewirkt ...'" – Gustav Ucicky's "Singende Engel" (1947) als Österreich-Apotheose', *Maske und Kothurn. Internationale Beiträge zur Theaterwissenschaft*, 46(1), 69–82.

Höhn, M. 2002. *GIs and Fräuleins: The German-American Encounter in 1950s West Germany*, Chapel Hill, N.C.: University of North Carolina Press.

Hofstätter-Schmidt, A. 1994. 'Die Entwicklung des Salzburger Fremdenverkehrs in der Zweiten Republik', in H. Haas, R. Hoffmann and K. Luger (eds), *Weltbühne und Naturkulisse. Zwei Jahrhunderte Salzburg-Tourismus*, Salzburg: Verlag Anton Pustet, 134–144.

Horak, J.C. and E. Tape. 1986. *Fluchtpunkt Hollywood. Eine Dokumentation zur Filmemigration nach 1933*, 2nd ed., Münster: MAKS.

Hornung, E. 1998. *'Penelope und Odysseus'. Erzählungen über 'Warten' und 'Heimkehren' nach 1945*, unpublished PhD thesis, University of Vienna.

Inglis, F. 2000. *Delicious History of the Holiday*, London: Routledge.

James, R. 2006. *Working-class Taste in 1930s Britain: A Comparative Study of Film and Literature*, unpublished PhD thesis, University of Portsmouth.

Jancovich, M. 1995. 'Screen Theory', in J. Hollows and M. Jancovich (eds), *Approaches to Popular Film*, Manchester: Manchester University Press, 123–150.

Jeancolas, J.-P. 1992. 'The Inexportable: The Case of French Cinema and Radio in the 1950s', in R. Dyer and G. Vincendeau (eds), *Popular European Cinema*, London: Routledge, 141–148.

Jeffords, S. 1989. *The Remasculinization of America: Gender and the Vietnam War*, Bloomington: Indiana University Press.

Jeffords, S. 1994. *Hard Bodies: Hollywood Masculinity in the Reagan Era*, New Brunswick: Rutgers University Press.

Kaes, A. 1995. 'German Cultural History and the Study of Film: Ten Theses and a Postscript', *New German Critique*, (65), 47–58.

Kaindl, K. 1988. "'Er geht an der Zeit nicht vorbei ...'" Realitätsdarstellung und Vergangenheitsbewältigung im österreichischen Film', in H.H. Fabris and K. Luger (eds), *Medienkultur in Österreich*, Vienna: Böhlau, 133–154.

Kapczynski, J.M. 2007. 'The Treatment of the Past: Geza von Radvanyi's Der Arzt von Stalingrad and the West German War Film', in J.E. Davidson and S. Hake (eds), *Framing the Fifties: Cinema in a Divided Germany*, New York: Berghahn Books, 137–150.

Kaplan, E.A. 1997. *Looking for the Other: Feminism, Film, and the Imperial Gaze*. New York: Routledge.

Karazman-Morawetz, I. 1996. 'Arbeit, Konsum, Freizeit. Veränderungen im Verhältnis von Arbeit und Reproduktion', in R. Sieder, H. Steinert and E. Tálos (eds), *Österreich 1945–1995: Gesellschaft, Politik, Kultur*, Vienna: Verlag für Gesellschaftskritik, 409–425.

Karner, C. 2005. 'The "Habsburg Dilemma" Today: Competing Discourses of National Identity in Contemporary Austria', *National Identities*, 7(4), 409–432.

Kaschuba, W. 1989. 'Bildwelten als Weltbilder', in W. Kaschuba and D. Bahlinger (eds), *Der deutsche Heimatfilm. Bildwelten und Weltbilder. Bilder, Texte, Analysen zu 70 Jahren deutscher Filmgeschichte*, Tübingen: Tübinger Vereinigung für Volkskunde, 7–13.

Kaschuba, W. and D. Bahlinger (eds). 1989. *Der deutsche Heimatfilm. Bildwelten und Weltbilder. Bilder, Texte, Analysen zu 70 Jahren deutscher Filmgeschichte*, Tübingen: Tübinger Vereinigung für Volkskunde.

Kerschbaumer, G. 1994. 'Die Wiederbelebung der Glanzzeiten in den Nachkriegsjahren', in H. Haas, R. Hoffmann and K. Luger (eds), *Weltbühne und Naturkulisse. Zwei Jahrhunderte Salzburg-Tourismus*, Salzburg: Verlag Anton Pustet, 129–144.

King, G. 2002. *Film Comedy*, London: Wallflower.

Kirkham, P. and J. Thumim. 1993. *You Tarzan: Masculinity, Movies, and Men*, New York: St. Martin's Press.

Knight, R. 2000. *Ich bin dafür, die Sache in die Länge zu ziehen. Wortprotokolle der österreichischen Bundesregierung von 1945–52 über die Entschädigung der Juden*, 2nd rev. ed., Vienna: Böhlau.

Koch, G., K. Konz, W. Öhrle, G. Schmidt, and B. Wilczek. 1989. 'Die Fünfziger Jahre. Heide und Silberwald', in W. Kaschuba and D. Bahlinger (eds), *Der deutsche Heimatfilm. Bildwelten und Weltbilder. Bilder, Texte, Analysen zu 70 Jahren deutscher Filmgeschichte*, Tübingen: Tübinger Vereinigung für Volkskunde, 69–95.

Kos, W. 1994. *Eigenheim Österreich: zu Politik, Kultur und Alltag nach 1945*, Vienna: Sonderzahl.

Kracauer, S. 1984 [1947]. *Von Caligari zu Hitler: Eine psychologische Geschichte des deutschen Films*, Frankfurt am Main: Suhrkamp Verlag.

Kreimeier, K. 1992. *Die Ufa-Story. Geschichte eines Filmkonzerns*, Munich: Hanser.

Kreimeier, K. 1996. 'Karl Hartl: Homo faber und Visionär', in R. Beckermann and C. Blümlinger (eds), *Ohne Untertitel: Fragmente einer Geschichte des österreichischen Kinos*, Vienna: Sonderzahl, 31–51.

Krenn, G. 1999. 'Der bewegte Mensch – Sascha Kolowrat', in F. Bono, P. Caneppele and G. Krenn (eds), *Elektrische Schatten. Beiträge zur österreichischen Stummfilmgeschichte*, Vienna: Filmarchiv Austria, 37–46.

Kühne, T. 1996. 'Kameradschaft – "das Beste im Leben des Mannes". Die deutschen Soldaten des Zweiten Weltkriegs in erfahrungs-und geschlechtergeschichtlicher Perspektive', *Geschichte und Gesellschaft*, 22, 504–529.

Kühne, T. (ed.). 1996. *Männergeschichte - Geschlechtergeschichte. Männlichkeit im Wandel der Moderne*, Frankfurt am Main: Campus.

Kühne, T. 1996. 'Männergeschichte als Geschlechtergeschichte', in T. Kühne (ed.), *Männergeschichte - Geschlechtergeschichte. Männlichkeit im Wandel der Moderne*, Frankfurt am Main: Campus, 7–30.

Kühne, T. 2001. 'Zwischen Vernichtungskrieg und Freizeitgesellschaft. Die Veteranenkultur der Bundesrepublik (1945–1995)', in K. Naumann (ed.), *Nachkrieg in Deutschland*, Hamburg: Hamburger Edition, 90–113.

Kühne, T. 2006. *Kameradschaft: die Soldaten des nationalsozialistischen Krieges und das 20. Jahrhundert*, Göttingen: Vandenhoeck & Ruprecht.

Kuhn, A. 2002. *An Everyday Magic: Cinema and Cultural Memory*, London: I.B. Tauris.

Lagny, M. 1997. 'Kino für Historiker', *Österreichische Zeitschrift für Geschichte*, 8(4), 457–586.

Lang, A. 1999. 'Comedy: Austria', in T. Elsaesser (ed.), *The BFI Companion to German Cinema*, London: BFI, 55.

Langthaler, E. 1996. 'Ländliche Lebenswelten von 1945 bis 1950', in R. Sieder, H. Steinert and E. Tálos (eds), *Österreich 1945–1995: Gesellschaft, Politik, Kultur*, Vienna: Verlag für Gesellschaftskritik, 35–53.

Lears, T.J.J. 1985. 'The Concept of Cultural Hegemony: Problems and Possibilities', *The American Historical Review*, 90(3), 567–593.

Lehmann, A. 1999. *Von Menschen und Bäumen. Die Deutschen und ihr Wald*, Reinbek: Rowohlt.

Loacker, A. 1992. *Die ökonomischen und politischen Bedingungen der österreichischen (Ton-) Spielfilmproduktion der 30er Jahre*, unpublished master's thesis (Diplomarbeit), University of Vienna.

Loacker, A. 1999. *Anschluss im 3/4-Takt. Filmproduktion und Filmpolitik in Österreich 1930–1938*, Trier: Wissenschaftlicher Verlag Trier.

Loacker, A. and M. Prucha. 2000. 'Die unabhängige deutschprachige Filmproduktion in Österreich, Ungarn und der Tschechoslowakei', in A. Loacker and M. Prucha (eds), *Unerwünschtes Kino: Der deutschsprachige Emigrantenfilm 1934–1937*, Vienna: Filmarchiv Austria, 11–65.

Lowry, S. 1994. 'Der Ort meiner Träume? Zur ideologischen Funktion des NS-Unterhaltungsfilms' [Electronic version], *montage/av. Zeitschrift für Theorie & Geschichte audiovisueller Kommunikation*, 3(2), 55–72.

Lowry, S. 2002. 'Heinz Rühmann – the Archetypal German', in T. Bergfelder, E. Carter and D. Göktürk (eds), *The German Cinema Book*, London: BFI, 81–89.

Manoschek, W. 1996. 'Verschmähte Erbschaft. Österreichs Umgang mit dem Nationalsozialismus 1945 bis 1955', in R. Sieder, H. Steinert and E. Tálos (eds), *Österreich 1945–1995: Gesellschaft, Politik, Kultur*, Vienna: Verlag für Gesellschaftskritik, 94–106.

Marksteiner, F. 1996. 'Quäl dich nicht mehr… Trost und Rat für Heimkehrer', in R. Beckermann and C. Blümlinger (eds), *Ohne Untertitel: Fragmente einer Geschichte des österreichischen Kinos*, Vienna: Sonderzahl, 229–244.

Martschukat, J. and O. Stieglitz. 2005. *'Es ist ein Junge!': Einführung in die Geschichte der Männlichkeiten in der Neuzeit*, Tübingen: Ed. Diskord.

Martschukat, J. and O. Stieglitz. 2008. *Geschichte der Männlichkeiten*, Frankfurt am Main: Campus.

Mast, G. 1979. *The Comic Mind: Comedy and the Movies*, 2nd ed., Chicago: University of Chicago.

Mattl, S. 1992. '"Aufbau" – eine männliche Chiffre der Nachkriegszeit', in I. Bandhauer-Schöffmann and E. Hornung (eds), *Wiederaufbau weiblich. Dokumentation der Tagung 'Frauen in der Österreichischen und Deutschen Nachkriegszeit'*, Vienna: Geyer-Ed., 15–23.

Menasse, P. 1985. 'Die grosse Synthese. Bemerkungen zur Produktion des Neuen Österreich', in L. Wächter-Böhm (ed.), *Wien 1945: davor/danach*, Vienna: C. Brandstätter, 25–49.

Mesner, M. 1997. 'Die "Neugestaltung des Ehe- und Familienrechts". Re-Definitionspotentiale im Geschlechterverhältnis der Aufbau-Zeit', *Zeitgeschichte*, 5–6, 186–210.

Meyer, S. and E. Schulze. 1992. 'Auswirkungen des Zweiten Weltkriegs auf Familien', in I. Bandhauer-Schöffmann and E. Hornung (eds), *Wiederaufbau weiblich. Dokumentation der Tagung 'Frauen in der Österreichischen und Deutschen Nachkriegszeit'*, Vienna, Salzburg: Geyer-Ed., 112–137.

Moeller, F. 1998. *Der Filmminister. Goebbels und der Film im Dritten Reich*, Berlin: Henschel.

Moeller, R.G. 1997. 'Reconstructing the Family in Reconstruction Germany: Women and Social Policy in the Federal Republic 1949/1955', in R.G. Moeller (ed.), *West Germany under Construction: Politics, Society, and Culture in the Adenauer Era*, Ann Arbor: University of Michigan Press, 109–133.

Moeller, R.G. 1998. '"The Last Soldiers of the Great War" and Tales of Family Reunions in the Federal Republic of Germany', *Signs*, 24(1), 129–145.

Moeller, R.G. 2001. 'Heimkehr ins Vaterland: Die Remaskulierung Westdeutschlands in den fünfziger Jahren', *Militärgeschichtliche Zeitschrift*, 2(1), 403–436.

Möller, O. 2004. 'Die Pastellfarben des Proletariats', *taz* [electronic version]. http://www.taz.de/index.php?id=archivseite&dig=2004/06/08/a0228, retrieved 18 February 2011.

Moltke, J.v. 2005. *No Place Like Home: Locations of Heimat in German Cinema*, Berkeley: University of California Press.

Mooser, J. 1998. 'Arbeiter, Angestellte und Frauen in der "nivellierten Mittelstandsgesellschaft". Thesen', in A. Schildt and A. Sywottek (eds), *Modernisierung im Wiederaufbau. Die westdeutsche Gesellschaft der 50er Jahre*, Bonn: Dietz, 362–376.

Morris, P. (ed.). 1994. *The Bakhtin Reader: Selected Writings of Bakhtin, Medvedev and Voloshinov*, London: Arnold.

Moser, K. 2002. 'Die Bilderwelt der ÖSTERREICH IN BILD UND TON – Die konstruierte Realität eines ständestaatlichen Propagandainstruments', in M. Achenbach and K. Moser (eds), *Österreich in Bild und Ton – Die Filmwochenschau des austrofaschistischen Ständestaates*, Vienna: Eigenverlag, 99–148.

Moser, K. (ed.). 2005. *Besetzte Bilder. Film, Kultur und Propaganda in Österreich 1945–1955*, Vienna: Filmarchiv Austria.

Mosse, G.L. 1998. *The Image of Man: The Creation of Modern Masculinity*, New York: Oxford University Press.

Mühlen-Achs, G. 2003. *Wer führt? Körpersprache und die Ordnung der Geschlechter*, München: Verlag Frauenoffensive.

Müller-Funk, W. 2004. 'Lächeln, Langeweile, Zorn. Überlegungen zur österreichischen Identität' [electronic version], *Medienimpulse*, 13–15, retrieved 10 October 2012, from www.mediamanual.at/mediamanual/themen/pdf/identitaet/50_Mueller.pdf.

Mulvey, L. 2004 [1975]. 'Visual Pleasure and Narrative Cinema', in L. Braudy and M. Cohen (eds), *Film Theory and Criticism: Introductory Readings*, Oxford: Oxford University Press, 837–848. First published in 1975 in *Screen*, 16(3), 6–18.

Munby, J. 1999. 'Strassenfilme', in T. Elsaesser (ed.), *The BFI Companion to German Cinema*, London: BFI, 230.

Neale, S. 1980. *Genre*, London: BFI.

Neale, S. 2000. *Genre and Hollywood*, London: Routledge.

Neale, S. and F. Krutnik. 1990. *Popular Film and Television Comedy*, London: Routledge.

Nichols, B. 2000. 'Film Theory and the Revolt against Master Narratives', in C. Gledhill and L. Williams (eds), *Reinventing Film Studies*, London: Arnold, 34–52.

Nierhaus, I. 1996. 'Haus und Heimat. Zur Geschlechterordnung in *Heimatfilm* und Wohnbau der Wiederaufbauzeit', *Frauen. Kunst. Wissenschaft*, 22, 18–29.

Öhner, V. 2004. 'ASPHALT und der Diskurs über "Jugendverwahrlosung" und "Jugendkriminalität"', in C. Dewald (ed.), *Der Wirklichkeit auf der Spur. Essays zum österreichischen Nachkriegsfilm ASPHALT*, Vienna: Filmarchiv Austria, 25–39.

Palfreyman, R. 2010. 'Links and Chains: Trauma between the Generations in the Heimat Mode', in P. Cooke and M. Silberman (eds), *Screening War: Perspectives on German Suffering*, Rochester, N.Y.: Camden House, 145–164.

Patterson, J.T. 1996. *Grand Expectations: The United States, 1945–1974*, Oxford: Oxford University Press.

Pavalko, E.K. and G.H. Elder, Jr. 1990. 'World War II and Divorce: A Life-course Perspective', *The American Journal of Sociology*, 5(March), 1213–1234.

Pelinka, A. 1985. 'Zur Gründung der Zweiten Republik. Neue Ergebnisse trotz personeller und struktureller Kontinuität', in L. Wächter-Böhm (ed.), *Wien 1945 davor/danach*, Vienna: Christian Brandstätter.

Peter, B. 2010. '"Wie es euch gefällt"? NS-Theaterpolitik und Theaterpraxis am Beispiel der "Josefstadt"', in G. Bauer and B. Peter (eds), *Das Theater in der Josefstadt*, Vienna: Lit Verlag, 113–135.

Pilgram, A. 1996. 'Die Zweite Republik in der Kriminalpolitik', in R. Sieder, H. Steinert and E. Tálos (eds), *Österreich 1945–1995: Gesellschaft, Politik, Kultur*, Vienna: Verlag für Gesellschaftskritik, 485–496.

Poiger, U. 1998. 'A New, "Western" Hero? Reconstructing German Masculinity in the 1950s', *Signs*, 24(1), 147–162.

Poiger, U.G. 2000. *Jazz, Rock, and Rebels: Cold War Politics and American Culture in a Divided Germany*, Berkeley: University of California Press.

Poiger, U.G. 2001. 'Krise der Männlichkeit. Remaskulinisierung in beiden deutschen Nachkriegsgesellschaften', in K. Naumann (ed.), *Nachkrieg in Deutschland*, Hamburg: Hamburger Edition, 227–263.

Powrie, P., A. Davies and B. Babington. 2004. *The Trouble with Men: Masculinities in European and Hollywood Cinema*, London: Wallflower.

Prucha, M. 1996. 'Agfacolor und Kalter Krieg. Die Geschichte der Wien Film am Rosenhügel 1946–1955', in R. Beckermann and C. Blümlinger (eds), *Ohne Untertitel: Fragmente einer Geschichte des österreichischen Kinos*, Vienna: Sonderzahl, 53–79.

Purdie, S. 1993. *Comedy: The Mastery of Discourse*, Hemel Hempstead: Harvester Wheatsheaf.

Rathkolb, O. 1988. 'Die "Wien-Film"-Produktion am Rosenhügel. Österreichische Filmproduktion und Kalter Krieg', in H.H. Fabris and K. Luger (eds), *Medienkultur in Österreich*, Vienna: Böhlau, 117–132.

Rathkolb, O. 1991. *Führertreu und gottbegnadet. Künstlereliten im Dritten Reich*, Vienna: ÖBV.

Reicher, I. and S. Schachinger. 1999. 'Heimat Film and Mountain Films', in T. Elsaesser (ed.), *The BFI Companion to German Cinema*, London: BFI, 133–135.

Rentschler, E. 1996. *The Ministry of Illusion: Nazi Cinema and its Afterlife*, Cambridge, MA: Harvard University Press.

Richards, J. 2000. 'Rethinking British Cinema', in J. Ashby and A. Higson (eds), *British Cinema, Past and Present*, London: Routledge, 21–34.

Rieser, S.E. 1995. 'Bonbonfarbene Leinwände. Filmische Strategien zur (Re-) Konstruktion der österreichischen Nation in den fünfziger Jahren', in T. Albrich, K. Eisterer, M. Gehler and R. Steininger (eds), *Österreich in den Fünfzigern*, Innsbruck: Österreichischer StudienVerlag, 119–133.

Rose, S.O. 2007. 'Fit to Fight but Not to Vote? Masculinity and Citizenship in Britain, 1832–1918', in S. Dudink, K. Hagemann and A. Clark (eds), *Representing Masculinity: Male Citizenship in Modern Western Culture*, New York: Palgrave Macmillan, 131–150.

Rosenstone, R.A. 2006. *History on Film/Film on History*, Harlow: Longman.

Roth, G.D. 1985. 'Nachrufe: Anton Kutter', *Mitteilungen der Astronomischen Gesellschaft*, 64, 9–10.

Russegger, A. 2001. 'Kino - Schule der Frauen. Bemerkungen zu "Das Herz einer Frau" (1951) und "Dunja" (1955)', *Maske und Kothurn. Internationale Beiträge zur Theaterwissenschaft*, 46(1), 99–112.

Sandgruber, R. 1995. *Ökonomie und Politik. Österreichische Wirtschaftsgeschichte vom Mittelalter bis zur Gegenwart*, Vienna: Ueberreuter.

Sarasin, P. 2003. *Geschichtswissenschaft und Diskursanalyse*, Frankfurt am Main: Suhrkamp.

Schachinger, S. 1993. *Der österreichische Heimatfilm als Konstruktionsprinzip nationaler Identität in Österreich nach 1945*, unpublished master's thesis (Diplomarbeit), University of Vienna.

Schechner, R. 1973. 'Performance & the Social Sciences: Introduction', *The Drama Review: TDR*, 17(3), 3–4.

Schissler, H. 1992. 'Männerstudien in den USA', *Geschichte und Gesellschaft*, 18(2), 204–220.

Schissler, H. 2001. '"Normalization" as Project: Some Thoughts on Gender Relations in West Germany during the 1950s', in H. Schissler (ed.), *The Miracle Years: A Cultural History of West Germany, 1949–1968*, Princeton: Princeton University Press, 359–375.

Schmale, W. 2003. *Geschichte der Männlichkeit in Europa (1450–2000)*, Vienna: Böhlau.

Schneider, F. 2001. '"Einigkeit im Unglück"? Berliner Eheberatungsstellen zwischen Ehekrise und Wiederaufbau', in K. Naumann (ed.), *Nachkrieg in Deutschland*, Hamburg: Hamburger Edition, 206–226.

Schulte-Sasse, L. 1996. *Entertaining the Third Reich: Illusions of Wholeness in Nazi Cinema*. Durham, London: Duke University Press.

Schwarz, U. 2002. *Wochenschau, westdeutsche Identität und Geschlecht in den fünfziger Jahren*, Frankfurt am Main: Campus.

Schwarz, W.M. 2003. *Kino und Stadt. Wien 1945–2000*, Vienna: Löcker.

Schwarz, W.M. 2004. 'ASPHALT und die Jugend- und Schulddiskurse in der österreichischen Nachkriegszeit', in C. Dewald (ed.), *Der Wirklichkeit auf der Spur. Essays zum österreichischen Nachkriegsfilm ASPHALT*, Vienna: Filmarchiv Austria, 11–23.

Schwarzer, A. 1998. *Romy Schneider. Mythos und Leben*, Cologne: Kiepenheuer & Witsch.

Scott, J.W. 1986. 'Gender: A Useful Category of Historical Analysis', *The American Historical Review*, 91(5), 1053–1075.

Seeßlen, G. 1982. *Klassiker der Filmkomik. Geschichte und Mythologie des komischen Films*, Reinbek bei Hamburg: Rowohlt.

Seeßlen, G. 1992. 'Sissi – Ein deutsches Orgasmustrauma', in H.A. Marsiske (ed.), *Zeitmaschine Kino. Darstellungen von Geschichte im Film*, Marburg: Hitzeroth, 65–79.

Seeßlen, G. 1996. 'Hans Moser oder Vom traurigen Dienstmann, dem alten Glück und der neuen Zeit', in R. Beckermann and C. Blümlinger (eds), *Ohne Untertitel: Fragmente einer Geschichte des österreichischen Kinos*, Vienna: Sonderzahl, 121–141.

Seeßlen, G. 2004. 'Triumph des Scheiterns', *Filmarchiv Filmprogramm*, 19(11–12), 8–25.

Seidl, C. 1987. *Der deutsche Film der fünfziger Jahre*, Munich: Heyne.

Shandley, R.R. 2001. *Rubble Films: German Cinema in the Shadow of the Third Reich*, Philadelphia: Temple University Press.

Sieder, E. 1983. *Die alliierten Zensurmaßnahmen zwischen 1945–1955*, unpublished PhD thesis, University of Vienna.

Sieder, R., H. Steinert and E. Tálos. 1996. 'Wirtschaft, Gesellschaft und Politik in der Zweiten Republik. Eine Einführung', in R. Sieder, H. Steinert and E. Tálos (eds), *Österreich 1945–1995: Gesellschaft, Politik, Kultur*, Vienna: Verlag für Gesellschaftskritik, 9–32.

Sorlin, P. 1980. *Film in History: Restaging the Past*, Oxford: Blackwell.

Sorlin, P. 1991. *European Cinemas, European Societies 1939–1990*, New York: Routledge.

Sorlin, P. 2001. 'How to Look at a "Historical" Film', in M. Landy (ed.), *The Historical Film: History and Memory in Media*, New Brunswick, N.J.: Rutgers University Press, 25–49.

Spicer, A. 2003. *Typical Men: The Representation of Masculinity in Popular British Cinema*, London: I.B. Tauris.

Spode, H. 2005. 'Deutsch-österreichischer Tourismus und nationale Identität', in Stiftung Haus der Geschichte der Bundesrepublik Deutschland (ed.), *Verfreundete Nachbarn: Deutschland - Österreich*, Bielefeld: Kerber, 144–153.

Stadler, K.R. 1971. *Austria*, London: Benn.

Staiger, J. 1992. *Interpreting Films: Studies in the Historical Reception of American Cinema*, Princeton, N.J: Princeton University Press.

Standún, R. 2011. 'National Box-office Hits or International "Arthouse"? The New Austrokomödie', in R. Dassanowsky and O.C. Speck (eds), *New Austrian Film*, New York: Berghahn, 320–331.

Stapleton, K. and J. Wilson. 2004. 'Gender, Nationality and Identity: A Discursive Study', *European Journal of Women's Studies*, 11(1), 45–60.

Steiner, G. 1984. *Der Sieg der 'Natürlichkeit'. Eine Motivgeschichte des österreichischen Heimatfilms von 1946 bis 1966 mit besonderer Berücksichtigung der filmwirtschaftlichen Strukturen*, unpublished PhD thesis, University of Vienna.

Steiner, G. 1987. *Die Heimat-Macher: Kino in Österreich 1946–1966*, Vienna: Verlag für Gesellschaftskritik.

Steiner, I. 2005. 'Österreich-Bilder im Film der Besatzungszeit', in K. Moser (ed.), *Besetzte Bilder. Film, Kultur und Propaganda in Österreich 1945–1955*, Vienna: Filmarchiv Austria, 203–255.

Stern, F. 2003. 'Tanz auf dem Vulkan. Das Kino Nazi-Deutschlands in der heutigen Filmkultur', in J. Distelmeyer (ed.), *Tonfilmfrieden, Tonfilmkrieg. Die Geschichte der Tobis vom Technik-Syndikat zum Staatskonzern*, Munich: Edition Text + Kritik, 9–24.

Stern, F. 2005. 'Durch Clios Brille: Kino als zeit- und kulturgeschichtliche Herausforderung', *Österreichische Zeitschrift für Geschichtswissenschaften*, 16(1), 59–87.

Street, S. 1997. *British National Cinema*, London: Routledge.

Strohmeier, G. 1999. 'Schneelandschaften. Alltag, romantische Bilder und politsche Ladungen' [electronic version], in R. Grossmann (ed.), *Kulturlandschaftsforschung*, vol. 5, Vienna: Springer. http://www.iff.ac.at/oe/ifftexte/band5gs.htm, retrieved 12 April 2012.

Sutton, D. 2000. *A Chorus of Raspberries: British Film Comedy 1929–1939*, Exeter: University of Exeter Press.

Tálos, E. 2005. *Vom Siegeszug zum Rückzug. Sozialstaat Österreich 1945–2005*, Innsbruck: Studienverlag.

Thumin, J. 2002. 'The "Popular", Cash and Culture in the Postwar British Cinema Industry', in C. Fowler (ed.), *The European Cinema Reader*, London: Routledge, 194–211.

Thurner, E. 1992. 'Frauen-Nachkriegsleben in Österreich - im Zentrum und in der Provinz', in I. Bandhauer-Schöffmann and E. Hornung (eds), *Wiederaufbau weiblich. Dokumentation der Tagung 'Frauen in der Österreichischen und Deutschen Nachkriegszeit'*, Vienna: Geyer-Ed., 3–14.

Thurner, E. 1995. 'Die stabile Innenseite der Politik. Geschlechterbeziehungen und Rollenverhalten', in T. Albrich, K. Eisterer, M. Gehler and R. Steininger (eds), *Österreich in den Fünfzigern*, Innsbruck: Österreichischer StudienVerlag, 53–66.

Tillner, G. 1996. 'Österreich, ein weiter Weg. Filmkultur zwischen Austrofaschismus und Wiederaufbau', in R. Beckermann and C. Blümlinger (eds), *Ohne Untertitel: Fragmente einer Geschichte des österreichischen Kinos*, Vienna: Sonderzahl, 175–195.

Tosh, J. 1998. 'Was soll die Geschichtswissenschaft mit Männlichkeit anfangen? Betrachtungen zum 19. Jahrhundert in Großbritannien', in C. Conrad and M. Kessel (eds), *Kultur und Geschichte. Neue Einblicke in eine alte Beziehung*, Stuttgart: Reclam, 160–206.

Tosh, J. 2004. 'Hegemonic Masculinity and the History of Gender', in S. Dudink, K. Hagemann and J. Tosh (eds), *Masculinities in Politics and War: Gendering Modern History*, Manchester: Manchester University Press, 41–58.

Trimborn, J. 1998. *Der deutsche Heimatfilm der fünfziger Jahre: Motive, Symbole und Handlungsmuster*, Cologne: Teiresias.

Trotter, D. 2000. *Cooking with Mud: The Idea of Mess in Nineteenth-century Art and Fiction*, Oxford: Oxford University Press.

Uhl, H. 2005. 'Vergessen und Erinnern der NS-Vergangenheit in der Zweiten Republik', in Stiftung Haus der Geschichte der Bundesrepublik Deutschland (ed.), *Verfreundete Nachbarn: Deutschland - Österreich*, Bielefeld: Kerber, 184–197.

Utgaard, P. 2003. *Remembering and Forgetting Nazism: Education, National Identity, and the Victim Myth in Postwar Austria*, New York: Berghahn Books.

Van Rahden, T. 2007. 'Wie Vati die Demokratie lernte. Zur Frage der Autorität in der politischen Kultur der frühen Bundesrepublik', *WestEnd. Neue Zeitschrift für Sozialforschung*, 4(1), 113–125.

Varga, M. 1953. *Die Jugendkriminalität in ihrer Behandlung durch die Wiener Tagespresse in den Jahren 1946–1950*, unpublished PhD thesis, University of Vienna.

Veigl, H. 2004. 'Geplantes Glück im Alltag. Der kulturelle Wandel der 50er und 60er Jahre aus der Sicht der Illustrierten'. http://www.alltagskultur.at/veigl01.doc, retrieved 7 December 2010.

Verband der Wiener Lichtspieltheater und Audiovisionsveranstalter. 1986. *90 Jahre Kino in Wien. 1896–1986. Vergangenheit mit Zukunft*, Vienna: Jugend & Volk.

Wächter-Böhm, L. (ed.). 1985. *Wien 1945 davor/danach*, Vienna: C. Brandstätter.

Wagnleitner, R. 1991. *Coca-Colonisation und Kalter Krieg. Die Kulturmission der USA in Österreich nach dem Zweiten Weltkrieg*, Vienna: Verlag für Gesellschaftskritik.

Walby, S. 1995. *Theorizing Patriarchy*, 6th ed., Oxford: Blackwell.

Watson, P. 2003. 'Critical Approaches to Hollywood Cinema: Authorship, Genre and Stars', in J. Nelmes (ed.), *An Introduction to Film Studies*, 3rd ed., London: Routledge, 129–184.

Wauchope, M. 2007. 'The Other "German" Cinema', in J.E. Davidson and S. Hake (eds), *Take Two: Fifties Cinema in Divided Germany*, New York: Berghahn Books, 210–222.

Weber, F. 1996. 'Wiederaufbau zwischen Ost und West', in R. Sieder, H. Steinert and E. Talos (eds), *Österreich 1945–1995: Gesellschaft, Politik, Kultur*, Vienna: Verlag für Gesellschaftskritik, 68–79.

Weber, M. 1968. *Economy and Society: An Outline of Interpretive Sociology*, ed. G. Roth and C. Wittich, New York: Bedminster Press, vol. 3.

Wedel, M. 1999. 'Frank Wysbar', in T. Elsaesser (ed.), *The BFI Companion to German Cinema*, London: BFI, 255.

Wedel, M. 2007. *Der deutsche Musikfilm. Archäologie eines Genres, 1914–1945*. Munich: Edition Text + Kritik.

Wegenstein, B. 2008. 'The Embodied Film: Austrian Contributions to Experimental Cinema', in R. Halle and R. Steingröver (eds), *After the Avant-Garde: Con-*

temporary German and Austrian Experimental Film, Rochester, N.Y.: Camden House, 50–68.

West, C. and S. Fenstermaker. 1995. 'Doing Difference', *Gender & Society*, 9(1), 8–37.

Wex, M. 1979. *'Let's Take Back Our Space': 'Female' and 'Male' Body Language as a Result of Patriarchal Structures*, Berlin: Frauenliteraturverlag Hermine Fees.

Wilhelm, W. 2005. 'Dossier zum Hintergrund der Verfolgung wegen sexueller Orientierung in der Zeit des Nationalsozialismus und danach'. http://www.publi-cartvienna.at/downloads/Dossier_morzinplatz_d.pdf, retrieved 18 February 2011.

Witte, K. 1995. *Lachende Erben, toller Tag: Filmkomödie im Dritten Reich*, Berlin: Vorwerk.

Witte, K. 1996. 'Der Violinschlüssel. Zur Produktion der Wien-Film', in R. Bek-kermann and C. Blümlinger (eds), *Ohne Untertitel: Fragmente einer Geschichte des österreichischen Kinos*, Vienna: Sonderzahl, 17–29.

Yuval-Davis, N. 1997. *Gender & Nation*, London: Sage.

FILMOGRAPHY

This list includes all commercially released, feature-length films produced or co-produced by Austrian film companies between 1946 and 1955. Films are listed chronologically by year of first release in Austria. The film titles given are those under which the films were released in Austria.[1]

Abbreviations: AT (alternative titles), P (production company), D (director), S (script), C (cinematography), AD (art director), M (music), A (key actors).

1946

Der weite Weg / The Long Way Home (Drama)
Premiere: 23 August 1946
AT: Schicksal in Ketten
P: Donau-Film (Vienna)
D: Eduard Hoesch
S: Karl Kurzmayer, Karl Jantsch
C: Karl Kurzmayer, Anton Pucher
AD: Julius von Borsody
M: Frank Fox
A: Hans Holt, Rudolf Prack, Maria Andergast

Glaube an mich / Believe in Me (Tourist Film)
Premiere: 15 November 1946
P: Löwen-Film (Vienna)
D: Géza von Cziffra
S: Géza von Cziffra
C: Hans Schneeberger
AD: Gustav Abel
M: Anton Profes
A: Marte Harell, Ewald Balser, Rudolf Prack

Praterbuben / Boys of the Prater (Musical)
Premiere: 26 December 1946
P: Vindobona-Film (Vienna)
D: Paul Martin
S: Hugo Maria Kritz, Edmund Strzygowski
C: Oskar Schnirch
AD: Julius von Borsody
M: Willy Schmidt-Gentner
A: Hermann Thimig, Pepi Glöckner-Kramer, Fritz Imhoff

Schleichendes Gift / Creeping Poison (Docudrama)
Premiere: 27 September 1946
P: Standard-Film (Vienna)
D: Hermann Wallbrück
S: Stefan Wolfram
M: Oskar Wagner
A: Alfred Neuhart, Eleonore Beck

1947

Am Ende der Welt / At the Edge of the World (Melodrama)
AT: Erbin der Wälder
Premiere: 4 July 1947 (*Überläufer*, produced 1943)
P: Wien-Film (Vienna)
D: Gustav Ucicky
S: Gerhard Menzel
C: Günther Anders
M: Willy Schmidt-Gentner

A: Brigitte Horney, Attila
Hörbiger, Boguslaw Samborski,
Trude Hesterberg

**Das unsterbliche Antlitz / Immortal
Face** (Historical Costume Film)
Premiere: 10 October 1947
P: Cziffra-Film (Vienna)
D + S: Géza von Cziffra
C: Ludwig Berger
AD: Friedrich Jüptner-Jonstorff
M: Alois Melichar
A: O.W. Fischer, Marianne
Schönauer, Helene Thimig

**Der Hofrat Geiger / Privy Councillor
Geiger** (Tourist Film)
Premiere: 19 December 1947
P: Willi-Forst-Film (Vienna)
D: Hans Wolff
S: Hans Wolff, Martin Costa
C: Rudolf Icsey, Ladislaus Szemte
AD: Friedrich Jüptner-Jonstorff
M: Hans Lang
A: Maria Andergast, Waltraut Haas,
Paul Hörbiger, Hans Moser

**Die Glücksmühle / The Mill
of Happiness** (Comedy)
Premiere: 9 May 1947
P: Belvedere-Film (Vienna)
D: Emmerich Hanus
S: Ernst Henthaler
C: Hans Nigmann
AD: Sepp Rothauer
M: Oskar Wagner
A: Erich Dörner, Paula Seitz-
Fielder, Thea Weis

**Die Welt dreht sich verkehrt /
The World Turns Backward**
(Historical Costume Film)
Premiere: 13 February 1947
P: Österreichische Wochenschau-
und Produktions KG J. A.
Hübler-Kahla & Co (Vienna)
D: J.A. Hübler-Kahla
S: Kurt Nachmann, J.A. Hübler-Kahla
AD: Werner Schlichting
M: Willy Schmidt-Gentner
A: Hans Moser, Josef Meinrad,
Marianne Schönauer, Karl Skraup,
Thea Weis, Alfred Neugebauer

Erde / Earth (*Heimatfilm*)
AT: Trotzige Herzen
Premiere: 17 October 1947
P: Austrian-Swiss co-production:
Tirol-Film (Innsbruck);
Omnia Film (Zürich)
D: Leopold Hainisch
S: Eduard Köck, Karl Schönherr (play)
C: Richard Angst
A: Eduard Köck, Ilse Exl, Anna Exl

**Liebe nach Noten / Love from
the Score** (Comedy)
AT: Du bist Musik für mich
Premiere: 18 November 1947
(*Überläufer*, produced 1944/45)
P: Wien-Film (Vienna)
D + S: Géza von Cziffra
C: Hans Schneeberger
AD: Gustav Abel, Max Fellerer
M: Michael Jary
A: Olly Holzmann, Hans
Olden, Rudolf Prack

**Macht im Dunkel / The Dark
Force** (Docudrama)
Premiere: 31 May 1947
P: Standard-Film (Vienna)
D: Hermann Wallbrück
S: Franz Ritschl, Karl Steurer,
Hermann Wallbrück
C: Hermann Wallbrück
A: Ivan Petrovich, Veit
Relin, Hilde Mikulicz

**Seine einzige Liebe / His Only
Love** (Historical Costume Film)
Premiere: 18 November 1947
P: Royal-Film (Vienna)
D: Emerich Hanus
S: Benno A. Haas, Walter Gynt
C: Willi Sohm
AD: Sepp Rothaur
M: Oskar Wagner
A: Franz Böheim, Klara Maria Skala,
Walter Gynt, Heinz Conrads

Singende Engel / Singing Angels
(Historical Costume Film)
Premiere: 19 December 1947
P: Vindobona-Film (Vienna)
D: Gustav Ucicky
S: Rolf Olsen, Gustav Ucicky

C: Walter Riml
AD: Otto Niedermoser,
    Walter Schmiedl
M: Willy Schmidt-Gentner
A: Hans Holt, Käthe Dorsch,
    Gustav Waldau

Sturmjahre / Stormy Years
    (Documentary)
Premiere: 14 November 1947
P: Pax-Film (Vienna)
D + S: Frank Ward Rossak,
    Hermann Heidmann

**Triumph der Liebe / Lysistrata
    - Triumph of Love** (Historical
    Costume Film)
Premiere: 18 April 1947
P: Wiener Mundus-Film (Vienna)
D: Alfred Stöger
S: Kaspar Loser
C: Oskar Schnirch
AD: Werner Schlichting
M: Alois Melichar
A: O.W. Fischer, Judith
    Holzmeister, Paul Kemp

Umwege zu dir / Detour to You
    (Historical Costume Film)
Premiere: 7 November 1947
    (*Überläufer*, produced 1944/45)
P: Wien-Film (Vienna)
D + S: Hans Thimig
C: Jaroslav Tuzar
AD: Julius von Borsody
M: Anton Profes
A: Marte Harell, Richard
    Romanovsky, Christl Mardayn

**Wer küsst wen? / Who Kisses
    Whom?** (Comedy)
AT: Die vertauschten Ehemänner
Premiere: 11 December 1947
P: Belvedere-Film (Vienna)
D: Wolf-Dietrich Friese
S: August Diglas
C: Sepp Ketterer
M: Oskar Wagner
A: Alexander Trojan, Trude
    Marlen, Thea Weis

**Wiener Melodien / Viennese
    Melodies** (Comedy)

Premiere: 3 June 1947
P: Donau-Film (Vienna)
D: Theo Lingen, Hubert Marischka
S: Kaspar Loser
C: Karl Kurzmayer
AD: Julius von Borsody
M: Frank Filip
A: Elfie Mayerhofer, Johannes
    Heesters, Fritz Gehlen

**Wintermelodie - Les Amours
    de Blanche Neige / Winter
    Melody** (Tourist Film)
Premiere: 14 August 1947
P: Austrian-French co-production:
    Wieser-Film (Vienna),
    Tarice Films (Paris)
D: Eduard Wieser
S: Werner Eplinius
C: Hans Staudinger, Walter Riml
M: Willy Schmidt-Gentner
A: Ilse Peternell, Rudolf Brix,
    Franz Eichberger, Rudi Matt

1948

Alles Lüge / All Lies (Comedy)
Premiere: 9 April 1948
P: Löwen-Film (Vienna)
D: E.W. Emo
S: Fritz Koselka, Lilian Belmont
C: Fritz Woditzka
AD: Friedrich Jüptner-Jonstorff
M: Willy Schmidt-Gentner
A: Wolf Albach-Retty, Senta
    Wengraf, Hedwig Bleibtreu

**An klingenden Ufern / On
    Melodious Shores** (Melodrama)
Premiere: 15 September 1948
P: Violanta-Film (Vienna)
D + P: Hans Unterkircher
S: Alexander Lernet-Holenia
C: Hans Staudinger
M: Karl von Pauspertl
A: Marianne Schönauer, Curd
    Jürgens, Cäcilia Kahr

Anni. Eine Wiener Ballade / Anni
    (Historical Costume Film)
Premiere: 4 June 1948
P: Styria-Film (Graz), Berna-Film (Wien)

D: Max Neufeld
S: Max Neufeld, Harald Röbbeling
C: Walter Riml
AD: Friedrich Jüptner-Jonstorff
M: Alois Melichar, Robert Stolz
A: Elfie Mayerhofer, Siegfried
   Breuer, Josef Meinrad

Arlberg Express /Arlberg
   Express (Drama)
Premiere: 8 June 1948
P: Donau-Film (Vienna)
D: Eduard von Borsody
C: Hans Androschin
S: Curt J. Braun
AD: Julius von Borsody
M: Wolfgang Russ-Bovelino
A: Paul Hubschmid, Elfe Gerhart,
   Iván Petrovich, Hans Putz

Das andere Leben / The
   Other Life (Drama)
AT: Der 20. Juli 1944
Premiere: 4 May 1948
P: Filmstudio des Theaters in
   der Josefstadt (Vienna)
D: Rudolf Steinböck
S: Alfred Ibach
C: Willi Sohm
AD: Herbert Ploberger
A: Aglaja Schmid, Robert Lindner,
   Gustav Waldau, Vilma Degischer

Das singende Haus / The
   Singing House (Comedy)
Premiere: 23 January 1948
P: Wien-Film (Vienna),
   Kollektiv-Film (Vienna)
D: Franz Antel
S: Aldo von Pinelli, Franz Antel
C: Helmuth Fischer-Ashley,
   Oskar Schnirch
AD: Julius von Borsody
M: Peter Kreuder
A: Hans Moser, Curd Jürgens, Walter
   Müller, Richard Romanowsky,
   Hannelore Schroth

Der Engel mit der Posaune /
   Angel with a Trumpet (His-
   torical Costume Film)
Premiere: 19 August 1948
P: Vindobona-Film (Vienna)

D: Karl Hartl
C: Günther Anders
S: Karl Hartl, Franz Tassié,
   Ernst Lothar (novel)
AD: Otto Niedermoser,
   Walter Schmiedl
M: Willy Schmidt-Gentner
A: Paula Wessely, Attila Hörbiger,
   Fred Liewehr, Hedwig Bleibtreu

Der Herr Kanzleirat / Sir
   Kanzleirat (Tourist Film)
AT: Der alte Herr Kanzleirat
Premiere: 21 May 1948
P: Donau-Film (Vienna)
D: Hubert Marischka
S: Hubert Marischka
C: Herbert Thallmayer
AD: Julius von Borsody
M: Hans Lang
A: Hans Moser, Susanne von
   Almassy, Egon von Jordan

Der himmlische Walzer / The
   Heavenly Waltz (Comedy)
Premiere: 4 September 1948
P: Cziffra-Film (Vienna)
D + S: Géza von Cziffra
C: Ludwig Berger
AD: Friedrich Jüptner-Jonstorff
M: Ludwig Schmidseder,
   Alois Melichar
A: Elfie Mayerhofer, Paul
   Hubschmid, Inge Konradi,
   Curd Jürgens, Paul Kemp

Der Leberfleck / The Freckle (Comedy)
AT: Die unmoralische Erbschaft
Premiere: 21 August 1948
P: Belvedere-Film (Vienna)
D: Rudolf Carl
S: Helmut Kemmerl
C: Rudolf Icsey
M: Oskar Wagner
A: Oskar Sima, Liesl Andergast,
   Erich Dörner, Lotte
   Neumayer, Fritz Imhoff

Der Prozess / The Trial
   (Historical Costume Film)
Premiere: 19 March 1948
P: Hübler-Kahla-Film (Vienna)
D: G.W. Pabst

S: Kurt Heuser, Rudolf
Brunngraber, Emeric Roboz,
Rudolf Brunngraber (novel)
C: Oskar Schnirch, Helmuth Ashley
AD: Werner Schlichting
M: Alois Melichar
A: Ernst Deutsch, Ewald Balser,
Marianne Schönauer, Josef
Meinrad, Ernst Waldbrunn

**Die Frau am Weg / The Woman
by the Road** (Melodrama)
Premiere: 12 October 1948
P: Willi-Forst-Film (Vienna)
D: Eduard von Borsody
S: Eduard von Borsody, Walter
Firner, Fritz Hochwälder (novel)
C: Walter Riml
AD: Julius von Borsody
M: Willy Schmidt-Gentner
A: Brigitte Horney, Robert
Freitag, Otto Wögerer

**Die Schatztruhe / The Treasure
Chest** (Comedy)
Premiere: 17 December 1948
P: Ring-Film (Vienna)
D +S: Carl Kurzmayer
S: Karl Kurzmayer
C: Sepp Ketterer
AD: A.J. Paulini
M: Hans Hagen
A: Karl Skraup, Rudolf Carl,
Theodor Danegger

**Die Sonnhofbäuerin / The Sonn-
hof Farmer** (*Heimatfilm*)
Premiere: 21 January 1948
P: Ring-Film (Vienna)
D: Wilfried Frass, Karl Kurzmayer
S: Wilfried Frass
C: Karl Kurzmayer
AD: Heinz Ludwig
M: Hans Hagen
A: Wolfgang Hebenstreit, Elisabeth
Höbarth, Willy Danek

**Die Verjüngungskur /
Rejuvenation Cure** (Comedy)
Premiere: 13 August 1948
P: Savoy-Film (Vienna)
D + S: Harald Röbbeling

C: Walter Riml
AD: Gustav Abel
M: Frank Fox
A: Hermann Erhardt, Josef
Egger, Lotte Lang, Olga von
Togni, Paul Löwinger

**Ein Mann gehört ins Haus / A
Man Is Needed** (Comedy)
AT: Der Jäger und die Tannhofwirtin
Premiere: 21 May 1948 (*Überläufer*,
produced 1944/45)
P: Wien-Film (Vienna)
D: Hubert Marischka
S: Alexander Lix, Anton Maly (story)
C: Hans Schneeberger
AD: Friedrich Jüptner-Jonstorff
M: Hanns Elin, Anton Profes
A: Magda Schneider, Paul Richter,
Maria Andergast, Carl Günther

Fregola / Fregola (Musical)
Premiere: 25 December 1948
P: Styria-Film (Vienna)
D: Harald Röbbeling
S: Harald Röbbeling, Karl Farkas
C: Günther Anders, Hans Staudinger
AD: Friedrich Jüptner-Jonstorff
M: Theo Nordhaus, Willy
Schmidt-Gentner
A: Marika Rökk, Rudolf Prack,
Siegfried Breuer, Gustav
Waldau, Josef Meinrad

**Gipfelkreuz / Summit
Cross** (*Heimatfilm*)
Premiere: 17 September 1948
P: Benesch-Film (Vienna)
D: Alfons Benesch
S: Alfons Plankensteiner
C: Alfons Benesch
M: Rudolf Kattnigg
A: Luis May, Margit Seeber, Walter
Weber, Michael Gnigler

**Gottes Engel sind überall / God's
Angels Are Everywhere** (Drama)
Premiere: 22 March 1948
P: Unitas-Film (Vienna)
D: Hans Thimig
S: Kurt Heuser, Peter Francke
C: Hans Schneeberger

AD: Werner Schlichting
M: Anton Profes
A: Attila Hörbiger, Heiki Eis, Paul
   Hubschmid, Susi Nicoletti

Hin und her / To and Fro (Comedy)
AT: Der Wind hat meine
   Existenz verweht
Premiere: 21 January 1948
P: Hübler-Kahla-Film (Vienna)
D: Theo Lingen
P: J.A. Hübler-Kahla
S: Franz Gribitz, Theo Lingen
C: Karl Kurzmayer
AD: Julius von Borsody
M: Frank Fox
A: Theo Lingen, Fritz Eckhardt,
   O.W. Fischer, Dagny
   Servaes, Ursula Lingen

**Im Banne des Monte Miracolo
/ Under the Spell of Monte
Miracolo** (Mountain Film)
Premiere: 19 November 1948
   (*Überläufer*, produced 1943/48)
P: Tirol-Film Luis Trenker (Innsbruck)
D + S: Luis Trenker
C: Umberto Della Valle, Vittorio Della
   Valle, Albert Benitz, Ernst Elsigan
AD: Alfredo Montori
M: Giuseppe Becce
A: Luis Trenker, Umberto
   Sacripante, Dora Bini Maria,
   Carla De Gara Graziella

**Kleine Melodie aus Wien / Little
Melody from Vienna** (Comedy)
Premiere: 29 October 1948
P: Excelsior-Film (Vienna)
D: E.W. Emo
S: E.W. Emo, Franz Tassié, Fritz Koselka
   (story), Lilian Belmont (story)
AD: Friedrich Jüptner-Jonstorff
M: Robert Stolz
A: Paul Hörbiger, Maria
   Andergast, Annie Rosar

**Königin der Landstrasse / Queen
of the Road** (Comedy)
Premiere: 8 October 1948
P: Circus-Film (Vienna),
   Löwen-Film (Vienna)

D + S: Géza von Cziffra
S: Géza von Cziffra
C: Hans Schneeberger
AD: Friedrich Jüptner-Jonstorff
M: Anton Profes, Hanns Elin
A: Rudolf Prack, Albin Skoda,
   Angelika Hauff, Dagny Servaes

Maresi / Maresi (Historical
Costume Film)
AT: Der Angeklagte hat das Wort,
   Maresi – Gefährtin meines Lebens
Premiere: 5 November 1948
P: Unitas-Film (Vienna)
D: Hans Thimig
P: Anton Profes
S: Peter Francke, Kurt Heuser,
   Alexander Lernet-Holenia (novel)
C: Oskar Schnirch
AD: Julius von Borsody
M: Anton Profes
A: Attila Hörbiger, Maria
   Schell, Siegfried Breuer

**Rendezvous im Salzkammergut
/ Rendezvous in the
Salzkammergut** (Tourist Film)
Premiere: 27 March 1948
P: Wiener Mundus-Film (Vienna)
D: Alfred Stöger
S: Aldo von Pinelli
C: Ludwig Berger
AD: Friedrich Jüptner-Jonstorff
M: Robert Stolz
A: Inge Konradi, Hertha Mayen,
   Hans Holt, Josef Meinrad,
   Theodor Danegger

**Ulli und Marei / Ulli and
Marei** (*Heimatfilm*)
AT: Wo die Alpenrosen
   blühen, Der Berghofbauer
Premiere: 23 April 1948 (*Überläufer*,
   produced 1944/45)
P: Wien-Film (Vienna)
D: Leopold Hainisch
S: Leopold Hainisch, Eduard Köck
C: Ernst W. Fiedler, Günther
   Anders, Richard Angst
A: Eduard Köck, Ilse Exl,
   Attila Hörbiger

**Verlorenes Rennen / Lost
Race** (Melodrama)
Premiere: 20 December 1948
P: Berna-Film (Vienna),
Donau-Film (Vienna)
D: Max Neufeld
S: Curt J. Braun
C: Willi Sohm, Hannes Staudinger
AD: Gustav Abel
M: Frank Fox
A: Elfe Gerhart, O.W. Fischer,
Curd Jürgens

Zyankali / Cyanide (Crime Film)
Premiere: 26 May 1948
P: Savoy-Film (Vienna)
D + S: Harald Röbbeling
C: Willy Riml
AD: Fritz Mögle
M: Willy Schmidt-Gentner
A: Siegfried Breuer, Maria
Andergast, Rudolf Prack

1949

Bergkristall / Rock Crystal (*Heimatfilm*)
AT: Der Wildschütz von Tirol
Premiere: 23 October 1949
P: Austrian-West German
co-production: Josef-Plesner-
Filmproduktion (Kufstein),
Hubert-Schonger-Filmproduktion
(Inning am Ammersee)
D: Harald Reinl
S: Harald Reinl, Hubert
Schonger, Rose Schonger
C: Josef Plesner
AD: Friedrich Jüptner-Jonstorff
M: Giuseppe Becce
A: Franz Eichberger, Maria
Stolz, Hans Renz

**Das Kuckucksei / The
Cuckoo's Egg** (Comedy)
Premiere: 26 January 1949
P: Willi-Forst-Film (Vienna)
D: Walter Firner
S: Walter Firner, Irma Firner
C: Günther Anders
AD: Friedrich Jüptner-Jonstorff
M: Peter Wehle

A: Käthe Dorsch, Annemarie
Blanc, Hans Holt

**Das Siegel Gottes / God's
Signet** (*Heimatfilm*)
AT: Schuld und Sühne
Premiere: 8 February 1949
P: Wiener Mundus-Film (Vienna)
D: Alfred Stöger
S: Alexander Lix
C: Sepp Kletterer
AD: Friedrich Jüptner-Jonstorff
A: Josef Meinrad, Hilde
Mikulicz, Robert Lindner

Doktor Rosin / Doctor Rosin (Drama)
Premiere: 2 September 1949
P: Belvedere-Film (Vienna)
D: Arthur de Glahs
S: Arthur de Glahs, Gustl Peuker
C: Gustl Peuker
A: Erika Berghöfer, Viktor Braun,
Hans Richter, Alfred Neugebauer

**Duell mit dem Tod / Duell
with Death** (Drama)
AT: Am Rande des Lebens, Der
Eid des Professor Romberg
Premiere: 2 December 1949
P: Pabst-Kiba-Filmproduktion (Vienna)
D: Paul May
S: Paul May, G.W. Pabst
C: Helmuth Fischer-Ashley
M: Alfred Schneider
A: Rolf von Nauckhoff, Anneliese
Reinhold, Ernst Waldbrunn

**Ein bezaubernder Schwindler / A
Charming Fraud** (Comedy)
Premiere: 16 December 1949
P: Excelsior-Film (Vienna)
D: Hans Wolff
S: Hans Wolff, Aldo von Pinelli
C: Fritz Woditzka
M: Robert Stolz
A: Wolf Albach-Retty, Elfe
Gerhart, Waltraut Haas, Inge
Konradi, Gustav Waldau

**Eins, zwei, drei – aus! / 1, 2,
3 – Out!** (Comedy)
AT: Meisterringer
Premiere: 2 December 1949

P: Pabst-Kiba-Filmproduktion (Vienna)
D: J.A. Hübler-Kahla
S: Frank Filip
C: Hans H. Theyer
M: Frank Filip
A: Hans Moser, Thea Weis,
   Franz Berndt

Eroica / Eroica (Historical
   Costume Film)
Premiere: 31 July 1949
P: Wiener-Kunstfilm (Vienna) for the
   Neue Wiener Filmproduktions
   GmbH (Vienna)
D + P: Walter Kolm-Veltée
S: Walter Kolm-Veltée, Franz
   Tassié, Norbert Kunze
C: Günter Anders
A: Ewald Balser, Marianne
   Schönauer, Judith Holzmeister

**Es lebe das Leben / Celebrate
   Life** (Drama)
Premiere: 23 September 1949
P: Löwen-Film (Vienna)
D: E.W. Emo
S: J.B. Tanko
C: Fritz Woditzka
AD: Friedrich Jüptner-Jonstorff
M: Willy Schmidt-Gentner
A: Geraldine Katt, Fritz
   Lehmann, Josef Menschik

**Geheimnisvolle Tiefe / Mysterious
   Depth** (Melodrama)
Premiere: 8 September 1949
P: Pabst-Kiba-Filmproduktion (Vienna)
D: G.W. Pabst
S: Trude Pabst, Walter von Hollander
C: Helmuth Fischer-Ashley,
   Hans Schneeberger
AD: Werner Schlichting,
   Isabella Schlichting
M: Roland Kovač, Alois Melichar
A: Ilse Werner, Paul Hubschmid,
   Elfe Gerhardt

Hexen / Witches (Comedy)
Premiere: 8 April 1949
P: Alpenfilm Austria (Graz)
D + S: Hans Schott-Schöbinger
S: Hans Schott-Schöbinger
C: Walter Riml, Willi Sohm

AD: Friedrich Jüptner-Jonstorff
M: Willy Schmidt-Gentner
A: Edith Mill, Margrit Aust,
   Curd Jürgens

**Höllische Liebe / Infernal
   Love** (Comedy)
Premiere: 17 November 1949
P: Cziffra-Film (Vienna) for the
   Neue Wiener Filmproduktions
   GmbH (Vienna)
D + S + P: Géza von Cziffra
C: Ludwig Berger
AD: Friedrich Jüptner-Jonstorff
M: Hanns Elin
A: Elfie Mayerhofer, Vera
   Molnar, Hans Holt

**Kleiner Schwindel am Wolfgangsee
   / Little Swindle at Lake
   Wolfgang** (Tourist Film)
Premiere: 11 November 1949
P: Alpenländische Filmgesellschaft
   (Vienna/Linz)
D: Franz Antel
S: Franz Antel, Gunther Philipp,
   G.V. Satzenhofen (idea)
C: Hans Theyer
AD: Sepp Rothauer
M: Ludwig Schmidseder
A: Waltraut Haas, Hans Holt, Susi
   Nicoletti, Gunther Philipp

**Lambert fühlt sich bedroht / Lambert
   Feels Threatened** (Crime Film)
AT: Das Haus im Nebel
Premiere: 4 March 1949
P: Cziffra-Film (Vienna)
D + S + P: Géza von Cziffra
C: Ludwig Berger
AD: Friedrich Jüptner-Jonstorff
M: Hanns Elin
A: Hannelore Schroth, Curd
   Jürgens, Leopold Rudolf

**Liebe Freundin / Dear
   Friend** (Melodrama)
AT: Zweimal verliebt
Premiere: 23 March 1949
P: Filmstudio des Theaters in
   der Josefstadt (Vienna)
D: Rudolf Steinböck
S: Curt J. Braun

C: Willi Sohm
AD: Herbert Ploberger
M: Alexander Steinbrecher
A: Vilma Degischer, Johannes
   Heesters, Erik Frey

Liebesprobe / Love Test (Comedy)
AT: Wilderernacht
Premiere: 3 November 1949
P: Ring-Film (Vienna)
D: Karl Leiter
S: Karl Pruckner, Toni Sayden (idea)
C: Carl Kurzmayer
AD: Hans Zehetner
M: Hans Hagen
A: Oskar Sima, Helly Lichten,
   Martha Wallner

**Liebling der Welt / Beloved of the
   World** (Historical Costume Film)
AT: Rosen der Liebe, Hoheit
   darf nicht küssen, Seine
   Hoheit darf nicht küssen
Premiere: 11 March 1949
P: Austrian-French co-production:
   Berna-Film (Vienna), Donau-Film
   (Vienna), Arta-Film (Paris)
D: Max Neufeld
S: Siegfried Breuer, Karl Farkas
C: Oskar Schnirch
AD: Gustav Abel
M: Nicolas Brodszky, Frank Fox
A: Nadja Gray, O.W. Fischer,
   Siegfried Breuer

**Märchen vom Glück / Kiss Me,
   Casanova** (Historical Costume Film)
AT: Traum vom Glück
Premiere: 9 September 1949
P: Belvedere-Film (Vienna)
D: Arthur de Glahs
S: Arthur de Glahs, Franz Krpata
C: Hans Nigmann
AD: Gustav Abel, Ferdinand Kollhanek
M: Franz Thurner
A: O.W. Fischer, Maria Holst,
   Erika Berghöfer

**Mein Freund, der nicht 'Nein'
   sagen kann / My Friend Who
   Can't Say No** (Comedy)
AT: Mein Freund Leopold

Premiere: 20 December 1949
P: Wiener Mundus-Film (Vienna),
   Helios-Film (Vienna)
D: Alfred Stöger
S: Georges Creux
C: Sepp Ketterer
AD: Friedrich Jüptner-Jonstorff
M: Robert Stolz
A: Josef Meinrad, Hans Olsen,
   Inge Konradi, Susi Nicoletti

**Nach dem Sturm / After the
   Storm** (Melodrama)
AT: Opfer aus Liebe
Premiere: 21 January 1949
P: Swiss-Austrian-Liechtenstein
   co-production: Cordial-Film
   (Zürich, Vaduz, Vienna)
D: Gustav Ucicky
S: Peter Wyrsch, Gustav
   Ucicky, Carl Zuckmayer
C: Konstantin Tschet, Otto Ritter
AD: Otto Niedermoser, Robert
   Furrer, Adolf Rebsamen
M: Robert Valberg
A: Marte Harell, Nicholas
   Stuart, Erwin Kalser

Vagabunden / Vagabonds (Melodrama)
AT: Vagabunden der Liebe
Premiere: 18 October 1949
P: ÖFA Österreichische
   Filmgesellschaft (Salzburg)
D: Rolf Hansen
S: Juliane Kay, Rolf Hansen, Tibor Yost
C: Oskar Schnirch
AD: Julius von Borsody
M: Anton Profes
A: Paula Wessely, Attila Hörbiger,
   Erik Frey, Elfe Gerhart

**Vom Mädchen zur Frau / From
   Girl to Woman** (Docudrama)
Premiere: 9 September 1949
P: Vita-Film (Vienna)
D: Alfred Renel
S: E. Valentinitsch
C: Fritz Friedl
M: Hans Pero
A: Erwin Strahl, Ernst
   Neuhardt, Steffi Hübl

Weisses Gold / White Gold (*Heimatfilm*)
AT: Angela
Premiere: 19 April 1949
P: Austrian-Swiss co-production:
ÖFA Österreichische
Filmgesellschaft (Salzburg),
Neue Interna Film AG (Zürich)
D: Eduard von Borsody
S: Eduard von Borsody, Alexander
Lix, Wolfgang Müller-Sehn (idea)
C: Fritz Friedl
AD: Julius von Borsody
M: Alois Melichar
A: Angela Salloker, Armin
Dahlen, Heinrich Gretler

**Wie ein Dieb in der Nacht / Like a
Thief in the Night** (Comedy)
Premiere: 23 September 1949
(*Überläufer*, produced 1944)
P: Wien-Film (Vienna)
D: Hans Thimig
S: Lilian Belmont, Fritz Koselka,
Hugo Maria Kritz
C: Jaroslav Tuzar, Carl Kurzmayer,
Bob Christbyn, Christian von Enk
A: Gusti Huber, Wolf Albach-
Retty, Hermann Thimig

Wiener Mädeln / Viennese Girls
(Historical Costume Film)
Premiere: 21 December 1949
(*Überläufer*, produced 1944/45)
P: Willi-Forst-Film (Vienna)
D: Willi Forst
S: Willi Forst, Franz Gribitz,
Erich Meder
C: Jan Stallich, Hannes
Staudinger, Viktor Meihsl
A: Willi Forst, Hans Moser, Judith
Holzmeister, Curd Jürgens

**Wir haben soeben geheiratet / We've
Just Got Married** (Comedy)
Premiere: 29 July 1949
P: Standard-Film (Vienna) D: Hans
Effenberger, Hermann Wallbrück
S: Hans Effenberger
C: Herbert Brunnbauer, Ludwig
Kerner, Herbert Thallmayer
A: Lotte Lang, Maria Eis, Hans Olden

1950

**Auf der Alm, da gibst koa
Sünd' / No Sin on the Alpine
Pastures** (Comedy)
Premiere: 20 November 1950
P: Berna-Film (Vienna),
Donau-Film (Vienna)
D: Franz Antel
S: Franz Antel, Aldo von Pinelli
C: Hans Theyer
AD: Gustav Abel
M: Hans Lang
A: Maria Andergast, Karl Skraup,
Annie Rosar

Cordula / Cordula (Melodrama)
Premiere: 23 October 1950
P: Paula-Wessely-Film (Vienna)
D: Gustav Ucicky
S: Gustav Ucicky, Max Mell
C: Hans Schneeberger
AD: Otto Niedermoser
M: Joseph Marx, Willy Schmidt-
Gentner, Heinz Sandauer
A: Paula Wessely, Attila Hörbiger,
Eduard Köck, Leopold Rudolf,
Jane Tilden, Hermann Ehrhardt

**Das Jahr des Herrn / The Year
of the Lord** (*Heimatfilm*)
AT: Kraft der Liebe, Der Wallnerbub
Premiere: 12 December 1950
P: Wiener Mundus-Film (Vienna)
D: Alfred Stöger
S: Karl Heinrich Waggerl, Ulrich Bettac
C: Sepp Ketterer
AD: Friedrich Jüptner-Jonstorff
A: Käthe Gold, Ewald Balser,
Karl Haberfellner

**Das vierte Gebot / The Fourth
Commandment** (Historical
Costume Film)
AT: Der Weg abwärts, Die Kupplerin
Premiere: 15 September 1950
P: Berna-Film (Vienna),
Donau-Film (Vienna)
D: Eduard von Borsody
S: Eduard von Borsody, Friedrich
Schreyvogel
C: Hans Schneeberger, Sepp Ketterer

AD: Gustav Abel
M: Wolfgang Russ-Bovelino
A: Attila Hörbiger, Dagny
    Servaes, Hans Putz

**Der keusche Adam / Chaste
    Adam** (Comedy)
Premiere: 16 November 1950
P: Helios-Film (Vienna)
D: Karl Sztollar
S: Carla Gidt, Gretl Löwinger
    (play), Paul Löwinger (play)
C: Julius Jonak
M: Bruno Uher
A: Paul Löwinger, Gretl
    Löwinger, Liesl Löwinger

**Der Seelenbräu / The Soul-
    Brewer** (Drama)
Premiere: 18 April 1950
P: Vindobona-Film (Vienna)
D: Gustav Ucicky
S: Alexander Lix, Theodor Ottawa
C: Hans Schneeberger, Sepp Ketterer
AD: Otto Niedermoser, Eduard Stolba
M: Willy Schmidt-Gentner
A: Paul Hörbiger, Heinrich
    Gretler, Aglaja Schmid

**Erzherzog Johanns grosse Liebe /
    Archduke Johann's Great Love**
    (Historical Costume Film)
Premiere: 3 December 1950
P: Patria-Filmkunst (Vienna)
D: Hans Schott-Schöbinger
S: Josef Friedrich Perkonig,
    Franz Gribitz
C: Günther Anders, Hannes Staudinger
AD: Werner Schlichting,
    Isabella Schlichting
M: Willy Schmidt-Gentner
A: O.W. Fischer, Marte
    Harell, Josef Meinrad

**Es schlägt dreizehn / That's
    the Limit!** (Comedy)
AT: Jetzt schlägt's dreizehn
Premiere: 18 September 1950
P: Helios-Film (Vienna)
D: E.W. Emo
S: Fritz Koselka, Lilian Belmont,
    E.W. Emo (idea)

C: Helmuth Fischer-Ashley
AD: Friedrich Jüptner-Jonstorff
M: Bruno Uher
A: Theo Lingen, Hans Moser,
    Susi Nicoletti

**Grossstadtnacht / Night in
    the City** (Drama)
AT: Diebe aus Liebe
Premiere: 8 September 1950
P: Helios-Film (Vienna)
D: Hans Wolff
S: Hans Wolff, Wilhelm
    Lichtenberg (novel)
C: Hans Theyer
AD: Friedrich Jüptner-Jonstorff
M: Bruno Uher
A: Wolf Albach-Retty, Inge
    Konradi, Hedwig Bleibtreu

**Gruss und Kuss aus der Wachau
    / Greetings and Kisses from
    the Wachau** (Musical)
Premiere: 18 December 1950
P: Viktoria Film (Vienna)
D: Fritz Schulz
S: Karl Farkas
C: Hans Schneeberger
AD: Eduard Stolba
M: Willy Schmidt-Gentner
A: Waltraut Haas, Marianne
    Schönauer, Gretl Schörg

**Kind der Donau / Child of
    the Danube** (Musical)
Premiere: 8 August 1950
P: Nova-Filmproduktion (Vienna),
    Wien-Film (Vienna)
D: Georg Jacoby
S: Friedrich Schreyvogel, Georg Jacoby
C: Hanns König, Walter Riml
AD: Julius von Borsody
M: Nico Dostal
A: Marika Rökk, Fred
    Liewehr, Fritz Muliar

**Küssen ist keine Sünd' / Kissing
    is No Sin** (Comedy)
AT: Das Lerchel von Salzburg
Premiere: 28 September 1950

P: Austrian-West German co-
production: Schönbrunn-Film
(Vienna), Aco-Film (Munich)
D: Hubert Marischka
S: Hubert Marischka, Rudolf
Österreicher
C: Franz Koch, Josef Illig
AD: Hans Ledersteger, Ernst Richter
M: Alois Melichar
A: Elfie Mayerhofer, Curd
Jürgens, Hans Moser

**Prämien auf den Tod / Bonus
on Death** (Crime Film)
Premiere: 13 January 1950
P: Alpenfilm Austria (Graz)
D: Curd Jürgens
S: Kurt Heuser, Curd Jürgens
C: Günther Anders
AD: Isabella Schlichting,
Werner Schlichting
A: Siegfried Breuer, Werner
Krauss, Judith Holzmeister

**Schuss durchs Fenster / Shot through
the Window** (Crime Film)
Premiere: 5 May 1950
P: Alpenfilm Austria (Graz)
D: Siegfried Breuer
S: Siegfried Breuer, Rolf Olsen
C: Helmuth Fischer-Ashley
AD: Werner Schlichting
M: Willy Schmidt-Gentner
A: Siegfried Breuer, Curd
Jürgens, Edith Mill

**Seitensprünge im Schnee / Escapades
in the Snow** (Tourist Film)
Premiere: 15 December 1950
P: Austrian-West German co-
production: Löwen-Film
(Vienna/Munich)
D: Siegfried Breuer
S: Siegfried Breuer, Marieluise Füringk
C: Oskar Schnirch
M: Franz Grothe
A: Doris Kirchner, Heinz
Engelmann, Jane Tilden

1951
Asphalt / Asphalt (Social
Problem Film)

AT: Minderjährig, Die Minderjährigen
Premiere: 19 June 1951
P: Savoy-Film
D + S: Harald Röbbeling
C: Walter Partsch
A: Maria Eis, Johanna
Matz, Inge Novak

**Das gestohlene Jahr / Stolen
Year** (Melodrama)
Premiere: 4 January 1951
P: Austrian-West German co-
production: Ring-Film (Vienna),
Kammerspiel-Film (Hamburg)
D: Wilfried Frass
S: Walter von Hollander, Wilfried Frass
C: Carl Kurzmayer
AD: Theo Zwierski
M: Alfred Uhl
A: Oskar Werner, Elisabeth
Höbarth, Ewald Balser

**Das Herz einer Frau / Heart
of a Woman** (Comedy)
Premiere: 17 August 1951
P: Nova-Filmproduktion (Vienna),
Wien-Film (Vienna)
D: Georg Jacoby
S: Johannes Mario Simmel,
Friedrich Schreyvogel
C: Hanns König, Viktor Meihsl
AD: Hans Rouc, Julius von Borsody
M: Nico Dostal
A: Marianne Schönauer, Stefan
Skodler, Kurti Baumgartner

**Das Tor zum Frieden / Gateway to
Peace** (Historical Costume Film)
Premiere: 19 March 1951
P: Lambach-Film (Lambach,
Upper Austria)
D: Wolfgang Liebeneiner
S: Leopoldine Kytka
C: Günther Anders, Willi Sohm
AD: Friedrich Jüptner-Jonstorff
A: Paul Hartmann, Hilde
Krahl, Vilma Degischer

Der alte Sünder / The Old Sinner
(Historical Costume Film)
Premiere: 19 March 1951
P: Schönbrunn-Film (Vienna)

D: Franz Antel
S: Franz Antel, Martin Costa
C: Hans Theyer
AD: Felix Smetana
M: Hans Lang
A: Paul Hörbiger, Maria
   Andergast, Johanna Matz

**Der blaue Stern des Südens / The
Blue Star of the South** (Comedy)
Premiere: 22 December 1951
P: Vindobona-Film (Vienna)
D: Wolfgang Liebeneiner
S: Heinrich Rumpff, Theodor Ottawa
C: Günther Anders
AD: Ernst H. Albrecht
M: Franz Grothe, Hans-
   Martin Majewski
A: Viktor de Kowa, Gretl
   Schörg, Gustav Knuth

**Der fidele Bauer / The Merry
Farmer** (Musical)
Premiere: 21 September 1951
P: Berna-Film (Vienna),
   Donau-Film (Vienna)
D: Georg Marischka
S: Hubert Marischka,
   Rudolf Österreicher
C: Hans Schneeberger
AD: Gustav Abel
M: Leo Fall
A: Paul Hörbiger, Erich Auer,
   Marianne Wischmann

**Der Fünf-Minuten-Vater / Father
for Five Minutes** (Comedy)
Premiere: 18 May 1951
P: Pilsner-Film (Kufstein)
D: J.A. Hübler-Kahla
S: Karl Fischer
C: Hans Theyer
AD: Otto Pischinger
M: Frank Filip
A: Karl Fischer, Fritz Eckhardt,
   Dagny Servaes

**Der Himmel sagt nein / Heaven
Says No** (Melodrama)
AT: Der schweigende Mund
Premiere: 30 November 1951
P: Excelsior-Film (Vienna)

D: Karl Hartl
S: Karl Hartl, Hugo Maria Kritz
C: Oskar Schnirch
AD: Friedrich Jüptner-Jonstorff
M: Anton Profes
A: Oskar Homolka, Gisela
   Uhlen, Curd Jürgens

**Der Loibnerbauer / The Loibner
Farmer** (*Heimatfilm*)
Premiere: 1951 (exact date unknown)
P: Austrian-West German co-
   production: Wifa-Filmproduktion
   (Linz), Marc Roland-
   Filmproduktion (Munich)
D: Peter Baldauf
S: Eberhard Frowein, Carl
   Emil Watzinger (novel)
C: Hans Jura, Fritz Reisinger
A: Hans Franz Pokorny, Trude
   Derntl-Pichler, Herta Scharizer

**Der Teufel führt Regie / The
Devil Directs** (Drama)
AT: Dämonische Liebe
Premiere: 27 April 1951
P: Austrian-West German co-
   production: Helios-Film
   (Vienna), HMK-Film (Munich)
D: Kurt Meisel
S: Karl Peter Gillmann, Fred Andreas
C: Helmuth Fischer-Ashley
AD: Robert Herlth, Willi Schatz
M: Friedrich Meyer
A: Margot Hielscher, Paul
   Hörbiger, Kurt Meisel

**Der Weibsteufel / A Devil of
a Woman** (*Heimatfilm*)
Premiere: 28 September 1951
P: Styria-Film (Vienna)
D + S: Wolfgang Liebeneiner
C: Günther Anders, Hannes Staudinger
M: Heinz Sandauer
A: Hilde Krahl, Kurt Heintel,
   Bruno Hübner

**Eva erbt das Paradies / Eva Inherits
Paradise** (Tourist Film)
Premiere: 21 September 1951
P: Alpenländische Filmgesellschaft
   (Vienna/Linz)

D: Franz Antel
S: Franz Antel, Kurt Maix,
  Gunther Philipp
C: Hans Theyer
AD: Sepp Rothauer
M: Hans Lang
A: Maria Andergast, Josef Meinrad,
  Susi Nicoletti, Gunther Philipp

Fräulein Bimbi / Miss Bimbi (Comedy)
AT: Das unmögliche Mädchen
Premiere: 9 November 1951
P: Helios-Film (Vienna)
D: Akos von Ratony
S: Werner Riedel
C: Albert Benitz
AD: Fritz Mögle
M: Michael Jary
A: Hans Holt, Hannelore
  Schroth, Paul Kemp

**Frühling auf dem Eis / Spring
  on Ice** (Musical)
Premiere: 10 February 1951
P: Nova-Filmproduktion
  (Vienna), Wien-Film
D: Georg Jacoby
S: Johannes Mario Simmel
C: Hanns König, Viktor Meihsl
AD: Julius von Borsody, Hans Rouc
M: Nico Dostal, Hanns Elin
A: Ewa Pawlik, Hertha Mayen,
  Hans Holt, Oskar Sima

**Gangsterpremiere / Gangster
  Premiere** (Comedy)
AT: So ein Theater
Premiere: 26 October 1951
P: Alpenfilm Austria (Graz)
D: Curd Jürgens
S: Curd Jürgens, Franz Gribitz
C: Hans Schneeberger
AD: Fritz Maurischat, Isabella
  Schlichting, Paul Markwitz,
  Werner Schlichting
M: Willi Mattes
A: Grethe Weiser, Bruni
  Löbl, Curd Jürgens

**Gesetz ohne Gnade / Law
  without Mercy** (*Heimatfilm*)
AT: Gipfelkreuz

Premiere: 17 February 1951
P: Austrian-West German co-
  production: Lichtfilm (Salzburg),
  Aafa-Filmproduktion (Wiesbaden)
D: Harald Reinl
S: Karl Loven
C: Josef Plesner, Franz Trager,
  Gerhard Deutschmann
M: Giuseppe Becce
A: Karl Loven, Harriet Geßner,
  Rudolf Schatzberg

**Hochzeit im Heu / Wedding
  in the Hay** (Comedy)
Premiere: 23 January 1951
P: Austrian-West German co-
  production: Schönbrunn-Film
  (Vienna), Cordial-Film (Berlin)
D: Arthur Maria Rabenalt
S: Hans Gustl Kernmayr, Alexander Lix
C: Hans Theyer
AD: Felix Smetana
M: Albert Fischer
A: Oskar Sima, Inge Egger, Kurt Seifert

Maria Theresia / Maria Theresia
  (Historical Costume Film)
Premiere: 19 December 1951
P: Paula-Wessely-Film (Vienna)
D: Emile Edwin Reinert
S: Paul H. Rameau
C: Friedl Behn-Grund
AD: Werner Schlichting
M: Alois Melichar, Joseph Haydn
A: Paul Wessely, Fred Liewehr,
  Attila Hörbiger

**Ruf aus dem Äther / Call
  over the Air** (Drama)
AT: Ein Wunder unserer Tage,
  Piraten der Berge
Premiere: 2 February 1951
D: G.W. Pabst, Georg C. Klaren
P: G.W. Pabst
S: Kurt Heuser
C: Willi Sohm
AD: Friedrich Jüptner-Jonstorff
M: Roland Kovač
A: Oskar Werner, Otto
  Wögerer, Heinz Moog

**Schwindel im Dreivierteltakt /
   Swindle in 3/4 Time** (Comedy)
Premiere: 28 September 1951
P: Ring-Film (Vienna)
D: Alexander von Slatinay
S: Christl Räntz
C: Carl Kurzmayer
M: Heinz Sandauer
A: Lotte Lang, Anni Korin, Hans
   Olden, Fritz Immhof

Stadtpark / City Park (Comedy)
AT: Kleiner Peter, grosse Sorgen
Premiere: 13 March 1951
P: Bera-Film (Vienna),
   Donau-Film (Vienna)
D: Hubert Marischka
S: Hubert Marischka, Frank Filip
C: Walter Riml
AD: Otto Pischinger
M: Frank Filip
A: Annie Rosar, Peter Czejke, Erik Frey

**Verklungenes Wien / Vienna
   as it Used to Be** (Historical
   Costume Film)
Premiere: 17 August 1951
P: Erma-Film (Vienna)
D + S: Ernst Marischka
C: Hans Schneeberger, Sepp Ketterer
AD: Friedrich Jüptner-Jonstorff
M: Bruno Uher, Ralph Benatzky
A: Paul Hörbiger, Wolf Albach-Retty,
   Marianne Schönauer, Fritz Imhoff

Wien tanzt / Vienna Dances
   (Historical Costume Film)
AT: Wiener Walzer
Premiere: 17 June 1951
P: Austrian-Liechtenstein co-
   production: Vindobona-Film
   (Vienna), Cordial-Film (Vaduz)
D: Emile Edwin Reinert
S: Jacques Companéez, Emile Edwin
   Reinert, Hans Gustl Kernmayr (idea)
C: Günther Anders, Hannes Staudinger
AD: Otto Niedermoser
M: Willy Schmidt-Gentner
A: Adolf Wohlbrück, Marte
   Harell, Lilly Stepanek

**Zwei in einem Auto / Two in
   a Car** (Tourist Film)

Premiere: 21 December 1951
P: Erma-Film (Vienna)
D +S: Ernst Marischka
C: Sepp Ketterer
AD: Friedrich Jüptner-Jonstorff
M: Hans Lang
A: Wolf-Albach Retty, Johanna
   Matz, Hans Moser

1952

1. April 2000 / April 1, 2000 (Comedy)
Premiere: 19 November 1952
P: Wien-Film (Vienna) sponsored
   by the Austrian government
D: Wolfgang Liebeneiner
S: Ernst Marbö, Rudolf Brunngraber
C: Fritz Arno Wagner, Sepp Ketterer
AD: Otto Niedermoser
M: Alois Melichar
A: Hilde Krahl, Josef Meinrad,
   Judith Holzmeister

**Abenteuer in Wien / Stolen
   Identity** (Film)
AT: Gefährliches Abenteuer
Premiere: 19 September 1952
P: Austrian-US co-production:
   Schönbrunn-Film (Vienna),
   Transglobe-Film (New York)
D: Emile Edwin Reinert
S: Franz Tassié, Michael Kehlmann
C: Helmuth Fischer-Ashley
AD: Friedrich Jüptner-
   Jonstorff, Fritz Mögle
A: Gustav Fröhlich, Cornell
   Borchers, Franz Lederer

**Das letzte Aufgebot / The Last
   Reserves** (Historical Costume Film)
AT: Der Bauernrebell
Premiere: 16 January 1952
P: Listo-Film (Vienna) D: Alfred Lehner
D: Alfred Lehner
C: Fritz von Friedl
A: Eduard Köck, Marianne Schönauer,
   Kurt Heintel, Leopold Rudolf

**Der Mann in der Wanne / The Man
   in the Bath Tub** (Comedy)
Premiere: 14 August 1952
P: Neusser-Wien (Vienna)
D: Franz Antel

S: Franz Antel, Fritz Koselka, Lilian
  Belmont, Gunter Philipp
C: Hans Schneeberger
AD: Friedrich Jüptner-Jonstorff
M: Hans Lang
A: Gunther Philipp, Wolf Albach
  Retty, Axel von Ambesser,
  Maria Andergast

Der Obersteiger / The Mine Foreman
  (Historical Costume Film)
Premiere: 26 December 1952
P: Patria-Filmkunst (Graz)
D: Franz Antel
S: Franz Antel, Friedrich
  Schreyvogel, Jutta Bornemann
C: Hans Theyer
AD: Werner Schlichting,
  Isabella Schlichting
M: Hans Lang
A: Hans Holt, Gunther Philipp, Josefine
  Kipper, Wolf-Albach Retty

**Der Sonnblick ruft / The
  Sonnblick Calls** (*Heimatfilm*)
Premiere: 8 April 1952
P: Austrian-West German co-
  production: Telos-Film (Vienna),
  Lifa-Filmgesellschaft (Munich)
D: Eberhard Frowein
S: Eberhard Frowein, Josef Prack
C: Carl Kurzmayer, Fritz Blaschko
AD: Gustav Abel
M: Heinz Sandauer
A: Eduard Köck, Marianne
  Wischmann, Fritz Friedl

**Die Wirtin von Maria Wörth / The
  Landlady of Maria Wörth** (Comedy)
AT: Die Wirtin vom Wörthersee
Premiere: 5 December 1952
P: Donau-Film (Vienna)
D: Eduard von Borsody
S: Eduard von Borsody, Fritz
  Böttger, Joachim Wedekind,
  Walter Forster (idea)
C: Walter Riml
AD: Gustav Abel
M: Hans Lang
A: Maria Andergast, Isa
  Günther, Jutta Günther

**Frühlingsstimmen / Voices
  of Spring** (Musical)
Premiere: 21 February 1952
P: Film Dillenz-Filmproduktion
  (Vienna)
D: Hans Thimig
S: Josef Kobliha, Max Mel
C: Herbert Thallmayer
M: Alfred Uhl
A: Hans Jaray, Paul Hörbiger,
  Senta Wengraf

**Hallo Dienstmann / Hello
  Porter** (Comedy)
Premiere: 18 January 1952
P: Schönbrunn-Film (Vienna)
D: Franz Antel
S: Rudolf Österreicher, Lilian
  Belmont, Paul Hörbiger (idea)
C: Hans H. Theyer
AD: Felix Smetana
M: Hans Lang
A: Paul Hörbiger, Maria
  Andergast, Hans Moser,
  Harry Fuß, Waltraud Haas

Hannerl / Hannerl (Comedy)
AT: Ich tanze mit dir in den
  Himmel hinein
Premiere: 22 December 1952
P: Wien-Film (Vienna)
D + S: Ernst Marischka
C: Sepp Ketterer
AD: Friedrich Jüptner-Jonstorff
M: Anton Profes, Franz Grothe,
  Friedrich Schröder, Willy
  Schmidt-Gentner
A: Johanna Matz, Paul Hörbiger,
  Adrian Hoven, Adrienne Gessner,
  Richard Romanowsky

**Ich hab mich so an dich gewöhnt
  / I Got Used to You** (Comedy)
AT: Geschiedenes Fräulein
Premiere: 14 November 1952
P: Donau-Film (Vienna)
D: Eduard von Borsody
S: Eduard von Borsody,
  Aldo von Pinelli
C: Günther Anders
AD: Julius von Borsody

M: Ludwig Schmidseder,
Wolfgang Russ-Bovelino
A: Inge Egger, O.W. Fischer,
Robert Lindner

**Ideale Frau gesucht / Looking for
the Ideal Woman** (Comedy)
Premiere: 30 September 1952
P: Schönbrunn-Film (Vienna),
Cziffra-Film (Vienna)
D: Franz Antel
S: Franz Antel, Jutta Bornemann,
Franz Beron (idea)
C: Hans Theyer
AD: Felix Smetana
M: Johannes Fehring, Willi Berking,
Werner Müller, Gerhard Froböss
A: Inge Egger, Wolf Albach-
Retty, Jeanette Schultze

**Knall und Fall als Hochstapler / Knall
and Fall as Impostors** (Comedy)
Premiere: 21 November 1952
P: Austrian-West German co-
production: Wiener Mundus-Film
(Vienna), Arena-Film (Munich)
D: Hubert Marischka
S: Walter Forster, Jo Hans Rösler
C: Walter Tuch, Walter Meichsel
AD: Friedrich Jüptner-Jonstorff
M: Hans Lang
A: Hans Richter, Rudolf
Carl, Waltraut Haas

**Nacht am Mont Blanc / Night on the
Mont Blanc** (Mountain Film)
AT: Weiße Hölle am Mont Blanc
Premiere: 25 January 1952
P: Austrian-West German
co-production: Hope-Film
(Vienna), Hope-Film Gebr.
Hoffmann (Munich)
D + S: Harald Reinl
C: Walter Riml
M: Giuseppe Becce
A: Dagmar Rom, Baldur von
Hohenbalken, Dietmar Schönherr

**Saison in Salzburg / Season
in Salzburg** (Comedy)
Premiere: 23 October 1952
P: Erma-Film (Vienna),
Wien-Film (Vienna)

D + S: Ernst Marischka
C: Sepp Ketterer
AD: Friedrich Jüptner-Jonstorff
M: Fred Raymond, Willy
Schmidt-Gentner
A: Johanna Matz, Adrian
Hoven, Walter Müller

**Schäm dich, Brigitte! / Shame
on you, Brigitte!** (Comedy)
AT: Wir werden das Kind
schon schaukeln
Premiere: 11 October 1952
P: Styria-Film (Vienna)
D: E.W. Emo
S: E.W. Emo, Karl Farkas,
Hugo Maria Kritz
C: Oskar Schnirch
AD: Gustav Abel
M: Heinz Sandauer
A: Heinz Rühmann, Theo
Lingen, Hans Moser

Seesterne / Starfish (Musical)
Premiere: 23 December 1952
P: Revue Nova-Filmproduktion
(Vienna), Wien-Film (Vienna)
D: J.A. Hübler-Kahla
S: Dr. Brand
C: Hans König, Viktor Meihsl
AD: Otto Pischinger
M: Nico Dostal
A: Eva Kerbler, Franz
Meßner, Edith Prager

**Symphonie Wien / Vienna
Symphony** (Docudrama)
Premiere: 25 June 1952
P: Schönbrunn-Film (Vienna)
D: Albert Quendler
S: Albert Quendler, Franz Theodor
Csokor, Felix Hubalek, Elio Carniel
C: Elio Carniel
A: Wilma Lipp, Raoul Aslan,
Ernst Deutsch

**Tanz ins Glück / Dance into
Happiness** (Musical)
Premiere: 27 February 1952
P: Wiener Mundus-Film (Vienna)
D: Alfred Stöger
S: Fritz Koselka, Lilian Belmont
C: Kurt Schulz, Herbert Geier

AD: Gabriel Pellon, Peter Schlewski
M: Michael Jary, Robert Stolz
A: Johannes Heesters, Waltraut
   Haas, Ursula Lingen

**Valentins Sündenfall / The Fall
   of Valentin** (Comedy)
Premiere: 4 January 1952
P: Schönbrunn-Film (Vienna)
D: Paul Löwinger
S: Gretl Löwinger, Karl
   Leitner, August Rieger
C: Carl Kurzmayer
AD: Gustav Abel
M: Gerhard Bronner
A: Josef Egger, Sepp Rist,
   Paul Löwinger

**Verlorene Melodie / The Lost
   Melody** (Comedy)
Premiere: 12 August 1952
P: Nova-Filmproduktion (Vienna)
D: Eduard von Borsody
S: Eduard von Borsody,
   Johannes Mario Simmel
C: Helmuth Fischer-Ashley
M: Willy Schmidt-Gentner
A: Robert Lindner, Elfie
   Mayerhofer, Annie Rosar

Wienerinnen / Viennese Women
   (Social Problem Film)
AT: Wienerinnen – Schrei nach
   Liebe, Wienerinnen im
   Schatten der Grossstadt
Premiere: 26 February 1952
P: Schönbrunn-Film (Vienna),
   Rex-Film (Vienna)
D: Kurt Steinwendner
S: Kurt Steinwendner
C: Elio Carniel, Walter Partsch
M: Paul Kont
A: Elisabeth Stemberger, Karlheinz
   Böhm, Kurt Jaggberg

1953

**Abenteuer im Schloss / Adventures
   in the Castle** (Musical)
Premiere: 17 February 1953
P: Nova-Filmproduktion (Vienna),
   Wien-Film (Vienna)
D: Rudolf Steinböck

S: Rudolf Örtel
C: Willi Sohm
AD: Hans Zehetner
M: Karl von Pauspertl
A: Doris Kirchner, Gerhard
   Riedmann, Herta Staal

**Auf der grünen Wiese / On the
   Green Meadow** (Comedy)
Premiere: 15 December 1953
P: Wiener-Mundus Film (Vienna),
   Wien-Film (Vienna)
D: Fritz Böttger
S: Hanns H. Fischer, Ulrich Bettac
C: Sepp Ketterer
AD: Friedrich Jüptner-Jonstorff
M: Frank Fox, Willi Meisel
A: Hannelore Bollmann, Walter
   Müller, Hans Holt, Erik Frey

**Der Feldherrnhügel / Grandstand
   for General Staff** (Historical
   Costume Film)
Premiere: 13 October 1953
P: Vindobona-Film (Vienna)
D: Ernst Marischka
S: Ernst Marischka, Alexander Roda-
   Roda (novel), Carl Rössler (play)
C: Sepp Ketterer
AD: Friedrich Jüptner-Jonstorff
M: Anton Profes
A: Annemarie Düringer, Adrienne
   Gessner, Hans Holt, Susi Nicoletti,
   Paul Hörbiger, Gretl Schörg

Der Verschwender / The Spendthrift
   (Historical Costume Film)
Premiere: 9 February 1953
P: Dillenz-Filmproduktion (Vienna)
D: Leopold Hainisch
C: Oskar Schnirch
AD: Gustav Abel
M: Alfred Uhl
A: Attila Hörbiger, Maria
   Andergast, Josef Meinrad

**Der Wildschütz / The
   Poacher** (*Heimatfilm*)
AT: Die grosse Schuld, Die große
   Schuld des Berghofbauern
Premiere: 6 October 1953 (Germany,
   date of Austrian premiere unknown)

P: Austrian-West German co-
production: Alba-Film (Munich),
Listo-Film (Vienna)
D: Alfred Lehner
S: Alfred Lehner, Franz Grohmann,
Hanns Marschall, Jürgen von Alten
C: Karl Kurzmayer
AD: Nino Borghi
A: Renate Mannhardt, Kurt
Heintel, Marianne Schönauer

Die Fiakermilli / Fiakermilli
(Historical Costume Film)
Premiere: 20 January 1953
P: Schönbrunn-Film (Vienna)
D: Arthur Maria Rabenalt
S: Martin Costa, Arthur Maria Rabenalt
C: Elio Carniel
AD: Felix Smetana
M: Hans Lang
A: Gretl Schörg, Paul Hörbiger,
Karl Schönböck, Fritz Immhof

**Die fünf Karnickel / The Five
Bunnies** (Comedy)
AT: Im Krug zum grünen Kranze
Premiere: 29 December 1953
P: Delta-Film (Vienna)
D: Kurt Steinwendner, Paul Löwinger
S: Gretl Löwinger, Kurt Steinwendner
C: Carl Kurzmayer
AD: Friedrich Jüptner-Jonstorff
M: Frank Filip
A: Ingrid Lutz, Rudolf Carl,
Lucie Englisch

**Die Regimentstochter /
Daughter of the Regiment**
(Historical Costume Film)
Premiere: 25 September 1953
P: Nova-Film (Vienna)
D: Georg C. Klaren, Günther Haenel
S: Georg C. Klaren, Margarete Göbel
C: Willi Sohm
AD: Hans Zehetner, Leopold
Metzenbauer
M: Karl von Pauspertl
A: Aglaja Schmid, Robert Lindner,
Hermann Erhardt, Gusti Wolf

**Die Todesarena / Arena of
Death** (Crime Film)

Premiere: 21 August 1953
P: Austrian-West German co-
production: Listo-Film (Vienna),
Bristol-Film Heinz Wolff (Munich)
D: Kurt Meisel
S: Hans Herbert, Raimund Warta
C: Elio Carniel
AD: Nino Borghi
A: Richard Häussler, Katharina
Mayberg, Friedl Hardt, Bert
Fortell, Elfe Gerhart, Fritz Imhoff

**Du bist die Welt für mich / The
Richard Tauber Story** (Drama)
Premiere: 27 October 1953
P: Erma-Film (Vienna)
D + S: Ernst Marischka
C: Sepp Ketterer
AD: Alexander Sawczynski,
Friedrich Jüptner-Jonstorff
M: Anton Profes, Richard Tauber
A: Rudolf Schock, Annemarie
Düringer, Richard Romanofsky

**Eine Nacht in Venedig / A
Night in Venice** (Musical)
AT: Komm in die Gondel
Premiere: 14 August 1953
P: Nova-Film (Vienna)
D: Georg Wildhagen
S: Rudolf Österreicher
C: Walter Tuch
AD: Eduard Stolba, Walter Schmiedl
M: Nico Dostal
A: Jeanette Schultze, Marianne
Schönauer, Peter Pasetti

**Einmal keine Sorgen haben
/ To Be without Worries**
(Historical Costume Film)
AT: Einen Jux will er sich machen
Premiere: 22 May 1953
P: Austrian-West German co-
production: Carlton-Film (Vienna),
Carlton-Film (Munich)
D: Georg Marischka
S: Hans Weigel, Georg Marischka
C: Friedl Behn-Grund
AD: Friedrich Jüptner-Jonstorff,
Alexander Sawczynski
M: Oscar Straus, Bruno Uher

A: Walter Müller, Hans Moser,
Fritz Imhoff, Nadja Tiller

Flucht ins Schilf / Brutality (Drama)
Premiere: 25 September 1953
P: Hoela-Film (Vienna)
D: Kurt Steinwendner
S: Kurt Steinwendner
C: Walter Partsch
M: Paul Kont
A: Heinz Altringen, Kurt
Jaggberg, Ilka Windisch

Franz Schubert / Franz Schubert
(Historical Costume Film)
AT: Franz Schubert – Ein unvollendetes
Leben, Franz Schubert – ein
Leben in zwei Sätzen
Premiere: 20 November 1953
P: Beta-Film (Vienna)
D: Walter Kolm-Veltée
S: Carl Merz, Walter Kolm-Veltée
C: Hanns König, Karl Kirchner
AD: Hans Zehetner, Leopold
Metzenbauer
A: Heinrich Schweiger, Aglaja Schmid,
Fritz Imhoff, Hans Thimig

**Fräulein Casanova / Miss
Casanova** (Comedy)
Premiere: 13 February 1953
P: Wiener-Mundus Film (Vienna)
D: E.W. Emo
S: Karl Hans Leiter
C: Fritz Arno Wagner, Karl Löb
AD: Fritz Mögle
M: Peter Igelhoff
A: Angelika Hauff, Gertrud
Kückelmann, Loni Heuser,
Paul Henckels, Josef
Meinrad, Walter Giller

**Geh mach dein Fensterl auf / Open
your Window** (Comedy)
Premiere: 1 December 1953
P: Austrian-West German
co-production: Bergland-
Film (Linz), Süddeutsche-
Filmproduktion (Munich)
D + S: Anton Kutter
AD: Heinz Ockermüller, Sepp Rothauer
M: Herbert Jarczyk

A: Peter Pasetti, Hans Olden,
Gunther Philipp, Elisabeth
Stemberger, Marianne Koch

**Hab ich nur deine Liebe / If
I Only Have your Love**
(Historical Costume Film)
Premiere: 15 December 1953
P: ÖFA Österreichische-
Filmproduktion (Vienna)
D: Eduard von Borsody
C: Bruno Mondi
AD: Hans Rouc, Julius von Borsody
M: Rudolf Kattnigg
A: Johannes Heesters, Margit
Saad, Egon von Jordan, Friedl
Hardt, Gretl Schörg

**Hereinspaziert / Step Right
Up!** (Comedy)
AT: Praterherzen, Tingeltangel,
Das Leben ist stärker
Premiere: 16 January 1953
P: ÖFA Österreichische
Filmgesellschaft (Vienna),
Schönnbrunn-Film (Vienna)
D: Paul Verhoeven
S: August Rieger
C: Elio Carniel
AD: Friedrich Jüptner-Jonstorff
M: Hans-Otto Borgmann
A: Gardy Granass, Curd Jürgens,
Christl Mardayn, Hans
Putz, Paul Verhoeven

**Hoch vom Dachstein / Dark Clouds
over the Dachstein** (*Heimatfilm*)
AT: Wetterleuchten vom Dachstein,
Die Herrin vom Salzerhof
Premiere: 20 March 1953
P: Austrian-West German
co-production: Telos-Film
(Vienna), Süddeutsche-
Filmproduktion (Munich)
D + S: Anton Kutter
C: Sepp Kirzeder, Gustav Weiß
M: Herbert Jarczyk
A: Gisela Fackeldey, Pero Alexander,
Eduard Köck, Marianne Koch

**Ich und meine Frau / Me and
my Wife** (Comedy)

Premiere: 28 August 1953
P: Paula-Wessely-Film (Vienna)
D: Eduard von Borsody
S: Eduard von Borsody, Friedrich
Schreyvogl, Karl Farkas
C: Günther Anders, Hans Staudinger
AD: Felix Smetana
M: Gerhard Bronner
A: Attila Hörbiger, Paula Wessely,
Isa Günther, Jutta Günther, Nicole
Heesters, Jane Tilden, Fritz Schulz

**Irene in Nöten / Irene in
Trouble** (Comedy)
AT: Wirbel um Irene
Premiere: 14 August 1953
P: Austrian-Yugoslav co-production:
Helios-Film (Vienna),
Triglav-Film (Zagreb)
D: E.W. Emo
S: Ernst Waldbrunn, Lilian Belmont
C: Oskar Schnirch
AD: Fritz Mögle
A: Bruni Löbel, Friedl Czepa,
Walter Giller, Hans Olden,
Susi Nicoletti, Helli Servi

Kaiserwalzer / The Emperor's Waltz
(Historical Costume Film)
Premiere: 10 September 1953
P: Neusser-Wien (Vienna)
D: Franz Antel
S: Franz Antel, Jutta
Bornemann, Gunther Philipp,
Friedrich Schreyvogl
C: Hans Heinz Theyer
AD: Sepp Rothauer, Heinz Ockermüller
M: Hans Lang
A: Rudolf Prack, Winnie Markus,
Gunther Philipp, Hans Holt

**Knall und Fall als Detektive / Knall
and Fall as Detectives** (Comedy)
Premiere: 4 September 1953
P: Austrian-West German co-
production: Wiener Mundus-Film
(Vienna), Arena-Film (Munich)
D: Hans Heinrich
C: Bruno Stephan
AD: Rolf Zehetbauer
M: Bert Grund, Hans Lang

A: Rudolf Carl, Hans Richter,
Fritz Wagner

Lavendel / Lavender (Comedy)
AT: Eine Ehe ohne Moral, Lavendel –
eine ganz unmoralische Geschichte
Premiere: 21 August 1953
P: Austrian-West German co-
production: Schönbrunn-Film
(Vienna), Rex-Film Bloemer (Berlin)
D: Arthur Maria Rabenalt
S: Arthur Maria Rabenalt, Fritz Böttger
C: Elio Carniel
AD: Felix Smetana
M: Hans Hagen
A: Gretl Schörg, Karl Schönböck,
Hans Holt, Erni Mangold, Hans
Putz, Elisabeth Stemberger

**Magdalena Percht / Magdalena
Percht** (*Heimatfilm*)
AT: Dein Herz ist meine Heimat
Premiere: 13 November 1953 (Germany,
date of Austrian premiere unknown)
P: Austrian-West German co-
production: Bela-Film (Vienna),
Primus-Film (Geiselgasteig)
D: Richard Häussler
S: Thea von Harbou
C: Walter Tuch
AD: Eduard Stolba, Walter Schmiedl
M: Anton Profes, O. Benedikt
A: Inge Egger, Erwin Strahl,
Viktor Staal, Elisabeth
Markus, Heinrich Gretler

**Pünktchen und Anton / Anna
Louise and Anton** (Comedy)
Premiere: 11 September 1953
P: Austrian-West German co-
production: Rhombus-Film
(Munich), Ring-Film (Vienna)
D: Thomas Engel
S: Erich Kästner, Maria Osten-
Sacken, Thomas Engel
C: Franz Weihmayr
AD: Friedrich Jüptner-Jonstorff
M: Heino Gaze, Herbert Trantow
A: Paul Klinger, Hertha Feiler,
Heidemarie Hatheyer, Sabine
Eggerth, Peter Feldt, Annie Rosar

1954

Bruder Martin / Brother Martin
(Historical Costume Film)
AT: Und der Himmel lacht dazu
Premiere: 11 October 1954
P: Neue Wiener-Filmproduktion
    (Vienna), Lux-Film (Vienna)
D: Axel von Ambesser
S: Erna Fentsch, Carl Costa (novel)
C: Sepp Ketterer
AD: Friedrich Jüptner-Jonstorff
M: Hans Lang
A: Paul Hörbiger, Marianne
    Koch, Gerhard Riedmann

Das Geheimnis der Venus / Secret
of the Venus (Docudrama)
AT: Spiegel der Schönheit
Premiere: 12 October 1954
P: Austrian-West German co-
    production: Schönnbrunn-Film
    (Vienna), Rex-Film (Munich)
D: August Rieger
S: August Rieger, Fritz Eckhardt
C: Anton Pucher, Walter Partsch
AD: Lorenz Withalm
M: Hans Hagen
A: Fritz Eckhardt, Lotte
    Lang, Rudolf Carl

Das Licht der Liebe / Light
of Love (Melodrama)
AT: Wenn du noch eine Mutter hast
Premiere: 3 September 1954
P: Paula-Wessely-
    Filmproduktion (Vienna)
D: Robert A. Stemmle
S: Gerhard Menzel, Robert A. Stemmle
C: Helmuth Fischer-Ashley
AD: Felix Smetana
M: Willy Schmidt-Gentner
A: Paula Wessely, Fritz Schulz,
    Waltraud Haas, Erich Auer,
    Heinrich Schweiger

Der erste Kuss / The First
Kiss (Comedy)
Premiere: 27 August 1954
P: Austrian-West German co-
    production: Donau-Film (Vienna),
    Melodie-Film (Berlin)

D: Erik Ode
S: Aldo von Pinelli, Juliane Kay
C: Richard Angst
AD: Gustav Abel
M: Peter Kreuder
A: Isa Günther, Jutta Günther,
    Erich Auer, Hans Nielsen,
    Adrienne Gessner

Der Komödiant von Wien / Girardi
(Historical Costume Film)
AT: Wiener Herzen
Premiere: 8 October 1954
P: Akkord-Film (Vienna)
D: Karl Paryla, Karl Stanzl
S: Theodor Ottawa, Karl
    Paryla, Karl Stanzl
C: Hannes Fuchs
M: Oskar Wagner
A: Karl Paryla, Christl Mardayn,
    Angelika Hauff, Marianne
    Schönauer, Alma Seidler

Der rote Prinz / The Red Prince
(Historical Costume Film)
AT: Das Geheimnis von Schloss Orth
Premiere: 12 March 1954 (Germany,
    date of Austrian premiere unknown)
P: Austrian-West German co-
    production: Patria-Filmkunst
    (Graz), Internationale Tonfilm-
    Produktion ITO (Munich)
D: Franz Antel, Hans Schott-Schöbinger
S: Aldo von Pinelli, Franz Antel
C: Oskar Schnirch, Klaus
    von Rautenfeld
AD: Eduard Stolba
M: Anton Profes
A: Inge Egger, Peter Pasetti, Richard
    Häussler, Rolf Wanka, Kurt Heintel

Der Weg in die Vergangenheit
/ Walking Back into the
Past (Melodrama)
Premiere: 28 December 1954
P: Paula-Wessely-
    Filmproduktion (Vienna)
D: Karl Hartl
S: Emil Burri, Johannes Mario Simmel
C: Konstantin Tschet
AD: Werner Schlichting
M: Willy Schmidt-Gentner

A: Paula Wessely, Willi
Forst, Willy Fritsch, Attila
Hörbiger, Josef Meinrad

**Die letzte Brücke - Poslednji Most /
The Last Bridge** (Anti-war Film)
Premiere: 6 May 1954
P: Austrian-Yugoslav co-
production: Cosmopol-Film
(Vienna), UFUS (Belgrad)
D: Helmut Käutner
S: Helmut Käutner, Norbert Kunze
C: Elio Carniel, Julius Jonak
AD: Otto Pischinger
M: Carl de Groof
A: Maria Schell, Bernhard Wicki,
Barbara Rütting, Carl Möhner

**Die Perle von Tokay / The
Pearl of Tokay** (Comedy)
Premiere: 26 February 1954
P: Donau-Film (Vienna)
D: Hubert Marischka
S: Hubert Marischka,
Rudolf Österreicher
C: Sepp Ketterer
AD: Friedrich Jüptner-Jonstorff
M: Frank Fox
A: Johanna Matz, Karl Schönböck,
Rudolf Carl, Paul Hörbiger,
Karl Hackenberg

**Echo der Berge / Echo of the
Mountains** (*Heimatfilm*)
AT: Der Förster vom Silberwald
Premiere: 25 November 1954
P: Rondo-Film (Vienna)
D: Alfons Stummer
S: Friedrich Schreyvogel, Alfons
Stummer, Alfred Solm
C: Sepp Ketterer, Walter Tuch
A: Rudolf Lenz, Anita Gutwell, Erik
Frey, Lotte Ledl, Karl Ehmann

**Ein tolles Früchtchen / A
Great Rascal** (Comedy)
Premiere: 22 January 1954
P: Styria-Film (Vienna)
D: Franz Antel
S: Karl Farkas, Fritz Böttger (idea)
C: Hans Heinz Theyer
AD: Sepp Rothauer

M: Erwin Halletz
A: Ingrid Pan, Hans Holt, Fritz Schulz,
Jane Tilden, Erika von Thellmann

**Glück ins Haus / A House
Full of Love** (Comedy)
AT: Ein Haus voll Liebe
Premiere: 10 September 1954
P: Austrian-West German co-
production: Wiener Mundus-Film
(Vienna), Bristol-Film (Munich)
D: Hans Schweikart
S: Egon Eis, Hans Schweikart
C: Willy Goldberger
AD: Friedrich Jüptner-Jonstorff
M: Werner Richard Heymann
A: Gertrud Kückelmann, Michael
Cramer, Erni Mangold

**Glück muss man haben / Strike
it Lucky** (Comedy)
AT: Drei, von denen man spricht
Premiere: 5 January 1954
P: Neue Wiener Filmproduktion
(Vienna), Lux-Film (Vienna)
D: Axel von Ambesser
S: Axel von Ambesser
C: Georg Krause
AD: Julius von Borsody
M: Peter Igelhoff, Erich Meder
A: Wolfgang Lukschy, Paul Kemp,
Theodor Danegger, Bruni Löbel,
Paul Hörbiger, Axel von Ambesser

**Hochstaplerin der Liebe / Marriage
Impostor** (Melodrama)
Premiere: 12 November 1954
P: Helios-Film (Vienna)
D: Hans H. König
S: Werner Eplinius, Janne Furch
C: Kurt Hasse
AD: Otto Pischinger, Herta Pischinger
M: Theo Nordhaus
A: Hilde Krahl, Viktor de Kowa,
Alexander Golling, Hans Nielsen

Kaisermanöver / Kaiser Manoeuvres
(Historical Costume Film)
Premiere: 7 September 1954
P: Hope-Film (Vienna),
Neusser-Film (Vienna)
D: Franz Antel

S: Jutta Bornemann, Karl Hans
   Leiter, Gunther Philipp
C: Georg Bruckbauer
AD: Julius von Borsody, Hans Rouc
M: Hans Lang
A: Rudolf Prack, Winnie Markus,
   Hans Moser, Hannelore Bollmann,
   Gunther Philipp, Walter Müller

**König der Manege / King of the
Circus Ring** (Comedy)
Premiere: 24 September 1954
P: Erma-Film (Vienna)
D + S: Ernst Marischka
C: Hans Schneeberger
AD: Friedrich Jüptner-Jonstorff
M: Anton Profes
A: Rudolf Schock, Germaine
   Damar, Fritz Imhoff, Elma
   Karlowa, Walter Müller, Hans
   Richter, Helmut Qualtinger

Maxie / Maxie (Comedy)
Premiere: 14 October 1954 (Germany,
   date of Austrian premiere unknown)
P: Ring-Film (Vienna)
D: Eduard von Borsody
S: Eduard von Borsody, Karl
   Hans Leiter, Maria von der
   Osten-Sacken (idea)
C: Otto Baecker
AD: Julius von Borsody
M: Karl de Groof
A: Sabine Eggerth, Willy
   Fritsch, Cornell Borchers, Fita
   Benkhoff, Paul Henckels

**Mädchenjahre einer Königin /
Victoria in Dover** (Historical
Costume Film)
Premiere: 23 December 1954
P: Erma-Film (Vienna)
D + S: Ernst Marischka
C: Bruno Mondi
AD: Friedrich Jüptner-Jonstorff
M: Anton Profes
A: Romy Schneider, Adrian Hoven,
   Magda Schneider, Karl Ludwig Diehl

Pepi Columbus / Pepi Columbus
(Information Film)
Premiere: 17 December 1954

P: US Information Service (Vienna)
D: Ernst Häusserman
S: Friedrich Torberg
C: Hans Schneeberger
M: Hanns Elin
A: Josef Meinrad

**Unsterblicher Mozart / Eternal
Mozart** (Opera Film)
Premiere: 30 November 1954
P: Wiener-Mundus-Film (Vienna),
   Thalia-Film (Vienna)
D: Alfred Stöger, Oscar Fritz
   Schuh, Herbert Waniek
S: unknown
C: Sepp Ketterer
M: Rudolf Moralt
A: Vilma Lipp, Emmy Loose, Hilde
   Güden, Rudolf Christ, Peter Klein

**Verliebte Leute / People in
Love** (Tourist Film)
AT: Verliebter Sommer
Premiere: 31 December 1954
P: Neusser-Wien (Vienna)
D: Franz Antel
S: Herbert Reinecker, Hans-Karl
   Kubiak, Jutta Bornemann
C: Hans Heinz Theyer
AD: Sepp Rothauer
M: Lotar Olias
A: Rudolf Platte, Peter Alexander,
   Hannelore Bollmann, Peter Pasetti

**Wenn ich einmal der Herrgott
wär / If I Was God** (Comedy)
Premiere: 5 November 1954
P: Austrian-West German
   co-production: Bergland-
   Film (Linz), Süddeutsche-
   Filmproduktion (Munich)
D + S: Anton Kutter
C: Sepp Kirzeder
A: Hans Holt, Gisela Fackeldey, Jutta
   Bornemann, Gustl Gstettenbauer

1955

**An der schönen blauen Donau /
The Blue Danube** (Musical)
Premiere: 15 April 1955

P: ÖFA Österreichische
Filmgesellschaft (Vienna),
Schönbrunn-Film (Vienna)
D: Hans Schweikart
S: Peter Berneis, August Rieger, Jacques
Companéez, Theodor Ottawa (idea)
C: Sepp Ketterer
AD: Friedrich Jüptner-Jonstorff
M: Franz Grothe
A: Hardy Krüger, Nicole Besnard,
Paul Hörbiger, Renée Saint-Cyr

Bel-Ami / Bel Ami (Drama)
AT: Der Frauenheld von Paris
Premiere: 9 April 1955
P: Projektograph-Film Oskar
Glück (Vienna)
D: Louis Daquin
S: Louis Daquin, Vladimir Pozner,
Roger Vailland, Peter Loos
C: Nicolas Hayer, Viktor Meihsl
AD: Léon Barsacq, Leopold
Metzenbauer
M: Hanns Eisler, Theo Mackeben
A: Johannes Heesters,
Marianne Schönauer, Christl
Mardayn, Gretl Schörg

**Das Geheimnis einer Ärztin / The
Doctor's Secret** (Melodrama)
AT: Liebe am Scheideweg, Rauschgift
– das Schicksal einer Ärztin
Premiere: 12 August 1955
P: Austrian-West German co-
production: Schönbrunn-Film
(Vienna), Rex-Film (Berlin)
D: August Rieger, Karl Stanzl
S: August Rieger, Hans Fritz
Köllner, Karl Stanzl
C: Walter Partsch
AD: Friedrich Jüptner-Jonstorff
M: Carl Loubé
A: Hilde Krahl, Ewald Balser, Erik
Frey, Rudolf Carl, Hans Putz

**Das Lied der Hohen Tauern / The
Song of the Hohe Tauern** (Drama)
AT: Das Lied von Kaprun
Premiere: 27 January 1955
P: Austrian-West German
co-production: Bergland-

Film (Linz), Süddeutsche
Filmproduktion (Munich)
D + S: Anton Kutter
C: Gustav Weiss
AD: Sepp Rothauer
M: Willi Mattes
A: Albert Lieven, Eduard Köck,
Waltraut Haas, Gustl Stark-
Gstettenbaur, Ida Krottendorf

**Das Mädchen vom Pfarrhof / The Girl
from the Vicarage** (*Heimatfilm*)
Premiere: 29 September 1955
P: Sonor-Film (Vienna),
Zenith-Film (Vienna)
D: Alfred Lehner
S: Hans Schott-Schöbinger
C: Sepp Ketterer
AD: Gustav Abel
A: Erich Auer, Waltraud Haas,
Albert Rueprecht, Attila
Hörbiger, Helene Thimig

**Der Kongress tanzt / The Congress
Dances** (Historical Costume Film)
Premiere: 12 December 1955 (Germany),
13 January 1956 (Austria)
P: Cosmos-Neusser-Film (Vienna)
D: Franz Antel
S: Kurt Nachmann, Jutta Bornemann
C: Georg Bruckbauer
AD: Werner Schlichting,
Isabella Schlichting
M: Werner Richard Heymann,
Robert Gilbert
A: Johanna Matz, Rudolf Prack,
Gertrud Kückelmann, Karl
Schönböck, Marte Harell,
Hans Moser, Josef Meinrad

**Der letzte Akt / The Last
Ten Days** (Drama)
Premiere: 15 April 1955
P: Cosmopol-Film (Vienna)
D: G.W. Pabst
S: Fritz Habeck, Erich Maria Remarque
(draft), Michael A. Musmano (novel)
C: Günther Anders, Hans Staudinger
AD: Werner Schlichting,
Otto Pischinger
A: Albin Skoda, Oskar
Werner, Erik Frey

**Die Deutschmeister / The
Deutschmeister** (Historical
Costume Film)
Premiere: 21 September 1955
P: Erma-Film (Vienna)
D: Ernst Marischka
S: Ernst Marischka, Gustav Holm
C: Bruno Mondi
AD: Friedrich Jüptner-Jonstorff
M: Robert Stolz
A: Romy Schneider, Magda
  Schneider, Siegfried Breuer Jr.,
  Josef Meinrad, Hans Moser

**Die lieben Verwandten / The
Dear Relatives** (Comedy)
AT: Oh, diese lieben Verwandten
Premiere: 2 August 1955
P: Austrian-West German
  co-production: Bergland-
  Film (Linz), Süddeutsche
  Filmproduktion (Munich)
D: Joe Stöckel
S: Jochen Kuhlmey, Hans Holt (idea)
C: Walter Tuch
AD: Felix Smetana
M: Willi Mattes
A: Joe Stöckel, Joseph Offenbach, Paul
  Heidemann, Erika von Thellmann

**Die Sennerin von St. Kathrein
/ The Dairy Maid of St.
Kathrein** (*Heimatfilm*)
Premiere: 11 November 1955
P: ÖFA Österreichische
  Filmgesellschaft (Vienna),
  Schönnbrunn-Film (Vienna)
D: Herbert B. Fredersdorf
S: Theodor Ottawa
C: Sepp Riff, Walter Tuch
AD: Friedrich Jüptner-Jonstorff
M: Anton Karas
A: Anita Gutwell, Rudolf
  Lenz, Rudolf Carl

**Die Wirtin zur Goldenen
Krone / The Landlady of the
Golden Crown** (Comedy)
Premiere: 23 December 1955
P: Paula-Wessely-Film (Vienna)
D: Theo Lingen

S: Karl Farkas, Hugo M. Kritz,
  Otto Dürer (idea)
C: Sepp Ketterer, Rudolf Sandtner
AD: Julius von Borsody, Heinz
  Ockermüller, Felix Smetana
M: Hans Lang
A: Paula Wessely, Albert Rueprecht,
  Christiane Hörbiger, Fritz Schulz

Don Juan / Don Juan (Historical
Costume Film)
Premiere: 12 August 1955
P: Akkord-Film (Vienna)
D: Walter Kolm-Veltée
S: Alfred Uhl, Walter Kolm-
  Veltée, Ernest Henthaler
C: Hannes Fuchs, Willi Sohm
AD: Hans Zehetner
A: Cesare Danova, Hans von Borsody,
  Josef Meinrad, Marianne Schönauer

**Drei Männer im Schnee / Three
Men in the Snow** (Tourist Film)
Premiere: 30 June 1955
P: Ring-Film (Vienna)
D: Kurt Hoffmann
S: Erich Kästner
C: Richard Angst
AD: Werner Schlichting,
  Isabella Schlichting
M: Sándor Slatinay
A: Paul Dahlke, Günther Lüders,
  Claus Biederstaedt, Nicole
  Heesters, Margarete Haagen

**Du bist die Richtige / You Are
the Right One** (Comedy)
Premiere: 21 January 1955
P: Austrian-West German co-
  production: Donau-Film (Vienna),
  Melodie-Film (Berlin)
D: Erich Engel, Josef von
  Baky (completion)
S: Juliane Kay, St. John Ervine (play)
C: Oskar Schnirch
AD: Julius von Borsody
M: Wolfgang Russ-Bovelino, Heino
  Gaze, Aldo von Pinelli
A: Curd Jürgens, Antje Weisgerber,
  Elma Karlowa, Hans Holt

Dunja / Dunja (Historical
  Costume Film)
Premiere: 22 December 1955
P: Sascha-Film (Vienna)
D: Josef von Baky
S: Emil Burri, Johannes Mario
  Simmel, Gerhard Menzel,
  Alexander Puschkin (novel)
C: Günther Anders
AD: Fritz Maurischat
M: Alois Melichar
A: Eva Bartok, Karlheinz Böhm,
  Ivan Desny, Walter Richter

**Ehesanatorium / Marriage
  Sanitarium** (Comedy)
AT: Ja, so ist das mit der Liebe
Premiere: 25 February 1955
P: ÖFA Österreichische
  Filmgesellschaft (Vienna),
  Schönnbrunn-Film (Vienna)
D: Franz Antel
S: Kurt Nachmann, Franz
  Antel, Gunter Philipp
C: Hans Heinz Theyer, Hanns Matula
AD: Friedrich Jüptner-Jonstorff
M: Lotar Olias
A: Adrian Hoven, Gunter Philipp,
  Maria Emo, Margit Saad,
  Hans Moser, Paul Hörbiger

**Götz von Berlichingen /
  Götz von Berlichingen**
(Historical Costume Film)
Premiere: 12 October 1955
P: Wiener Mundus-Film (Vienna),
  Thalia-Film (Vienna)
D: Alfred Stöger, Josef Gielen
S: Johann Wolfgang von Goethe (play)
C: Anton Pucher, Walter Tuch
AD: Theo Otto
M: Walter Heidrich
A: Albin Skoda, Ewald Balser, Fred
  Liewehr, Judith Holzmeister

Heimatland / Heimat (*Heimatfilm*)
Premiere: 24 August 1955
P: Sascha-Film (Vienna),
  Lux-Film (Vienna)
D: Franz Antel
S: Kurt Nachmann, Josef Friedrich
  Perkonig, Hans Holt

C: Hans Heinz Theyer, Hanns Matula
AD: Sepp Rothauer
M: Willy Schmidt-Gentner
A: Adrian Hoven, Marianne
  Hold, Rudolf Prack

**Hofjagd in Ischl / Royal Hunt in
  Ischl** (Historical Costume Film)
AT: Zwei Herzen und ein Thron
Premiere: 8 December 1955
P: Austrian-West German co-
  production: Patria-Filmkunst
  (Graz), Tonfilm GmbH (Munich)
D: Hans Schott-Schöbinger
S: Rudolf L. Koerner
C: Klaus von Rautenfeld
AD: Herta Pischinger, Otto Pischinger
M: Karl Bette
A: Elma Karlowa, Herta Staal,
  Adrienne Gessner, Gunther Philipp

**Ihr erstes Rendezvous / Her
  First Date** (Comedy)
Premiere: 23 September 1955
P: Austrian-West German co-
  production: Donau-Film (Vienna),
  Melodie-Film (Berlin)
D: Axel von Ambesser
S: Max Kolpe, Axel von Ambesser
C: Willi Sohm
AD: Julius von Borsody,
  Heinz Ockermüller
M: Peter Kreuder, René Sylviano
A: Adrian Hoven, Nicole Heesters,
  Paul Dahlke, Karl Schönböck

**Mozart / The Lives and Loves of
  Mozart** (Historical Costume Film)
AT: Reich mir die Hand, mein Leben
Premiere: 20 December 1955
P: Cosmopol-Film (Vienna)
D: Karl Hartl
S: Karl Hartl, Franz Tassie
C: Oskar Schnirch
AD: Werner Schlichting
M: Wolfgang Amadeus Mozart
A: Oskar Werner, Johanna Matz, Erich
  Kunz, Gertrud Kückelmann

**Omaru – Eine afrikanische
  Liebesgeschichte / Omaru – An
  African Love Story** (Docudrama)

Premiere: 4 October 1955
P: Wien-Film (Vienna)
D + S: Albert Quendler
C: Elio Carniel
A: Omaru, Jindaray, Mairama

Sarajevo / Sarajevo (Historical
Costume Film)
AT: Um Thron und Liebe
Premiere: 17 October 1955
P: Wiener Mundus-Film (Vienna)
D: Fritz Kortner
S: Robert Thoeren
C: Heinz Hoelscher
AD: Felix Smetana
M: Winfried Zillig
A: Ewald Basler, Luise Ullrich,
Klaus Kinski, Karl Skraup, Franz
Stoss, Erik Frey, Hans Olden

**Schicksal am Lenkrad / Fate
at the Steering Wheel**
(Social Problem Film)
Premiere: 3 May 1955
P: Akkord-Film (Vienna)
D: Aldo Vergano
S: Ruth Wieden
C: Walter Tuch, Karl Kirchner
AD: Leopold Metzenbauer
M: Hanns Eisler
A: Winfried Schatz, Harry
Fuss, Hermann Erhardt

**Seine Tochter ist der Peter / His
Daughter Is Called Peter** (Comedy)
Premiere: 2 September 1955
P: ÖFA Österreichische
Filmgesellschaft (Vienna),
Schönnbrunn-Film (Vienna)
D: Gustav Fröhlich
S: Gustav Fröhlich, Ilse von
Gasteiger, Ernst A. Welisch
C: Sepp Riff

AD: Friedrich Jüptner-Jonstorff
M: Erwin Halletz
A: Sabine Eggerth, Wolf Albach-Retty,
Gretl Schörg, Josef Meinrad

Sissi / Sissi (Historical Costume Film)
Premiere: 21 December 1955
P: Erma-Film (Vienna)
D + S: Ernst Marischka
C: Bruno Mondi
AD: Friedrich Jüptner-Jonstorff
M: Anton Profes
A: Romy Schneider, Karlheinz Böhm,
Magda Schneider, Gustav Knuth,
Vilma Degischer, Josef Meinrad

**Sonnenschein und Wolkenbruch
/ Sunshine and Cloudburst**
(Tourist Film)
Premiere: 4 November 1955
P: Wien-Film (Vienna)
D: Rudolf Nussgruber
S: Franz Gribitz, Jutta Bornemann,
Kurt Nachmann
C: Elio Carniel, Sepp Ketterer
AD: Walter Schmiedl
M: Hanns Elin
A: Jester Naefe, Hans Holt, Helli
Servi, Rudolf Vogel, Hans Olden

Spionage / Espionage (Historical
Costume Film)
AT: Oberst Redl
Premiere: 18 April 1955
P: Neusser-Hope-Film (Vienna)
D: Franz Antel
S: Alexander Lernet-Holenia,
Kurt Nachmann
C: Hans Theyer, Hanns Matula
A: Ewald Balser, Oskar Werner, Barbara
Rütting, Rudolf Forster, Attila
Hörbiger, Erik Frey, Marte Harell

Index Names and Film Titles

INDEX